The authors of this edited volume are to be congratulated for insightfully addressing the complex challenges of translating well-intended laws and policies on women's health into effective outcomes.

—Rebecca J. Cook, Professor of Law Emerita,
University of Toronto, Canada

Women's Health and the Limits of Law: Domestic and International Perspectives is an important book. Dr. Iyioha (ed.) and the book's contributors provide a critical analysis of the promise of, and limits to, the role of law in furthering women's health. This thoughtful and provocative book will be of interest to scholars, policy-makers, and advocates who are concerned with women's health, human rights, feminist jurisprudence, intersectionality, and global perspectives on health.

—Mary Anne Bobinski, Professor and Dean,
School of Law, Emory University, USA

This edited collection is timely, original and a true interdisciplinary contribution. The whole collection is structured on a strong, common theoretical foundation that provides a novel lens through which to view and understand the deeply entrenched debates within feminism regarding culture, gender, and legal orders around the globe. This book contains a broad range of topics and perspectives on a wide variety of subjects related to women's health, and brings together a diverse and accomplished group of scholars to address empirical, political, legal and cultural aspects of women's health in a global context. It will add to the scholarly debates within legal theory, feminism, health law and ethics, and will be of interest to students, researchers, academics and law-makers around the globe.

—Dr. Angela Cameron, Associate Professor,
Sheryl Greenberg Chair of Women and
the Legal Profession, Faculty of Law,
University of Ottawa, Canada

# Women's Health and the Limits of Law

Despite some significant advances in the creation and protection of rights affecting women's health, these do not always translate into actual health benefits for women. This collection asks: 'What is an effective law and what influences law's effectiveness or ineffectiveness? What dynamics, elements and conditions come together to limit law's capacity to achieve instrumental goals for women's health and the advancement of women's health rights?' The book presents an integrated, co-referential and sustained critical discussion of the normative and constitutive reasons for law's limited effectiveness in the field of women's health. It offers comprehensive and cohesive explanatory accounts of law's limits and, for the first time in the field, introduces a distinction between Formal and Substantive *Effectiveness* of laws. Its approach is trans-systemic, multi-jurisdictional and comparative, with a focus on six countries in North America, Europe, Asia and Africa and international human rights case law based on matters arising from Hungary, Portugal, Spain, Slovakia, the Czech Republic, Peru and Bolivia.

The book will be a valuable resource for educators, students, lawyers, rights advocates and policymakers working in women's health, socio-legal studies, human rights, feminist legal studies and legal philosophy more broadly.

**Irehobhude O. Iyioha**, LL.B., LL.M., BL., Ph.D., is an Assistant Professor at the Faculty of Law, University of Victoria, Canada and an Associate Adjunct Professor at the Dossetor Centre, Faculty of Medicine and Dentistry, University of Alberta. She has held teaching positions at the Faculties of Law at Western University, the University of British Columbia, and the University of Alberta, Canada. She is the recipient of the 18th World Congress on Medical Law Award from the World Association for Medical Law for her seminal work on legal effectiveness and the Canadian Association of Law Teachers (CALT) Award, 2017 for scholarly work that makes a substantial contribution to legal literature for her theory of Substantive (Legal) Effectiveness.

# Routledge Research in Human Rights Law

**Challenging Territoriality in Human Rights Law**
Building Blocks for a Plural and Diverse Duty-Bearer Regime
*Wouter Vandenhole*

**Care, Migration and Human Rights**
Law and Practice
*Siobhán Mullally*

**China's Human Rights Lawyers**
Advocacy and Resistance
*Eva Pils*

**Indigenous Peoples, Title to Territory, Rights and Resources**
The Transformative Role of Free Prior and Informed Consent
*Cathal M. Doyle*

**Civil and Political Rights in Japan**
A Tribute to Sir Nigel Rodley
*Edited by Saul J. Takahashi*

**Human Rights, Digital Society and the Law**
A Research Companion
*Edited by Mart Susi*

**Criminal Theory and International Human Rights Law**
*Steven Malby*

**Women's Health and the Limits of Law**
Domestic and International Perspectives
*Edited by Irehobhude O. Iyioha*

For more information about this series, please visit: www.routledge.com/Routledge-Research-in-Human-Rights-Law/book-series/HUMRIGHTSLAW

# Women's Health and the Limits of Law

## Domestic and International Perspectives

Edited by Irehobhude O. Iyioha

Routledge
Taylor & Francis Group

LONDON AND NEW YORK

First published 2020
by Routledge
2 Park Square, Milton Park, Abingdon, Oxon OX14 4RN

and by Routledge
52 Vanderbilt Avenue, New York, NY 10017

*Routledge is an imprint of the Taylor & Francis Group, an informa business*

First issued in paperback 2021

*British Library Cataloguing-in-Publication Data*
A catalogue record for this book is available from the British Library

*Library of Congress Cataloging-in-Publication Data*
A catalog record for this book has been requested

ISBN: 978-1-138-54964-7 (hbk)
ISBN: 978-1-03-208204-2 (pbk)
ISBN: 978-1-351-00238-7 (ebk)

Typeset in Galliard
by Apex CoVantage, LLC

# Contents

Table of cases                                            ix
Table of legislation, treaties and instruments            xi
List of figures                                           xv
List of table                                             xvi
Notes on contributors                                     xvii
Acknowledgements                                          xxii

1  Introduction: within and beyond the hedge—form,
   substance and the limits of law on women's health       1
   IREHOBHUDE O. IYIOHA

2  Law, normative limits and women's health: towards
   a jurisprudence of substantive effectiveness            17
   IREHOBHUDE O. IYIOHA

3  Feminism, morality, and human rights: assessing the
   effectiveness of the United Kingdom's FGM Act           65
   JENAYE M. LEWIS, IREHOBHUDE O. IYIOHA, AND DEXTER DIAS

4  Abortion law in China: disempowering women
   under the liberal regulatory model                      99
   WEI WEI CAO

5  Forced sterilizations: addressing limitations of
   international rights adjudication through
   an intersectional approach                             122
   CHARLOTTE H. SKEET

6  Tilted interpretations: reproductive health law
   and practice in the Philippines                        152
   AMPARITA STA. MARIA

7 Economics and the limits of law: an international analysis
of persistent gaps in women's reproductive health 182
KAREN A. GRÉPIN, JENI KLUGMAN AND MATTHEW MOORE

8 Indigenous feminist legal theory: a multi-juridical analysis
of the limits of law on Indigenous women's health
in relation to HIV in Canada 212
EMILY SNYDER

9 Domestication and reception of international reproductive
health law and the limits of law: perspectives
from Nigeria and South Africa 232
BABAFEMI ODUNSI AND OLUWAYEMISI A. ADEWOLE

10 On the margins of law: examining the limits of legislative
initiatives on maternal mortality in South Africa
and Nigeria 260
AROOJ SHAH, SIMISOLA O. AKINTOLA AND
IREHOBHUDE O. IYIOHA

*Index* 288

# Cases

*A, B, and C v Ireland*, No. 25579/05 Eur. Ct. H.R. (2010).
*Abacha v Fawehimi* (2000) 6 NWLR (pt 660) 228.
*Abdulaziz, Cabales and Balkandali v. The United Kingdom* (1985) 7 EHRR 471.
*Ahamefule v Imperial Medical Centre and Molokwu*, Appeal No. CA/L/514/ 2001, delivered on 21 April 2004.
*Ahamefule v Imperial Medical Centre and Molokwu*, Suit No. ID/1627/2000 (Ikeja Judicial Division of the Lagos High Court, Nigeria).
*Airey v Ireland* (1979–1980) 2 EHRR 305.
*Alliance for the Family Foundation Philippines, Inc. (ALFI) and Atty. Maria Concepcion S. Noche, in her own behalf as president of ALFI et al. v Dr. Janette L. Garin, Secretary-Designate of the Department of Health et al., G.R. No. 217872* (Temporary Restraining Order) (Supreme Court of the Philippines 2015, 17 June).
*Andrews v. Law Society of British Columbia and the Attorney General of British Columbia* [1989] 1 S.C.R. 143 (Can.).
*AP Garcon and Nicot v France* ECHR (application nos. 79885/12, 52471/13 and 52596/13).
*AS v Hungary* (2004) Communication No. 4/2004, CEDAW/C/36/ D/4/2004.
*Chavez v Peru*, I-A CHR Report No 71/03 Petition 12.191, Friendly Settlement, Maria Mam'erita Mestanza *Chavez v. Peru*, October 22, 2003.
Commission on Human Rights Resolution to Case No. 2015–0411, entitled *In the Matter of the Issuance by Mayor Sally Lee of Executive Order No. 003, Declaring Sorsogon City a "Pro-Life City", the alleged effects thereof, and the Violation of the Women's Right to Reproductive Health*, dated June 27, 2017.
*Corte Inter Americana De Derechos Humanos I.V. v BOLIVIA*, Report 72/14 Case 12.655 Merits I.V. Bolivia (August 15, 2014).
*DH v Czech Republic* [2007] ECHR 922.
*Dudgen v UK [1981] 4 EHRR 149.*
*Ebralinag v Division Superintendent of Schools* G.R. No. 95770, March 1, 1993.
*Eldrige v. British Columbia (Att. Gen.)* [1997] 3 SCR 624, 151 DLR (4th) 577.
*Estrada v. Escritor*, A.M. No. P-02–1651, August 4, 2003.
*Gonzales v. Carhart*, 550 U.S. 124 (2007).

*Ibidapo v Lufthansa Airlines* (1997) 4 NWLR (Part 498) 124.

*Jaitun v Maternal Home MCD, Jangpura & Others*, W.P. (C) 8853/2008 & 10700/2009, Delhi High Court (2010).

*James M. Imbong et al. v Hon. Paquito N. Ochoa*, G.R. No. 204819 (Supreme Court of the Philippines April 8, 2014).

*L.C. v Peru, Committee on the Elimination of Discrimination against Women Views on Communication No. 22/2009*, CEDAW, 50th Sess, CEDAW/C/50/D/22/2009 (2011).

*Laxmi Mandal v Deen Dayal Harinagar Hospital & Others*, W.P. (C) No. 8853/2008.

*MHWUN v Minister of Health & Productivity & Ors* (2005) 17 NWLR (Pt. 953) 120.

*Pimentel v Brazil, Committee on the Elimination of Discrimination against Women Views on Communication No. 17/2008*, CEDAW, 49th Sess, CEDAW/C/49/D/17/2008 (2011).

*R. v. Morgentaler* [1988] 1 S.C.R. 30, 44 D.L.R. (4th) 385 (Supreme Court of Canada).

*Roe v. Wade*, 410 U.S. 113 (1973).

*Sandesh Bansal v Union of India* W.P. (C) 9061/2008, High Court of Madhya Pradesh (2012).

*Silguero v Portugal*, ECHR application no. 33290/96 [1999].

*State v. Astou Diop*, Judgement n 88/09, Kaolack Regional Court (18 February 2009).

*State v. Landing Massaly*, Judgement n 1544/08, Dakar Special Regional Court (23 April 2008).

*State v. Mouscoye Sane (known as Mamy)*, Judgement n 2067/2008, Dakar Special Regional Court (16 May 2008).

*Symes v. Canada* [1993] 4 SCR 695.

*The Diocese of Bacolod, represented by the most Rev. Bishop Vicente M. Navarra and the Bishop himself in his personal capacity v. Commission on Elections and the Election Officer of Bacolod City, Atty. Mavil V. Majarucon*, G.R. No. 205728 (Supreme Court of the Philippines 2015, 21 January).

*The Mental Health Trust, Acute Trust & The Council v DD and BC*, Reported as *Re DD (No 4) (Sterilisation)* [2015] EWCOP 4).

*The X Case: Attorney General v X* [1992] IESC 1; [1992] 1 IR 1 (5 March 1992).

*Toonen v Australia* (1994) Human Rights Committee Communication 488/1992.

*Towne v. Eisner*, 245 U.S. 418, 425 (1918).

*VC v Slovakia* [2009] Application no (18968).

*Whole Woman's Health v. Hellerstedt*, 579 U.S., 136 S. Ct. 2292 (2016).

*Xákmok Kasek Indigenous Community v Paraguay* (2012) Judgment, Inter-Am Ct HR (Ser C).

# Legislation, treaties and instruments

*Abortion Act* of 1967 (UK).

*African Charter on Human and Peoples' Rights on the Rights of Women in Africa* (Maputo Protocol), 2004.

*An Ordinance Providing for the Safety and Protection of the Unborn Child within the Territorial Jurisdiction of Barangay Ayala Alabang*, Barangay Ordinance No. 01, Series of 2011, Sanggunian Barangay of Ayala Alabang (3 January 2011).

*Beijing Declaration and Platform for Action, Fourth World Conference on Women*, 15 September 1995, A/CONF.177/20 (1995) and A/CONF.177/20/Add.1 (1995).

*Canada Health Act*, R.S.C. 1985, c. C-6.

*Canadian Criminal Code*, R.S.C. 1985, c. C-46.

*CEDAW General Recommendation 19*, 11th Session 1992.

*CEDAW General Recommendation 24, Article 12 of the Convention (Women and Health)*, A/54/38/Rev.1, OCHCR, 20th Sess (1999).

*CEDAW Recommendation* 28 CEDAW/C/2010/47/ GG.2.

*CERD* 56th session (2000) General Recommendation XXV on Gender Related

*Cheaper Medicines Act*, 2008, Republic Act No. 9502 ('Act Providing for Cheaper and Quality Medicines').

*Child Rights Act*, Act No. 26 of 2003.

*Choice on Termination of Pregnancy Act* (CTOPA), No 92 of 1996, as amended.

*Code of Medical Ethics*, Art. 35 of decree n 67–147 of 10 February 1967.

*Constitution of 1982* (China), current version adopted by the 5th National People's Congress on December 4, 1982, with revisions in 1988, 1993, 1999, 2004 and 2018.

*Constitution of the Federal Republic of Nigeria*, No. 24 LFN 1999.

*Constitution of the Federal Republic of Nigeria* (Third Alteration) Act, 2010.

*Constitution of the Republic of South Africa*, No 109 of 1996.

*Convention Against Torture and Other Cruel, Inhuman and Degrading Treatment or Punishment*, GA res. 39/46, annex, 39 UN GAOR Supp. (No. 51) at 197, UN Doc. A/39/51 (1984); 1465 UNTS 85.

*Convention on Rights of Persons with Disabilities*, General Comment 3, 2016 CRPD/C/GC/3.

*Convention on the Prevention and Punishment on the Crime of Genocide* 1948, Art 11(d).

*Council of Europe Convention on preventing and combating violence against women and domestic violence Council of Europe Convention 210, Istanbul 11.V.2011.*

*Criminal Practice Direction*, 2015, EWCA, Crim 1567, 3D.2 (UK).

*Criminal Procedure Rules*, 2015 ('CPR'), Rule 1 (UK).

*Criminal Procedure Rules*, 3.9(7)(b) (UK).

*Declaration on Social Progress and Development*, UN General Assembly Resolution 2542, U.N. Doc. A/7630. Adopted by the General Assembly in resolution 2542, 1969, affirmed the Tehran Proclamation of the International Conference on Human Rights, Tehran, Republic of Iran (22 April to 13 May 1968).

*Declaration on the Elimination of Violence Against Women*, A/RES/48/104.

*Dimensions of Racial Discrimination in Report of the Committee on the Elimination of Racial Discrimination* 56th and 57th Session a /55/10.

European Convention on Human Rights and Fundamental Freedoms, ETS 5; 213 UNTS 221.

*Executive Order* (E.O.) No. 003, issued by former Manila Mayor Jose L. Atienza (City of Manila).

*Executive Order* (E.O.) No. 3 of 2015, "An Executive Order Declaring Sorsogon City as a Pro-Life City" (City of Sorsogon).

*Factories Act*, Cap 126 LFN 1990.

*Female Genital Mutilation Act of 2003*, c. 31 (United Kingdom).

*General Principles of the Civil Code, 1986* (Effective January 1, 1987) (China).

*General Recommendation of CERD Committee*, No. 25, 56th Session (2000).

*Guidelines on Medical Management of Victims of Violence, Post-Abortion Care Training Manual* (Nigeria).

ICCPR General Comment 28 CCPR/C/21/Rev.1/Add.10.

ICESCR General Comment 5.

*Integrated Maternal, Newborn and Child Health Strategy*, Federal Ministry of Health (Nigeria).

*Inter-American Convention on the Prevention, Punishment, and Eradication of Violence against Women* (Convention of Belém do Pará), 9 June 1994.

*International Convention on Civil and Political Rights* (ICCPR), 19 December 1966, 999 UNTS 171 (entered into force 23 March 1976).

*International Covenant on Economic, Social and Cultural Rights* (ICESCR), GA res. 2200A (XXI), 21 UN GAOR Supp. (No. 16) at 49, UN Doc. A/6316 (1966); 993 UNTS 3; 6 ILM 368 (1967).

*International Covenant on Economic, Social, and Cultural Rights*, 19 December 1966, 993 UNTS 3.

*International Covenant on the Elimination of all forms of Racial Discrimination* (ICERD).

*Law of the People's Republic of China on Maternal and Infant Health Care* (Order No.33 of 1994) (Code on Maternal and Infant Health Care, 1994).

*Law on Reproductive Health*, Art. 15, law n 2005–18 of 5 August 2005.

*Marriage Act*, Cap 219 LFN 1990.

*Maternal and Child Health Strategic Plan for 2012–2016* (South Africa).
*Matrimonial Causes Act*, Cap 220 LFN 1990.
*Matrimonial Causes Act*, Cap M7 LFN 2010.
*National Adolescent Health Policy, 1995* (Nigeria).
*National Family Planning/Reproductive Health Service Protocol* (Nigeria).
*National Health Act*, No 12 of 2013 (South Africa).
*National Health Act*, No. 8 of 2014 (Nigeria).
*National Health Act*, No. 8 of 2014.
*National Health Insurance Act of 1995*, Republic Act No. 7875 (Philippines).
*National Policy on Maternal and Child Health, 1994* (Nigeria).
*National Policy on the Elimination of Female Genital Mutilation (1998 and 2002).*
*National Reproductive Health Policies (2010 and 2017).*
*National Reproductive Health Policy, 2017* (Nigeria).
*National Reproductive Health Policy and Strategy, 2002.*
*National Training Manual on Integration of Reproductive Health and HIV Services* (Nigeria).
*Nigerian Criminal Code*, Cap 77 LFN 1990.
*Nigerian Labour Act*, Cap L1 LFN 2010.
*Nigerian Penal Code*, Cap 89 LFN 1963.
*Optional Protocol to CEDAW*, entered into force December 2000.
*Partial-Birth Abortion Ban Act*, 18 USC s. 1531 (2007).
*Population and Family Planning Law of the People's Republic of China* (Order of the President No. 63) (Code on Population and Family Planning, 2002).
*Prohibition of Female Circumcision Act*, 1985, c. 38.
*Protocol to the African Charter on Human and People's Rights on the Rights of Women in Africa*, Maputo, Mozambique on 11 July 2003.
*Reproductive Health Policy and Strategy, 2001*, Federal Ministry of Health (Nigeria).
*Resolution XVIII: Human Rights Aspects of Family Planning, Final Act of the International Conference on Human Rights*, U.N. Doc. A/CONF. 32/41.
*Responsible Parenthood and Reproductive Health Act of 2012*, R.A. 10354.
*Same Sex Marriage (Prohibition) Act*, 2014.
*Serious Crimes Act*, 2015 c.9.
*The 2030 Agenda for Sustainable Development*, adopted by all United Nations Member States in 2015.
*The Act for Collecting and Managing the Social Maintenance Fee, 2002*, Decree No. 357, State Council of the People's Republic of China, August 2, 2002.
*The Constitution of the Republic of the Philippines, 1987* (in force Feb. 11, 1987; approved Oct. 12, 1986).
*The Council of Europe Convention on Preventing and Combatting Violence Against Women and Domestic Violence*, 11.V.2011.
*The Programme of Action of the UN International Conference on Population and Development* (ICPD), 1993.
*The Protection of Life During Pregnancy Act*, 2013 (Act No.35 of 2013; previously Bill No.66 of 2013).

*The Right to the Highest Attainable Standard of Health*, UN Committee on ESCR General Comment, UN Doc. EC/12/2000/4.

*The Strasbourg Declaration on Roma*, Council of Europe High Level Meeting on Roma Strasbourg, 20 October 2010.

*Trafficking in Persons (Prohibition) Law Enforcement and Administration Act*, 2003, No. 24, as amended by Act No. 14 of 7th December, 2005.

*Transforming Our World: The 2023 Agenda for Sustainable Development*, GA Res A/RES/70/1, UNGOAR, 70th Sess, Supp No 49, UN Doc 15–16301 (E) 1 at 16 (2015).

*UN Committee on the Convention on the Rights of the Child*, General Comment 13.

*UN Convention against Torture and other Cruel, Inhuman or degrading Treatment or Punishment*, GA res. 39/46, annex, 39 UN GAOR Supp. (No. 51) at 197, UN Doc. A/39/51 (1984); 1465 UNTS 85.

*UN Convention on the Rights of the Child* (CRC), GA res. 44/25, annex, 44 UN GAOR Supp. (No. 49) at 167, U.N. Doc. A/44/49 (1989); 1577 UNTS 3; 28 ILM 1456 (1989).

UN Economic and Social Council, *General Comment No. 14: The Right to the Highest Attainable Standard of Health (Art. 12 of the Covenant)*, E/C.12/2000/4, CESCR, 22nd Sess, UN Doc GE.00–43934 (E) (2000) at para 14.

*United Nations Millennium Declaration*, GA Res A/RES/55/2, UNGOAR, 55th Sess, Supp No 49, UN Doc 00 55951 (2000).

*United Nations, Committee on the Elimination of Discrimination against Women* (2014 August), Summary of the inquiry concerning the Philippines under Article 8 of the Optional Protocol to the Convention on the Elimination of All Forms of Discrimination against Women.

*Universal Declaration of Human Rights* (General Assembly Resolution 217 A (III) of 10 December 1948).

*Vienna Declaration and Programme of Action*, 1993.

*Violence Against Persons (Prohibition) Act*, 2015 (Nigeria).

# Figures

7.1  Trends in Maternal Mortality and Attended Births                              183
7.2  Maternal Mortality: Regional Averages and Country
     Outliers, 2015                                                              184
7.3  Relationship between Education and Share of Women
     Who Lack Sexual Autonomy                                                     191
7.4  Limited Progress in Reproductive Health Is Explained
     by Mutually Reinforcing Constraints                                          193
7.5  Trends in Girls' Net Secondary Enrollment by Region,
     1995–2016                                                                    200
7.6  Trends in Contraceptive Prevalence by Region, 1990–2014      206

# Table

7.1     Selected Agency Deprivations in Developing Countries      190

# Contributors

## Editor/Author

**Irehobhude O. Iyioha**, LL.B., LL.M., B.L., Ph.D., is an Assistant Professor at the Faculty of Law, University of Victoria, Canada and an Associate Adjunct Professor at the John Dossetor Health Ethics Centre, Faculty of Medicine and Dentistry, University of Alberta. She has held teaching positions at the Faculties of Law at Western University, the University of British Columbia, and the University of Alberta, Canada. She has also served in research and senior policy positions with the governments of Ontario and Alberta, respectively. She is co-editor of the book *Comparative Health Law and Policy: Critical Perspectives on Nigerian and Global Health Law* (Ashgate, 2015) (with R.N. Nwabueze). Her work has been published in edited collections and leading Canadian and international law journals, including Oxford University's *Statute Law Review,* *Canadian Journal of Law and Society* (Cambridge University), Edinburgh University's *African Journal of International and Comparative Law* and York University's *Transnational Human Rights Review.* Dr. Iyioha is a past Nathanson Visiting Fellow at Osgoode Hall Law School and Visiting Scholar at the Faculty of Law, University of Toronto. She holds a Ph.D. from the University of British Columbia, an LL.M. from the University of Toronto and an LL.B. (with highest honours) from the University of Benin. Her scholarship and service to the local and global communities have been recognized nationally and internationally through numerous awards, including the 18th *World Congress on Medical Law Award* from the World Association for Medical Law for her formative work on legal effectiveness and the *Canadian Association of Law Teachers (CALT) Award,* 2017 (co-recipient) for scholarly work that makes a substantial contribution to legal literature for her theory of Substantive (Legal) Effectiveness.

## Contributing authors

**Oluwayemisi A. Adewole**, LL.B., LL.M., B.L., M.Phil Cand., is a lawyer and a law teacher at Obafemi Awolowo University, Ile-Ife, Nigeria. She obtained her Bachelor's and Master's Degrees from Obafemi Awolowo University, where she is currently a candidate for the M.Phil Degree. She is also a graduate of the Nigerian Institute of Management (Chartered). Adewole's scholarly interest is in alternative dispute resolution, the promotion and protection of women's rights and reproductive health law. She is a member of the Nigerian Bar Association, National Association of Law Teachers and the Nigerian Institute of Management. She was a member of the Legal Aid Council during her National Youth Service Corps, where she worked with colleagues pro bono to secure the release of unlawfully detained suspects from prison.

**Simisola O. Akintola**, LL.B., LL.M., B.L., Ph.D., is an associate professor of law at the University of Ibadan as well as an adjunct professor at the School of Medicine of the University of Ibadan. She obtained a doctorate (Ph.D.) in Law from the University of Southampton, UK, and a Master of Laws Degree in Global Health Law from Georgetown University Law Center, Washington, DC. She is a member of the University of Ibadan Research Ethics Review Board. She has over 30 publications in peer-reviewed journals and has authored and co-authored several books in her field. She is editor of several journals including *Current Pharmacogenomics* and *Personalised Medicine.*

**Wei Wei Cao**, LL.M., M.Phil, Ph.D., is a professor and Director of the Biomedical Law and Ethics Center at the School of Law, Hunan University, China. Appointed in 2018 on a two-year term, she serves as the vice chair of the Hunan Women's Federation. Professor Cao obtained her law Degree and a Master of Laws from Hunan University and a Ph.D. in law from the University of Keele in England. She served part-time as a research assistant in England and was a visiting scholar at the University of British Columbia and the University of Keele. Her research areas are the legal regulation of reproduction, comparative health care law and ethics and feminist legal studies. The National Social Science Fund of China (Grant no. 17CFX043) supported her research, which culminated in her chapter in this book.

**Dexter Dias**, QC, is an award-winning human rights lawyer, Queen's Counsel and Deputy High Court Judge and is specially authorised to sit at the Old Bailey and on cases of serious sexual offending. He is a Visiting Researcher at Cambridge University and recently Harvard. At Cambridge he was awarded the Lopez-Rey Prize for ranking first in his research degree. During the last 30 years, he has been involved in some of the biggest legal cases involving murder, terrorism, crimes against humanity and genocide. He does pro bono human rights work around the world protecting the rights of the most vulnerable, and was principal author of the influential Bar Human Rights report to the UK Parliamentary Inquiry on Female Genital Mutilation that played a pivotal part in changing the law to better safeguard at-risk young women and girls. He is Chair of the Global Media Campaign to End FGM and Special Adviser on Human Rights to UNICEF UK. His book *The Ten Types of Human* (Penguin Random House, 2018) was a bestseller on Amazon in a dozen categories, selected for the BBC's prestigious non-fiction book club and is being published internationally, including in China and Taiwan. He is currently working with the UN on a substantial project to eradicate FGM and child marriage.

**Karen A. Grépin**, Ph.D., is an Associate Professor at the School of Public Health at the University of Hong Kong and the former Canada Research Chair in Global Health Policy and Evaluation at Wilfrid Laurier University, Canada. Her research focuses on institutional factors affecting the demand and supply of health services, the politics and effectiveness of development assistance for health and the role of routine health information systems in strengthening health systems. She has a Ph.D. in Health Policy (economics) from Harvard University and an S.M. in Health Policy and Management from the Harvard School of Public Health.

**Jeni Klugman**, Ph.D., is Managing Director at the Georgetown Institute for Women, Peace and Security. Previous positions include a fellowship at the Kennedy School of Government's Women in Public Policy Program at Harvard University, Director of Gender and Development at the World Bank, and director and lead author of three global Human Development Reports published by the United Nations Development Programme. She has published widely on poverty, inequality, human development and gender issues. She sits on several boards and panels, including for the World Economic Forum and the *Journal of Human Development and Capabilities*. She holds a Ph.D. in Economics from the Australian National University and postgraduate degrees in both Law and Development Economics from the University of Oxford, where she was a Rhodes Scholar.

**Jenaye M. Lewis**, B.A., J.D., holds a law Degree from the University of Alberta, Canada. Prior to this degree, Jenaye earned a Bachelor of Arts with Distinction at the same university, double-majoring in English and Women's and Gender Studies. During her undergraduate studies, she volunteered with the Center to End All Sexual Exploitation (CEASE) in Edmonton, Alberta. She prepared and delivered a research paper delineating the latest feminist methodologies regarding issues of sexual violence to be utilized in augmenting harm-prevention and harm-reduction programs already in existence, and in influencing the development of new initiatives. She was chosen to present a research paper on the history of feminist thought at the International Women's Day Conference at the University of Alberta in 2013. She has continued to follow her passion for women's issues and rights throughout her J.D. degree, most notably through enrolment in courses such as Women's Health and the Law – Global Perspectives, introduced and taught by Dr. Irehobhude O. Iyioha at the University of Alberta, and membership in the Women's Legal Forum.

**Amparita Sta. Maria**, LL.B., LL.M., is Director of the Graduate Legal Studies Institute and Director of the Urduja Women's Desk, Human Rights Centre, Ateneo de Manila University School of Law. She graduated with honors from the Ateneo Law School (LL.B.) and obtained her Master of Laws

(LL.M.) at the University of Toronto, Canada, under a Reproductive Health Law Fellowship as part of the Women's Rights and Reproductive Health Graduate Scholarships of the Faculty of Law, University of Toronto. She joined the Ateneo Law School in 1991 and in 2002 introduced an elective course, Gender and the Law. She also teaches family law, human rights law and women's rights. She is a professorial lecturer in international and human rights law at the Philippine Judicial Academy and, from 2007 to 2011, served as member of the Committee on Gender Responsiveness in the Judiciary, Supreme Court of the Philippines. She has been involved in the training of judges, court lawyers and personnel in human rights, women's rights and gender sensitivity, and continues to lecture on these topics and on other emerging human rights and gender-related issues. She specializes in women's rights, human rights and family law.

**Matthew Moore**, J.D., M.A., is the Hillary Rodham Clinton Law Fellow at the Georgetown Institute for Women, Peace and Security, where his research focuses on the role of international law in promoting women's rights and on legal and policy strategies to combat violence against women. He has published on the history of international law and human rights and the legal consequences of Brexit, and has conducted field research on peacebuilding in Medellín, Colombia. He was articles editor of the *Georgetown Journal of International Law* and editor of the *Columbia Journal of International Affairs*. He holds a J.D. from Georgetown University Law Center and a Master's Degree from Columbia University's School of International and Public Affairs.

**Babafemi Odunsi**, LL.B., B.L., LL.M. (Ife), LL.M. (Toronto), Ph.D., Cert. [IHL] (Pretoria), is Dean of the Faculty of Law at the Obafemi Awolowo University, Ile-Ife, Nigeria, where he holds full professorship in law. He has taught courses at undergraduate and postgraduate levels, including medical law/medical jurisprudence, environmental law, military law and law of insurance at the Obafemi Awolowo University. He is a McArthur Fellow of the Faculty of Law, University of Toronto, Canada. He has also been a research associate with the AIDS and Human Rights Research Unit (Centre for Human Rights and Centre for the Study of AIDS), Faculty of Law, University of Pretoria, South Africa (2006–2007). He served as a research fellow at the Faculty of Law, University of the Free State, Bloemfontein, South Africa (2011). His scholarly interests and activities revolve principally around Medical Law and Medical Jurisprudence. His professional and academic affiliations include membership of the Nigerian Bar Association, Nigerian Association of Law Teachers, American Society of Law Medicine and Ethics (Web), International Union of Scientific Studies of Population, International Institute for Research in Ethics and Biomedicine and the International Union for the Conservation of Law (IUCN) Academy of Environmental Law.

**Arooj Shah**, J.D., B.A., is a lawyer in Alberta, Canada. She, holds a J.D. with distinction from the University of Alberta. Prior to law school, Arooj received a Specialized Honours Bachelor of Arts with distinction in Human Rights and Equity Studies from York University in Toronto, Ontario. During law school, she competed in the Philip C. Jessup International Law Moot, volunteered with a student organization to provide legal information and referrals to low-income individuals, interned with the Alberta Human Rights Commission, and worked as a research assistant on mental health and bankruptcy law.

**Charlotte H. Skeet**, Ph.D., is a lecturer-in-law and a co-director of the Sussex Centre for Human Rights Research in the School of Law, Politics and Sociology at the University of Sussex. She is the academic convenor and lecturer for the Women and Human Rights module on LL.M. and M.A. programmes in International Human Rights, and for the Feminism, Law and Society module on the M.A. Gender Studies at the University of Sussex. At the undergraduate level, she runs options in Law and Development and Canadian Constitutional Law. Her Ph.D. (2005) developed a thesis on Gender and Constitutional Change in the UK. Current research interests focus on gender and constitutionalism, post-colonial feminist legal theory and intersectionality theory. She convened the Intersectionality Stream for the Socio-Legal Studies Conference from 2010–2016. Prior to her appointment at Sussex Law School, she co-edited *Education Law Monitor* and focused her writing on equality and discrimination cases in education, particularly on the role of the Local Government Commissioner (Ombudsman). She also worked as a research assistant for projects on Gender and Constitutions at the Cunliffe Centre for the Study of Constitutions at the University of Sussex. She is a member of Rights of Women (ROW), Human Rights Lawyers Association (HRLA), British Association of Canadian Studies (BACS), Socio-Legal Studies Association (SLSA), Society of Legal Scholars (SLS) and the Feminism and Institutionalism International Network.

**Emily Snyder**, Ph.D., is an assistant professor in Indigenous Studies and Women's and Gender Studies at the University of Saskatchewan. Her research interests are in the areas of Indigenous legal issues, Indigenous feminisms, HIV criminalization, gendered violence and anti-colonial feminist approaches to legal education. She is the author of *Gender, Power, and Representations of Cree Law* and has published in the *Dalhousie Law Journal, UBC Law Review, Alberta Law Review, The Ethics Forum* and the *Canadian Journal of Women and the Law*. She has also published reports, in collaboration with All Nations Hope Network, on the impacts of the criminalization of HIV on Indigenous people who are HIV-positive. She completed her Ph.D. in Sociology at the University of Alberta, and was awarded a Social Sciences and Humanities Research Council of Canada Postdoctoral Fellowship which she held at the Indigenous Law Research Unit in the Faculty of Law at the University of Victoria. Emily is a white settler originally from Haudenosaunee and Anishinaabe territories in the Waterloo region in southern Ontario, Canada.

# Acknowledgements

There is a community of people to thank for the successful completion and publication of this book. I thank the contributing authors for their painstaking and thoughtful work and for their patience through the several stages of the editing process. For their early and long-standing commitment to the project, I offer special thanks to Jeni Klugman, Wei Wei Cao, Karen Grépin, Amparita Sta. Maria, Simisola O. Akintola, and Charlotte Skeet. I am particularly grateful to Wei Wei for her insights on the theory of Substantive Effectiveness through comments and the application of the theory in her work on Chinese law in important ways that helped refine the theory. The commissioning editor, Alison Kirk, and the editorial assistant, Emily Summers, were patient and understanding, and offered helpful advice in the publication process. I am also grateful to our blind reviewers for their comments and suggestions.

I am hugely indebted to Dr. Angela Cameron, Associate Professor and the Shirley Greenberg Chair of Women and the Law at the University of Ottawa, for her untiring support of this project and for the helpful comments. Professor (Emeritus) Bernard Dickens and Professor (Emerita) Rebecca Cook, Co-directors of the Reproductive Health Law Program at the Faculty of Law, University of Toronto, deserve my heartfelt thanks for comments made on the second chapter during presentations of this work at the University of Toronto and for resources offered. I thank Professor Mary Anne Bobinski, former Dean, Allard School of Law, University of British Columbia and current Dean, Emory University School of Law, from whom, along with Angela and Rebecca, we requested additional critical comments after the initial peer review process conducted by our blind reviewers. While I was prepared to further delay the publication process to address any critical comments, the statements they issued following the painstaking read of the rather lengthy manuscript were generous endorsements: for these I am truly grateful.

Finally, I owe an enormous debt of gratitude to some truly outstanding friends and family members who provided moral and intellectual support during my work on this book. For their enduring faith and kindness, I say a profound *thank you*.

# 1 Introduction

## Within and beyond the hedge: form, substance and the limits of law on women's health

*Irehobhude O. Iyioha*

### Background: form, substance and law's limits

In the last several years, the world has experienced significant advances in the recognition and protection of women's health rights. Rule-based advances have come in the form of new and amended legislation, and in some cases, through constitutional guarantees – mostly state responses to commitments made to an international human rights regime that is at the forefront of expanding and promoting women's rights and interests. Even in the more conservative parts of the world, including Africa, Latin America and the Middle East, there are progressive legislation guaranteeing some rights to reproductive health services and prohibiting violence and harmful traditional practices against women.

Yet, progressive laws recognizing women's rights and agency do not always translate into actual health benefits for women. Data on several social and medical problems that impair women's physical, mental and reproductive health reveal that millions of women around the world are still subject to harmful cultural practices and adverse gender norms, while many others in repressive regimes are faced with prohibitive conditions for the exercise of their rights, especially those pertaining to their reproductive health. The challenges women face are numerous and substantial. Violence against women around the world[1] remains a considerable problem. In Canada, for example, violence against Indigenous women in particular has reached epidemic proportions, a situation Amnesty International has described as a "national human rights crisis".[2]

High rates of maternal mortality – caused by several factors, including poor healthcare access, HIV infections and the criminalization of abortion – is another major problem.[3] The use of the criminal law to regulate access to abortion is

---

1 UN Women, *Facts and Figures: Ending Violence Against Women,* available at www.unwomen. org/en/what-we-do/ending-violence-against-women/facts-and-figures.

2 Amnesty International, *Violence Against Indigenous Women and Girls in Canada: A Summary of Amnesty's International's Concerns and Call to Action* (Feb. 2014), available at www. amnesty.ca/sites/amnesty/files/iwfa_submission_amnesty_international_february_2014_-_ final.pdf (accessed 11 May 2019).

3 *Trends in Maternal Mortality: 1990 to 2015: Estimates by WHO, UNICEF, UNFPA, World Bank Group and the United Nations Population Division* (Geneva: World Health Organization, 2015),

particularly limiting of women's agency and autonomy over their reproductive health, as are non-legal or systemic limits in jurisdictions where the procedure is liberalized. Beyond these measurable factors, an intractable and arguably insidious cause of maternal mortality relates to the governance of women's lives through customary legal orders that conflict with international reproductive health rights recognizing women's full agency and control over their bodies. Another problem that has gained the attention of the international community relates to the prevalence of female genital cutting and its unremitting, surreptitious migration as a cultural transplant among some practicing immigrant communities in Western nations.[4] These and other emerging data suggest that women's bodies remain sites of social, political, cultural and legal contests.

Stated simply, there is a fundamental gap – perhaps more clearly evident in the global South – between the lived experiences of millions of women and the transformative goal of substantive equality sought through legal reform that has animated the scholarship on women's reproductive health and the feminist legal project. Although there are indications that several legislative reforms and targeted programs at the domestic level[5] as well as international efforts such as the Convention on the Elimination of All Forms of Discrimination Against Women (CEDAW) have been effective,[6] other observers question the overall effect of this and other treaties and domestic laws on women's rights.[7]

A book on the limits of law in the field of women's health law and policy is necessitated not only by the dearth of critical scholarship with a marked theoretical bent but also by the nature of the times in which we live. In the last few years, the persistence of religious illiberalism and the conflation of judicial roles with religious orthodoxy and obligation, as well as the rise and open acceptance of authoritarian populism and the resultant adverse consequences for women's reproductive health have incrementally eroded women's rights. This development demands a focus on the limits of domestic and international human rights law – a focus situated markedly in both the philosophy of law and empirical analyses.

---

available at http://apps.who.int/iris/bitstream/handle/10665/194254/9789241565141_ eng.pdf;jsessionid=B8ABEE8724C8F98410176BE00F4738CA?sequence=1 [*Trends in maternal mortality*].

4  United Nations News Centre, *UN Report Reveals Increasing Incidents of Female Genital Mutilation in Guinea, Including on Infants* (April 25, 2016), available at www.un.org/apps/ news/story.asp?NewsID=53775#.V9HYJfkrK70; Jazmin Chavez, *Female Genital Mutilation on the Rise in the United States* (March 18, 2016), Human Rights Brief, available at http:// hrbrief.org/2016/03/female-genital-mutilation-on-the-rise-in-the-united-states/.

5  For a discussion of some successful grassroots initiatives for improving women's reproductive health, see analysis of economics and the limits of law in Grépin et al., Chapter 7 of this volume.

6  N. A. Englehart and M. K. Miller, "The CEDAW Effect: International Law's Impact on Women's Rights" (2014) 13:1 *Journal of Human Rights* 22–47; N. Englehart, "Women's Rights, International Law and Domestic Politics: Explaining CEDAW's Effectiveness" *APSA 2011 Annual Meeting Paper*.

7  Andreea Maria Serbu, "From the CEDAW to the Istanbul Convention: Effectiveness in tackling Violence Against Women" (Università Ca' Foscari Venezia, 2017). Eric A. Posner, *The Twilight of Human Rights Law* (New York: Oxford University Press, 2014).

Enquiry into the limits of law aligns with the feminist legal project, which aims for equality for all women through legal reform. Therefore, interrogating the limits and effectiveness of law – an undertaking central to the realization of substantive equality – furthers the ultimate aims of the feminist legal project and the more immediate goals of incremental legislative and systemic reforms. Towards these goals, it is expected, as Charles Ngwena has noted, that norms in a "plural democracy" would allow for consensus on the importance of equality under the law.[8] A general level of consensus is foundational not only to securing "effective" and "accessible" justice, but also to "securing equality"[9] in both procedural and substantive terms. The reasons for and consequences of a lack of consensus on legal and policy reform, with particular reference to the impact on reception of and compliance with law, animate the discussions in this book.

While questions about the limits of human rights law are only a part of the broader discourse on the limits and effectiveness of law, they are a significant part of the discourse. Campaigns promoting women's interests and health, especially women's reproductive health, draw pivotally on the framework and language of human rights as argumentative tools for guiding the discourse on rights as well as for negotiating and advancing women's health rights. Given their intrinsically persuasive logic, it is not unexpected that human rights are conceived of as universal and objective, though dependent on a progressive state or one sympathetic to the shared values of dignity and equality for women to effectuate its promises.

However, opposition has been mounted against the idea of universalism of human rights on account of the diversity of cultures and ideologies on rights. Ideological and cultural relativisms – of which much has been said and written – demand a conception of ethical issues and women's rights through lenses qualified by differences in value systems. While laws in many nation-states, including in some of the states discussed in this book, actively embody norms that reflect this relativist notion of rights, the narrative of universalism and immutability of human rights has helped sustain advocacy for legislative and policy reform as well as large-scale structural changes across populations in many other jurisdictions. As UN member states negotiate their ideological stance with regards to internationally prescribed norms, scholars and advocates must also find ways to address the consequences of conflicting ideologies for women – consequences that cannot be completely disassociated from the strategic limitations inherent in a top-down and universalized approach to reform that is embodied in human rights advocacy. The nature, foundations and manifestations of these consequences and the reasons for the underlying limits as they apply within human rights law and progressive domestic law on women's healthcare are the subjects of focus in this book.

Limitations to the successful use of international human rights and domestic law to improve women's health are framed in this book as the derivatives

---

8 Charles G. Ngwena, "Reforming African Abortion Laws and Practice: The Place of Transparency" in R. J. Cook, J. N. Erdman and B. M. Dickens, eds., *Abortion Law in Transnational Perspective: Cases and Controversies* (Philadelphia: University of Pennsylvania Press, 2014) at 178.
9 Ibid.

of multiple traversing factors. Limits may be conceptualized as arising from the much-disputed nature of law recognized within the non-positivist school of juris-prudence as a system of rules defined by the formality of the procedures central to its formulation and interpretation as well as by its aspiration for justice or for doing right – what legal philosopher Robert Alexy describes as 'correctness'.[10] However, while Alexy considers human rights to be "absolute" and "objective" and contends that "necessary moral elements do exist",[11] the diversity of moral viewpoints around the world that challenge any assumption of a single concep-tion of 'correctness' sits at the root of the problems of legal effectiveness, espe-cially with regards to women's reproductive health rights. This is one of the primary ideas connecting the diverse chapters of this book.

Against the problem of different ideologies on what constitutes 'human rights', the extent to which women's reproductive health should be protected by state law and the nature of the protections to be secured by the state, this book asks: What is an effective law and what determines legal effectiveness or ineffectiveness? Are there limits that specifically arise due to the nature of the field of women's health law and policy? On this latter question, an observer only needs to consider the historical and continuous policing of women's bodies, and the significant legal and political debates over women's bodies and their repro-ductive health rights to understand that a perceived exceptionality of women's bodies and reproductive role in society provokes the inordinate interference with women's agency and autonomy. Fundamentally, the book asks: How might these limits (whether or not unique to the field of women's health law) be theorized? Specifically, what dynamics, elements and conditions come together to limit law's capacity to achieve instrumental goals for women's health and the advancement of women's health rights?

While there are no easy answers to these questions, what is at least clear is that addressing them requires an engagement with the nature of law. The con-nection between the subject of law's limits and law's claimed nature can be discerned from a study of the field, especially through insights from the philo-sophical debates about the factors essential to law's validity, as well as through a close study of the claims made about law within mainstream Western legal jurisprudence. Central to this jurisprudence is the philosophical framework of legal positivism, within which law is defined by certain structural qualities, such as autonomy, certainty, generality, universality, neutrality and uniformity.[12] This structural form of law – expressed in *legal formalism* – offers a legal methodology

---

10 See generally Robert Alexy, *The Argument from Injustice: A Reply to Legal Positivism* (Oxford: Clarendon Press, 2002); Robert Alexy, "On the Concept and the Nature of Law" (Sept. 2008) 21:3 *Ratio Juris* 281–299. See Chapters 2 and 3 of this volume for a further exploration of this term.

11 Alexy, Robert, "Law, Morality, and the Existence of Human Rights" (2012) 25:1 *Ratio Juris* at 3.

12 Margot Stubbs, "Feminism and Legal Positivism" (1986) *Australian Journal of Law and Society* at 65.

in which the application of law is grounded on a sequence of logical decision-making based on predetermined legal rules.[13] Several problems have been identified with this approach to the application and study of law. A major problem is that it offers an approach to understanding law in practice that is not reflected in the actual social circumstances that circumscribe women's experiences. Furthermore, legal formalism's "highly formalistic and apolitical understanding of law" ultimately produces conservative political outcomes for women that typically do not serve their best interests.[14]

Part of the feminist legal undertaking has long been to expose the ways in which this *"form* of law" regulates women's lives and the oppression that they experience.[15] This structural and adjudicative form of law, which – it must be emphasized – traditionally defines the very nature of the Western legal order, has historically served to "reinforce and reproduce existing" sex-based social and economic imbalances in relationships between men and women.[16] Thus, central to exposing the operations and real-life consequences of law – and a primary part of the goals of this project – is the task of challenging the very ideological foundations of law as defined in Western jurisprudence. On this, Margot Stubbs notes:

> An acceptance of the understanding of the law presented in mainstream Western jurisprudence (as defined by the "science of legal positivism") limits the development of a political critique of law as it presents the law as an autonomous, self-contained system, fuelled by its own logic, which is supposedly uninvolved in the processes of class production and reproduction.[17]

Beyond the adjudicatory problems arising from the conceptual construct of law within the Western legal tradition, a study of the procedural and substantive qualities of law also reveal entrenched limits. As Douglas, Sarat and Umphrey have noted, law itself is defined by "the very idea of limits".[18] In the definitive elements of law – its procedural and substantive elements – are to be found the very limits that constrain law in its operation. For example, the 'nature' of law as a system of rules that have been authoritatively passed, the social facts embodied within law, as well as the language that conveys law's purpose and commands can complicate compliance with law. Inhering in these elements – which are only one part of the elements of law on a non-positivistic account – are influences that bear upon the workings of law and whether a given law is regarded as legitimate. The potency of the limits embodied in these and other elements of law in predicting

13 Ibid. at 65.
14 Ibid. at 67, 64.
15 Ibid. at 68.
16 Ibid. at 65.
17 Ibid. at 67.
18 L. Douglas, A. Sarat and M.M. Umphrey, "At the Limits of Law: An Introduction" in Austin Sarat, Lawrence Douglas and Martha Merrill Umphrey, eds., *The Limits of Law* (Stanford, CA: Stanford University Press, 2005) at 9.

or determining the effectiveness of law, and the outcomes when applied against data on women's health and experiences across multiple jurisdictions, has actuated a classification of theories of law's limits into *formal* and *substantive* legal effectiveness – a classification proposed in this book for the first time in the field.

Also emerging from a majority of the chapters is an understanding that celebrated conceptualizations about law – whether as a pliant ordering growing organically from prevailing social norms and the values underpinning them or as an inflexible and predictable system of rules independent of the morality of their content – have implications for law's capacity to rise to the expectations of improving women's health and achieving gender equality. Embracing a comprehensive understanding of law's nature – one that recognizes law's binary qualities of procedural and moral correctness, several of the chapters demonstrably or implicitly explore the limits or problems traceable to this nature, which contribute to ineffectiveness in law.

For example, as evident in the overall discussions in Chapter 2,[19] law's seeming structural incoherence – arguably manifest in the historical and continuous scholastic debates about its nature and limits – reveals itself in its internal struggle to be reflective of transmutable social norms that are understood to be the foundational ethical blocks upon which a society stands and yet be immutable, predictable and independent of those same norms in its formulation, application and implementation. Unfortunately, the conventional Western understanding of law as 'formal state law' or 'positive law' that is 'textual', 'precedent based' and therefore 'predictable', obeys preset rules of interpretation and applies objectively and universally to all within its dominion often fails to capture the manifold social and customary law systems that (sometimes in the case of customary law and most times in the case of social norms) do not share these characteristics. That this conventional understanding of law influences the interpretation and application of state law raises significant problems for women and is, therefore, a legitimate subject for engagement in Chapter 2 as well as several other chapters of the book.

Beyond the interpretive and applicative impact of social and customary norms on domestic and international laws on women's health, the manner in which state law is implemented and the level of its success are also affected by the structural and infrastructural resources available within the health system of a given country. Laws are rendered ineffective where the system within which it ought to function lacks basic infrastructure for the implementation of the substantive rights. Much like non-legal norms, resource-based factors are important determinants of the effectiveness of legislation. In this book, resource-based factors, the influence of public perceptions about law's moral character and the internal elements traceable to law's contested nature that (1) affect the ability of a country and its legal system to effectuate its international human rights commitments; (2) impact the design and implementation of domestic laws; and (3) dictate the level of receptiveness to reforms on women's health, are all critically examined. Classifying the

19 See Iyioha, Chapter 2 of this volume.

interaction of these factors and other determinants of effectiveness within the typologies of '*internal* and *external* elements and limits of law' in Chapter 2, the chapters of the book broadly discuss the influence of these dynamics on law's capacity – in its conception, interpretation and implementation – to create transformative change in women's health.

## Design and methodology

This book aims to provide a sustained critical analysis of the limits of law's effectiveness in the specific context of women's health. The choice of a critical analysis significantly drawing on legal theory is deliberate and inevitable: not only is scholarship of this nature on the subject considerably sparse, the choice is also necessitated – as stated above – by the pressing need to interrogate the ways in which old orthodoxies about women and their personhood find renewed expression in restrictive and pseudo-liberal laws that have been spawned by the rising tide of populism and religious orthodoxy.

In light of this, the analysis is conducted through a multi-dimensional study (in terms of approaches, fields and theories) of law's operation in relation to several healthcare problems that women experience. In working towards the realization of its primary goal, the authors of the chapters have striven to be integrative and co-referential, where possible, in their analyses. With the focus (as noted) largely being on specific health problems and on a given jurisdiction (or multiple jurisdictions in some cases), each chapter offers a unique and distinct thesis, which – while referencing points of shared meanings in other chapters – stays true to the field of expertise, ideological leanings and thesis of the author(s).

The choice of comparative and multi-jurisdictional analyses was designed to test the several interrelated hypotheses of the limits of law offered in this book through trans-systemic analyses. Six countries (Canada, United Kingdom, China, the Philippines, South Africa, and Nigeria) are studied alongside human rights case law based on matters arising from Hungary, Portugal, Spain, Slovakia, the Czech Republic, Peru and Bolivia adjudicated in the international human rights system. Specifically, the human rights jurisprudence examined is from the Inter-American Commission on Human Rights, the European Court of Human Rights, the African Commission on Human Rights, and the Committee for the Convention of the Elimination of All Forms of Discrimination Against Women. The strategic selection of these analytically important states and regions has allowed us to assess the broader utility of the ideas and theories proposed in this book in a manner attentive to the plural legal systems in some of the states, as well as those legal cultures, as in the case of China, that are clearly different from those in Western democracies.

The analyses are critical and aim at reform, and in line with this combined approach the authors have drawn on a rich body of data, including scientific and social science data on health outcomes, successful on-the-ground reproductive health initiatives in the global South, records of parliamentary debates, judicial precedent, legislation and parliamentary committee inquiries. Most of the chapters analyze specific laws or selected legal provisions along with case law regarding specific health challenges or issues adversely impacting women's health; specific issues examined include female genital cutting, abortion, forced sterilizations, HIV and maternal mortality along with general issues pertaining to women's reproductive, physical and mental well-being. In addressing these issues and health problems, some chapters offer more sustained theoretical contributions, while others apply existing theoretical approaches in feminist legal studies and in the broader field of legal philosophy to support their analyses. All chapters of the book explore the discrepancies between theory and practice – the gap between the conceptual visions of a transcultural human rights strategy and the public health and normative challenges that women face daily within national jurisdictions.

## The chapters: mapping limits within and beyond the borders of law

The chapters of this book offer a range of interrelated explanatory accounts of law's limits – in each case focusing primarily on one or a few selected strands of the broader discourse on the limits of law. Without limiting the breadth of work accomplished in each chapter in this introductory paragraph (and the chapter summaries that follow in the next paragraph indeed offer a closer preview of the scope of each chapter), a quick review of the chapters reveals their primary leanings. For example, the approach in Chapter 2 – a chapter drawing in depth from jurisprudence – is necessarily holistic because of its aim for an explanatory theory. Chapter 3, which centres on the claimed morality that underlies law and human rights norms, draws significantly on philosophical views about law and morality in the field of jurisprudence. While the analysis in Chapter 4 is multifactorial because it addresses the overlapping influences of politics, the economy and communist culture, its primary focus on the problems of what is purportedly a liberal law places political philosophy and distinctive ideas on citizenship and rights at the core of its analysis. Chapter 5 examines intersectionality's contributions to the discourse on the limits of law through an exploration of the limitations of adjudicative strategies under the international human rights system. Chapter 6 focuses on the determinative influence of culture, religion and tradition and the ways in which these overlapping factors are simultaneously shaped by and deployed to shape a nation's laws and its national identity. Chapter 7 concentrates on economic limits to law's effectiveness and women's reproductive health outcomes, as well as the far-reaching impact of improved reproductive health on a nation's economic growth. Chapter 8 addresses a range of intersecting social determinants embodied in or created and/or perpetuated by law impacting on the health of a historically marginalized population. Chapter 9 examines legal, political and cultural factors critical to the reception and domestication of, and compliance with, international reproductive health laws. While the crux of analysis in Chapter 10 is primarily on legislative and systemic limits, it also engages with theoretical debates on the relationship between law and socio-cultural norms and the effect on the shape and outcome of legislative initiatives.

The task of mapping law's limits in this book begins with an exploration of the notional hedges within which scholars and jurists have historically situated their discussion of law's limits – a discussion outlined in Chapter 2. The chapter examines the dynamics that influence law's effects and explores whether the nominal returns from law can be explained by the conceptual structure of law or other external factors. Discussions on the nature of law centre predominantly on what makes law valid, what constitutes the 'borders' of law and what is possible within those borders. The chapter begins on the trajectory of this traditional discourse, exploring the meaning and nature of law as consequential to determining law's limits and its effectiveness. It applies the result of this analysis to the proposition that limits to the effectiveness of domestic law and international human rights law regarding women's health are traceable to a range of intersecting factors that include conflicting norms and values in various cultural contexts, influences on perception, reception and compliance exerted by factual, moral and scientific correctness, as well as internal limits created by asymmetries between law's objectives, its language and substance, and the needs, contexts and identities of legal subjects. These and other allied influences are pulled together in a principled three-part theory of Substantive Legal Effectiveness (SLE).

The SLE theory is developed around the normative reasons for legal ineffectiveness as a method of explaining and determining legal effectiveness. The chapter classifies these reasons or factors into the binary categories of *internal* and *external* limits of law, setting out how they challenge the legal reform project on women's health. In mapping limits to law, the chapter draws on empirical examples from a number of health and social issues that women face in their daily lives, such as violence against women, the regulation of abortion in Canada, the United States and countries in the global South – summarily discussing the role of science and scientific opinions in limiting women's access to abortion services in these countries, as well as female genital cutting.

The aims in this chapter are neither to provide an absolute account of the ways in which law has perpetuated or failed to resolve women's inequality nor to provide alternative explanations of accepted and fundamental understandings of law's contributions to women's challenges in society and the concepts that already capture those explanations. Recognizing the manifold systemic issues that contribute to poor health outcomes for women, as well as the contributions of current theories in feminist legal studies and the broader field of legal philosophy, the chapter focuses centrally on the scholarship on law's limits and on the effectiveness of law, offering a conceptual account of limits that both draws on proven ideas in the field and extends the discourse beyond the frontiers of those ideas.

The ideas central to the thesis in Chapter 2, outlined in three interconnecting principles in the concept of *substantive legal effectiveness*, suggest that the effectiveness of legislation or policy for women's health can be significantly improved through heightened attention to the implications of the element of *correctness* of a law and to the diverse identities, needs and social contexts of the beneficiaries of the law, and how these and elements constitutive of law shape the design, interpretation and implementation of legal rules.

For Jenaye Lewis, Irehobhude O. Iyioha and Dexter Dias, central to the ineffectiveness of the United Kingdom's Female Genital Mutilation Act is the problem of correctness – the problem of law's persistent struggle with "defining its relationship with morality" – and the manifold ways in which this substantive problem manifests in legislation, its interpretation and implementation. Thus, Chapter 3 expounds on the role of morality in lawmaking and adjudication on women's health and how discourses on and differences in the conception of morality creates problems for feminist legal work and the human rights agenda. In exploring problems associated with the diversity of moral views and with the concept of the universality of human rights, and what these mean for feminist legal work and its theoretical bent in legal philosophy, the authors draw on the works of philosophers Robert Alexy, Gustav Radbruch and Hans Kelson.

The authors examine how opposing moral views about women's rights and differences in the ways women's reproductive rights are addressed in different parts of the world problematize the notion of universality of human rights and complicate the agenda on making laws effective for women. Through a summary analysis of formal theories of effectiveness, they argue that a lack of attention to the fluxes in moral judgements often engendered by political, social and cultural considerations in any theorization on law's effectiveness can lead to an "inaccurate" and at best "incomplete" view of the consequences of law for women, especially marginalized women. The authors demonstrate the real-life manifestations and implications of these problems through a close examination of the UK Female Genital Mutilation (FGM) Act. By examining the reasons for the ineffectiveness of the UK FGM Act through an application of the three-part principle of *substantive legal effectiveness* first introduced in Chapter 2, the authors provide insights on the specific ways in which the factors outlined in the SLE concept manifest in a statute, its interpretation and execution, as well as in its impact on legal subjects and the targeted harm. In this, they offer an analysis that can be useful in the evaluation of other domestic laws on female genital cutting.

While the ways in which cultural norms (and their underlying moralistic character) limit the effects of the UK's law on female genital cutting is a major undercurrent in Lewis et al.'s analysis in Chapter 3, the problem that Wei Wei Cao confronts in Chapter 4 on abortion regulation in China includes the cultural as intertwined in politics, economics and demographic concerns – and significantly – as devoid of any of the moral or ontological sentiments of anti-abortion advocacy. Cao's discussions of Communist political and cultural ideology and the concept of rights in China as part of a series of intersecting formative influences on the nature of Chinese abortion law reveal a deontological view of the law – more aptly understood as a law creating a moral duty deriving from the assumed rightness or rationality of the underlying (utilitarian) obligation, regardless of the consequences of the act itself.

Legal access to abortion is typically perceived as a sign of autonomy and empowerment for women, more so in the case of unrestrained access. The law on termination of pregnancy in China is thought of as the most liberal abortion regulation in the world because it has no limits on the statutory grounds on which, and the time when, abortion can be lawfully performed. In a historical and cultural analysis of China's constitutionalized abortion regulatory regime, Cao demonstrates the inconsistencies between the law's putative liberalism and its actual effect on the reproductive autonomy and equality of millions of Chinese women. Cao argues that the enactment and implementation of China's ostensibly liberal abortion law is designed to serve the state's demographic and population needs – an objective accomplished through the manipulation of female fertility and the institutionalization of punitive financial consequences.

The chapter provides an in-depth analysis of the historical influences of Communist ideology in the definition of women's role in Chinese society and how Chinese traditional family values requiring women to lead maternal and self-sacrificing lives according to the needs of others encroaches on women's personal autonomy and right to self-determination. These gendered values, derived from the Confucianism-dominated culture, operate in tandem with the authoritative passage of state law to ensure China's abortion law is widely accepted as formally valid and 'correct' and, therefore, deserving of compliance. Supporting the framework of 'the state knows best' that underlies compliance with China's abortion law is an awareness and popular acceptance of citizen rights as dependent on (the primacy of) a duty to the state in terms of an obligation to act for the collective good. Cao rejects this deontological view of abortion rights – which manifestly conflicts with Western society's conceptual notion of universal human rights – as legitimizing a system that infringes on Chinese women's autonomy and reproductive health rights.

Fundamental to her rejection of the logic behind Chinese state law and practices on abortion are the insidious ways in which the workings of the law and its effects buoy up a false sense of effectiveness when assessed through what is described in this book as 'formal' theories of effectiveness. The formal effects of the law are apparent from the data – for example, there were about 13 million state-sanctioned surgical abortions in 2013 (not including backstreet procedures or abortions by other methods) and 10 million terminations annually by unregistered providers. In engaging strategically with the effects of China's abortion law through a broad and interlocking strip of legal, historical, political, economic and cultural analyses, Cao reveals the intrinsic limits of traditional approaches to assessing legal effectiveness.

Intertwined as an undercurrent in Cao's thesis on the ineffectiveness of China's abortion law for millions of Chinese women seeking autonomy in their reproductive choices is the intersectional harm that the law inflicts on Chinese women of poorer economic classes. Charlotte Skeet's analysis in Chapter 5 applies the concept of intersectionality to expose the limits of International Rights Adjudication of forced sterilizations among poor and economically disadvantaged women. Skeet systematically explores the intersectional disadvantages that result when state law and international rights adjudication fail to adopt or apply an intersectional approach. Skeet examines the issues through cases brought before the Committee for the Convention on the Elimination of All Forms of Discrimination Against Women (CEDAW), the European Court of Human Rights

(ECt.HR), the Inter-American Commission of Human Rights (IACHR), and the Inter-American Court of Human Rights (I/A Court HR). Skeet asserts that the "absence of an intersectional understanding of the women's claims" limits "effective standards setting" and the importance and effect of recommendations from these forums.

In reaching this conclusion, Skeet makes a number of important observations. She recognizes the sometimes conflicting rhetoric from women's rights advocacy groups regarding forced sterilization in which the language of rights is used to simultaneously justify the incidence of forced sterilization as well as vilify the practice. Skeet observes that these rhetorical/strategic practices, which (as Chapter 3 argues) raise questions about legal feminism's ideological commitments and, indeed, coherence, fundamentally fail to address the expectations and needs of law's diverse subjects.[20] According to Skeet, conflicting opinions on human rights norms and strategies for affirming human rights for women in relation to forced sterilization are due to a number of fallacies, such as essentialized ideas about gender, paternalistic ideas advancing a notion of what is supposedly best for women, or the promotion of a "corporate view of women's rights", which advances a view of rights as serving "the greater good of [all] 'women'", even in cases where particular rights limit the autonomy of already marginalized women.

Skeet's observations go to the core of the theoretical contributions that connect many of the chapters of this book: that notions of factual, moral and scientific correctness vary and can significantly influence the formulation, articulation, and adjudication of rights. Thus, Skeet admonishes that in articulating rights norms, non-governmental organizations (NGOs) and rights activists must be sensitive to how their "approaches to morality and correctness can be determinative of the outcomes for women's rights".

The swinging pendulum of what is acceptable and consequently a legitimate subject for feminist legal analysis and the problems engendered when unproductive connections are made between historically problematic policies (such as eugenics) and women's reproductive health rights resurfaces in Amparita Sta. Maria's analysis of Philippine reproductive health law and practice in Chapter 6. In spite of recent progressive legislative reforms on women's health in the Philippines, there remains a dichotomy between national policy and legislation on reproductive healthcare and established political and cultural practices that influence governance in the country. Maria examines the cultural, religious and traditional (CRT) factors as well as the political dynamics that create discrepancies between law and practice in women's healthcare in the Philippines. She undertakes this analysis through an examination of the Philippines' Responsible Parenthood and Reproductive Health Act (RPRHA). Known as the Magna Carta of Women, the RPRHA provides simultaneously for "comprehensive health

---

20  Citing Iyioha, Chapter 2 of this volume.

services" in harmony with women's religious beliefs and the "protection of the life of the unborn".

In spite of the legal reforms achieved through the RPRHA, political and social norms embedded in Philippine culture and governance especially at the local government level allow skewed interpretations of the Act that claw back rights guaranteed under the Act. Central to Maria's analysis of the multiple interpretations to which the RPRHA has been subjected is the 2015 Ordinance, enacted by the Sorsogon city mayor, declaring the city "Pro-Life" on the authority of the Magna Carta of Women. On the basis of the ordinance, the local government removed reproductive health services not deemed "pro-life" from local health facilities – an act illustrating the disconnect between national law and policy and local, politically and socially influenced implementation.

Maria conducts a methodic analysis of excerpts of parliamentary debates on the RPRHA, the constitutional challenges against the statute and the decision of the Philippine Supreme Court to show how the religious and socio-cultural landscapes of the Philippines enable parliamentarians and heads of government units, such as the mayor of Sorsogon City, to make their personal moral convictions the determinative policy of entire constituencies. While underscoring the ways that some members of the Philippine Parliament used the historical connection between population control and eugenics to justify their opposition to the passage of the reproductive health law on the ground that they were "protecting" women, Maria's analysis reveals the multiple strategies and conflicting logic adopted by politicians whose moral persuasions conflict with the notion of reproductive rights. Maria's analysis of the statements of parliamentarians further shows how the same set of facts can be interpreted inversely and used to deprive women access to reproductive health services under the veil of 'protecting women'.

The legislative pretext of 'protection' offered by parliamentarians as an objective for questionable laws and sometimes accepted in deference to legislative intent by courts adjudicating women's rights is problematic for several reasons. One reason is the considerable and compelling evidence that supports the position that women and nations do better overall when there is recognition of and respect for women's reproductive health rights. Through discussion of a rich body of "micro-level" evidence on the impact of poor economic status on women's reproductive health in Chapter 7, Karen Grépin, Jeni Klugman and Matthew Moore effectively demonstrate the connections between improved economic status and better reproductive health and the impact of economic factors on law's effectiveness, while establishing the positive impact of improved access to reproductive health services on a nation's economy.

Grépin et al. undertake an expansive multi-jurisdictional analysis that outlines the economic evidence explaining persistent gaps in women's reproductive health, highlighting how fiscal and economic challenges intersect with social and cultural factors to limit law's capacity to be an effective instrument for realizing women's reproductive health rights in practice. Conceptualizing these collective influences as 'external limits' to the realization of women's reproductive rights, the authors offer evidence-based suggestions on policies and programs for improving reproductive health outcomes, particularly in the global South, where the need is most evident.

As Grépin et al.'s broader recommendations for improving women's health outcomes reveal, economic advancements – consequential as they are to improved health outcomes – do not necessarily translate to progressive or effective laws, for a repressive state that is economically advanced would most likely produce laws that work against women's reproductive rights and, consequentially, engender poor health outcomes. The results can be the same for a progressive state where laws and policies are not attentive to many of the factors – unique needs, diversity of legal subjects, historical contingencies and situational realities – identified in Chapter 2 as central to the effectiveness of laws for women. Indeed, even in a Western liberal democracy – such as Canada – with legislated and constitutionalized recognition of women's equality, there is substantial evidence of the adverse consequences of law for racialized women, especially Indigenous and black women who carry an unfair burden of those consequences. Emily Snyder's analysis in Chapter 8 explores these consequences for Indigenous women living with HIV in Canada, not only as the consequences emanate from and are manifest in legal rules, but also as enduring limits deriving from entire legal orders. These limits, especially as entrenched in legal orders, are particularly problematic because they, as Snyder explains, are "shaped by social norms" that are "intimately woven into social problems".

Facing a number of health challenges as well as systemic and psychological barriers to accessing healthcare services, Indigenous women also carry a significant burden of HIV infections in Canada. Snyder's analysis is grounded on the available research on the health and legal issues faced by Indigenous women living with HIV in the country. Snyder addresses these issues – as created or sustained by law – from a multi-juridical perspective. While the focus of analysis in relation to the impact of law on the health of Indigenous women is often on Canadian State law – analysis which often prompts calls for changes to Canadian health laws and policies, Snyder directs attention to the importance of centring analysis of the limits of law for Indigenous women's health on both state and Indigenous legal orders. In this regard, she argues that "Indigenous legal responses also need to be central in discussions on the relationship between law and Indigenous women's health".

Thus, while examining how Canadian law has historically created or fostered deep-rooted and long-lasting healthcare challenges for Indigenous women, Snyder advances the need for equal attention to the ways that legal norms set within Indigenous customs might negatively impact, even as they support, Indigenous women's health. On this point, she suggests the necessity for a "practical" and "critical" approach to the adoption of Indigenous legal order in the protection of Indigenous women's health. Rejecting the practice of complete idealizations or total deprecation of Indigenous legal orders, she draws on the Indigenous Feminist Legal Theory (IFLT) – a theory that connects feminist legal theory, Indigenous feminist theory, and Indigenous legal theory in important interactive ways – to highlight the "gendered power dynamics" and social problems inherent in both state and Indigenous laws, which limit the effect of these laws for Indigenous women. She further applies IFLT to underscore why a "complex" assessment of these entrenched limits is necessary for ensuring laws are substantively effective for Indigenous women's health.

Babafemi Odunsi and Oluwayemisi Adewole in Chapter 9 and Arooj Shah, Simisola O. Akintola and Irehobhude O. Iyioha in Chapter 10 offer prelusive insights into the type of comprehensive trans-systemic analysis that Snyder advances in Chapter 8. Odunsi and Adewole's assessment of the theoretical and practical limitations to the reception and domestication of international reproductive health laws in Nigeria and South Africa reiterates some of the observations in the preceding chapters on the determinative influence of normative ideologies on lawmaking and the implementation of laws – especially in a multi-juridical legal system. The authors trace the conceptual, legal and practical limits to implementing international reproductive health laws in member states, identifying these as including legislated rules on reception (that is, whether the states operate a monist or dualist approach), the influence of moral correctness in lawmaking and implementation, and legal pluralism based on the multiple customary legal orders co-existing with state law.

Employing several indications of law's limits in reproductive health practice in Nigeria and South Africa to support their observations, Odunsi and Adewole suggest that the same underlying issue of moral correctness that constrains the will of legislators to implement international reproductive health laws is crucial to citizenry compliance with the laws – if at all domesticated. The diverse customary legal orders (typically embodying socio-cultural norms with their conservative moral leanings) that make up the pluralistic legal systems in many African states further complicate the implementation of international reproductive health laws even when domesticated.

While acknowledging states' legitimate interest in their sovereignty as the underlying factor in the choice of the respective reception rules, the authors – drawing on the opinions of other scholars in the field – question the continued relevance of the dualist approach in a globalized world, as well as its compatibility with the notion of universality of human rights. The authors offer a number of recommendations that lawmakers could adopt to reform current approaches to the reception and domestication of international reproductive health laws.

In Chapter 10, Arooj Shah et al. demonstrate how the same problems (regarding adverse cultural norms and practices) arising from the jurisdiction of customary laws over women – part of the themes in Odunsi and Adewole's discussion in Chapter 9 – contribute to poor maternal health outcomes in many African states and complicate the effectiveness of law and policymaking to address maternal mortality in the region. Focusing on South Africa and Nigeria as case studies, the authors identify the legal and systemic problems that are major contributors to the burden of maternal deaths in both countries. These problems include the framing of legal rights and entitlements in laws affecting women, abortion criminalization in Nigeria, legislative omissions in South Africa's abortion law, the quality of health services, the consequential impact of HIV infections on maternal health and the impact of customary practices relating to pregnancy and childbirth.

To appreciate the impact of customs and customary legal orders on maternal health in the two countries, it is important to understand the "relationship between law and social norms" and how this intricate relationship influences citizens to comply with or reject domestic and international reproductive health laws. The authors explore a few different philosophical perspectives on the relationship between law and socio-cultural norms to highlight some underlying issues arising from the relationship between law and norms, as well as to draw attention to problems with theorizations about the impact of this relationship.

Following an assessment of domestic and international laws and policies in South Africa and Nigeria on women's reproductive health, including the constitutions of both countries, South Africa's Choice on Termination of Pregnancy Act,[21] the National Health Act of South Africa[22] and Nigeria,[23] as well as relevant healthcare policies in Nigeria, the authors proceed to consider the extent to which these laws and policies address the problems of inaccessible and inadequate healthcare services. One of such critical services is abortion and post-abortion care, which – when lacking, inadequate or inaccessible – contribute to unacceptably high maternal mortality rates. Within this context, the authors summarily examine the reasons why South Africa's liberal laws on abortion have failed to ameliorate the problem of illegal and clandestine abortions among South African women.

Finally, the authors draw on *substantive legal effectiveness* (SLE) set out in Chapter 2 to explain the problems with these legislated attempts at addressing maternal mortality. Specifically, they assess whether there can be significant reduction of mortality among pregnant women through legislative and on-the-ground efforts without holistic attention to a range of issues that determine the effectiveness of laws and policies.

## Conclusion

This book aims to offer insights into the limits of law in the field of women's health law and policy. It adopts an analytical approach that recognizes the combined contributions of theory and empiricism on law's limits in response to the gap in scholarship (especially comparative scholarship that is manifestly theoretical) on the subject. The expectation is that in charting the influences that constrain law's effectiveness for women through trans-systemic and critical legal analysis that combines a range of empirical data and interdisciplinary approaches, the book can reach a wider audience beyond the legal field.

The target audience are specialists, comprising legal, medical and bioethical scholars, scholars in the field of reproductive health and gender studies, women's rights advocates, policy experts at both local and international levels, lawyers and practitioners in relevant fields, and professionals interested in the intersections of law, sociology, culture, politics, economics and religion. In spite of the (arguably) technical nature of the subject, it is hoped that a general audience of interested readers, including students from the social sciences and humanities and the inquisitive public, find its content useful in both current and future engagement with the issues addressed.

21  No 92 of 1996, as amended [CTOPA].
22  No 12 of 2013 [South Africa NHA].
23  No 8 of 2014 [Nigeria NHA].

# 2 Law, normative limits and women's health

## Towards a jurisprudence of substantive effectiveness[α]

*Irehobhude O. Iyioha*

## Introduction

Much has been written about the nature of law and what animates law as an authoritative system that regulates transactions and daily living. At the heart of legal doctrine and practice is a sustained interest and preoccupation with law's limits and effectiveness, with a focused interest on how law can be effectively implemented[1] and achieve projected results. Historically, law and socio-legal scholars have deeply engaged with and theorized on the limits of law as an instrument for regulation, reform and control. Most writings on the limits of law and the factors that curtail law's capacity for creating and sustaining change have revolved largely around law's regulatory role in several areas, including terrorism, international humanitarian law, discrimination and pollution, to name a few.[2] While there is a growing list of scholarly works that engage the subject of law's role in regulation and even in dispute resolution, less common are works that confront the limits of law in its protective or "symbolic" role.[3] In the specific area of women's health and law, this observation – outlined by Claes, Devroe and Keirsbilck in their book on the limits of law – raises two relevant points: the limited scope of the type of books available on the subject of law's limits and the type of academic analysis that has been pursued.

Although a few authors have produced incisive articles on the subject of law's limits in the field of women's health, there has not been a sustained analysis – in a book-length form that adopts a multi-jurisdictional and trans-systemic approach through critical legal analysis – that investigates the effectiveness of law and its limits in the specific context of law's protective and reformative function in the field of women's health law and policy. More common in the field of reproductive and sexual health law and policy and the broader field of women's health law

---

α Winner, Canadian Association of Law Teachers (CALT) Award, 2017 given for a scholarly paper that makes a substantial contribution to legal literature (co-recipient).

1 Erik Claes, Wouter Devroe and Bert Keirsbilck, eds, *Facing the Limits of Law* (Berlin; London: Springer, 2009) at p. xv ('Claes et al.').
2 Ibid.
3 Ibid.

and policy are inquisitions into the intersections of social norms and women's reproductive health, as well as assessments of advances in specific subjects of importance in the field. Itself an important analysis, the links between women's reproductive health and such non-legal factors as culture, social contexts, politics, economics, religion and tradition reveal much about the concept or nature of law. A study of these connections and how each strengthens or topples a legislative agenda designed to protect women's health is itself part of the inquiry into the constitutive elements of law. An examination of the limits and effectiveness of law on women's health of necessity demands a closer look at these issues: the nature of law, its constitutive elements, and its borders.

This inquiry is important because of the role of law (or societal expectations of law) in modern society. Law regulates an astounding scope of socio-cultural, political and economic behaviour in society and acts upon virtually all areas of human endeavours. There appears to be as much law as there is reliance on law and expectations of it to fix major problems and challenges in almost every society ruled by law. There is pervasive belief in the capacity of law to solve a vast range of issues that affect society.[4] Perceived ineffectiveness and actual lack of effectiveness in law's ability to live up to this expectation diminish law's reputation[5] and question the basis for more law. Indeed, this question is particularly relevant as the international human rights system continues to advance solutions to address the endemic problem of gender inequality. Elevated estimations about law's function in societal ordering and its assumed capacity for effecting lasting reform are particularly evident in this area. The struggle for gender equality has been mounted primarily on the front steps of law. The human rights agenda for gender equality relies heavily on the normative force of law for attaining its lofty goals. Therefore, the question whether law (including international human rights instruments incorporated into local legislation) is an effective mechanism for the social justice objective of protecting women's health and what accounts for law's limits are legitimate and momentous questions for examination.

Before further addressing the nature of the task undertaken in this chapter, it is necessary to first examine prefatorily the empirical grounds for this inquiry. More than 20 years after the United Nations Declaration on the Elimination of Violence Against Women, the statistics on the trend remain staggering: at least 1 in 3 women worldwide has experienced physical or sexual violence by an intimate partner or sexual violence by a non-partner.[6] Some national studies show up to 70% of women have been victims of sexual and physical violence perpetuated by an intimate partner. Women who have been victims of physical and sexual abuse

---

4 W.A. Bogart, *Consequences: The Impact of Law and its Complexity* (Toronto: University of Toronto Press, 2002) ('Bogart, *Consequences*').
5 Peter H. Schuck, *The Limits of Law: Essays on Democratic Governance* (Boulder, CO: Westview Press, 2000) at 420 ('Schuck, *The Limits of Law*').
6 UN Women, *Facts and Figures: Ending Violence Against Women*, available at www.unwomen. org/en/what-we-do/ending-violence-against-women/facts-and-figures.

are more than twice as likely to obtain an abortion.[7] In Canada, the alarming scope and extremity of violence against Indigenous women "constitutes a national human rights crisis".[8]

Outside the cases of sexual and physical violence, millions of women across Africa, Latin America, the United Kingdom, the United States and Canada seeking abortion services as a medically necessary procedure, whether for the protection of their health, lives or for other necessary purposes, face a range of barriers, including legal, institutional and infrastructural barriers, in spite of the 'decriminalization' of abortion services in some of these jurisdictions. In many African and Latin American states, abortion remains regulated through the criminal law system, creating a regulatory approach in which the procedure is allowed only on the basis of statutory exceptions to what is otherwise a criminalized procedure.

The 2015–2016 spread of the sexually transmittable Zika virus and the risks to pregnant women and their foetuses highlighted yet another gap between women's basic health rights and the implementation of those rights. Pregnant women in both the United States and parts of Latin America faced the multiple and intersecting challenges of limited abortion access or outright abortion bans and parliamentary rejection of funding bills to fight the spread of the virus.[9]

For a number of United Nations member states, the ratification of international human rights conventions affecting women's health and their enactment or incorporation into domestic law has not yielded the high returns expected. In spite of the ratification of the Convention on the Elimination of all Forms of Discrimination Against Women (CEDAW) by Canada and many African countries, violence against Indigenous women in Canada, as is the case of violence against women generally in the African and Latin American regions, remains significantly high. Also, female genital cutting remains on the rise, especially on the African continent and in many immigrant-receiving societies in the West.[10]

---

7  Ibid.

8  Amnesty International, *Violence Against Indigenous Women and Girls in Canada: A Summary of Amnesty International's Concerns and Call to Action* (February 2014), available at www.amnesty.ca/sites/amnesty/files/iwfa_submission_amnesty_international_february_2014_-_final.pdf (accessed 11 May 2019).

9  As more instances of locally transmitted cases of the Zika virus were reported in the United States, Congress engaged in political theatre with the Republican-backed Senate funding bill, which contained a Republican wish to end funding for the pro-abortion group Planned Parenthood, to fight the spread of the virus in Puerto Rico: BBC News, *Zika Outbreak: US Congress Blocks Zika Funding Bill*, available at www.bbc.com/news/world-us-canada-37293329 (accessed 11 May 2019). In the case of Latin America, women face the additional problem of poor healthcare access for financial and other reasons.

10  United Nations News Centre, *UN Report Reveals Increasing Incidents of Female Genital Mutilation in Guinea, Including on Infants* (April 25, 2016), available at https://news.un.org/en/story/2016/04/527632-un-report-reveals-increasing-incidents-female-genital-mutilation-guinea (accessed 11 May 2019); Jazmin Chavez, Female Genital Mutilation on the Rise in the United States, *Human Rights Brief* (March 18, 2016), available at

Against these data, this chapter asks: What is an effective piece of legislation? By what parameters do we define effectiveness? In the particular context of women's health law and policy, what factors are responsible for limiting law's capacity to improve women's health and advance women's health rights? The answers to these questions are neither straightforward nor easy. However, one finds some consensus in the scholarship on a causative relationship between a lack of effectiveness of both local and international legal norms on women's health and a lack of appreciation – by the artisans of the former – for the broad range of factors, inclusive of the context of laws, that determine legal effectiveness. Although one popular strand of the problem of context is articulated in the universalist versus relativist debate about human rights, a less explored, more intractable, though by no means unrelated problem is that of the inherent constitutive and normative limits to law's ability to deliver on its mandate.

The process of unravelling the problem of law's limits invites us of necessity to wade into the terrain of theory and conceptualizations about law and its disputed nature. This is because "law is constituted by the very idea of limits", and for this reason, a study of law's normative limits is inseparable from a study of its definition and nature.[11] However, while discussions of this nature tend to be categorized as theoretical, questions concerning the nature of law and its normative and constitutive limits can have significant practical implications not only for the practice of law, but on women's actual well-being. I will adopt a comprehensive understanding of law in establishing the practical effects of the nature of law[12] on advancements in the field of women's health. A comprehensive view of law recognizes the binary and yet interconnected nature of law and how this nature influences its functional capacity for social justice reform.

Debates on the nature of law have more generally been bifurcated along the positivistic and non-positivistic axis, captured most clearly by the Hart-Fuller debate. Ideas emerging from and expanding on this debate provide insights on whether some practices, laws and norms in the global South – often ideal targets of human rights conventions – can rightly be called law for the purposes of compliance. On the reverse side of the debate is the question of the validity of laws ratifying and domesticating human rights treaties, specifically in cases where those laws are a reflection of international legal norms, and differ from and seek

---

http://hrbrief.org/2016/03/female-genital-mutilation-on-the-rise-in-the-united-states/ (accessed 11 May 2019); Mart Tran, Female Genital Mutilation Increase in England 'Only Tip of Iceberg' (April 30, 2015) *The Guardian*, available at www.theguardian.com/society/ 2015/apr/30/female-genital-mutilation-england-fgm-girls (accessed 11 May 2019).

11 L. Douglas, A. Sarat and M. M. Umphrey, "At the Limits of Law: An Introduction" in Austin Sarat, Lawrence Douglas and Martha Merrill Umphrey, eds., *The Limits of Law* (Stanford, CA: Stanford University Press, 2005) at 9 ('Douglas et al., "At the Limits of Law"').

12 The use of the descriptor 'the nature of law' is not intended to impose a singular conception of or theorization about law's nature on all others. While recognizing the existence of different theories on the nature of law, I use the expression to acknowledge that I am herein making a conscious choice to align myself with one conception, shared by many, and which accepts law as comprising both positive norms and a moral aspect.

to supplant local norms and established behavioural patterns. An equally potent debate arises in the context of laws, such as China's abortion law, that enjoy compliance based on formal and cultural validity and mimic liberal values, even though their effect, on a closer look, is antithetical to conventional notions of freedom and reproductive autonomy. The anomaly of such laws incentivizes a distinction – conducted in this chapter and for the first time on this subject – between *formal* and *substantive* effectiveness of law. The necessary distinctions between form and substance, as well as questions of validity and what can be labelled 'law' – themselves questions about the nature of law – are fundamental components of my assessment of the reasons for legal ineffectiveness in the field of women's health law and policy.

The discussion continues in the next section with an examination of the meaning of law and legal effectiveness. I begin the discussion by exploring the meaning and nature of law because discussions of law's nature centre predominantly on what is valid law, what are the borders of law and what is possible within those borders. Next I examine the meaning of effectiveness, the borders of the discourse in relation to equality jurisprudence, as well as theories of legal effectiveness; and within this context I explore the concept of formal legal effectiveness. Part of the issues arising from formal legal effectiveness is the problem of the sometimes indeterminate nature of legislative objectives as captured in the categories of 'patent' and 'latent' objectives. I summarily address the problems associated with analyzing a law with patent and latent objectives through formal legal effectiveness.

Following the above, I examine the range of normative and prescriptive reasons for legal ineffectiveness – reasons that I classify in the binary categories of *internal* and *external* limits of law. Following this analysis, I examine in more detail internal and external limits to law, which capture the binary nature of law, and from which I set out the factors, inherent in the nature of law, that limit (whether in themselves or by application) law's capacity to protect women's health. In defining limits to law, I draw on empirical examples from the regulation of abortion in Canada, the United States and other countries in the global South while summarily discussing the role of science and scientific arguments in limiting women's access to abortion services in these countries. Underlying my analysis in this chapter is the thesis that an appreciation of, and heightened attention to, the significance of the element of moral and factual *correctness* of law's normative standards, as well as the diverse identities and social contexts of law's subjects – and how these impact on lawmaking (in its language and composition), legal interpretation, and implementation of laws – are critical to the effectiveness of legal rules.

## Law, meaning and effectiveness

The question 'What is law?' is fundamental to addressing the meaning of legal effectiveness. This is because the meaning or nature of law itself, as well as historic academic thoughts on the nature of law, is defined by elements that play a pivotal role in whether a given law enjoys popular compliance,[13] achieves its objectives and is therefore regarded as 'effective'. Scholars of legal philosophy have acknowledged the intricate alliance between the problem of law's limits (or the problem of (in)effectiveness) and the meaning and nature of law.[14] Indeed, inherent in the nature of law is the very idea of limits, and this arises from the fact that the factors that define law and its nature are inseparable from the elements that limit law's capacities.[15] To place this in a starker perspective, the meaning, nature and validity of law are determined based on combinations of at least three major elements – *authoritative issuance, social efficacy* and *correctness*.[16] Within each element are the internal and external factors that can significantly affect compliance with law and the outcomes of law and by implication law's effectiveness. Thus, the elements of law – the qualities that define law and determine the validity of law – are in themselves central to the actual effectiveness of law in practice. What, then, is law?

### The meaning of law

There are several competing ideas about law. To ask about the meaning of law is to ask about the nature of law. As Alexy aptly states, "To define the concept of law or to determine its nature is to say what law is".[17] Indeed, any study of the concept and the nature of law is a study of "necessary truths"[18] about law.

---

13  On the reasons why citizens comply with law, Charles Sampford argues that "[T]he reasons for compliance [with authority] will tend to be mixed and the mix will vary from individual to individual. This is uncontroversially true of citizens and has been shown to be true of officials by compliance theorists. Some [citizens] respond more to the threats of sanctions for breaches (coercion), some respond more to a belief in the right of the institutions to require certain forms of behavior (legitimate authority), and yet others respond more from a belief in the benefits of compliance (inducement and competent authority) . . . The individual may independently believe in the correctness of a legal prescription": Charles Sampford, *The Disorder of Law: A Critique of Legal Theory* (Oxford and New York: Basil Blackwell, 1989) at 229 ('Sampford, *The Disorder of Law*'). While Sampford's statement accurately accounts for the elements of law (specifically the elements of "authoritative issuance" and "correctness") which, as set out in this work, influence compliance, it remains debatable as some authors, including Anthony Allott, have observed whether sanctions truly compel obedience to law in the majority of cases. Of this, more is said in the course of this analysis.

14  For example, see Douglas et al., "At the Limits of Law".

15  Douglas et al., "At the Limits of Law" at 9.

16  Robert Alexy, *The Argument from Injustice: A Reply to Legal Positivism* (Oxford: Clarendon Press, 2002) ('Alexy, *The Argument from Injustice*'): Alexy uses the phrase 'social efficacy' to describe what I refer to here simply as 'effectiveness'. Correctness, according to Alexy, could mean moral correctness or social correctness. I introduce a new category here, 'scientific correctness'. In his book, *The Argument from Injustice*, Robert Alexy draws a distinction between moral and social validity, as well as between the implications of the conflicts between social and moral norms and law: see Alexy, *The Argument from Injustice* at 89.

17  Robert Alexy, "On the Concept and the Nature of Law" (Sept. 2008) 21:3 *Ratio Juris* 281–99 at 281 ('Alexy, "On the Concept and Nature of Law"').

18  Ibid. at 284.

Questions about law's nature and its validity are themselves questions about the relationship between the form of law and its content, or as it has historically been posited, between law and morality. It is at this mandatory foundation that the analysis here must begin.

The foundational question is in what ways does the relationship between law and morality and law and other so-called social factors affect the validity of law and the manner in which members of a society react to law? Centuries of analyses have brought us broadly speaking two philosophical schools of thought on the relationship between law and morality and how this relationship determines the validity of law: These are positivism and non-positivism. At the centre of the ensuing analysis in this chapter is positivism's core position that there is no "conceptual connection" between law and morality, between law and the correctness of its content, or between law as it has been promulgated and law as it ought to be.[19] While positivism has had various conceptual mutations, H.L.A. Hart conceives of positivism as grounded on five tenets, which – drawing on Margot Stubbs' succinct outline – presupposes that:

1   All laws are commands issuing from a sovereign.
2   There is no necessary connection between law and morals – a tenet drawing a line between law as it is and law as it should be.
3   The analysis of legal concepts should be differentiated from historical analysis of the causes and sources of law, and should be distinguished from sociological investigation of the relationship or connections between law and other social phenomena.
4   The legal system is a closed and logical system of rules through which "correct legal decisions can be deduced by logical means from predetermined legal rules, without reference to social aims, policies, or moral standards."
5   Moral judgements, unlike statements of facts, cannot be "established or defended" through "rational argument, evidence or proof".[20]

This conceptual framework, which "constitutes the methodological infrastructure of Western legal discourse", conceives of law as universal, neutral, "autonomous" and "self-contained".[21] Of particular importance, it also posits that the validity of law does not rest on the correctness[22] of its content. Accordingly, as long as a piece of legislation has been validly issued – that is its promulgation complies with procedural rules regarding the passage of a law – and as long as it has a "minimum" level of social efficacy, it is a valid piece of law regardless of the

---

19  Alexy, *The Argument from Injustice* at 3.
20  Margot Stubbs, "Feminism and Legal Positivism" (1986) *Australian Journal of Law and Society* at 64 ('Stubbs, "Feminism and Legal Positivism"').
21  Ibid. at 63.
22  At this stage of my analysis, correctness includes moral correctness. In my subsequent discussion, I will expand the meaning of correctness to include moral, factual and scientific correctness, as well as correctness in the context of non-legal norms and factors.

moral repugnancy of its content.[23] Thus, central to the positivistic concept of law are authoritative issuance and practical efficacy.[24] Within this framework, a law that denies women access to standard contraceptive methods of birth control in preference for natural approaches to birth control, if formally passed, is valid law regardless of the injustice it might perpetrate against women. Indeed, as feminist legal scholar Margot Stubbs notes, a positivist conception of law has "a *conservative* political consequence" in its separation of the critical analysis of law from broader social enquiries,[25] and this consequence often has grave ramifications for women's health.

Feminist legal scholarship outlines the origins and nature of these consequences. At its core, the feminist legal undertaking studies the various ways in which law, in its effect, harms women and the methods through which law can be reformed to ensure women's best interests are served.[26] As part of this inquiry, legal feminism challenges Western positivist theories of law that portray law as an "autonomous entity" that is distinct from the society it governs, and the legal system as "different from a political or economic system" that "operates on the basis of abstract rationality" – a characteristic that affords it the quality of universality.[27] By this logic, law is considered to be capable of being neutral and objective in its application[28] – a characterization that forms the 'dominant' conceptualization of law in Western theories of law.

One of the key tenets of non-positivism, on the other hand, is the concept of an essential connection between law and the quality of its content. Non-positivism in its various forms subscribes to the idea that the validity of law rests on a necessary connection between law that is authoritatively issued, its practical effectiveness and the moral correctness of its content. A piece of legislation that fails to account for moral correctness is, according to non-positivism, legally defective.[29] In order

---

23  Some variations of positivism offer different theories regarding the level of depravity that will thereby invalidate a law; for example Radbruch's conception treats the "extreme injustice" of a law as constituting a defect that goes to the validity of the law: for more exposition on this, see Alexy, "On the Concept and the Nature of Law", *supra*.

24  Alexy, ibid. See also Alexy, *The Argument from Injustice, supra*.

25  Stubbs, "Feminism and Legal Positivism" at 64.

26  Ngaire Naffine, "In Praise of Feminism – Butterworths Inaugural Legal Studies Lecture" (2002) 22 *Legal Studies* 71–101 at 72 ('Naffine, "In Praise of Feminism"'). As Naffine puts it, "the general purpose of legal feminism is to make sense of the many ways gender shapes law, to reveal the many ways that law, as a consequence, harms women, and to try to change law so that women are helped". Ibid. at 72.

27  Hilary Charlesworth, Christine Chinkin and Shelley Wright, "Feminist Approaches to International Law" (Oct. 1991) 85:4 *American Journal of International Law* 613–645 ('Charlesworth et al.').

28  Ibid. at 613.

29  Lon L. Fuller describes eight principles of legality, which any system of rules must satisfy as "internal" qualities that constitute 'morality' – an argument rejected by H.L.A Hart. Here, I focus on the tenets of positivism and non-positivism that centre on questions of validity as based on the existence (or lack thereof) of an external moral quality of law on which law's validity depends.

to explain the practical significance of these accounts of the concepts of law in the context of laws dealing with women's health, it is important to briefly examine the philosophical perspectives they offer and which are inherent in definitions of law.

## Philosophical perspectives and definitions of law

Definitions of law are as numerous as they are diverse. Law has been defined or described variously as "prophecies of what the courts will do in fact"[30], and as "the social system of a centrally organized, broadly inclusive community", which is based on a "sanction-apparatus implemented monopolistically by particular organs".[31] This sampling of definitions contains identifiers of the formal character of law which flow from formal, authoritative issuance, the element of sanction that is integral to compliance (at least at a theoretical level),[32] as well as the element of effectiveness. Robert Alexy describes definitions of law similar to the above as "efficacy-oriented concepts of law".[33] This means that such definitions highlight the importance of compliance: basically, they define law that is valid as one that enjoys the compliance of societal members. The principle at the core of such definitions is that norms to which we ascribe the label 'law' must command compliance by virtue of internal and formally prescribed rules compelling obedience to the provisions of law.[34]

Beyond the above formalistic definitions, there are definitions that support a connection between compliance with law and societal expectations of conduct. For example, Bierling proposes that "law in the juridical sense is generally everything that human beings who live together in some community or another mutually recognize as norm and rule of their life together".[35] In a similar vein, Luhmann draws on norm-based behavioural expectations to define law as the

---

30  Oliver Wendell Holmes, "The Path of the Law" (1896–7) 10 *Harvard Law Review* 457–78 at 461.

31  Theodor Geiger, *Vorstudien zu einer Soziologie des Rechts* (1st pub. 1947), 4th edn, ed. Manfred Rehbinder (Berlin: Duncker & Humblot, 1987) at 297.

32  Several scholars have argued that the relationship between sanctions and compliance is theoretical because there is no hard evidence that sanctions induce the subjects of a law to comply with it. The case of capital punishment for murder is often cited to support the argument that people will continue to commit crimes, even those with the harshest punishments. This argument devalues the theory of the deterrence effect of criminal sanctions. See Anthony Allott, "The Effectiveness of Laws" (1981) 15:2 *Valparaiso University Law Review* 229–242 ('Allott, "The Effectiveness of Laws"'); Eric Posner, *Law and Social Norms* (Cambridge: Harvard University Press, 2002) ('Posner, *Law and Social Norms*'); Bogart, *Consequences, supra*.

33  Alexy, *The Argument from Injustice* at 15.

34  Note, however, that this formal tenet does not require effectiveness or compliance with law to be based on an agreement between the provisions or content of the law and popularly accepted 'social norms'. According to formal, positive definitions of law, the fact that law might reflect accepted social norms is inconsequential to legal validity and is simply what it is: an existential fact that has no relation whatsoever to the formal validity of the law: See Alexy, *The Argument from Injustice* at 16.

35  Ernst Rudolf Bierling, *Juristische Prinzipienlehre*, vol. 1 (Freiburg i. Br. and Leipzig: J.C.B. Mohr, 1894, repr. Aalen: Scientia, 1979), 19, cited in Alexy, *The Argument from Injustice* at 16.

"structure of a social system" that is "based on the congruent generalization of normative expectations of behaviour".[36] And, although Hans Kelsen's definition of law as a "normative coercive order" emphasizes the element of authoritative issuance, the definition, importantly, also emphasizes that legal validity rests on the combination of authoritative issuance and efficacy that flows from the fact that the given law reflects commonly accepted patterns of behaviour. In fact, without the latter, according to Kelsen's definition of law, an "individual legal norm" can "forfeit its validity".[37] Also noteworthy is Anthony Allott's broader expositions about law. Although he defines law simply as a "normative provision or set of provisions in a legal order", his expatiation on law and the reasons that account for legal ineffectiveness suggest a view of law that derives its effectiveness from (among other factors) an agreement between the provisions of the law and the 'social norms' prevalent in the society in which the law is to operate.[38]

Regardless of scholastic differences on the relationship between law and the moral or social content of law and how this relationship affects law's validity, it is noteworthy that the definitions recognize the importance of *legal compliance*. As I explain shortly, different accounts of law (and indeed the overall debate on law's meaning, nature and validity) have real world consequences for women and their healthcare needs, as well as for legal administration and the delivery of "social"[39] goods. Arising from these theories of law – particularly in their convergence on the importance of legal compliance – are questions central to this and several other chapters in this book, such as: Can a law that is deemed morally and factually incorrect and fails to meet established behavioural expectations enjoy compliance and be effective? Can a law that fails to engage a community's moral sensibilities or compel its obedience be regarded as socially efficacious? And should a law, depraved as it may be, that meets the formal or procedural hallmarks of 'effective-ness' be regarded as '*effective*' if it produces disadvantageous results that negatively affect the health and well-being of the target population? These questions compel a reassessment of the traditional constellation of elements – as between *authoritative issuance, social efficacy* and *correctness* – that define law and legal validity.

In his works,[40] Robert Alexy argues that law has a dual nature: a real/factual nature and an ideal/critical nature. The real/factual dimension of law is captured by the elements of authoritative issuance and social efficacy. On the other hand, the ideal aspect of law is reflected in the element of moral correctness. According to Alexy, authoritative issuance of law and social efficacy are social facts, and the claim that social facts alone are sufficient for grounding law's nature and validity is a positivistic definition of law.[41] However, the element of

---

36  Ibid.
37  Ibid.
38  Allott, "The Effectiveness of Laws" at 232.
39  Alexy, "On the Concept and the Nature of Law" at 284.
40  Ibid. See also Robert Alexy, "The Dual Nature of Law" (2010) 23 *Ratio Juris* 167–82 ('Alexy, "The Dual Nature of Law"').
41  Alexy, "The Dual Nature of Law" at 167.

correctness, which is the second dimension of Alexy's dual-nature thesis, reflects a non-positivistic perspective of law. Recognizing the rationality of the dual-nature thesis and the fact that "law's claim to correctness always has reference not only to social facts but also to morality",[42] I herein adopt an explanation of law's nature that reflects the binary character of law. Specifically, I espouse the centrality of factual and moral correctness to perceptions about law and its validity, and by extension, their critical role in the determination of law's effectiveness (that is, whether law enjoys popular acceptance and compliance and whether its objectives are realized).

In achieving the central objective of this chapter – to explore the possible reasons for legal ineffectiveness and fashion a new approach to determining effectiveness, I emphasize the (1) the importance of *compliance* and *substantive outcomes* to legal effectiveness and (2) the critical role of *correctness* (or perceptions about correctness) in engendering these outcomes.[43] Broadly defined, *correctness* captures the aspirational nature of law that reflects the reasons for obedience to law. Thus, correctness denotes both moral correctness and factual or scientific correctness. While classifying *correctness* as an extrinsic or external element of law that builds "an outermost limit"[44] into and around law, the element of authoritative issuance, the social norms/facts that form law's content and the language through which the content is delivered constitute the internal elements of law. Taken together, these aspects of law – the internal and the external – mediate the way citizens relate to law. As I will further explain, beyond the outcomes of a relational analysis of legislative objectives and citizens' response to law (in terms of compliance or obedience), which is only one part of the basis of a theory of substantive legal effectiveness (SLE), equally important to an assessment of substantive effectiveness is a determination whether law's content reflects the diversity of identities and needs of those subject to it.

I adopt the view that law has a binary nature and that central to its effectiveness is the moral and factual/scientific correctness of its content because law's validity is not simply a function of its constitutional legitimacy and procedural fairness; it is also a function of its social effectiveness,[45] which can be expressed in terms of its morality, factuality, logicality and informational content[46] – that, as some scholars suggest, lead citizens to comply with law. It is my contention that

---

42  Ibid. at 171.
43  This does not discount the importance of "authoritative issuance" to legal effectiveness, which is herein taken as a given, or the fact that there are people who will obey a law they deem to be incorrect because of the fear of sanctions. While scholars remain in disagreement on the exact impact of sanctions on behaviour, my thesis and emphasis on 'correctness' is based on analysis of the types of responses, objections and limitations encountered by laws that address women's reproductive and overall health needs in both Western and non-Western societies.
44  Alexy, "On the Concept and the Nature of Law" at 282.
45  Schuck, *The Limits of Law* at 432.
46  Richard H. McAdams, *The Expressive Powers of Law: Theories and Limits* (Cambridge, MA: Harvard University Press, 2015) ('McAdams, *The Expressive Powers of Law*').

a perceived lack of correctness can affect legal compliance in a manner significant enough to diminish social effectiveness and thereby unsettle the foundations of traditional accounts of law. At a practical level, perceptions of moral, factual or scientific incorrectness among societal members or adjudicators can and have had an impact on the everyday operation of law in the lives of women.[47] Take, for example, the opposition to abortion in North America, specifically Canada and the United States. The opposition in these jurisdictions was, and continues to be, founded on moral and religious convictions about the procedure. Emerging research shows quite clearly a link between morally founded, scientifically packaged arguments and unfavourable judicial decisions in abortion cases in the United States.[48] Canadian medical historians are also uncovering the strong connection between the extreme opposition to abortion in Canada's Prince Edward Island and ethical-medical or scientific foundations for the opposition. By contending that a permissive legal framework for abortion services contradicted the supposed scientific fact that life begins at conception, pro-life groups were gradually able to use their position and voices to block access to abortion services in Prince Edward Island.[49] Thus, whether opposition is simply at the level of street demonstrations based on perceptions about the moral incorrectness of a law or in the courtroom manifested in judicial decisions invalidating (in some respects) women's ability to freely access abortion, we find an unmistakable link between some of the elements that are applied towards explicating the nature and validity of law – in this case, moral, factual and scientific correctness – and the extensive impact of those elements on women's lived experiences. Thus, the elements of law are at the heart of the effectiveness and functioning of a piece of legislation.

Parliaments often grapple with the role and implications of social facts or social norms when adjudicating issues affecting women's right to health services and products. As Babafemi Odunsi has observed, the lawmaking process typically involves consideration of conflicting philosophical positions on an issue.[50]

---

47  Note that Alexy asserts that the "mere fact that individual norms that are legally valid according to constitutional criteria for validity lose their social validity does not by itself mean that the whole constitution, and with it its system of norms as a whole, forfeits legal validity": Alexy, *The Argument from Injustice* at 89. Drawing a distinction between 'systems of norms' and 'individual norms', Alexy argues that the "threshold" of validity "is crossed only *if the norms belonging to the system of norms are no longer by and large socially efficacious, that is, no longer by and large complied with or a sanction is no longer by and large imposed for non-compliance*": see Alexy, *The Argument from Injustice* at 90–91, emphasis added. Notably, the author asserts that the "legal validity of a legal system as a whole depends more on social validity than on moral validity". Most of the analysis in this book resolves around social validity.

48  Caitlin E. Borgmann, "Judicial Evasion and Disingenuous Legislative Appeals to Science in the Abortion Controversy" (2008) 17:1 *Journal of Law and Policy* 14–56 ('Borgmann, "Judicial Evasion and Disingenuous Legislative Appeals to Science"').

49  Katrina Ackerman, "In Defence of Reason: Religion, Science, and the Prince Edward Island Anti-Abortion Movement, 1969–1988" (2014) 31:2 *CBMH* 117–138.

50  Babafemi Odunsi, "Abortion and the Law" in I.O. Iyioha and R.N. Nwabueze, eds., *Comparative Health Law and Policy: Critical Perspectives on Nigerian and Global Health Law* (London: Ashgate, 2015) at 207.

In reproductive health matters, the debate can include conflicting theological and scientific viewpoints as well as the perceived social norms prevalent in the society. The given law that is the outcome of such parliamentary debates does not of itself in general reflect the viewpoints of every member of the class that will be subject to it. Furthermore, the process of parliamentary debate involves negotiations, concessions and amendments. Thus, from its conception and formation, "built into the very nature of the legal norm, is a sufficient explanation of ineffectiveness".[51]

The complexities and inefficiencies of law are evident in the tasks of law-makers and jurists who must make and interpret laws; and in these official processes, there is often a balancing act between the objectives of a given law and the context within which the law will be implemented. Although not all national congresses or parliaments are, perhaps, as vocal as the Philippine Congress about the morality and context of laws as Sta. Maria's chapter highlights, nonetheless a close examination of specific bodies of laws (including but not limited to those restricting access to abortion services) reveals laws on reproductive health that do not reflect the actual realities of women's healthcare needs. It is against this noisy legislative and adjudicatory background of interacting philosophies and norms that draw on moral conceptions to (in)validate law that I outline the reasons for and associated theories of legal effectiveness below, beginning with a discussion of the meaning of legal effectiveness.

### The meaning of legal effectiveness

Concerns about legal effectiveness, especially in relation to a substantive law setting out entitlements and rights, can arise for various reasons. For example, a law might fail to achieve the legislated objective, whether that objective seeks a measurable outcome or simply compliance. Of particular concern here is how a formally valid system of norms may be rendered *invalid* because they are, to borrow Alexy's words, "by and large" not efficacious due to the fact that they do not enjoy popular compliance in spite of the sanctions for non-compliance. Perhaps a more complicated question pertains to how a law that is formally valid (because it is authoritatively issued and enjoys compliance) can be invalidated on other grounds beyond these formal grounds of validity. The problem with this hinges on the fact that the law, on the strength of a positivistic theory of law, is formally valid and socially effective. What, then, are the grounds upon which we can hinge a finding of *substantive* ineffectiveness? In other words, how does a law that is formally valid and enjoys compliance become *substantively* ineffective? My concern, therefore, is about *why* and *what*. That is, *why* might a law fail to gain acceptance? *What* are the legal and social norms that lead to non-compliance or,

---

51 Allott, "The Effectiveness of Laws" at 233.

short of non-compliance, account for the design and content of laws that limit women's access to comprehensive health services, including reproductive and sexual health services?[52] *Why* is a concept of substantive effectiveness necessary? *What* is legal ineffectiveness and what makes a law ineffective?

### Defining effectiveness

The task of defining 'effectiveness' is complex and the definitions of the concept are notoriously varied. There have been fervent debates on the definition of legal effectiveness among scholars from different interdisciplinary fields,[53] and different terminologies have been employed to capture the apparently elusive meanings with which the effectiveness of law has been associated. The concept has been described with the terms 'efficiency', 'validity' and 'efficacy'[54] as well as in terms of outcomes and compliance. The manifestly vague terminology of 'effectivity' has also been used in the literature.

A common meaning of 'effectiveness' suggests that a rule is effective "if it achieves the goals for which it was adopted".[55] Lawrence Friedman defines effectiveness as the "power to make an intended result occur, or the capacity to produce effects".[56] For Vincenzo Ferrari, legislation is deemed effective when there exists a "correspondence between the political plan" and the effects of the statute.[57] As Verena Zoppei explains, Ferrari's political plan is a broader concept than the statutory objectives intended by the lawmakers; it includes "intentions that are not explicitly expressed" by the lawmakers.[58] For Anthony Allott in his work, "The Effectiveness of Laws", "[a] general test of the effectiveness of a law (a particular provision of a legal system) is . . . to see how far it realizes its objectives, i.e. fulfils its purposes".[59]

Definitions of legal effectiveness and the terms employed for its description often reveal a focus on patent outcomes and compliance with law, that is, an emphasis on the end products of law. And perhaps this is to be expected in light of the nature of the discourse. However, as Allott has rightly observed, built into the very nature of a legal rule is an explanation for ineffectiveness,[60] a fact that necessitates recognition and assessment of the factors that account for ineffectiveness from the beginning of the life-cycle of a rule. There is support for this approach

---

52  This chapter does not pretend to provide a full and complete thesis on reasons for 'compliance' with law; but offers critical insight that is central to understanding compliance with law.
53  V. Zoppei, *Anti-Money Laundering Law: Socio-Legal Perspectives on the Effectiveness of German Practices* (International Criminal Justice Series 12, The Hague, The Netherlands: T.M.C. Asser Press, 2017) at 9 ('Zoppei, *Anti-Money Laundering Law*').
54  Ibid. at 10.
55  Ibid.
56  Lawrence M. Friedman, *The Legal System: A Social Science Perspective* (New York: Russell Sage Foundation, 1975) at 45 ('Friedman, *The Legal System*').
57  V. Ferrari, *Le Funzioni Del Diritto* (Laterza, Bari, 1992) at 148.
58  Zoppei, *Anti-Money Laundering Law* at 15.
59  Allott, "The Effectiveness of Laws" at 233.
60  Ibid.

in Zoppei's "elastic" concept of legal effectiveness, which takes into consideration the broader factors affecting the formulation, application and reception of a given law.[61] Additionally, the breadth and complexity of factors accounting for ineffectiveness and the fact that many of these factors are grounded in the very nature of law mandate a conceptualization of legal effectiveness that explores the unique character of law.

### *The borders of the discourse: on equality and effectiveness*

Substantive equality – first argued by the Women's Legal Education and Action Fund in the Canadian case of *Andrews v. Law Society of British Columbia*[62] – embodies the fact that at the core of the inequality experienced by women is the problem of hierarchy.[63] It invites an understanding that central to the substance of inequality "is always a social relation of rank ordering", which is "actualized concretely in specific domains for each inequality", in ways that are "often intersecting and overlapping".[64] The substance of each enumerated inequality is the "domain" within which the inequality "operates as a hierarchy"; thus, social hierarchy or hierarchy *simpliciter* "defines the core" of the problem of inequality[65] and constitutes the "social content" of the disadvantages that women experience.

Recognizing the challenges with defining the equality concept, former Chief Justice Beverley McLachlin of the Canadian Supreme Court asserts that substantive equality is one of three "rocks of certainty" in modern equality doctrine and on which the "evolving jurisprudence" on equality can be anchored.[66] The first rock, according to the chief justice, is 'substantive or material equality', which is to be differentiated from 'formal Aristotelian equality'.[67] The second rock of modern equality doctrine is "the idea that equality is concerned not with the letter of the law, but also with effects".[68]

Although the issue of "social effects" is equally at the core of gender-specific (or issue-specific) and gender-neutral laws,[69] yet the traditional discourse on legal

---

61 Zoppei, *Anti-Money Laundering Law* at 15.
62 *Andrews v. Law Society of British Columbia and the Attorney General of British Columbia* [1989] 1 S.C.R. 143 (Can.).
63 See generally Catharine MacKinnon, "Substantive Equality: A Perspective" (2011) 96:1 *Minnesota Law Review* 1–27 ('MacKinnon, "Substantive Equality"').
64 Ibid. at 11.
65 Ibid. at 12.
66 Beverley McLachlin, "Equality: The Most Difficult Right" (2001) 14 *S.C.L.R.* (2d) at 18 and 20.
67 Ibid. at 20.
68 Ibid. at 22. The third rock of equality doctrine is "the concept that the right to like treatment invokes a comparable right to unlike treatment": ibid. at 22. On this point, McLachlin states that "[it] is not enough to treat those in substantially similar situations alike; the law must also treat those in substantially different situations differently to avoid inappropriate distinctions and discrimination" – an idea that "has attained virtual consensus in modern equality doctrine": ibid.
69 The inequality problems generated by these two situations are two of four factors that Beverley Baines identifies as the reasons why women lose sex equality cases in Canada. The other

effectiveness aligns with assessment of the *effectiveness* of laws that purport to fulfil a defined objective, as in the case of issue- or gender-specific laws. Generally, the subject of the effect of law may be studied in multiple scenarios: first, it can be understood as addressing *results* based on expectations that a piece of legislation will produce the promised outcomes or effect (the typical purview of the scholarship on legal effectiveness);[70] second, it may be understood as speaking to *significances* with specific reference to the sometimes-unintended outcomes of legislation (an effects-based analysis at the heart of McLachlin CJ's theorization). A possible third scenario, which involves examining an issue- or gender-specific law in relation to declared (patent) and undeclared (latent) objectives, is subsumed below under the first category of *results-based* effectiveness analysis.

In the first scenario, the discourse on law's effect is concerned with gender-specific laws that are promulgated to address specific challenges women encounter. Some examples are laws prohibiting violence against women, criminalizing female genital cutting, abrogating involuntary sterilization or a law decriminalizing abortion.[71] This first scenario or category of laws – involving gender-specific laws that purport to be reformative – is the traditional focus of effectiveness scholarship, where laws are assessed against stated objectives and examined for the various ways in which their effectiveness is limited by the nature of the legal process itself or by factors external to the legal process.[72]

The case of laws regulating abortion providers and clinics that purport to 'protect women's health' within a jurisdictional context in which abortion is decriminalized – as in the case of US 'TRAP' laws (Targeted Restrictions on Abortion Providers) – falls within this first scenario. These laws raise the issue – critical to an effectiveness analysis – of the importance of discerning the true intent or purpose of a law, especially one that declares an objective different from a second underlying or latent goal. This issue is captured by discussions around patent and latent objectives, and the question at the core of the discussion of these forms of objectives in this chapter is whether traditional modes of effectiveness analysis are sufficient where a law has a latent or undeclared objective different from its patent or declared objective.

---

two factors are intersectionality and the s. 1 limitations clause of the Canadian Charter of Rights and Freedoms: See generally Beverley Baines, "Gender Equality in the Constitution: The Canadian Experience" (Anayasa'da Kadın-Erkek Eşitliği: Kanada Tecrübesi) in Fatih Ozturk, ed., *Road Map for the New Constitution (Yeni Anayasa İçin Yol Haritası)* (Istanbul, 2012) ('Baines, "Gender Equality in the Constitution"').

70  Friedman, *The Legal System* at 48.

71  These laws are typically modeled after, or inspired by, international treaties.

72  It is important to emphasize that the sense in which a 'gender-specific law' is used here is different from a law that makes a direct, specific distinction on the basis of gender in which, for example, women are banned from carrying out an activity: This is a problem easily remediable through a formal equality analysis [Beverley Baines, "Constitutionalizing Women's Equality Rights: There is Always Room for Improvement" (2015/2016) 37.2:1 *Atlantis* at 116]. My use of the phrase is to denote reformative laws that are designed to remedy a problem affecting women. Here and elsewhere in this volume, I describe them interchangeably as 'issue-specific laws' (see Chapter 3 for example).

In the second scenario, a sex/gender neutral legislation can have the "effect" of actually discriminating against women even while it purports to apply neutrally to the whole population.[73] Although an important issue in equality litigation, and one that is also addressed within traditional discourses on effectiveness, issues of immediate relevance, the scope of this chapter, and the volume of important work already carried out on the subject of 'adverse effects' precludes an assessment of this category of cases within the current framework of this chapter.[74] In the design of this project and in an early draft of this chapter, the focus of analysis was, and still is, primarily on exploring and pushing the boundaries of legal effectiveness analysis in relation to the first scenario, with an interest in exposing the ways in which feminism's equality and reform-based project might fail to hit the target due to law's limits.

The ensuing analyses explore the possibilities of a principle-based approach to determining effectiveness in the first scenario delineated above in which questions of the effectiveness of a law designed to advance women's best interests and equality are at play. Specifically, the goals are to examine the nature of the factors that account for discrepancies between the promises of a reform-based law that proposes to improve the conditions of women's lives and the actual effects of the law; explore the reasons why law may have a differential impact on racialized and marginalized women than it has on Caucasian women; and from these, extract a three-part principle on which we can ground a determination

---

73 A good example of this, though outside the health context, is the case of *Symes v. Canada* ([1993] 4 SCR 695), where a female lawyer challenged the income tax law, which did not recognize childcare costs paid to a caregiver as a business expense deduction, as infringing on her equality rights on the ground of sex. While non-inclusion of childcare deduction applied equally to men and women – which meant that men also could not claim this deduction, the plaintiff, Symes, needed the court to understand the adverse effect that this 'exclusion' had on her as a business woman for whom childcare is a significant expense. Her claim highlighted the fact that what constitutes an acceptable business expense did not consider the lived experiences of a woman with childcare needs and who had incurred childcare costs. The court rejected her claim, holding that this neutral legislation had not violated her equality right. In this decision, the court failed to see how this otherwise neutral law generated a gendered and problematic result, and had a disparate impact on the plaintiff as a woman than it had on men. This problematic result raises the question regarding the appropriate tools for assessing the neutral language and provisions of the legislation in order to unearth its disparate effect on women. For an example of a Canadian case involving a health issue where an adverse effects claim was successful, see *Eldrige v. British Columbia (Att. Gen.)* [1997] 3 SCR 624, 151 DLR (4th) 577.

74 Indeed, some scholars consider this analysis to be wholly within a traditional legal effectiveness analysis as 'unintended effects' of law – and rightly so. Its non-inclusion (in terms of an exhaustive treatment) in the present discussion is because of the chapter's general focus on gender-specific laws or laws that purport to advance reforms that are in women's best interests, as well as for reasons of scope and fair treatment. On this note, I owe particular thanks to Professor Lorraine Weinrib, constitutional law scholar at the University of Toronto who served as Commentator on this chapter at the University of Toronto Faculty of Law's Mary and Philip Seeman Health Law, Ethics, and Policy Seminar curated by Professor Trudo Lemmens, and whose incisive comments and insights helped to shed further light on this aspect of the work.

of legal effectiveness. In this exercise, the goal is very much connected to the broader goals of the scholarship on law's limits and legal effectiveness and as reflected in the hopes of the feminist enterprise in law: that law works to achieve substantive equality for marginalized peoples generally and, in the case of the feminist project, to achieve same for women given their historical marginalization in society.

Indeed, as Naffine has observed, legal feminists have long worked towards these goals. Legal feminists' understanding of the "limitations of law", and their dedication to law reform is owed in part to their "continuing frustration with the pace and efficacy of law reform for women".[75] In working towards these goals, legal feminists are acutely aware that while substantive equality is a transformative doctrine, yet – as originator MacKinnon, observes – a substantive approach to equality is "no silver bullet just because it is called that" and "can also fail to hit the target".[76]

The discussions of effectiveness, a fitting analytical framework or theory, and the necessity for a concept of substantive effectiveness that follow in the rest of this chapter reveal the contributions of effectiveness analysis to understanding some of the ways in which courts in and beyond Canada, as well as adjudicative bodies in the international legal system, have failed to hit the target of achieving equality that is truly substantive in lawmaking, interpretation and implementation.

### Theories of legal effectiveness

There are a few dominant theories of legal effectiveness among several postulations in the literature. Here, I explore the *Compliance* and *Outcomes* Theories, as well as the *Socio-legal* Theory, which offers an explanation of effectiveness based on the claimed equivalence of law and societal norms.

### Outcomes, compliance and socio-legal theories of legal effectiveness

The Outcomes Theory of legal effectiveness postulates that law is effective when there is congruity between the objectives or goals outlined in the law and the actual results produced by the law. The test of effectiveness is the assessment of the extent to which law attains the stated objectives or purpose. Based on this outline of the Outcomes Theory, it follows that a law with an underlying objective of changing behavioural patterns, which is well accepted and attracts popular

---

75  Naffine, "In Praise of Feminism" at 78.
76  MacKinnon, "Substantive Equality" at 10. Other critics of Canadian equality law have noted that "judges give lip service to substantive equality in Charter cases" while actually applying formal equality: see Baines, "Constitutionalizing Women's Equality Rights" at 116, citing Sheila McIntyre, "Answering the Siren Call of Abstract Formalism with the Subjects and Verbs of Domination" in Fay Faraday, Margaret Denike and M. Kate Stephenson, eds., *Making Equality Rights Real: Securing Substantive Equality under the Charter* (Toronto, ON: Irwin Law, 2006) at 99–122.

compliance with the stated objective, has met its goal and is therefore effective. Thus, both the outcomes and the compliance theories bear a similarity in terms of the underlying emphasis on legislated outcomes.

The Compliance Theory of law posits that law is effective when there is congruence between law's commands and societal behaviour. When behaviour differs from legal provisions, a law is considered ineffective. Underlying this theory is the view that law is effective when it enjoys "sufficient compliance to be accepted by all".[77] This theory – to the extent that it emphasizes compliance as sufficient to ground legal validity – is reminiscent of the positivist notion of law. Socio-legal theorists on legal effectiveness firmly reject this formulation of the concept of legal effectiveness.

Socio-legal explanations of effectiveness draw on social change and the "congruence of law with societal norms".[78] Socio-legal theorists identify law as originating from commonly accepted norms and values,[79] emphasizing how these affect societal response to law. For the socio-legal theorist, laws that are closely constructed to fit societal norms and values are effective laws.[80] The socio-legal thesis on effectiveness rejects the positivistic approach for failing to explain law's origin and how laws that are readily accepted, and are therefore effective, can best be created.[81] An example of the operations of a socio-legal theory in terms of an explanation for ineffectiveness may be found in South Africa's Choice on Termination of Pregnancy Act (CTOPA),[82] where moral disagreements regarding the content of the law have translated into restrictive practices in healthcare settings that deny women access to abortion. While other problems intrinsic to the statute feed into this problem, the overall disparity between social norms and values and the law's content has generated adverse outcomes for women, including turning women seeking abortion services to backstreet and illegal providers.

These accounts of legal effectiveness reflect philosophical views about law that are easily traceable to theories of law's nature, and to the extent that they originate from foundational ideas about law and its origin, they also carry some of the burdens associated with conceptual accounts of law. For example, a formal rule-based positivist model of legal effectiveness, as aptly captured by compliance and outcomes theory, fails to account for the role of social norms and values, as well as the definitive role of perceptions about law in the determination of legal effectiveness. While persuasive on the surface, these accounts of law without more fail to address the vagaries of implementation and how implementation is

---

77  W. B. Bradnee Chambers, "Towards an Improved Understanding of Legal Effectiveness of International Environmental Treaties" (2003–4) 16 *Geo. International Environmental Law Review* 501 at 502 ('Chambers, "Towards an Improved Understanding of Legal Effectiveness of International Environmental Treaties"').

78  Ibid. at 508. Note that Zoppei describes what is termed here the 'compliance theory' as an example of a 'socio-legal' definition of effectiveness. I align my analysis here with Chambers' exposition on these three theories of effectiveness.

79  Ibid.

80  Ibid.

81  Ibid.

82  No 92 of 1996, as amended.

itself affected by the social, cultural, political, religious and economic dynamics in a country. Furthermore, to accept the compliance theory as sufficient explanation for effectiveness is to accept an approach to law's effectiveness that fails to give a full account of whether the overall objectives of a law are being met,[83] or whether broader objectives related to fairness and justice are being addressed.

To the extent that the socio-legal theory of effectiveness emphasizes the necessity for congruity between laws and societal norms, it sheds an important light on the impact of perceptions about law on whether a society complies with law. However, a mere agreement between law and societal norms discounts the important issue of whether broader, equally important and often universal objectives of law are met. For example, is a law that conforms with societal expectations and yet works injustice to marginalized members of society an effective law? Should the fact of popular compliance with and acceptance of the law take precedence over a consideration of the rights of other members of society for whom the law is unjust and fundamentally ineffective?

Although beyond the scope of this article, the theory of intersectionality[84] can be applied to facilitate an understanding of how some groups of women defined by their race and other social factors experience adverse outcomes from a law that is otherwise effective for the general population. From the poor health experiences of Indigenous women in Canada to the experiences of women living in countries where there is liberal access to certain reproductive health services, there are ample examples of disparities in outcomes (for different groups of women in a society) of *formally* effective law that conforms with societal norms. The next subsection takes a closer look at formal legal effectiveness.

### *The case of formal legal effectiveness*

Traditionally, law seeks to regulate or shape the conduct of members of a society and it attempts to achieve this through prescriptive methods as well as through empowerment.[85] Thus, inherent in law as a "normative provision or set of provisions" are "objectives" or "purposes" sought to be achieved through the enactment of the law in its entirety or of specific provisions. To the extent that a law is a living norm that grows and develops and is subject to (re)interpretations, we may infer its purpose either through plain declarations in the body of the legislation or based on its most current iteration by a competent adjudicatory authority.[86]

---

83 Chambers, "Towards an Improved Understanding of Legal Effectiveness of International Environmental Treaties" at 504.
84 The term "intersectionality" was coined in 1989 by Black American Scholar of Critical Race Theory, Kimberlé Williams Crenshaw, to identify the ways that race, gender and other factors, including class, disability and sexuality, amongst others, intersect in a context of systemic subordination to create discrete forms of inequality. See Kimberlé Williams Crenshaw, "Mapping the Margins: Intersectionality, Identity Politics, and Violence Against Women of Color" (1991) 43:6 *Stanford Law Review* 1241–1299.
85 Allott, "The Effectiveness of Laws" at 233.
86 Ibid.

Whatever the purpose or objective of a law, the traditional test of effectiveness of a law at a *formal* level is the assessment of the extent to which it attains its objective or purpose, whether it attains this through compliance or other metrics.

For example, we may assess a law guaranteeing women's right to abortion on the basis of how many women who need the procedure are actually able to access it in a given community. Or, the effectiveness of a law that prohibits violence against women may be assessed through the lenses of the data on reduction of incidences of violence since the passage of the law; such a law may also be assessed based on the rate of prosecution of offenders against the data on incidences of the prohibited act. However, in each of these cases, we could examine the data in a different way. We may question whether the easy accessibility of abortion services fulfils a purpose different from that of reproductive autonomy or protecting the expectant mother's health or life. We may assess the data in the context of the broader policies, such as population control, behind the law liberalizing abortion services; and this exercise may reveal that, though the law formally achieves its purpose, it has a negative impact on women's reproductive autonomy and even health. In the case of laws on violence against women, we may consider whether the reduced incidence of violence is due to underreporting or other social factors.

Similar assessments may be made in the context of 'compliance' with law. Thus, effectiveness in a formal sense may be determined by the degree of compliance by members of the given society whose conduct the law regulates with what the law prohibits or mandates. For prescriptive laws, such as those on female genital cutting (FGC)[87] and laws prohibiting violence against women, effectiveness may be measured by the data on prosecution of offenders alongside a comparison between the data on the number of women who have been cut since the passage of the law and the data before the passage of the law. This methodology would provide information that helps determine the degree to which legal subjects are obeying the legislative injunction against FGC and other forms of violence against women and the extent to which the police is prosecuting offenders. An increase in the number of procedures carried out since the passage of the law or poor prosecutorial efforts pitted against a rising number of procedures will be a sign of non-compliance or ineffectiveness with particular reference to the law.

Yet, the data on the number of women who have been cut since the passage of the law may be coloured by underground practices, secrecy and collusion between families and physicians – all factors that can distort information on whether there is actual compliance or whether practitioners have simply developed new ways to avoid compliance and being caught. These contextual factors, as is the case with the preceding examples on abortion and violence against women, capture the line between formal effectiveness and a more substantive notion of effectiveness. In the latter case, any analysis of data or records towards the goal of determining whether a law fulfils its objective(s) cannot be done in isolation from the context within which the law exists or was created.

---

87 See Lewis et al., Chapter 3 in this volume, for a fuller discussion of female genital cutting.

In the case of curative or facilitative laws, such as a law guaranteeing the right to abortion, where compliance is measured by the extent to which women seeking the procedure are able to access it without significant bureaucratic or institutional obstacles, a context-based analysis of legal effect would require not only an assessment of the underlying purpose behind the liberalization of the right but also its actual impact on women. Where a significant number of women in a given state or province have their decision to have an abortion subjected to scrutiny by a board or committee, or their journey to a facility for the procedure is unnecessarily clandestine and fraught with transportation, distance-related, informational and other hurdles,[88] we can rightly argue that the permissive law on abortion has not fulfilled its purpose for the affected women. In this case, effectiveness is measured against compliance by those entrusted with the implementation of the law.

Scholars have rightly noted that the assessment of effectiveness based on rates of compliance and deviance is hugely flawed; indeed, the evaluation of the effectiveness of a law or rule cannot be a quantitative exercise.[89] However, many traditional methods of effectiveness analysis, which can fall within the umbrella of 'formal legal effectiveness', incorporate both quantitative and qualitative methods that identify the differential impact of law on different identity groups, as well as the unintended effects of a policy.[90] Nevertheless, besides unnecessarily conflating issues of 'efficiency' with effectiveness – a conflation, arguably, offering helpful[91] but limited insights into the more substantive issues at the core of legal effectiveness, formal methods of effectiveness analysis often embody many of the flaws of formalist conceptions of law. Specifically, a close examination of formal or traditional assessments of legal effectiveness – which are typically cast as 'policy-analysis' within a political science perspective – reveals underlying assumptions about the supposed clarity, objectivity and rationality of law, as well as about legal language, law's intent and legislative goals. Of course, all of these assumed or claimed qualities of law are contested.

As Zoppei has observed:

> Certain typologies of policy-analyses assume typically that legislative intent is capable of being made clear and known, that language itself is transparent,

---

88  See generally Christabelle Sethna and Marion Doull, "Spatial Disparities and Travel to Freestanding Abortion Clinics in Canada" (2013) 38 *Women's Studies International Forum* 52–62 ('Sethna and Doull, "Spatial Disparities"'); Christabelle Sethna and Marion Doull, "Accidental Tourists: Canadian Women, Abortion Tourism, and Travel" (2012) 41 *Women's Studies* 457–475 ('Sethna and Doull, "Accidental Tourists"'); Christabelle Sethna, Beth Palmer, Katrina Ackerman and Nancy Janovicek, "Choice, Interrupted: Travel and Inequality of Access to Abortion Services since the 1960s" (Spring 2013) 71 *Labour/Le Travail* 29–48 ('Sethna et al., "Choice, Interrupted"').

89  Zoppei, *Anti-Money Laundering Law* at 13.

90  Florence Morestin, "A Framework for Analyzing Public Policies: Practical Guide" (National Collaborating Centre for Healthy Public Policy Briefing Note, September 2012).

91  See Zoppei, *Anti-Money Laundering Law* at 13, where the author acknowledges that, while efficiency analysis is not "exhaustive", it also provides information on effectiveness.

and that the policy-making process is rational and geared towards attaining stipulated goals.[92]

This approach to analyzing law and its effects mirrors the legalism that is entrenched in a positivistic concept of law in which law is expected to operate with certainty and neutrality, and with a commitment to universality and generality in its operations.[93] Just as the qualities of legalism in the application of law "frustrate the use of law as an instrument for social change", so also traditional, formalist methods of analyzing effectiveness exclude the "qualitatively different interests and social origins of individuals from entering into the calculus of political exchange".[94] Furthermore, much like positivism's "analytical focus" on the "internal consistency" of legal rules "to the exclusion of their substantive content and social effect",[95] formalist analyses of effectiveness – in their focus on mapping quantitative and qualitative outcomes of rules defined by positivism's structural qualities – limit understanding of the social phenomena underlying the outcomes of their analysis.

Basically, this follows from the fact that while they identify problems with a law's effectiveness, formal legal assessments of law's effectiveness through traditional metrics are not explanatory and, therefore, do not provide the reasons for law's disparate or adverse impact. They also do not offer an account of the endemic nature of ineffectiveness within law – a quality necessitating a theory that is not only retrospective but is pre-emptive in its prescriptions on law's effectiveness.

As has already been discussed in the foregoing, another consequence that arises from these deficiencies is their distortion of the true effect of otherwise 'formally effective' laws on women's lives – a distortion that hinders a truly qualitative assessment of the consequences of law. If legal effectiveness in a formal sense is primarily about producing legislated objectives or purposes, that is, about achieving projected results, measurement based on compliance is basically an assessment of the extent to which behavioural patterns are modified because of a new law or legal norm. Therefore, compliance induced by the formal validity of the law and even that produced by erroneous assumptions regarding the correctness of the law says nothing about the actual impact of the law on women. In this sense, formal compliance that does not reflect the core ideals underlying reproductive health and freedom can produce as much negative consequences as non-compliance.

Notably, scholars of law and criminology have expressed diverse opinions on whether law actually compels action. In his view, Anthony Allott argues that

---

92 Ibid.
93 See Stubbs, "Feminism and Legal Positivism" at 69.
94 Stubbs, "Feminism and Legal Positivism" at 69, citing I. Balbus, "Legal Form and Commodity Form: An Essay on the Relative Autonomy of the Law" (1977) 11 *Law and Society Review* 71.
95 Stubbs "Feminism and Legal Positivism" at 78, citing J. Wallace and J. Fiocco, "Recent Criticisms of Formalism in Legal Theory and Legal Education" (1980–81) 7 *Adelaide Law Review* 309.

law cannot compel anyone to observe it, even when the law is mandatory and issues sanctions for non-compliance. Allott contends that "all that a law can do is to try to *induce* someone to a particular course of action" through "threats or rewards".[96] Views such as this gain credence when we examine the case of crimes that attract capital punishment. Another example, more relevant to the context of this analysis, is the case of FGC laws. Available data show a subsisting practice that has defied the criminal laws and (sometimes) steep sanctions against the procedure in practising communities.[97]

The question, then, necessarily turns on the reasons for this. Why would a legal norm with an in-built system of enforcement and steep sanction(s) fail to command obedience or compliance? Although many UN member states ratified the Convention on Elimination of All Forms of Discrimination Against Women (CEDAW) and some have made various attempts to implement the Convention in their jurisdictions, the results of these efforts have been less than definitive.[98] Even in the area of civil and social rights, local implementation has at best produced chequered results. From South Africa to Kenya and to Nigeria, attempts at guaranteeing some health and social rights have either failed completely as in the case of Nigeria where abortion largely remains a crime;[99] or where they have succeeded (as in the case of South Africa which guarantees women the right to abortion), the successful passage of a law guaranteeing reproductive and sexual health services to women may still be tainted by problems of access due to resource and infrastructural limitations[100] and the overwhelming moral bias of service providers.

## *Reasons for Ineffectiveness*

### *Law's objectives*

PATENT AND LATENT OBJECTIVES AND THE LIMITS
OF FORMAL THEORIES OF EFFECTIVENESS

Part of the goal of legal reform involves challenging law through the invocation of "law's own objectives and stated intentions".[101] Indeed, entrenched in the nature of law is its aspirational goal to "do right to everyone" and "be fair and impartial".[102] This aspirational attribute of law demands clarity in the law, as well

---

96  Allott, "The Effectiveness of Laws" at 235. Emphasis is mine.
97  See note 10.
98  See, however, Neil A. Englehart and Melissa K. Miller, "The CEDAW Effect: International Law's Impact on Women's Right" (2014) 13:1 *Journal of Human Rights* 22–47, where the authors argue that CEDAW has been effective for women's rights.
99  Abortion is permitted only where a continuation of the pregnancy would pose a risk to the health or life of the mother.
100  See Rachel Rebouché, "The Limits of Reproductive Rights in Improving Women's Health" (2011) 63 *Alabama Law Review* 1.
101  Naffine, "In Praise of Feminism" at 78.
102  Ibid.

as linguistic objectivity in the laying out of the objectives of law. Yet, in practice, this is not always the case.

The objectives of a law may not always be clear or declared. In fact, a legislature may offer a false objective while concealing – usually ineffectively – the true purposes of the law. This true purpose (a latent objective) of the law may be the opposite of the declared purpose (or otherwise patent objective). Here, "lawmakers . . . say one thing" even though they "mean another".[103] Thus, guided by moral or other political considerations, lawmakers may intend or desire results that are not expressly stated.[104] One area in the field of women's reproductive health law and policy in which latent objectives are commonplace is abortion law. Several states in the United States have tried to claw back abortion rights by passing legislation with the declared or patent intent of 'protecting' women's health. Laws imposing strict and often unnecessary requirements on clinics and providers described as 'TRAP' – Targeted Restrictions on Abortion Providers – are an example of such laws.

On closer examination of these laws, what emerges is the latent objective of limiting women's access to abortion. In the landmark case of *Whole Woman's Health v. Hellerstedt*[105] decided on 27 June 2016, the US Supreme Court in a 5–3 decision struck down Texas' House Bill 2 (H.B. 2), which placed several restrictions on abortion clinics and providers. Among other restrictive provisions, the law required providers to have admitting privileges at a hospital within 30 miles of an abortion clinic – a provision purporting to guarantee a woman quick access to emergency help upon complications following an abortion, even though this risk is not borne out by the data. When this provision took effect, the number of clinics providing abortion dropped from 42 to 19.[106] In striking down the law, the Supreme Court observed that the law "provides few, if any, health benefits for women, poses a substantial obstacle to women seeking abortions, and constitutes an 'undue burden' on their constitutional right to do so".[107] The underlying question in *Whole Woman's Health* settled on whether the court would defer to the legislature's claim that the challenged provisions were enacted to protect women's health or whether the court would scrutinize the law to ascertain this declared objective for its real effects.[108] In choosing to lift the veil on the *patent* or declared purpose of the law, the court was able to ascertain the actual or real effects of the law on women – that of placing a significant obstacle on women's access to

103 Friedman, *The Legal System* at 55.

104 V. Aubert, "Alcune Funzioni Sociali Della Legislazione" (1965) 14 *Quaderni di Sociologia* 313–338 at 329 ('Aubert, "Alcune Funzioni Sociali Della Legislazione"').

105 *Whole Woman's Health v. Hellerstedt*, 579 U.S. __, 136 S. Ct. 2292 (2016).

106 Lindsey Cook, "Explaining the *Whole Woman's Health v. Cole Abortion* Case" *U.S. News* (January 11, 2016).

107 Cook, *Whole Woman's Health, supra*.

108 Cary Franklin, "*Whole Woman's Health v. Hellerstedt* and What it Means to Protect Women" in *Reproductive Rights and Justice Stories* (Foundation Press, 2019 – forthcoming); *University of Texas Law, Public Law Research Paper* No. 691.

abortion,[109] which was the law's *latent* objective. A decision such as *Whole Women's Health* further confirms that procedural limitations, such as those in H.B. 2, are often symptoms of normative or substantive objection to the core issue that the law purports to regulate or an issue already regulated by a different law.[110]

Latent objectives, which can often be discerned from the parliamentary records of debates on a bill or by studying its "real effects"[111] in practice, can be problematic when they are intended to curtail rights granted by other bodies or sources of law. The existence of patent and latent objectives further complicates the assessment of legal effectiveness because of the importance of determining the core or real objectives of the relevant legislation and the different ways its latent objectives operate or are manifest.

Importantly, discernment of the actual or latent objectives of a law has a real impact on whether or not a given law is deemed effective, and therefore renders even more critical the choice of an appropriate method of analysis. What this means is that an outcomes- or compliance-based approach to legal effectiveness might readily find a law with questionable objectives such as Texas' H.B. 2 to be quite effective at achieving their patent and latent goals based on traditional metrics,[112] even though those very goals worsen health outcomes for women and limit their constitutionally protected reproductive health rights. An alternative effectiveness analysis of the same law – one that is attentive to the dynamics of legislative objectives, language choice, and moral and scientific correctness (to name a few of the metrics in a substantive effectiveness approach) – would reveal the law's ineffectiveness for women in spite of its declared goal of protecting women's health.

### Internal and external limits

Compliance with law is about human behaviour. Compliance is also about perceptions, whether or not the perceptions are non-factual or factually based. The perceptions that influence a legal subject's views and reaction to a law are often influenced, generally speaking, by the individual's opinion of the correctness of the law and by the individual's conscious or subconscious reaction to prevailing social, cultural, traditional, political and economic factors (non-legal norms), which may conform or conflict with the law. While correctness of a law

---

109 *Whole Woman's Health v. Hellerstedt*, available at www.scotusblog.com/case-files/cases/whole-womans-health-v-cole/ (accessed 11 May 2019).

110 See J.N. Erdman, "The Procedural Turn: Abortion at the European Court of Human Rights" in R.J. Cook, J.N. Erdman and B.M. Dickens, eds., *Abortion Law in Transnational Perspective: Cases and Controversies* (Philadelphia: University of Pennsylvania Press, 2014) at 122, where the author notes that, "procedure is always related to some substantive end, but often in indirect and complex ways, and sometimes in defiance of intention and expectation".

111 Zoppei, *Anti-Money Laundering Law* at 18.

112 H.B. 2 was indeed effective at reducing the number of abortion clinics from 42 to 19 upon coming into effect.

(concerning law's moral and factual/scientific qualities and the context-based perceptions of societal members) – that often influence legislative and judicial decision-making, implementation of law, and individuals' perceptions of legal validity – relate to the contextual and *external* character of law, the intrinsic qualities of authoritative issuance, social facts/norms and language speak to the content and *internal* character of laws. Therefore, legal compliance goes to the heart of the *content* and *context* of laws.[113]

As will be recalled, law and its validity are primarily defined by any of two constellations of the elements of authoritative issuance, social efficacy and correctness. These three elements, as noted, form the basis of Alexy's dual-nature thesis: that law has a real/factual aspect based on authoritative passage and on social effectiveness and an ideal/critical aspect defined by the correctness of its content.[114] Taking authoritative issuance (a procedural limit) as a fixed value, which needs no further analysis in the context of this essay, I focus on social efficacy and correctness, applying the standard of correctness to both the factual and moral character of law. These two elements of law – social efficacy and correctness – contain the conceptual tools for my analysis of legal effectiveness. Arguing that 'effectiveness' is greatly influenced by the perceived correctness of both the moral and factual bases of law, I outline two categories of limits to law's effectiveness that are produced by the element of correctness: *Internal* and *External* Limits. The former deals primarily with factors (language and social facts/norms) that are content-based, that is, based on qualities *internal* to law itself. These factors are critical to how a law is interpreted and applied to those whose conduct is to be governed and how it is received, and the extent of compliance by the governed. The latter addresses factors (moral and factual/scientific correctness) that form the backdrop of law in a given society – and which "[build] into law an outermost limit".[115] These external factors and limits to law capture perceptions as well as objective and non-objective explanatory grounds for the acceptance and operation of law. The context of laws, as manifest in diverse societal norms and factors, including social, cultural, traditional, religious, political and economic, as well as considerations of history, race and identity, are equally relevant to how a given law is or ought to be interpreted, applied and received; but more specifically they have the innate capacity to influence and shape the design, content and implementation of law, as well as compliance with law. These factors, as well as how they affect the making, interpretation and reception of law, can assist the analyst in determining effectiveness. The next section examines the first of the two primary limits to legal effectiveness: *internal limits*.

---

113 This brings the analysis back to the nature of law. In aligning non-legal norms with *context*, I do not hereby ignore the sociological fact of the constitutive relationship between law and non-legal norms. Rather, I consider this fact implicit in my account of non-legal norms as constituting the context of laws.

114 Alexy also observes that "the claim of law to correctness always has reference not only to social facts but also to morality": Alexy, "The Dual Nature of Law" at 171.

115 Alexy, "On the Concept and the Nature of Law" at 282.

*Internal limits*

LANGUAGE AND LAW'S NORMATIVE ENDS

Internal elements of law reflect the content of a law or legal norm as well as the authoritative nature of law. They refer to the law's "distinctive nature and forms".[116] The internal elements of law include the language of legislative instruments with its attendant ambiguity, complexity and technicality as well as the interpretative problems that can arise from these. I refer to these attendant problems arising from law's internal elements as *internal limits* affecting law's capacity for effectiveness. Language is the "most elemental limitation"[117] of criticisms of the (in)effectiveness of law. Like other elements outlined below, functionalist criticisms of law that target law's ineffectiveness and limits are often based on the "inherent properties of law".[118] Under the rubric of internal limits, therefore, are the problems (or limits) that are generated by the operation of law's internal properties.

The problem of language is most evident in the process of interpretation. In order for a legal instrument to fulfil its purpose(s), it is necessary for the language of the law to be intelligible and capable of effective transmission. The fact that legal provisions are to be interpreted in the context of a diverse range of societal norms heightens the need for intelligibility.[119] As further discussed below, interpretative ambiguities are capable of harming, and have indeed harmed, women's interests in different contexts. In one instance, parliamentarians who opposed the Philippines' Responsible Parenthood and Reproductive Health Act[120] used ambiguities in the choice of language in the Act to advance their own moral view of the legislation.[121] Most laws addressing concerns in the area of women's health are couched in legal language that prescribes or commands and in a form that affirms what are believed to be accepted norms or what the drafters of the law wish to set as new normative standards. The next two subsections examine the normative content of law and problems inherent in use of language to convey law's normative goals.

LINGUISTIC AND INTERPRETATIVE LIMITS

The theoretical analysis of the meaning of law and legal validity at the outset provides some insight into the different schools of thought on what makes a law deserving of its name and what makes it valid. With the differences in thoughts

116 Schuck, *The Limits of Law* at 426.
117 Ibid. at 427.
118 Ibid.
119 See ibid.
120 *Responsible Parenthood and Reproductive Health Act of 2012*, R.A. 10354.
121 See Sta. Maria, Chapter 6 of this volume, for a discussion of this and the impact of culture, religion and traditional values in the reproductive health law and policy landscape of the Philippines.

about law come variations in the ways a decision may be reached on a set of facts in a court. While more complicated facts give rise to greater difficulty in the adjudicative process, difficulties may arise as well with seemingly everyday cases involving contentious issues of morality and ethics. Thus, decision-making does not simply rest on what has been authoritatively passed into law; jurists must confront vagueness of language, ambiguities of language, and the "indeterminacy of the law-maker".[122] While law's "intelligibility", "effectiveness" and validity "require the use of written words" that are determinate and clear in legal instruments, "legal language is a frail support for these goals".[123] Law's "irreducible ambiguity", complicated by the necessity for contextual application, often renders legal instruments unintelligible to the average legal subject.[124] Effective understanding and application of law flows from both the lucidity of its content and its transmission. For Allott, linguistic problems and issues with the "originating and transmitting end" are the first of several reasons for the ineffectiveness of laws.[125] According to Allott:

> All verbal formulations, legal as well as non-legal, are subject to the defects of every linguistic message. . . . It is not only the inherent limitations of linguistic expression which get in the way of the efficient formulation of a legal message: it is also the fact that, in developed legal systems, the linguistic register and structure used for such messages is an artificial one. It corresponds only fragmentarily with the language habitually employed by ordinary persons in communicating. In ordinary communications systems we try to ensure greater effectiveness for our messages by various devices . . . through better design, and through feedback. Legal systems are generally deficient in each of these areas. The message has little chance of getting to its intended recipients, and needs reinforcement by education and parallel communication. Statutes are ill-adapted as instructional messages, needing special decoders (lawyers) which most citizens do not have available by their side.[126]

A legislative provision that is "weak" or "distorted" in the process of transmission may not be received or understood as it was intended,[127] or worse, may open the room for flawed or skewed interpretations. Thus, beyond the act of lawmaking, effective communication and monitoring of the law's reception are crucial to ensuring effectiveness.[128]

---

122 Alexy, "On the Concept and the Nature of Law" at 283.
123 Schuck, *The Limits of Law* at 427.
124 Ibid. Schuck cites Oliver Wendell Holmes Jr., who aptly expresses this problem as follows: "A word is not a crystal, unchanged and transparent, it is the skin of a living thought and may vary in color and content according to the circumstances and the time in which it was used": *Towne v. Eisner*, 245 U.S. 418, 425 (1918).
125 Allott, "The Effectiveness of Laws" at 236.
126 Ibid.
127 Schuck, *The Limits of Law* at 427.
128 Allott, "The Effectiveness of Laws" at 236.

It has been suggested that the choice of the language of a law can be part of a political plan to create an ineffective law.[129] In Zoppei's analysis, vagueness or "mistaken legal formulation" may be attributed to a political decision with the purpose of deliberately creating an ineffective law.[130] In the author's view:

> The use of complex language, while at first sight may seem like a guarantee of impartiality, precision, and credibility, and thus legitimise the legislator's action, can be used to achieve latent functions. A 'bad formulation' may be a technical issue linked to the appropriateness of the legislation, but it can also be a part of a planned ineffectiveness.[131]

This suggests that the lawmaker's intentions can affect the choice of vocabulary in the framing of legal rules. Vocabulary that is not "appropriate"[132] for the intended subjects of the law can result in incomprehensible rules and prevent legal subjects from recognizing the existence of a right or entitlement. Equally important are deliberate gaps in the law, which allow for a skewed implementation of the law in ways unintended by the law.[133]

Schuck also highlights the problem of binary categories, through which regulatory law often attempts to govern complex situations. Such "artificial" and "reductionist" categories may be addressed through the use of contextual standards.[134] In confronting a range of facts, complex fact situations and possibly conflicting legal norms or multiple interpretations of a legal norm, the adjudicator may have recourse to social norms or non-legal reasons,[135] which include questions of justice,[136] or stated differently in the context of the foregoing discussion, the question of correctness, including both moral and factual correctness. The very process of reaching for non-legal forms of reasoning to build a case to support a law is inherently fraught with the possibility of ineffectiveness. Beyond the obvious reason that social norms or factors are not often scientifically precise, as well as the problems of arbitrariness and reduced legal predictability,[137] there is also the problem of the inherent philosophical bias that each jurist brings into the analysis.

Particular constructions of legislative provisions and the exercise of interpretation in general have an impact on the effectiveness of laws on women's health. This impact occurs at two levels: first, the level of specific words, language and

---

129 Zoppei, *Anti-Money Laundering Law* at 22; Aubert, "Alcune Funzioni Sociali Della Legislazione" at 313–338.
130 Ibid.
131 Zoppei, *Anti-Money Laundering Law* at 22.
132 Ibid.
133 For further discussion of this in the context of external limits of law, see the discussion on South Africa's Choice on Termination of Pregnancy Act (CTOPA) in the next section.
134 Schuck, *The Limits of Law* at 428.
135 Alexy describes these as non-authoritative reasons: Alexy, "On the Concept and the Nature of Laws" at 283.
136 Ibid.
137 Schuck, *The Limits of Law* at 428.

interpretations of language used in the body of the law; second, at the broader level of the meaning ascribed to a legal norm and provision. In the former case, easy examples may be drawn from the vagueness of particular words used in a statute, which give rise to ambiguities or multiple meanings. For example, scholars point to the ambiguities around the use of the word 'health' in the mandate given to the now defunct Therapeutic Abortion Committees (TAC) in Canada. In the years of their operation, TACs were tasked with the responsibility to decide whether or not a woman should be allowed to have an abortion on the basis that the continuation of the pregnancy would be adverse to her health. Such ambiguities in policy leave an open door for interpretations that adversely impact women. The requirement for physicians sitting on the TAC to determine the meaning of "health" required a case-by-case assessment of the circumstances of the application. In the face of "innumerable requests" from women seeking the procedure for "socioeconomic, psychological, and physical reasons", the Canadian Medical Association had to issue directive statements on what grounds women could seek abortions.[138] These attempts at clarifying the policy, in one case to permit women to seek abortions on "non-medical social grounds", created further opposition.

The ambiguity surrounding the word 'health' raises questions about the appropriate criteria for determining its meaning. Do non-medical social reasons that may affect a woman's physical and psychological health in the event of a continuation of the pregnancy count? Such a decision would be left to the whims of a committee such as the TAC, with variable impressions and interpretations of the case before them. The problem of interpretation confronted by such a committee continues to manifest itself in present times in any policy regime, such as the United Kingdom's, that fails to grant a formal right to abortion and requires an assessment by physicians of whether a woman's pregnancy would affect her mental or physical health before she is allowed to have an abortion.[139]

Ambiguities in a law on women's health can produce conflicting interpretations and lead to decisions that are adverse to the interest and well-being of women. Let us examine one example from Senegalese law on women's reproductive health. Characterized by "a certain ambiguity of legal texts" and by "inconsistency of the legal rules",[140] at least two Senegalese statutory provisions on women's reproductive health rights, which are based on the Criminal Code and the Law on Reproductive Health, capture a clear case of conflicting domestic laws, the resolution

138 Ackerman, "In Defence of Reason" at 121.
139 See the UK's Abortion Act of 1967. The lawmakers and leaders of UK's professional medical associations are said to have carefully ensured that the law did not contain any language that could have been interpreted as establishing the right to abortion: Sally Sheldon, *Beyond Control: Medical Power and Abortion Law* (London: Pluto Press, 1997) at 27–28.
140 Mamadou Badji, "Regulating Biomedical Practices on Women in Senegal" in Brigitte Feuillet-Liger, Kristina Orfali and Therese Callus, eds., *The Female Body: A Journey Through Law, Culture and Medicine* (Brussels: Bruylant, 2013) at 230 ('Badji, "Regulating Biomedical Practices on Women in Senegal"').

of which has not been in women's favour. The Criminal Code criminalizes the provision of abortion services in Senegal, treating induced abortions, voluntary pregnancy terminations, attempted terminations, the incitement of abortions by means of communication or advertising and any other form of pregnancy terminations as crimes that attract severe consequences, including prison terms for doctors.[141] However, these provisions are in conflict with the Code of Medical Ethics,[142] the Law on Reproductive Health,[143] and the Protocol to the African Charter on Human and People's Rights on the Rights of Women in Africa ('the Protocol').[144] The Protocol, which was ratified by Senegal,[145] permits abortion in the specific cases of possible harm to the life and health of the mother upon continuation of the pregnancy, strong likelihood that the unborn child would suffer from a serious medical condition or where the pregnancy is as a result of rape, sexual assault or incest.

These conflicts were called into issue in several cases decided in Senegal. In the *State v. Astou Diop*,[146] a pregnant woman was found guilty of self-induced abortion. The defendant had allegedly induced her own abortion with the use of drinks and medicinal products. In the *State v. Mouscoye Sane (known as Mamy)*,[147] the accused pregnant minor was charged with voluntarily performing her own abortion. She was found guilty and sentenced under Article 305 of the Criminal Code and Article 565 of the Code of Criminal Procedure. A charge of complicity to commit abortion was laid against the defendant in the *State v. Landing Massaly*[148] and following a guilty verdict, the defendant was sentenced under Articles 45, 46 and 305 of the Criminal Code. In each of these cases, the courts' ruling was based on the provisions of the Criminal Code – especially on Article 305, and on the basis of which the women were found guilty of crimes that were excused by other legislative provisions. The anomaly of the situation is aptly put by Mamadou Badji, who states that "the courts are inclined to rule in favour of the application of the criminal code, without referring to the law on

---

141 Law n 80–49 of 24 December 1980, supplementing law n 65–60 of 21 July 1965, introducing article 305(a) in the Criminal Code. Article 2 of the 1980 law repeals decree of 30 May 1933 and implements the law of 31 July 1920, which prohibited any propaganda in favour of birth control and incitement to abortion. For fuller exposition, see Badji, "Regulating Biomedical Practices on Women in Senegal" at 228 and at 225–241.

142 Art. 35 of decree n 67–147 of 10 February 1967, which established the Code of Medical Ethics. Art. 35 provides that a therapeutic abortion may be performed if it is likely to save the life of the pregnant woman.

143 Art. 15, law n 2005–18 of 5 August 2005. Art. 15 prohibits the voluntary termination of pregnancy except in the cases allowed by the law.

144 Signed in Maputo, Mozambique, on 11 July 2003, the protocol became effective on 25 November 2005.

145 The protocol entered into force in Senegal on 30 November 2005.

146 Judgement n 88/09, Kaolack Regional Court (18 February 2009).

147 Judgement n 2067/2008, Dakar Special Regional Court (16 May 2008).

148 Judgement n 1544/08, Dakar Special Regional Court (23 April 2008).

reproductive health which derogates from it and legalises abortion in the situations provided for by law".[149] According to Badji:

> The courts are expected to interpret the law, taking into account all legal texts, in order to give a concrete basis to the texts authorising legal abortion, to make abortion effective and to integrate it into public reproductive health policies. As there are numerous high risk pregnancies for various reasons (reality of early marriages, frequent childbearing, difficult and late pregnancies), the State must ensure that women have access to means to control their fertility.[150]

Another major problem is the nature of the legislative framework and associated linguistic devices employed in 'liberalizing' access to abortion. Pseudo-permissive abortion regimes that involve some form of 'decriminalization', such as in Nigeria, Senegal, Canada in 1969, and the United Kingdom, are problematic to the extent that they create an ostensibly permissive regime without guaranteeing a right in any concrete form. As Sethna et al. have observed, liberalization does not guarantee access. Presently, Canadian law, through the constitutional supplant of the criminal law on abortion in 1969, declares without more that the repealed s. 251 of the Canadian Criminal Code on abortion was a violation of a woman's constitutional right to security of the person to the extent that it created an unfair and arbitrary procedure for access to abortion services. What such laws that merely decriminalize abortion in exceptional cases and those, such as Canada's, that make constitutional declarations without more do is merely create (often speciously) a permissive environment that leaves ample spaces for infringement of the law.

This has been the case in Canada's New Brunswick and Prince Edward Island for over the last 30 years. Fundamentally, laws that merely decriminalize abortion in limited cases, as we find in the UK and in many countries in Africa and Latin America, merely create defences to what is otherwise a criminalized practice. By merely repealing existing criminal law on abortion and creating defences to the criminal law, the legislature writes into the law an inherently defective pathway for accessing an important medical procedure. This, in other words, is an inherent defect in the structure of the law itself that limits the ability of the law to effectively respond to women's health needs.

Indeed, this argument is aptly reflected in the decision of the Supreme Court of Canada in *R. v. Morgentaler*, where the court recognized that the injustice women faced was one created by law itself, one embedded in the very nature of the law. According to the court:

> The Crown argues in its supplementary factum that women who face difficulties in obtaining abortions at home can simply travel elsewhere in Canada

---

149 Badji, "Regulating Biomedical Practices on Women in Senegal" at 231.
150 Ibid.

to procure a therapeutic abortion. That submission would not be especially troubling if the difficulties facing women were not in large measure *created by the procedural requirements of* s. 251 *itself.* If women were seeking anonymity outside their hometown or were simply confronting the reality that it is often difficult to obtain medical services in rural areas, it might be appropriate to say 'let them travel'. But the evidence establishes convincingly that it is *the law itself* which in many ways *prevents* access to local therapeutic abortion facilities. The enormous emotional and financial burden placed upon women who must travel long distances from home to obtain an abortion is a burden created in many instances by Parliament.[151]

Scholars within the field of international human rights law have also highlighted jurisprudential barriers arising from court judgements that impede the ability of the marginalized to launch an effective human rights struggle against rights violations. Writing in the broader context of the poor in Nigeria, Okafor and Ugochukwu observe that

> the fact that sometimes government policies and judicial attitudes align to perpetuate rather than ameliorate the factors that hinder the poor from exercising their agency to resist their oppression through the utilisation of the institutions and processes of human rights law, requires us to take a closer look at the ways in which these dramas of oppression are *enacted* and *legitimized.*[152]

Another instance of a taxing legislative problem that arises, in this case from the Canada Health Act,[153] has to do with the 'portability' requirement under the Act and its requirement for consent for elective insured health services, as well as its definition of 'elective insured health services'. The portability requirement allows reciprocal billing when certain medical procedures are obtained with the health coverage of the patient's home province though outside the patient's province of residence. Abortion is one of 16 medical procedures that are exempted from the portability requirement. This is disadvantageous to young women in their mid-twenties who have low income and who – as is the case with many students – attend school outside their home provinces.[154] According to Sethna and Doull,

---

151  *R. v. Morgentaler,* [1988] 1 S.C.R. 30, 44 D.L.R. (4th) 385 (Supreme Court of Canada) at 71. Emphasis supplied.
152  O.C. Okafor and B. Ugochukwu, "Raising Legal Giants: The Agency of the Poor in the Human Rights Jurisprudence of the Nigerian Appellate Courts, 1990–2011" (2015) 15 *African Human Rights Law Journal* 397–420, referencing H. Yusuf, "Oil on Troubled Waters: Multi-national Corporations and Realising Human Rights in the Developing World, with Specific Reference to Nigeria" (2008) 8 *African Human Rights Law Journal* 79. Emphasis supplied.
153  R.S.C. 1985, c. C-6.
154  Sethna and Doull, "Spatial Disparities" at 60.

these women are "most likely to fall through the cracks created by the federal government's reluctance to enforce the principles of the Canada Health Act".[155]

A further example of the problems that can arise from the interpretation of language used in a law on women's health, especially when the provisions of the law are either ambiguous or deemed ambiguous may be found within Philippines' Reproductive Health Law.[156] As Sta. Maria highlights in Chapter 6, interpretation of Philippines's Responsible Parenthood and Reproductive Health Act has been fraught with ambiguities at the judicial level and in its implementation by local government officials who favour a pro-life interpretation of the provisions of the law. Following a skewed interpretation of the provisions, which were intended to ensure Philippine women have access to "comprehensive, *culture-sensitive*, and gender responsive" healthcare,[157] a mayor of a major city in Philippines declared the city a "Pro-Life City".[158] Along with this declaration came bans on women's access to contraceptives; the only forms of contraceptives allowed had to be based on natural family planning methods.[159]

LAW'S NORMATIVE CONTENT

Law regulates a vast amount of social behaviour and relationships.[160] The behaviours, collective values, shared philosophies, "common practices" and "mutual expectations" among members of a society which law regulates are often denoted as *social norms*.[161] Social norms are behavioural symmetries that occur among members of a group; they are "modes of social ordering in all collectivities, including states, families, and friendships".[162] Whether they draw on religious or secular

---

155  Ibid. at 59–60.
156  Responsible Parenthood and Reproductive Health Act of 2012, *supra.*
157  Emphasis mine.
158  Executive Order (E.O.) No. 3, "An Executive Order Declaring Sorsogon City as a Pro-Life City". See Sta. Maria, Chapter 6 of this volume.
159  See Sta. Maria, Chapter 6 of this volume. A different problem bearing on the content of a law, and less on the language and its interpretation, involves the choices made by the legislature on the manner in which women may have access to a needed health service. For example, access to abortion may be conditioned on the consent of a spouse or partner, or in the case of minors, a parent. Regardless of the merit of such consent (which, in the case of spouses or partners, is arguably based on the relational virtues of a shared experience), the imposition of consent conditions can limit women's ability to access timely and effective medical care. In the specific case of abortion, a woman who lives under conditions of violence and wishes to quietly seek an abortion may be inhibited by the provisions of the law.
160  Schuck, *The Limits of Law* at 419. Schuck describes this as the 'quantitative' aspect of law, as opposed to the qualitative aspect of law, which deals with law's "distinctive nature and forms": see Schuck, 426.
161  Ibid. at 434.
162  Ibid.

values, norms have the power to shape behaviour.[163] They shape behaviour through people's interest in being accepted within their communities.[164]

The relationship between law and norms is intricate.[165] Norms are crucial to effective laws: they secure the moral duty to comply with law on which law's legitimacy rests, and they provide the "substantive standard for many legal rules".[166] As a formal system of rules, law "aspires to insularity, to closing itself off, to establishing boundaries, delineations and hermetic enclosures".[167] This aspiration defines its independent nature and allows it to authoritatively control and regulate the very acts upon which its decrees are based. These acts are the whole gamut of matters affecting everyday living and human activity and upon which laws are formulated.

While law aspires to "close itself off" from the social, cultural, political and other related norms from which it draws its content, there is little doubt that these factors continue to interact with the way in which laws are drafted, interpreted and implemented by legislators, jurists and enforcement agencies. This is because the values held by individuals, including legislators and adjudicators, "are vital in affecting the content of their actions, in creating relations of legitimate authority and in limiting the power of certain key actors".[168] Thus, compositional equivalence between social norms and law that is issued by a recognized authority can create the right conditions for acceptance of, and compliance with law. Indeed, as one scholar has observed, the support of the public, those to whom the law applies, is "critical in law" attaining its own objectives.[169] Yet, public backing is not always adequate to enable law fulfil its "underlying" goals.[170]

Law is not vacuous; law rests on a base of social facts or social norms and acts upon them to generate autonomous rules that draw from law's formal validity to effectuate change. To the extent that these norms are the substratum of law, the backdrop against which laws are made, interpreted and implemented, they are *constitutive* of law. This is not to say that they are the same as law. While law may reflect social norms, social norms are not synonymous with law. On the contrary, they are distinct from law to the extent that law retains an autonomous legal force by virtue of its independent and distinct institutional authority, authoritative issuance and power of coercion.

This rather complicated relationship between law and norms is one in which law "sponsor[s] an existing or new norm" and "transfer[s] to the norm some

---

163 Schuck, *The Limits of Law* at 434.
164 Ibid. at 437.
165 Ibid. at 435. Bogart, *Consequences* at 3.
166 Ibid.
167 Douglas et al., "At the Limits of Law" at 9.
168 Sampford, *The Disorder of Law* at 227.
169 Bogart, *Consequences* at 8.
170 Ibid.

of its own prestige and power".[171] Law has also been said to "discover" and "refresh" social norms[172] and, through formal processes, fortifies them as *legal* norms. Although generally categorized as 'social norms' or 'social facts',[173] a diverse range of norms and factors that form the foundation of law and influence the operation of law are described throughout this book. Across this section and indeed across the rest of this book, the terms used and discussed in their particular contexts include social, cultural, religious and traditional norms as well as economic and political factors. A constellation of these norms and factors helps define a society's standards, giving it its unique character and form, and generating systems of legal norms that are largely accepted by members of a given society. Often, law-makers work within the "presuppositions, practices, and limits of acceptance of community members".[174] In this case, the legal norm draws on accepted practices and lifestyles. Where, however, a newly minted legal norm deviates from "the mores and aspirations of the governed", a conflict may arise that could manifest itself in non-compliance.

Yet, it remains necessary to recognize that there are diverse norms in every society with equally different meanings and levels of compatibility with the West's 'universal' human rights norms.[175] This reality makes room for the fact that progressive laws that challenge extant social, cultural or other norms can still find room to take root and grow in the given society. Indeed, as Cowan et al. have admonished, it is helpful "to think of culture as a field of creative interchange and contestation", and as a process involving ongoing "transformation" in values or practices.[176] This possibility for cultural and, therefore, perceptual change creates much needed room for legal reform.

## *External limits*

CORRECTNESS AND THE LIMITS OF LAW

The prescriptive character of law offers a vision of how law advances its normative objectives about how a system should operate and how law attempts to govern or regulate behaviour to conform to that vision. This vision may be described as an 'ideal' or an 'anticipated norm'. In laws that prescribe codes of conduct – for

---

171 Schuck, *The Limits of Law* at 435.
172 This argument by Robert Post "simplifies", as Schuck argues, what is actually a very complex process or relationship between law and norms: see Schuck, *The Limits of Law* at 435, citing Robert Post, *The Social Foundations of Privacy: Community and Self in the Common Law Tort* (1989) 77 *California Law Review* 957 at 970.
173 Notably, Schuck sometimes describes them as "informal norms".
174 Allott, "The Effectiveness of Laws" at 237.
175 See Shah et al., Chapter 10 in this volume, for further discussion of the relationship between law and norms.
176 See J.K. Cowan, Marie-Bénédicte Dembour and R.A. Wilson, "Introduction" in J.K. Cowan, Marie-Bénédicte Dembour and R.A. Wilson, eds., *Culture and Rights: Anthropological Perspectives* (Cambridge: Cambridge University Press, 2001) at 5.

example one criminalizing the performance of an act that violates a woman's physical integrity – there is a declaration of a normative standard (with its underlying message about the wrongfulness of the act) to which the law commands its subjects to aspire. Douglas, Sarat and Umphrey suggest that the "laws that govern human conduct are ineluctably prescriptive and normative"[177] and the "prescriptive nature of law . . . raises its own specialized questions – are there distinctly normative limits to the laws that govern human conduct?"[178] According to the authors, "[a] study of law's prescriptive limits is further, and perhaps ruinously, complicated by the fact that one's position on the question depends crucially on one's very definition of law itself".[179]

According to non-positivistic definitions of law, morality places normative limits on law or its validity. This view of law, contested by scholars leaning towards a more positivist view of law, invites an assessment of the correctness of a law – more commonly on grounds of morality – to determine whether it can rightly be called law and thereby deserving of compliance. The practical relevance of this view is that laws that are deemed immoral by those subject to it may receive little compliance. The stronger the belief in the immorality of the legal norm, the more likely it is that its provisions will be disobeyed or ignored. Hence, the perceived immorality of law may manifest in "widespread disobedience".[180]

Beyond the role of morality in defining the limits of a law in terms of how it is received and applied, members of a society may also assess the content of a law based on factual and scientific correctness. The belief that a new or given norm is factually or scientifically accurate or that it expresses information that is logical and meaningful[181] can have the impact of creating behavioural changes that reflect the given norm. The effect of such a law may be "hermeneutic"[182] – that is, it changes a community's belief – and thereby leads to changes in practice.[183] However, so-called moral or ethical stances are sometimes based on scientific data, whether such data is contested or contestable, thereby creating a symbiotic relationship between these two elements.

Shared perceptions about the moral content of a law can limit or improve the effectiveness of a given law. In Latin America, the Middle East and Africa, as well as in the Western countries of Canada, the United States and Ireland, opposition to abortion and (in the case of non-Western societies) to reproductive health laws, is historically founded on perceptions about the supposed moral and religious incorrectness of abortion law. In many countries, the doctrine of conscientious objection affords healthcare practitioners who oppose contraception and abortion the right to refuse service to patients in need of these services.

177 Douglas et al., "At the Limits of Law" at 6.
178 Ibid.
179 Ibid.
180 Schuck, *The Limits of Law* at 433.
181 McAdams, *The Expressive Powers of Law, supra.*
182 Posner, *Law and Social Norms* at 33.
183 See McAdams, *The Expressive Powers of Law, supra.*

However, along with this right comes – or ought to come – the duty of referral. While legal and value judgements about the referral duty of objecting physicians are beyond the scope of this section, what is of immediate relevance is the deleterious impact of the practice on women's health and the fact that dereliction of the duty to refer further limits women's legitimate access to needed health services. The United Kingdom's Abortion Act of 1967 permits healthcare practitioners to refuse to participate in a treatment that the law itself authorizes if they deem such treatment to be conscientiously objectionable.[184] Thus, a law itself that purports to allow women a very restricted access to abortion in predetermined cases – an offering that itself falls short of a right, further creates the legal room for the curtailment, denial, or abridgement of access based on perceptions of moral and religious correctness. While at this time there is no specific legislation dealing with conscientious objection in Canada, healthcare professionals in Canada can object to a procedure on conscientious grounds.

Another manifestation of this problem is in the case of South Africa's Choice on Termination of Pregnancy Act (CTOPA).[185] In spite of the progressive nature of the law, which grants South African women liberal access to abortion until up to 12 weeks of pregnancy, deliberate gaps in the framing of the law on the issue of conscientious objection and the lack of a provision on referral have led many healthcare practitioners, convinced of the immorality of the medical procedure, to deny women access to it without a corresponding provision of information on relevant options and providers. Thus, while the law as a whole is otherwise well-intentioned, the intentional lapses in its framing open the pathway for "informal"[186] regulation of abortion procedure by frontline workers who are morally opposed to the law. As Ngwena has observed in the case of abortion rights, whether women have achieved equality is to be "measured not only by ascertaining whether the letter of the law recognizes reproductive agency", but also whether the rights granted can be realized in reality "by women of all backgrounds and means, especially those that are most vulnerable and marginalized".[187]

Religious opposition to abortion services and high-level, carefully staged resistance mounted by pro-choice movements has also significantly affected access to abortion services in different parts of Canada. Historically, access to abortion services in Canada has – implicitly and explicitly – been filtered through, and regulated based on, moral ideas of the rightness or wrongness of the procedure. A close look at the history of the law on abortion in Canada unravels a powerful and successful grassroots pro-life movement in Prince Edward Island (PEI)

---

184 S. 4, Abortion Act, 1967.
185 See Shah et al. Chapter 10 in this volume, for further discussion of the Act; and Odunsi and Adewole, Chapter 9 in this volume, which offers an abridged discussion.
186 For use of this term, see R. J. Cook, J. N. Erdman and B. M. Dickens, *Abortion Law in Transnational Perspective: Cases and Controversies* (Philadelphia: University of Pennsylvania Press, 2014) ('Cook et al., *Abortion Law in Transnational Perspective*').
187 C. G. Ngwena, "Reforming African Abortion Laws and Practice: The Place of Transparency" in Cook et al., ibid. at 180.

that would greatly shape the laws and policies regarding abortion services in that province. Related histories in Nova Scotia and New Brunswick as well as varied attempts across Quebec and British Columbia highlight the instrumental role of religion and morality as limiting norms in legislative efforts on women's health.

Religion and morality also play a critical role in abortion litigation.[188] In a number of US decisions, the courts have covertly framed their decisions in abortion cases around moral arguments.[189] This was the case in *Gonzales v. Carhart*,[190] where the court indicated a willingness to uphold legislative attempts to restrict abortion services based on moral grounds disguised as scientific. In this case, the court upheld a federal statute, the Partial-Birth Abortion Ban Act,[191] which banned the abortion procedure known as partial-birth abortion even though the law did not contain an exception for a woman's health. Arguing on medical/scientific grounds that "[T]here is documented medical disagreement whether the act's prohibition would ever impose significant health risks on women",[192] the court stated, quite tellingly, that a ban on one or more methods of abortion is legally acceptable in order to ensure "respect for the dignity of human life".[193] In this, the court effectively sneaks in its opinion about the morality of the impugned procedure.

While the religious and moral undertones of opposition remain intact, there is now ample evidence that opposition to the decriminalization of abortion in Canada also draws significantly on, and relies upon, arguments based on science and technology. Beyond the courtroom, the nature of abortion as a topic that at once touches on moral, ideological, theological and philosophical beliefs has had implications for the effectiveness of the legal system as a path to accessing the procedure. While society has a lot of faith in the ability of courts to right wrongs and implement change through the adjudicatory process, the effectiveness of judicial decisions in the particular context of women's access to specific reproductive health services and products, such as abortion and contraceptives, remains contestable. The question whether judicial decisions are effective instruments for change, as Schuck has observed, is "complicated, contextual and mixed", with appraisals fluctuating based on the standards employed, the assessor, the given courts under study, and the specific legal or policy field under study.[194]

Cases, such as *Roe v. Wade*[195] and *R. v. Morgentaler*[196] are extolled for their norm-breaking and reformative character. Yet the mere fact that a decision is momentous and has expanded, bestowed or recognized a right does not translate

---

188  An in-depth analysis of this role in the Philippines has also been addressed by Sta. Maria in Chapter 6 of this volume.
189  Borgmann, "Judicial Evasion and Disingenuous Legislative Appeals to Science", *supra*.
190  550 U.S. 124 (2007).
191  Partial-Birth Abortion Ban Act, 18 USC s. 1531 (2007).
192  *Gonzales v. Carhart* at 162.
193  Ibid. at 157.
194  Schuck, *The Limits of Law* at 430.
195  *Roe v. Wade*, 410 U.S. 113 (1973).
196  *Morgentaler, supra*.

naturally into positive advancement of the interests or well-being of those pro-tected by the decision. There are a number of "causal indeterminacies" and "implementation barriers" that can limit the realization of the protected interests or right.[197]

One explanation for these barriers has much to do with the fact that the courts lack the tools to shape or control behaviours and attitudes.[198] Standard tools available to the courts, such as mandamus or the injunction, are ill-fitting for changing the attitudes and behaviours that stand in the way of genuine reform.[199] This point is reiterative of the earlier observation that laws and rules, including judicial decisions, cannot of themselves compel people to obedience. While peo-ple may obey a law simply because of the subconscious respect for legal authority or because of law's expressive and informative functions, which are signals of its logical character,[200] such obedience cannot be equated with a perceptual change. In fact, the belief that a law, authoritatively issued, is morally offensive can spur citizens to find quiet ways to defy the law.

The seminal US case of *Roe v. Wade* illustrates the point effectively. While advocates of abortion access hail *Roe v. Wade* as pivotal to establishing the con-stitutional right of American women to abortion services, the same case has become a rallying cry for what Schuck describes as "a militantly conservative grassroots movement"[201] whose stringent opposition to abortion has generated ever-expanding pockets of resistance and restrictive laws across the United States.

LAW'S LIMITS AND WOMEN'S HEALTH

The elements of law – its normative content, language and composition, for-mal passage, and the moral and factual correctness of its content – reflect law's distinctive virtues and what separates it from social norms *simpliciter*. Citizens attach much significance to correctness. Individuals reject laws that appear to "violate their moral principles or their fundamental interests".[202] A law that dras-tically attempts to transform accepted norms[203] or behavioural patterns in a given community would likely meet with opposition, as has been the case in Nigeria from the 1980s to 2006, when successive reproductive health bills, designed to preserve and improve women's health, were introduced before the House of Representatives but were vehemently rejected as legislative attempts to overturn

197 Schuck, *The Limits of Law, supra* at 430.
198 Ibid.
199 Ibid.
200 McAdams, *The Expressive Powers of Law, supra.*
201 Ibid. at 431.
202 Schuck, *The Limits of Law* at 433.
203 Within Nigerian socio-cultural politics, there is an unwritten 'perception' that societal living – constitutionally required to be governed by secular norms – is founded on deeply held moral and religious beliefs. In spite of this veil of religiosity, the practice of (illegal and clandestine) abortion is widespread, a fact that comes to light because of the staggering number of maternal deaths from illegal abortions.

long-standing values and beliefs in the society. As explained earlier, the constitutive elements that animate law also constitute limits to its effectiveness.

Social, cultural and traditional norms are often the most ingrained attitudinal norms that can affect perceptions of a law. In the practice of female genital cutting, for example, long-held beliefs about the culturally valuable nature of the practice has hindered legislative efforts to eradicate it. Similarly, age-old gender norms that ascribe roles and aspirations on the basis of gender frustrate legal efforts towards eradicating violence against women. Even when a new legal norm takes a reformative shape and is touted as a remedial instrument against a norm or practice widely agreed to be unacceptable, such as violence against women, it may still receive lethargic support and compliance as well as poor implementation – the latter of which can arise due to a police force's assessment of the relative importance of the prohibited act. For example, it is not surprising to find the police force in societies where gender inequality is the norm being reluctant to investigate domestic violence on the erroneous assumption that the state has no business in policing the domestic affairs of a home, or that the act itself is legitimate because women are understood to be the 'property' of men. Herein lies the importance of an in-built system of enforcement, one that recognizes the fundamental connections between ingrained normative patterns of behaviour and legal compliance.

Beyond popular opposition arising from dissonance between a law and established norms, the internal and external elements of law and the ways in which they limit law's effectiveness manifest at the legislative level where parliamentarians must defend their choices regarding a new law. In the Philippines, we have found vivid examples of heated parliamentary debates offering conflicting notions and visions of the Philippines' cultural and traditional life. In these debates, we find a negotiation on what rights can be offered within a new law on women's reproductive health – specifically, the Responsible Parenthood and Reproductive Health Act,[204] as well as a barter of opinions and dissents, some of which were ultimately incorporated into the law and now define what healthcare products and services are available to women. In this manner, law's constitutive elements affect the very process of creating a law for women's health as much as it affects, as already discussed, how the law is interpreted by the courts.

Political norms and factors can also affect lawmaking on women's health. The abortion procedure provides an apt example of the influence of the political on women's health. In their study on the impact of Prince Edward Island's (PEI's) abortion policies on women published in 2014,[205] MacQuarrie, MacDonald and Chambers highlight a number of intersecting factors that hinder PEI women's access to abortion services in the province. Among these are political factors, such as the deliberate institutional silence about abortion by the government and the lack of information from government establishments on access to the procedure,

204 Responsible Parenthood and Reproductive Health Act of 2012, *supra*.
205 MacQuarrie et al., "Trials and Trails of Accessing Abortion in PEI: Reporting on the Impact of PEI's Abortion Policies on Women" (January 2014).

anti-choice structures (strengthened by the intolerant political atmosphere and policy frameworks in the province) ensuring a lack of local access and multiple levels of marginalization[206] arising from the pro-life orientation of the province's politicians.

Women's need for and right to abortion have also been used as instruments for population politics. Some nations have used what is superficially a liberal stance on abortion to achieve other political and economic goals for the country as a whole. The most common example is the case of liberalization of abortion to curb unacceptable increases in population growth or the tightening of abortion laws when politicians see the need to instigate population growth. Needless to say, such policies are also an economic control tool to regulate the fiscal outcomes of the rate of population growth. Wei Wei Cao fully addresses the implications of this trend for women's autonomy in China. Cao's careful examination of the socio-cultural and traditional foundations of such policies in China and implications of the trend for Chinese women's autonomy[207] illuminates the intersecting nature of social norms, in this case the socio-cultural, traditional and the political, as traversing factors that undermine women's true autonomy. A study of the historical and political outline of China's abortion laws thus uncovers the disingenuous foundations of a supposedly liberal abortion regime.

The impact of politics on women's health is also deeply evident in the endless speculations and slavering over who should be appointed to the US Supreme Court – the highest court in the country's judicial system – whenever there is vacancy on the court. This is due to the expected impact that the choice of successor to the court would have on abortion rights in the country. For conservatives, a right-leaning composition of the court would likely guarantee an overturn of what little formal victory was obtained through *Roe v. Wade* or at least ensure an affirmation or approval of the incremental peeling back of rights that takes place at the state level.

Another noteworthy factor relevant to women's access to needed health services are economic factors. As Grépin, Klugman, and Moore's analysis demonstrates,[208] the economic context of a nation significantly influences the availability of necessary health resources and services, as well as women's access to these services. Poverty, fiscal constraints and budgetary decisions have significant impacts on the services a country or government is able to provide to its citizens and this in turn might affect the legal responsibility that a government is willing to accept. Take, for example, the case where the right to health (much less to reproductive health services) is non-justiciable on grounds of the limited infrastructural and financial resources of a country.[209]

---

206  Ibid.
207  See Cao, Chapter 4 of this volume, for analysis of abortion law in China.
208  See Grépin et al., Chapter 7 of this volume.
209  See, for example, the Fundamental Objectives and Directive Principles of State Policy, Chapter II, Constitution of the Federal Republic of Nigeria, 1999.

In countries such as Nigeria where the right to health is non-justiciable, women are offered a right without content, preventing millions of women from using the law and the courts to advance their healthcare rights.

## Towards a jurisprudence of substantive effectiveness

The objective of a concept of 'substantive effectiveness' is to offer a method to determine whether a law fulfils the underlying objective for an optimal level of reproductive health and overall wellness within the context of a woman's particular needs.[210] Effectiveness, therefore, requires an assessment of the progress (or lack thereof) that women have made through law – not through formal, generalized standards of analysis and in global, decontextualized terms as between women of varying experiences and aspirations but with specific regards to the unique context(s) of individual experiences, needs and aspirations as well as with a clear appreciation of the workings of law. Against this background, a jurisprudence of 'substantive effectiveness' aims towards advancing a method of assessing the factors that interact to influence decision-making (whether at the legislative, adjudicative or administrative levels) on women's health. The goal in every case is to direct the assessment towards the advancement of women's health rights in ways that affirm and guarantee women's need for comprehensive health services without yielding to arguments that reify gender inequality. Against this backdrop, what then are the qualities of the concept or theory of substantive effectiveness?

### The concept of SLE

Substantive effectiveness offers a perspective of law and an approach to understanding law and the operation of law in context. More fundamentally, it is aimed at advancing a method for assessing legal effectiveness. In the foregoing, I have outlined the centrality of moral and factual correctness to perceptions about law, and how perceptions affect compliance with laws. In the particular instance of laws affecting women's health, there is much evidence, discussed above, of law's limited effectiveness in the area of women's health. Simple positivistic accounts of law as effective as long as there is compliance provide no information about the factors that motivate compliance. Similarly, a social-legal account that defines as effective any law that simply reflects shared societal norms discounts broader facts and phenomena – including identity, historical facts and class – that can create adverse outcomes for some members of the population or target group. Against this background, the concept of substantive effectiveness seeks to bridge a gap between theories of law and effectiveness that give little theoretical or practical value to the aspirational or ideal aspect of law and those that recognize that law

---

210  I recognize the possibilities of a wider application of the concept to broader issues around sex equality or perhaps beyond. Indeed, preliminary applications of the concept to areas outside the current field suggest its amenability to other areas of law.

of necessity has an ideal aspect that aspires to correctness without addressing the broader objectives of fairness and justice, which are critical to a determination of effectiveness.

Based on expositions in the foregoing analysis, a major reason for legal ineffectiveness arises in the context of the conflict between the aspirations of the legislator and the context within which the laws are established, that is, the nature of the society in which the legislator intends the laws to operate. Societies are populated by members with diverse characteristics and identities, and inattention to the disadvantage that can result from multiple, intersecting factors, including factors based on identity and status, can lead to laws with poor and disparate outcomes. While millions of Chinese women of a certain class, region and ethnicity may not experience, and may in fact support China's abortion law, millions of other Chinese women who lack the financial ability to pay their way out of the penalty for breaching China's abortion and family-planning policies or whose needs conflict with the state's policy would find the policy and associated laws to be deeply oppressive and restrictive.[211] While a traditional analysis of this policy and its associated laws through the compliance theory would support a conclusion that China's abortion law is effective, yet the law and associated family planning policies fail to meet basic human rights law concerning fairness, justice and reproductive autonomy.

Drawing on a different example, Canada professes to be a leader in advancing women's human rights; yet, while the non-Indigenous female population largely enjoys the basic right to health, Indigenous women experience poorer health status when compared to their non-Indigenous counterpart.[212] Some of the factors that account for this disparity include Indigenous women's social, political and economic status, as well as their gender, identity and historical experiences.

Placed within the context of my earlier conceptual analysis of the meaning and nature of law, the foregoing examples reveal that law's effectiveness cannot simply be assessed formalistically from the perspective of compliance or of congruence between its directives and societal norms. In making a determination of effectiveness, we must also address the overall legislative objectives (inherently complicated as these sometimes can be), addressed through particular attention to societal responses to law and its content, the importance of moral and factual correctness in mediating such responses, and the diverse identities of societal members and the contexts of their existence. Taking these into consideration, a substantive concept of effectiveness first conceives law that is formally promulgated as possessing a twofold character, the first of which is its *internal* character that is reflective of law's content, that is *language* and *social norms* (which have a significant impact on law's effectiveness based on the nature of their content as

---

211  See Cao, Chapter 4 of this volume, for a full discussion of China's abortion law and why this policy is substantively ineffective for millions of Chinese women.
212  Yvonne Boyer, "First Nations, Métis, and Inuit Women's Health" (Discussion Paper Series in Aboriginal Health: Legal Issues, National Aboriginal Health Organization, 2006).

well as on perceptions about the correctness of their content); and the second of which is the *external* character (edicts that are assumed to be morally, factually or scientifically and contextually correct and cohesive). Second, drawing on this conception of law, a substantive notion of effectiveness posits that in every case of congruence between law's content – content that reflects the *diverse identities* of the targeted group and their normative perceptions – and the *diverse needs* of the targeted group, law's aspiration for and achievement of the ideal (that is, for *correctness* and *effectiveness*) is clearly evident.

On the basis of this understanding, a concept of SLE offers tools for lawmaking and legal and policy reform, as well as for evaluation of proposed legal rules. In the context of communities where the prevailing norms or dominant normative perceptions are antithetical to universal or external perceptions of fairness and justice, the concept of substantive effectiveness offers the perspective that a new legal norm (that is designed to supplant the prevailing norm) is most likely to obtain the compliance of legal subjects when it is fashioned out of an understanding of the contextual nature of law and of the importance of correctness to compliance with law. While attempting to supplant such pre-existing norms, the concept of substantive effectiveness tasks the legislative process with facilitating a community's recognition of women's unique place in the community, the centrality of their well-being to cohesiveness and order in the community, and the promises of advancement in the well-being of the women and the community from new legal norms. Promises of advancement, in keeping with the concept of substantive effectiveness, would be effectuated through a combination of coercive and non-coercive mechanisms, as well as non-legal incentives (especially economic incentives) that are incorporated into law. As Grépin et al. incisively demonstrate in their discussion of the role of economic factors in legal effectiveness in Chapter 7, economic-based policies and incentives are often more effective in creating positive results for women's health than are punitive methods that do not deter many lawbreakers.

By building into a law incentives for compliance alongside punitive methods for non-compliance where necessary, legislators signal that a new legal norm, itself building upon the commonly accepted positive aspects of a system, aspires to improve a society and its women, rather than supplant in punitive ways that which a society has held true for ages. To explain this point, the criminal act of FGC provides a useful example. Current prohibitions against the practice are supported by sanctions, severe in many cases, which include financial penalties and jail terms. Substantive effectiveness in this particular case advances an approach that recognizes law's inherent need to "appeal"[213] to citizens' expectations of legal correctness and their "self-interest"[214] by crafting reciprocal incentives to change individual behaviour. By reciprocity in this context is meant the provision of a benefit for compliance. Substantive effectiveness thus advances the formation of

---

213 Schuck, *The Limits of Law* at 437.
214 Ibid.

law that iterates and acknowledges the benign (admittedly a value judgement) aspects of the rituals and practices that are celebrated alongside the FGC procedure, affirms the need for cultural subsistence for such practices, outlines the medical or scientific case for eradication of the surgical aspect of the practices, offers economic incentives for compliance[215] (with compliance being monitored through medical visits as is the case in Canada and other Western countries), and caps it with penalties couched as the outcomes for contrary conduct.

Regardless of the specifics of the legislative approach adopted, what this approach does is allow the law to grow organically from existing norms even while supplanting some or most of those norms. Notably, economic benefits for compliance, where public resources allow, can significantly displace the excuses of excisors, whose actions are often economically grounded. The emphasis on the contextual nature of law and the need for legislators to advance an understanding of the unique place of women in society is based on the fact that generalized policies and established patterns of behaviour that have hitherto gone unquestioned often disadvantage women in particular ways where they may seem fair to the broader population. I return to the practice of FGC to illustrate this point. Drawing on the strengths of law's normative and constitutive characteristics which help to induce compliance, the emphasis of substantive effectiveness on contextuality is geared towards ensuring that state action (by way of criminalization) and other initiatives inform about the implications of the procedure for women's reproductive health (even when done clinically), educate about the factual and scientific correctness of a ban, and the implications of a woman-centric protective policy for improved health outcomes.[216]

In the area of judicial or quasi-judicial interpretation, adjudicators charged with construing legal norms can draw on the notion of SLE in ensuring that the adjudicative process draws on the context of laws, the role of social norms in defining and shaping women's experiences, and the need to reach decisions that advance the core goals of protecting and improving women's health. Recognition of the practical difficulties that many women in Canada and beyond continue to face in accessing abortion services and the real impact of social norms on women, manifested through (sometimes violent) activism, adverse policies, and blatant politicization of abortion services, should lead adjudicative authorities and lawmakers to, respectively, reach decisions or legislate to prevent the subsistence and disadvantageous influence of problematic non-legal norms, especially as actuated or perpetuated by legal rules.

Summarily, therefore, a theory of SLE first identifies the inequalities that are possible when the *objectives* of law, its framing and its provisions are asymmetrical

---

215 Grépin, Klugman and Moore suggest (in other contexts) scholarships and free tuition for compliance: see Chapter 7 of this volume.

216 See Irehobhude O. Iyioha, "Public Health, Cultural Norms and the Criminal Law: An Inconvenient Union? A Case Study of Female Genital Cutting" (2012) 31 *MedLaw* at 453, *supra.*

and fail to consider lived experiences and needs of those subject to law, especially historically marginalized individuals *(objectives, composition and content – addressing identity, needs, and context of legal subjects)*. Second, the theory finds application where the *language* of law and the *social facts* that are constitutive of law allow or create gaps, meanings and interpretations that defeat the purpose and administration of law *(internal limits – language, interpretation and social facts and the creation of legislative and interpretive loopholes)*. And third, the theory articulates how perceptions of moral, factual and scientific *correctness* impact the reception of and compliance with law *(external limits – moral, factual and scientific correctness and its impact on reception of and compliance with law)*.

The theory of SLE assesses effectiveness not simply on the basis of disaggregated outcomes and on the traditional standards that go into formal legal effectiveness, but also evaluates effectiveness as an inseparable exercise from the very formulation of a legal rule, given that embodied in the formulation and life cycle of every legal rule are the impurities that constitute the ingredients of ineffectiveness. More importantly, a theory of SLE addresses the challenge with traditional outcomes or compliance-based theories that fail to explain the 'why' of ineffectiveness or effectiveness. While *identifying* the outcomes of law – that is, the outcome that *is* 'ineffectiveness', formal legal theories do not *explain* why this is so. Factors such as 'context' and 'identity' (as well as 'social facts' and 'correctness', were these to be included in a formalistic analysis) do not by themselves explain the latent grounds for the relevance of these categories. Thus, formal legal effectiveness may show or indicate that the outcomes are different, but not 'why' they are. And to explain why they are different is to go beyond the traditional metrics of analysis to an approach that begins the assessment from the factors and processes involved in rulemaking. In this, SLE is both forward-looking – addressing the criteria of effectiveness pre-emptively at the creation of a law, as well as retrospective, assessing the results of law in ways allegiant to the legal process through interpretation and implementation.

In addressing law's limits in this encompassing manner, SLE aims to stay true to the binary nature of law – the analysis of legal effectiveness being very much about law's nature, its validity and constitutive parts. Through this approach, the legal or policy analyst's assessment of effectiveness is mediated by awareness of and attention to the distinctive ways that law's manifestations in drafting, interpretation and in practice – far from its claimed clarity and objectivity – affect women's realization of their rights.

It is hoped that the concept of substantive effectiveness of law emerges as both a theory that aids in the understanding of law and its operation and a method for assessing laws with due consideration to the consequential impact of the legal process on women's health and on the way women's health and interests are negotiated.

# 3 Feminism, morality, and human rights

## Assessing the effectiveness of the United Kingdom's FGM Act[β]

*Jenaye M. Lewis, Irehobhude O. Iyioha, and Dexter Dias*

## Introduction

Despite numerous international initiatives, including the establishment of the UN Commission on the Status of Women in 1946, the adoption of the Convention on the Elimination of All Forms of Discrimination Against Women (CEDAW) by the UN General Assembly in 1979 and, recently, the launch of the Sustainable Development Goals in 2015 to promote gender equality and equal participation, and to end violence against women, the plight of women in the world continues to be distressing. Women comprise about "70% of the world's 1.3 billion absolute poor" and continue to be disproportionately deprived of food, medicine, and education.[1] As of 2018, the WHO estimates that, globally, 35% of women have experienced "physical and/or sexual violence" from an intimate partner or a non-partner.[2] The WHO further estimates that "approximately 830 women die from preventable causes related to pregnancy and childbirth every day", with 99% of those women located in the developing world.[3] Indeed, scholars have appropriately wondered "whether being female, itself, threatens one's survival in the world".[4]

Given the alarming statistics above, it is unsurprising that Western feminists, particularly Western feminist legal scholars, have taken up the charge in advocating for women's rights on a global scale. In the hope of developing an elusive "global feminist theory",[5] Western feminists have endeavored to temper their critique of the lived experiences of women in other parts of the world – particularly

β Special thanks to Dr. Obiora Chinedu Okafor, Professor and York Research Chair in International and Transnational Legal Studies at Osgoode Hall Law School, York University and UN Independent Expert on Human Rights and International Solidarity for his insightful views on an important strand of our argument in this chapter.

1 Nancy Levit and Robert R.M. Verchick, *Feminist Legal Theory: A Primer*, 2nd ed. (New York: New York University Press, 2016) (EBSCOhost eBook Collection) at 223 ('Levit and Verchick, *Feminist Legal Theory*').
2 World Health Organization Fact Sheets: *Violence Against Women*, 2018.
3 World Health Organization Fact Sheets: *Maternal Mortality*, 2018.
4 Levit and Verchick, *Feminist Legal Theory* at 223.
5 Ibid. at 222.

the cultural and legal norms of their states – with an "anti-essentialist" approach that respects cultural, political, and religious diversity.[6] It has proven to be exceedingly challenging, however, to create a "feminism for all",[7] as the reality is that Western feminist ideas and models endorsing the betterment of women globally tend to be premised upon, and/or implicitly promote, Western values and conceptions of what constitutes a flourishing, autonomous life for women. While there may be examples where the transposition of Western ideals onto non-Western settings has "amount[ed] to an improved measure of women's well-being", the potential for harm caused by "an inappropriate endorsement of a particular cultural perspective"[8] is a real and pressing issue.

This chapter aims to expound some of the ways in which all concepts and beliefs, including both Western feminist ideologies, and, more generally, Western societal ideas about morality, are inescapably fraught with a moral relativism that clouds the feminist legal project. Drawing on foundational theories regarding law, morality and legal validity, the chapter illuminates the ways in which the multiplicity of moral perspectives complicates the agenda on making laws effective for women. We draw on evidence from traditional analyses of the effectiveness of laws – described for the first time in this book as "formal theories of effectiveness"[9] – to show how a lack of attention to the vagaries in moral judgments in theorizing law's effectiveness can lead to an incomplete and inaccurate picture of the real-world effects and consequences of law, particularly for members of marginalized groups. We also explore the arguments of philosophers Robert Alexy, Gustav Radbruch, and Hans Kelson to assess the connections between the nature of moral norms and law's validity, and the role this plays in assessing law's limits and its effectiveness.

The chapter explores the above using the UK law on female genital cutting (FGC) as a case study. We examine the reasons for the ineffectiveness of the UK law on FGC using the concept of SLE, introduced in Chapter 2, and offer an analysis that is transferrable to other domestic laws and international legal provisions on the practice.[10] The choice of FGC as a case study is based on the starkly divided moral viewpoints surrounding the practice as well as on the contentious cultural notions regarding women's rights to health, sexuality, and bodily

---

6 Ibid. at 224.
7 Ibid.
8 Ibid. at 235.
9 See Iyioha's analysis in Chapter 2 of this volume.
10 Although the World Health Organization (WHO), Amnesty International, and various state laws refer to the collection of cutting procedures done on women and girls as "female genital mutilation", the "value neutral" term "female genital cutting" or "FGC" is used throughout this paper in order to "depict the nuances involved in the procedure without the subjective judgement attached to the term "mutilation": Irehobhude O. Iyioha, "Public Health, Cultural Norms and the Criminal Law: An Inconvenient Union? A Case Study of Female Genital Cutting" (2012) 31 *MedLaw* at 453 ('Iyioha, "Public Health, Cultural Norms and the Criminal Law"').

autonomy engendered by the subject of FGC. As will be discussed, the factors underlying the lack of effectiveness of the UK law on FGC reflect some of the main theoretical factors identified in this book as constituting limits to law's effectiveness; and at the heart of these factors is the problem of correctness: the problem of law's enduring struggle with defining its relationship with morality and morality's myriad forms.

## On foundational concepts of law: positivism versus non-positivism

As feminist legal theory and, certainly, global feminist theory, are relatively novel concepts – the term "feminist jurisprudence" having been coined in the late 1970s – it is important as a foundational step to ground both theories within the broader discussion of the fundamental theoretical debate on the nature of law: the conflict between positivism and non-positivism. As noted in Chapter 2, an understanding of the nature and elements of law are key in ultimately assessing the effectiveness and functionality of any piece of legislation,[11] and a key concern of Western feminist ideology regarding laws that affect women's rights, well-being, and lives is the extent to which these laws safeguard women's autonomy and lead to women's advancement.

The concepts of "positivism" and "non-positivism" are legal theories that promulgate "very different theses" regarding the relationship between law and morality.[12] Proponents of positivism contend that, in order for a law to be valid, it need only be formally passed and obeyed. Positivism and its variants have often been described as offering an account of law that regards the moral context of laws as inconsequential to law's validity. Conversely, proponents of non-positivism posit that laws must, of necessity, possess a moral aspect – a deficiency of which *can* invalidate law. Theorist Robert Alexy explains that the distinction between positivism and non-positivism turns on "the relations between and among three elements: First, authoritative issuance, second, social efficacy, and third, correctness of content, which includes moral correctness".[13] All positivistic theories address only the first two elements, whereas all non-positivistic theories consider all three elements of the equation that arguably define and validate law. The absence of the third element in positivistic theories forms the basis of the "separation" or "separability" thesis, which eschews any "necessary connections" between law and morality;[14] or, in other words, which posits that there is "no

---

11 See Iyioha, Chapter 2 of this volume.
12 Robert Alexy, "Law, Morality, and the Existence of Human Rights" (2012) 25:1 *Ratio Juris* at 3 ('Alexy, "Law, Morality, and the Existence of Human Rights"').
13 Ibid.
14 Green, Leslie, "Positivism and the Inseparability of Law and Morals" (2008) *New York University Law Review*/Oxford Legal Studies Research Paper No. 15/2008 (TWEN) at 7.

necessary connection between the law as it is and the law as it ought to be".[15]
Non-positivism upholds the contrasting viewpoint – that of a necessary connection between law and morality or between law as it is or law as it ought to be.
According to Alexy:

> [A]ll non-positivists defend the connection thesis, which says that there is a necessary connection between legal validity or legal correctness on the one hand, and moral merits and demerits or moral correctness and incorrectness on the other.[16]

There are two streams of positivistic theory (exclusive and inclusive positivism) and three strands of non-positivistic theory (exclusive non-positivism, super-inclusive non-positivism, and inclusive non-positivism).[17] We focus here on the elucidation of the three strands of non-positivistic theory as necessary to understanding the workings of ideas around morality and the impact of such ideas on women's rights. Exclusive non-positivism, super-inclusive non-positivism, and inclusive non-positivism differ in their conceptions of the effects that moral defects in a law have on the validity of the law.[18] Alexy considers both exclusive non-positivism – which contends that *every* moral defect results in legal invalidity, and super-inclusive non-positivism – which posits that legal validity is *in no way affected* by moral defects, to be too radical to support.[19] Instead, Alexy argues that inclusive non-positivism, which states that legal validity is "lost in some cases and not in others", is the most appropriate and most defensible form of non-positivism.

This stance on inclusive non-positivism reflects Alexy's broader thesis on the nature of law, captured within his "dual-nature thesis" of law. This thesis claims that "law necessarily comprises both a real or factual dimension and an ideal or critical one",[20] the real/factual dimension identifying the elements of authoritative passage and the efficacy of law and the ideal/critical dimension capturing law's moral claims – or its claim to correctness. Alexy explains that

> the dual nature of law is expressed, on the one hand, by the Radbruch formula, which says that extreme injustice is not law and, on the other, by the correctness argument, which says that law's claim to correctness necessarily includes a claim to moral correctness. Thus, what the law is depends not only on social facts, but also on what the law ought to be.[21]

---

15  Robert Alexy, "On the Concept and the Nature of Law" (2008) 21:3 *Ratio Juris* 281–299 (TWEN) at 284 ('Alexy, "On the Concept and the Nature of Law"').
16  Ibid. at 285.
17  Ibid. at 285–290.
18  Ibid. at 287.
19  Alexy, "Law, Morality, and the Existence of Human Rights" at 5–7.
20  Alexy, "On the Concept and the Nature of Law" at 281. See also Iyioha, Chapter 2 of this volume, for an analysis of Alexy's dual-nature thesis.
21  Ibid.

On this basis, Alexy contends that the dual-nature thesis is exclusively compatible with inclusive non-positivism.[22]

What then is the relevance of this understanding of law – either as determined by passage and efficacy or by passage, efficacy, and correctness – to discourses around moral judgments in women's health? We return to our introductory commentary that the effectiveness of laws impacting women's lives, which is a core concern at the heart of the feminist project and of modern equality doctrine, turns in part on notions of moral correctness – that is, whether a given law meets the moral standards of lawmakers, adjudicators, or implementers. The next section explores this further.

## Feminist legal theory, the nature of law, and legal effectiveness

To understand the connections between foundational philosophical thoughts about law and feminist legal theory and the subject of legal effectiveness, it is necessary to track the historical trajectory of Western feminist thought. Though often referred to as "waves" of feminist thought in the field of women's and gender studies, this chapter adopts the terminology of feminist legal scholars Levit and Verchick, as their enumerated categories work as descriptive subsets within the greater umbrella terms of the second and third waves of feminism. What follows is a brief delineation of a few key streams as identified by Levit and Verchick: "liberal" feminism, "cultural" feminism, "critical race" feminism, "pragmatic" feminism, and "post-modern" feminism.[23]

"Liberal" or "second wave" feminism emerged in the 1960s, with the recognition that women's rights continued to be curtailed by patriarchal and sexist beliefs, values, systems, and norms. The movement emphasized the equal treatment of men and women under the law based on the principle of formal equality, and this tactic was "usually successful in eliminating explicit barriers to equal treatment" in the United States and Canada.[24] The focus on the "purely formal equality of opportunity" in the drafting of laws that affected women's rights and lives, which failed to consider any cultural and/or socioeconomic nuances and outright ignored marginalized identities, evidently indicates an initial trend towards positivism.[25]

The emergence of "cultural" feminism in the 1970s, which first recognized that the promise of formal equality did not often result in substantive equality, signaled what can be seen as a shift from an acceptance of positivism to non-positivism.[26] Feminist legal scholars under this school of thought recognized that gender-neutral laws and/or laws drafted without consideration of the unique

---

22 Ibid.
23 Levit and Verchick, *Feminist Legal Theory* at 12–39.
24 Ibid. at 14.
25 Ibid.
26 Ibid. at 15.

context of women's lived experiences forced women to adhere to "male norms", which were not only inappropriate, and often inapplicable, but also often upheld and even contributed to women's continued oppression.[27] The possibilities of substantive equality thus rose to the forefront of feminist concerns.

Levit and Verchick identify the seedlings of one of the key tenets of third wave feminism, intersectionality,[28] as having been sown in the 1980s, with the emergence of "critical race feminism". Proponents of critical race feminism eschewed second wave feminists' universal assertions about women's lived experiences and pointed out that neglecting factors such as race, socioeconomic status, and sexual orientation "stifled the voices" of marginalized women.[29] The core tenets of "pragmatic" and "post-modern" feminism, also born of the third wave of feminist thought, began to explicitly problematize the nature, elements, and effects and/ or effectiveness of law, specifically regarding the betterment of the lives of women on a global scale. Pragmatic legal feminism, which recognizes that "a search for contextual solutions is typically more useful than abstract theorizing",[30] nods not only to a support of non-positivism but, as will be discussed later, also to the idea of substantive legal effectiveness – a theory advancing understanding of a major component of modern equality doctrine regarding the significance of the *effect* of laws.[31] The idea of substantive effectiveness of laws and policies offers a précis of the conditions for law's effectiveness based on how symmetry between (1) law's objectives, its composition and substantive elements; (2) its structural qualities and administration;[32] and (3) the correctness, reception of, and compliance with law[33] are determinative of law's capacity to "ameliorate or exacerbate the conditions of women's lives".[34] The focus of the idea of substantive legal effectiveness (SLE) on (among others) law's structural elements comprising social facts and the language of law and its interpretation may, arguably, be interpreted as an awareness of the post-modern feminist trend toward challenging the foundations of law as rooted in positivism and the ways in which law – its creation, interpretation, and implementation – perpetuate or reinforce inequality, especially against marginalized and

---

27  Ibid. at 16.
28  Kimberlé Crenshaw, "Mapping the Margins: Intersectionality, Identity Politics, and Violence Against Women of Color" (1991) 43:6 *Stanford Law Review* at 1241–1299.
29  Levit and Verchick, *Feminist Legal Theory* at 24.
30  Ibid. at 33.
31  The first principle of modern equality doctrine, according to former Chief Justice Beverley McLachlin of Canada, is 'substantive equality' and the second sheds light on the importance of assessing a law's actual effect. McLachlin CJ notes that the second arm of the equality doctrine recognizes that law is to be determined by its effect rather than by its letters: see generally Beverley McLachlin, "Equality: The Most Difficult Right" (2001) *Supreme Court Review* 14 S.C.L.R. (2d).
32  Denoted as internal elements and internal limits: see Iyioha, Chapter 2 of this volume.
33  Denoted as external elements and limits: see ibid.
34  Irehobhude Iyioha, "Substantive Effectiveness, Women's Health and the Limits of International Human Rights Law" in Anna Kirkland and Marie-Andree Jacobs, eds., *Research Handbook on Law, Medicine and Society* (Edward Elgar, 2019 – Forthcoming) ('Iyioha, "Substantive Effectiveness, Women's Health and the Limits of International Human Rights Law"').

vulnerable groups. Yet, SLE does not pretend to represent or align itself with any particular theoretical schools, whether within feminism or beyond. In its framing, it seeks to better understand the way law is created, the way law works, and the ways in which law impacts particular marginalized population groups.

Notably, "post-modern" feminists, with a focus on language and discourse, "challenge the modernist idea of an unchangeable rule of law".[35] Under this school of thought, "post-modern" feminist legal scholars contend that "laws are not objective or impartial – they are crafted from political biases, so reliance on laws and on traditional ways of [creating and] practising law, can reinforce inequalities".[36] This contention directly recognizes a necessarily moral component to law, in the sense that lawmakers' personal biases regarding how "the law ought to be" always influence the law as it is.

Thus, it is inarguable that, from the perspective of "cultural" feminism, and all subsets subsumed under the category of the third wave of feminism, laws passed under the auspice of legal positivism would be largely dissatisfactory in upholding *all* women's rights, particularly those relating to their reproductive health and autonomy, and particularly for women of color, women of lower socio-economic status, women with lower levels of education, and women living in rural rather than urban areas, for example. Positivism's disregard for moral correctness as a necessary component of law has, in actuality, impacted both the lawmaking process and the judicial interpretation of reproductive health law, and this influence has often led to dire social, political, economic, and health-related consequences for women globally. There are a chilling number of cases wherein women's rights, autonomy, and lives were lost to "the deep chasm between 'the law on the books' and 'the law as applied'".[37] For example, India adopted a constitution in 1949 banning sex discrimination in all forms, a reform "officially extending equal rights much further than does the U.S. Constitution";[38] and yet, despite this commitment to formal equality, women and girls in India remain deprived of their proportionate share of food, medicine, and educational and career opportunities.[39]

Another example is the high rate of unsafe abortions and deaths from abortion complications in Latin America. As of 2011, Latin America had the "highest rate of unsafe abortions in the world", with "39 unsafe abortions per 100 live births" and 2,000 women dying due to abortion-related complications per year, "45% of whom [were] under the age of 24".[40] The criminalization of abortion has clearly resulted in an unjust public health crisis in Latin America. And one of the most poignant examples of the gap between the letter of the law and its effect on the ground is the death of Savita Halappanavar in Ireland in 2012. She was denied

35 Levit and Verchick, *Feminist Legal Theory* at 37.
36 Ibid.
37 Ibid. at 232.
38 Ibid.
39 Ibid.
40 Emma Richardson and Anne-Emmanuelle Birn, "Sexual and Reproductive Health and Rights in Latin America: An Analysis of Trends, Commitments and Achievements" (2011) 19:38 *Reproductive Health Matters* 183–184.

an emergency abortion, despite the death of the fetus and the imminent threat to her life due to the septic pregnancy, as doctors were unwilling to deviate from the country's hard-line abortion laws.

The opposing theory of law, non-positivism, which – in terms of its tenets and interpretive methodology – appears to align best with the tenor of the critical legal analysis that inspires Western feminist theories, would then seem to be capable of providing a solution to the problems and a means of preventing the types of tragedies condoned by positivistic approaches to law, as illustrated above. One imagines, for example, that it would be impossible for a child victim of rape to be forced to carry a pregnancy to term, or for a woman to be forced to terminate a pregnancy as in the case of Feng Jianmei[41] under laws infused with, and recognized as possessing, a supposed moral aspect. These circumstances arguably involve extreme injustices and, according to the Radbruch formula, "extreme injustice is not law".[42]

It is important to note that, according to Alexy, "anyone who endorses [Radbruch's] formula has not only accepted non-positivism as a theoretical view, but is also advocating a substantive legal thesis with direct practical consequences".[43] Thus, when Western feminists are appalled by the law's treatment of women such as Savita Halappanavar and Feng Jianmei and demand legal reform and justice, they are performing the implicit support of theories or approaches that enable recognition of how positive law in formulation and interpretation can perpetuate injustice and foster unfair or biased outcomes – approaches such as that embodied in non-positivism as described by Alexy. Cases such as the *X Case*,[44] *A, B, and C v Ireland*,[45] and *AS v Hungary*,[46] wherein judicial interpretation arguably favoured a non-positivist accounting of morality, and thereby advanced law's aspirational goal of realizing justice, could be framed as victories from a Western feminist perspective. On the surface, then, current Western feminist legal theory – to the extent that it aims to end the bias and inequality faced by women through reform of traditional Western legal jurisprudence (as embodied in positivism and formalism) – would seem to have an easy alliance with and find theoretical support

---

41  In 2012, Feng Jianmei of China was kidnapped by local family planning officials and was forced to terminate her seven-month pregnancy. This was allowed to occur under the auspices of China's strict family planning laws: see Cao, Chapter 4 of this volume.

42  Alexy, "On the Concept and the Nature of Law" at 281.

43  Ibid. at 283.

44  A 14-year-old girl became pregnant as a result of rape, and she subsequently fell into a suicidal depression. An exception was built into Ireland's abortion laws whereby a pregnancy could be lawfully terminated if a "real and substantial risk" to the mother's life, such as suicide, presented itself and termination was the only means of avoidance: *The X Case: Attorney General v X* [1992] IESC 1; [1992] 1 IR 1 (5th March, 1992).

45  No. 25579/05 Eur. Ct. H.R. (2010). The European Court of Human Rights found that the UK's failure to give legislative effect to the *X Case* violated the European Convention for Human Rights: Maeve Taylor, "Women's Right to Health and Ireland's Abortion Law" 2015) 130 *International Journal of Gynecology and Obstetrics* at 94.

46  Compulsory, non-consensual sterilization was found to violate the author's rights under Article 12 of the Convention: *AS v Hungary* (2004) Communication No. 4/2004, CEDAW/C/36/D/4/2004.

in a critical legal framework such as non-positivism – specifically *inclusive non-positivism* – with particular reference to non-positivism's constitutive connections to the idea of the moral element of law.

Yet, in this expected alliance between Western feminism and inclusive non-positivism are the broken threads of an unstable ideological relationship. A variety of cases across the globe illustrate that theoretical and interpretive recognition of the moral element of law can often be an ineffective tool in safeguarding women's reproductive health, rights, and autonomy, when laws are enacted in socio-political, cultural, and religious climates that do not protect, or are, at best, ambivalent about women's health and autonomy. This concern arises because of the procedural and substantive issues involved in lawmaking and adjudicative processes in both conservative and progressive regimes that manifest in statutory gaps or weak language in statutes,[47] "judicial evasion", or cases involving the judiciary's inappropriate abdication of its role through "blind judicial deference",[48] high-stakes lobbying by wealthy and powerful interest groups,[49] and deeply entrenched cultural, traditional, and religious norms and ideals which police women's bodies and undervalue women's health, wellness, and autonomy.[50] In regards to the last concern, it bears mentioning that despite legal reform, "once supporting social attitudes have solidified around [legal] norms, and especially once they become entrenched by religion and forms of ideology, we cannot just 'repeal' the gut feeling" that something is morally wrong.[51]

In this sense, adverse ideas about women, women's rights, and women's reproductive health and autonomy can continue to hamstring new laws – even progressive ones. The moral element of law thus seems to be able to twist the interpretation of laws in either direction – both toward and away from women's empowerment in the realm of reproductive health, rights, and autonomy.

---

47  See the wordiness and purposeful omission of the terms: "abortion" and "termination of pregnancy" in Ireland's Protection of Life During Pregnancy Act; see also the lack of recommendations for doctors: Taylor, "Women's Right to Health and Ireland's Abortion Law", *supra* at 93–97. See generally Iyioha, Chapter 2 of this volume, which discusses the problems of legislative gaps, legal uncertainties, and vagaries of statutory interpretation as part of the internal, structural limits confronting law.

48  Caitlin E. Borgmann, "Judicial Evasion and Disingenuous Legislative Appeals to Science in the Abortion Controversy" (2008) 17:1 *Journal of Law and Policy* 14–56 at 55.

49  See the success of the anti-abortion lobbyists in Prince Edward Island, Canada, in the 1960s: Katrina Ackerman, "In Defence of Reason: Religion, Science, and the Prince Edward Island Anti-Abortion Movement, 1969–1988" (2014) 31:2 *CBMH* 117–138; See also the deference to the "floodgates" concerns of conservatives in Ireland's *Protection of Life During Pregnancy Act*, 2013 (Act No. 35 of 2013; previously Bill No. 66 of 2013): Taylor, "Women's Right to Health and Ireland's Abortion Law", *supra* at 94.

50  See the twisting of scientific information and the purposeful dissemination of misinformation to suit the aims of religious norms and ideals in the United States: Henry A. Waxman, "Politics and Science: Reproductive Health" (2006) 16:1 *Health Matrix* 5–25. See also the fervent opposition of the Catholic Church to *any* lawmaking on reproductive health and rights in the Philippines: Manaloto, Renato, "The Philippine Reproductive Health Legislation: Politics Beyond Metaphysics" (2014) 6:4 *Asian Bioethics Review* at 343.

51  Leslie Green, "The Morality in Law" (2013) *New York University Law Review*/Oxford Legal Studies Research Paper No. 12/2013 at 14.

Indeed, one wonders at the efficacy of the Radbruch formula in safeguarding women's reproductive health, rights, and autonomy in an ideological environment that views the death of the fetus, for example, as the extreme injustice, and not the death of the woman. And one of the key tenets of "pragmatic" feminism, that "all observations are relative to perspective", including "the time and place where they occur . . . [and] the set of prior beliefs and attitudes that are held by the observing party", lends itself to the notion that one's ideas, even one's ideas about morality, are derived from one's own lived experience.[52] The question ultimately is: 'Is the idea of morality "parochial?" '[53] Is it the "the product of a specific culture – a Western culture internationalized through the international human rights system?"[54] Western feminism appears to be inherently fraught with an ideological bias in its approach to women's rights, particularly when viewed from a global context. A similar ideological bias can be said to complicate any approach to law that predicates law's validity on the nature of its moral content and the interconnections between law and other social phenomena, such as with non-positivism's claims to 'moral correctness'. This problem finds expression in the fact that even the conceptual and interpretive framework of non-positivism can produce inconsistent consequences for women's rights when the social, cultural, and religious climate in which it is implemented is taken into consideration.

Even while recognizing the diversity of Western feminism's theories and methods, yet the above concerns lead back to the point flagged earlier about the tenability of the substantive connections between non-positivism (in its recognition of law's moral quality and aspiration for justice) and Western feminism's ideological leanings. In light of the foregoing, we ask whether there is a universality to morality that ensures both of these critical approaches to the study and application of law are aligned. If there is not, what does this mean for non-positivism, especially in its thesis on law's moral character and aspirational quality of justice? What would an understanding of the nature of morality as *subjective* mean for the existence and universality of human rights and, by extension, women's rights?

## Morality, human rights, and the universality of difference: implications for law's effectiveness

Hans Kelson has explored the questions regarding the nature of morality posed earlier through the "argument from relativism",[55] or the "cultural pluralism"[56] argument. Kelsen's contention can be summarized as follows:

---

52 Levit and Verchick, *Feminist Legal Theory* at 33.
53 The term is connected to Joseph's Raz's work on legal positivism, as discussed in Alexy, Robert, "The Dual Nature of Law" (2010) 23:2 *Ratio Juris* at 291 ('Alexy, "The Dual Nature of Law"').
54 Ibid.
55 Alexy, "Law, Morality, and the Existence of Human Rights" at 2.
56 Robert D. Sloane, "Outrelativizing Relativism: A Liberal Defense of the Universality of International Human Rights" (2001) 34:3 *Vanderbilt Journal of Transnational Law* at 527 ('Sloane, "Outrelativizing Relativism" ').

First, that a necessary connection between law and morality presupposes the existence of absolute, objective, or necessary moral elements, and, second, that no such absolute, objective, or necessary moral elements exist.[57]

Alexy's counterargument is that "absolute, objective, or necessary moral elements do exist, for human rights exist, and human rights exist because they are justifiable".[58] Alexy also contends that "the moral or normative reasons standing behind the Radbruch formula comprise human or fundamental rights" and that a "non-positivistic concept of law must of necessity be applied in order to protect the fundamental rights of the citizen".[59] This links the debate on the nature of morality to the nature and reach of human rights in the discourse on non-positivism.

Another complicating question, in line with these discussions of cultural relativism, arises when one considers the applicability of non-positivism to theories of law, morality, and human rights in non-Western states. Can non-positivism be applied to the legal norms of a country such as China, for example, which has an entirely different conception of morality and human rights? In China, the concept of rights is generally known to refer to "citizen rights, rather than human rights", which are "granted by the state".[60] As Wei Wei Cao notes in this volume, the exercise of rights in China – rights having been defined in relation to citizenship rather than as human entitlement – "is reliant on [the] fulfilment of relevant obligations".[61] The "macrocosm of the social and political order", rather than the individuals who make up the system, is "recognized as the fundamental unit of social organization" in post-Maoist China.[62] This concept is in direct conflict with the emphasis on individualism in the West. As Cao further notes in Chapter 4, another difference between the Western notion of human rights and the Chinese concept of citizen rights is that "the content of citizens' rights can change depending on the state's needs".[63] Perhaps the clearest example of this difference is the sharp shift from a complete ban on contraceptives and abortion services in Maoist China to the liberalized right, and even *duty*, to access contraceptives and abortion services in modern-day China.[64]

Given this swift and overt mutation in abortion regulation and its subjectivity to factors external to the demands of 'justice' – at least from the perspective of Chinese women denied reproductive freedom – it is then no surprise that China's abortion law has been deemed ineffective and problematic for women whose personal aspirations differ from the needs of the state. That economic and fiscal

---

57 Alexy, "Law, Morality, and the Existence of Human Rights" at 2.
58 Ibid.
59 Alexy, "The Dual Nature of Law" at 296.
60 Wei Wei Cao, "The Law of Abortion in China" in Chapter 2 of this volume.
61 Ibid.
62 Lock, Margaret, "Situating Women in the Politics of Healthcare" in Susan Sherwin, ed., *The Politics of Women's Health: Exploring Agency and Autonomy* (Philadelphia: Temple University Press, 1998) at 53.
63 Cao, "The Law of Abortion in China" at 17.
64 Ibid.

concerns, politics, and population size, as well as other matters, are central to the chameleonic nature of China's abortion policy leads back to the issue of the role of externalities in the creation and implementation of law – an issue that forms a key substratum of the concept of substantive legal effectiveness.

The applicability of non-positivism to Chinese legal norms is thus problematic given Alexy's supposition that "absolute, objective, or necessary moral elements do exist".[65] This supposition, in line with the argument that "human rights exist, and human rights exist because they are justifiable", implies that the absolute, objective, or necessary moral elements of morality are manifested in human rights.[66] As human rights and citizen rights bear multiple important differences, the efficacy of international treaties such as CEDAW, intended to create, protect, and guarantee the implementation of women's reproductive rights and autonomy, is certainly dubious, at least in certain jurisdictions.

Robert D. Sloane is a proponent of the idea that international human rights are the "appropriate and universal functional concept to promote human dignity internationally".[67] Though Sloane frames the discussion of human rights in different terms than the theories on the nature of law (specifically, Sloane relies on Liberal or Kantian theory), his reverence for international human rights mirrors Radbruch's view that human rights are "higher" or "supra-positive law".[68] According to Radbruch, it is a matter of "willful skepticism" when "people question why certain things are extreme injustice", and he argues that people must "accept that there is a core area of human rights such that harm to it amounts to extreme injustice".[69]

One feminist project, emerging from the endeavor to create a "global feminist theory", which stems from the "post-modern" feminist contention that "practical effects in a localized context" should be emphasized over universal principles such as human rights, stands in contention with the reliance on international legal instruments to address women's plights on a global scale. Rather than focusing on human rights violations, this theory attends to the "broader and more basic challenge of satisfying women's practical and materials needs" – a method known as the "practical well-being approach".[70] The approach recognizes that official, formal rights are not always enforced. Indeed, many human rights advocates and scholars have expressed the concern that "the rule of law is broken or lacking the capacity to address systemic, persistent discrimination in societies", as it requires a kind of rigorous implementation which frequently does not occur.[71] Additionally,

---

65 Alexy, "Law, Morality, and the Existence of Human Rights".
66 Ibid.
67 Sloane, "Outrelativizing Relativism"' at 528.
68 Robert Alexy, "A Defence of Radbruch's Formula" in David Dyzenhaus, ed., *Recrafting the Rule of Law: The Limits of the Legal Order* (Oxford: Hart Publishing, 1999), 15–39 at 34 ('Alexy, "A Defence of Radbruch's Formula"').
69 Ibid.
70 Ibid.
71 Michele Goodwin and Whelan, Allison M, "Reproduction and the Rule of Law in Latin America" (2015) 83:5 *Fordham Law Review* at 2579.

the success of enforcement itself relies very much on a state's acceptance of the substantive rights to be enforced, such that even a state with a legal order that embodies the tenets of non-positivism can stand in the way of citizens' realization of substantive rights when they do not align with the state's moral values. Thus, it is not surprising that a growing number of activists and scholars in local spaces are questioning the efficacy of "the rule of law in advancing women's rights".[72] In regards to the practice of FGC in particular, governments of numerous countries, including the United States, Egypt, and Senegal, have recognized the need to implement "outreach efforts [. . .] aimed at changing perceptions and attitudes regarding FGM" prior to or in accompaniment with any legislation on the subject[73] – this being in effect a recognition of the importance of addressing moral perceptions about the substance of the law.

Determination of the success, or lack thereof, of a law regarding women's reproductive health, rights, and autonomy of necessity involves methods of analysis described as 'theories of legal effectiveness'. The foregoing examination of the nature of law and comparison between positivist and non-positivist accounts of law are critical to understanding theories of legal effectiveness and their utility in explaining why a law fails to work as designed. In other words, a valid and functional theory of effectiveness must itself derive from a recognition of the unique "binary"[74] character of law – an account of law's nature most closely linked with non-positivism – and the oscillations and context-dependency of its claimed moral content; it must also be developed from a necessary "re-evaluation of positivist conceptions about law's character".[75] Part of the demands involved in exploring a new way of thinking about or theorizing effectiveness is the significant breadth of factors that are interwoven into law's limits. For example, it is important to examine, among a number of other factors, the relationship between legislative objectives and the real-world effects and consequences of laws on women's lives, the ways in which this relationship is influenced by the cultural, religious, economic, and political backdrops of women's lived experiences, and other accounts of *how* and *why* these particular consequences and effects occur.

As has been discussed in Chapter 2, legal scholars have postulated a few key theories of legal effectiveness – the Compliance Theory, the Outcomes Theory, and the Social Legal Theory.[76] In this book, the concept of Substantive Legal Effectiveness has also newly been proposed as both a theory that assists in the understanding of law and its application, and as a means of measuring laws with "due consideration to the consequential impact of the legal process on women's health and on the way women's health and interests are negotiated".[77] What fol-

---

72 Ibid.
73 Iyioha, "Public Health, Cultural Norms and the Criminal Law" at 470–471.
74 See Iyioha, Chapter 2 of this volume; see also Iyioha, "Substantive Effectiveness, Women's Health and the Limits of International Human Rights Law", *supra*.
75 Ibid.
76 See Iyioha, Chapter 2 of this volume.
77 Ibid. at 51.

lows is an in-depth examination of the issue of female genital cutting (FGC) and an inquiry into the (in)efficacy of the United Kingdom's Female Genital Mutilation Act, 2003,[78] promulgated to tackle this issue using the tools provided within the concept of Substantive Legal Effectiveness. As will be seen, application of the substantive theory of legal effectiveness provides the most accurate means of drawing back the curtain of apparent legal validity and efficacy surrounding FGC laws worldwide, and exposing the aggregate of socio-legal norms which work to inhibit, rather than promote, the eradication of the practice and the protection and improvement of women's health in this context.

## Case study: assessing the effectiveness of FGC prohibition laws

According to the current World Health Organization (WHO) Fact Sheet on FGC, "more than 200 million girls and women alive today have been cut in 30 countries in Africa, the Middle East and Asia" where the practice of FGC is commonplace.[79] Additionally, "more than 3 million girls" are projected to be at risk for FGC yearly in their countries of origin, as well as in nations, such as the United Kingdom (UK), which receive a high proportion of migrants from states in which FGC is more concentrated.[80] The practice is usually carried out on girls at some point "between infancy and adolescence", and can involve a variety of different procedures.[81] Type 1, often referred to as clitoridectomy, involves the full or partial removal of the clitoris; Type 2, often referred to as excision, involves the full or partial removal of the clitoris and labia minora; Type 3, often referred to as infibulation, involves the "cutting and repositioning" of the labia minora and labia majora to create a "seal", which is often stitched closed and may or may not also involve a clitoridectomy; and Type 4, which refers generally to any other non-medical procedures done to the female genitalia, including, but not limited to "pricking, piercing, incising, scraping and cauterizing the genital area".[82] The WHO identifies a plethora of common short- and long-term complications and consequences from the procedures, including severe pain and bleeding, genital tissue swelling, fever and infections, urinary problems, menstrual problems, sexual dysfunction, irreversible injuries to the genital tissue, psychological problems including shock, increased risk of complications during childbirth and infant mortality, as well as an increased rate of mortality for the women and girls who undergo FGC, particularly immediately after the procedure is done and during childbirth.

To Western sensibilities, the severity of the physical and mental health consequences of FGC and the perceived lack of women's autonomy, particularly sexual

---

78 Female Genital Mutilation Act, 2003, c. 31.
79 World Health Organization Fact Sheets: *Female Genital Mutilation*, 2018.
80 Ibid.
81 Ibid. See also Iyioha, "Public Health, Cultural Norms and the Criminal Law" at 454.
82 Ibid.

autonomy, engenders outrage. From a Western perspective, the criminalization of FGC appears to be an appropriate step towards eradicating the procedure. As "extreme injustice is not law",[83] so, too, activities which are deemed by society to be extremely unjust – at least by Western society in the present context – cannot be legal. Yet, as has been discussed, "conceptions of justice vary greatly between communities".[84] Where many Western feminists' articulated horror at the procedure generates a desire for retributive justice, many non-Western women who have undergone FGC do not view the practice as wrong, do not view themselves as mutilated, and thus would likely oppose the common use of sensational descriptors such as 'mutilation'[85] or object to the criminalization of the practice.

Despite some women's approval of the practice, the institutional cultural acceptance and/or tolerance of FGC appears to be waning in at least some of the African, Middle Eastern, and Asian countries in which the practice originates and is most concentrated. For example, multiple Nigerian states have adopted FGC-specific legislation criminalizing the practice[86] and, recently, in Somalia, the death of a 10-year old girl due to complications from FGC prompted the country's first-ever FGC prosecution.[87] Additionally, European nations such as the UK have enacted FGC-specific legislation in response to the growing populations of migrants from Africa, the Middle East, and Asia. While the domestic laws within these nations of origin still suffer largely from the same efficacy issues as are expounded below in our discussion of UK's FGC laws, we adopt the UK FGC law specifically as a case study due to the added tensions around the incendiary collision of Western and non-Western ideals (aptly exemplified by the clandestine practice of FGC in the UK), alongside the mix of social, cultural, political, economic, and religious factors which affect laws and lawmaking.

Despite pre-existing criminal offences regarding grievous bodily harm, including mutilation, UK lawmakers determined that the severity of the FGC issue demanded extra protection under the law.[88] An exploration of general criminal law theory would seem to support the implementation of a piece of legislation of this kind, as issue-specific statutes arguably best define prohibited acts and provide public notice that said specific acts are prohibited.[89] Additionally, specific, narrowly written laws arguably best provide for proportionality and limit prosecutorial discretion.[90] And lastly, FGC-specific offences are potentially the most effective in changing societal attitudes and commanding compliance, as specific

83 Alexy, "On the Concept and the Nature of Law" at 281.
84 Iyioha, "Public Health, Cultural Norms and the Criminal Law" at 469.
85 Ibid. at 452.
86 Ibid. at 454.
87 Kate Hodal, "Death of 10-year-old Girl Prompts First FGM Prosecution in Somalia's History", *The Guardian* (26 July 2018), available at www.guardian.co.uk.
88 Lynne Townley and Professor Susan Bewley, "Why the Law Against Female Genital Mutilation Should be Scrapped", *City University of London* (7 November 2017), available at www.city.ac.uk.
89 Iyioha, "Public Health, Cultural Norms and the Criminal Law" at 456.
90 Ibid.

offences make clear the government's position on the issue and place an emphasis on the "public interest in responsible behaviour".[91]

But how do we assess whether the supposed advantages of specific criminal offences are actually working practically as theorized? While laws may, on the surface, seem perfectly designed to tackle the issue of FGC and contribute to the eradication of the practice, how do we ensure that the true underlying goals of such laws – the safeguarding of women's rights to health, wellness, and sexual and reproductive autonomy and the betterment of the quality of women's lives – are being met? This is where a discussion of legal theories of effectiveness comes into play, and it is to this we now turn.

## Theories of effectiveness and the limits of the UK Female Genital Mutilation Act

An Outcomes Theory of Legal Effectiveness posits that a law is effective as long as it meets its underlying objective, whether this is in regard to changing behavioral patterns or achieving clearly defined outcomes in social phenomena.[92] Similarly, through the lens of Compliance Theory, a law is effective when it "enjoys 'sufficient compliance to be accepted by all'".[93] Thus, a lack of prosecutions, and consequently, a lack of convictions (as has been the case in the UK since the inception of the FGC law)[94] could conceivably be construed as evidence of legal effectiveness – specifically, the effectiveness of the UK law on female genital cutting. In theory, the enactment of the FGM Act could (or should) have ousted the practice of FGC, as people, in theory, aim to obey laws.

However, even a cursory glance at some of the social facts/non-legal norms surrounding FGC – particularly the socio-cultural climate – would indicate otherwise. As Iyioha discusses in Chapter 2, a perceived lack of correctness, whether moral, factual, scientific, or otherwise, "can affect legal compliance in a manner significant enough to diminish social effectiveness and thereby unsettle the foundations of traditional accounts of law".[95] While we acknowledge that even positivistic theoretical prescriptions on legal effectiveness can report on the differential impact of the law on women's lives, in this "retrospective" analysis of the social impact of a given law, such a theory inherently fails to give a necessary account of why the law has failed. In this lack of rationalization, which trails the trend of modern impact analyses to report on differences in impact among different groups without more, the Outcomes and Compliance theories fail to address the intricate layers of factors involved in the legal process that "diminish social effectiveness", thereby falling short of offering an explanatory theory for law's failure.

---

91  Ibid.
92  See Iyioha, Chapter 2 of this volume.
93  Ibid.
94  Townley and Bewley, "Why the Law Against Female Genital Mutilation", *supra*.
95  See Iyioha, Chapter 2 of this volume.

And herein lies what is fatally problematic about both of these theories, particularly from a feminist legal perspective that values the betterment of women's lives as the primary ideal. As both theories represent the formal rule-based positivistic approach to legal effectiveness, which fails to account for the role of the plethora of nuances regarding social, cultural, economic, political, and religious factors impacting laws and lawmaking, the Outcomes Theory and the Compliance Theory cannot be relied upon to provide an accurate, realistic picture of women's lived experiences of the law(s) in question. This complacency with the perceived success of such laws is, in all likelihood, a more dangerous state of affairs for those most vulnerable and most drastically affected by the inefficacy of the laws. A proper understanding of legal effectiveness must thus involve an understanding of the social contexts of law and the impact of context in lawmaking, adjudication, and implementation – a point, as Iyioha notes in Chapter 2, that the Supreme Court of Canada has recognized with particular reference to the adjudication of equality claims brought forward by women.

Where the Social Legal Theory is laudable for its recognition of the significance of the interactions/interfaces between societal norms and law, it remains a problematic theory for accounting for the effectiveness of laws purporting to advance women's rights because its emphasis on "congruity between laws and societal norms" and "popular compliance" can overlook the oscillatory character of morality and the diverse nature of societal norms.[96] The UK's FGC law, for example, likely fits with the dominant Western ideals and judgments of the nation regarding the practice of FGC, but it is also likely completely at odds with the beliefs and values of some members of the migrant population practicing it. The moral stance of the UK Parliament is evident in the language of the legislation, especially in the choice of the terminology of "mutilation". Indeed, a law that directly labels the issue in this way and makes certain what it criminalizes bends, even prelusively, towards effectiveness; yet a law that both targets and arguably alienates a specific, marginalized group is likely to contend with some ideological challenges around what it proscribes and the manner in which it does so. As is likely the case with migrant populations practicing or likely to practice FGC in the UK, "where a newly minted legal norm deviates from the 'mores and aspirations of the governed'", conflicts often arise which culminate in non-compliance with the law.[97] Indeed, the "perceived immorality of [a] law may manifest in 'widespread disobedience'".[98]

This point is clearly evident in many of the problems that scholars and activists have identified with the UK's law on FGC. These problems reflect the core factors that constitute limits to law outlined in the theory of substantive legal effectiveness. Summarily, some of these problems with regard to the UK law on FGC are a reluctance on the part of victims to speak up about their experiences based on allegiance to the authority (moral and institutional at a familial level) of

96 Ibid.
97 Ibid.
98 Ibid.

parents and relatives; social ethos and economic reasons that discourage reports from disapproving family members; a lack of certainty by health professionals on the significance of the practice and the appropriate way to define and act on the law's provisions; a lack of "criminal propensity" and, as has been contentiously argued, "criminal intent"[99] to commit the act; and gaps in the law.[100] What follows is a discussion of the prevalence and severity of the FGC issue in the UK, as well as a brief discussion of the history of the FGC law in the UK, to ground this theoretical analysis and further propound the necessity for a more nuanced look at the actual effectiveness of the UK's FGM Act.

### The UK FGM Act: scale and history

The scale of the 'problem' of FGC in the UK remains contested. The issue subdivides into two broad categories: (1) the number of women and girls resident in the UK who are living with FGC; and (2) the number of young females in the UK who are sent back to countries of origin to be cut. A further figure sought to be identified is the number of young women and girls in the UK at risk of FGC. None of these figures is known with any precision and the roots of this are methodological, among other culturally linked factors.

As to the latter, the UK has a complex history of migration. In previous centuries the UK has been a major, and, for a time, *the* major colonial power in the world. The British Empire, and latterly the British Commonwealth, have spanned the globe and touched several of the countries with known high prevalence rates of FGC or significant absolute numbers of FGC survivors (such as Nigeria, a former colony). There are substantial migrant communities from such countries in the UK. The numbers of UK residents from affected areas is complicated by the UK's historic and once sympathetic approach towards receiving asylum-seekers. This has changed with the perceived migration 'crisis' that has affected much of Europe; nevertheless, there are large populations from countries such as Somalia in parts of the UK. A further factor, and even harder to quantify, comes from the fact that the UK sits at the end of long, arduous, and dangerous migration routes

---

99  Some activists such as Nahid Toubi and Anika Rahman have noted that FGC family members lack "violent intent" or, in other words, the requisite criminal intent that makes up the *mens rea* element of a criminal offence: N. Toubia, "Editorial: Female Circumcision/ Female Genital Mutilation" (1998) 2:2 *AJRH* and Anika Rahman and Nahid Toubia, *Female Genital Mutilation: A Guide to Laws and Policies Worldwide* (New York: Zed Publications, 2000). However, as Iyioha has observed elsewhere, it is important to distinguish between "criminal intent" and "motive" in these cases, and the deliberateness of the conduct of excisors or practitioners would seem to meet the element of "criminal intent" as their motivation for the practice – that of raising a child in a manner that ensures her marital viability – falls within the purview of 'motive', an irrelevant subject for criminal liability: Iyioha, *supra* note 81. This is also the case with the FGC law in the UK. See also Dexter Dias, Felicity Gerry and Hilary Burrage, "10 Reasons Why Our FGM Law Has Failed – and 10 Ways to Improve It", *The Guardian* (7 February 2014), available at www.theguardian. com ('Dias et al., "10 Reasons Why Our FGM Law Has Failed"').
100  Dias et al., "10 Reasons Why Our FGM Law Has Failed".

for those seeking economic betterment. Thus, at Calais, on the French coast, an informal migrant camp (the 'Jungle') came into existence for people from Africa, Eastern Europe, the Middle East and Asia seeking entry into the UK by any means possible.

In 2007, the non-governmental organization (NGO) FORWARD carried out research in England and Wales to estimate the prevalence of FGC. The report suggested that 24,000 girls in the UK were at risk of FGC. In 2014, researcher Julie Bindel was commissioned by the New Culture Forum to provide an updated prevalence estimate. Bindel's study, "An Unpunished Crime", assessed the figure of women and girls living in the UK to have suffered FGC to be 170,000. She found that 65,000 girls were at risk of genital cutting. At about the same time, a report by another NGO, Equality Now, in association with City University, London, found that the number of affected females resident in the UK was around 137,000.

These reports have generally extrapolated from census and population figures from countries in which FGC is known to be prevalent. They provide a starting point and possible order of magnitude but must be viewed in light of clear limitations. Assumptions have been made that, for example, the migrant diaspora are broadly of the same attitude towards FGC as the Indigenous population in the country of origin; further, that the attitude towards FGC is substantially the same in new countries as in country of origin.

In July 2018 the government published figures based on the 'Enhanced Dataset' collected by healthcare providers in England, including hospitals, mental health providers, and general practitioners (GPs). This prevalence study sought to build the empirical picture across the nation. From the beginning of the year to March 2018, 6,195 women and girls attended healthcare facilities where FGC was identified. Of these, 4,495 were 'newly recorded' – not previously appearing in the dataset. Thus, the scale of the existence of females living with FGC in the UK is slowly emerging. These figures do not specify when or where the procedure was performed. FGC is notoriously a transnational phenomenon. The affected population groups are dispersed throughout the UK but generally gravitate towards the major cities. These urban concentrations have been the focus of government poster campaigns and the investment of community engagement funds (although the latter have been limited). They have focused on London, Bristol, Birmingham, Manchester, Leicester, Liverpool, Sheffield, and Cardiff.

FGC is, of course, *prima facie* a criminal offence. The UK criminal law has long deemed the infliction of acts of serious harm and bodily injury to be a crime, notwithstanding situations wherein there may be consent from the victim, such as during acts of more extreme sadomasochism.[101] This is a policy decision. Conceivably the kind of genital cutting that constitutes the typologies of the more severe forms of FGC as defined by the WHO taxonomy would constitute

---

101  *R v Brown* [1993] UKHL 19 (sadomasochistic acts among gay men); *R v Emmett* [1999] All ER 641, CA (heterosexual defendants).

criminal offences under the Offence Against the Person Act, 1861: Victorian legislation that codified much more antiquated common law.

The UK's initial legal response to FGC arose as a result of the international movement to provide enhanced protection of women and girls from discrimination and violence. The UK was one of the 189 states to ratify CEDAW in 1981. It is in this wider global context that the UK passed the Prohibition of Female Circumcision Act, 1985.[102] It purported to comply with the UK's obligations under CEDAW to outlaw FGC by criminalizing acts of female genital cutting in the UK.

No prosecutions resulted from this statute. In the next two decades, a more nuanced understanding of the nature of the phenomenon led to the 1985 Act being repealed and replaced with the Female Genital Mutilation Act, 2003. The new legislation extended the scope of the offence, creating a transnational jurisdiction for acts of FGC committed abroad by UK nationals or permanent residents. It also increased the maximum sentence to 14 years' imprisonment. In the subsequent decade, however, no prosecutions were brought.

Whatever the actual empirical figure of the prevalence of FGC in the UK, given the existence of the very substantial affected migrant communities, it was an irresistible inference that there must have been acts of FGC either perpetrated in the UK or arranged in the UK to be executed in countries of origin. Such crimes either did not exist – an unlikely possibility – or were going undetected and unpunished. Frontline workers in affected communities and embedded members of these communities confirmed that the practice existed in the UK in both senses, but the UK's institutional response displayed a dangerous vacillation between cultural indifference and moral confusion and paralysis.

In response to this state of affairs, a roots-up social justice movement began to exert pressure on the UK government. An online petition in 2013 secured the necessary 100,000 signatures for parliamentary debate. In 2014, the groundswell of concern and outrage at the lack of prosecution resulted in a Parliamentary Inquiry into FGC undertaken by a high-level parliamentary committee, the Home Affairs Select Committee (HASC). It sought submissions from stakeholders across civil society, affected communities, and concerned parties and interest groups. It received written evidence from 53 entities. One of these was from one of the UK's prime human rights organizations, the Bar Human Rights Committee of England and Wales (BHRC). It undertook a systematic appraisal of the UK Act and critically evaluated it against the UK's international treaty obligations under international law. Several of the BHRC's key recommendations were adopted by the HASC and developed into changes in the UK's FGC law.[103]

---

102 Prohibition of Female Circumcision Act, 1985, c. 38.
103 In the interest of full disclosure, one of the authors of this chapter, Dexter Dias, QC, was chair of the BHRC's 'FGM' working group. Dias, QC co-wrote – with the organization's overall Chair, Kirsty Brimelow QC – an open letter to the Parliamentary Inquiry. The letter stated that: "The UK has an obvious and urgent need to protect young women and girls far more effectively from the risk of genital mutilation. The BHRC has grave concerns about

The principal recommendations from the BHRC included the creation of 'FGM Protection Orders' to equip the courts with a series of preventative powers to safeguard girls before they undergo the procedure (Recommendation 1). This became law under the Serious Crime Act 2015 (SCA),[104] which became the new section 5A of the 2003 FGM Act. The SCA received its Royal Assent on 3 March 2015 and was enacted on 3 May 2015. The High Court now regularly imposes such orders. Since the new law's inception, dozens of girls who might otherwise have been cut have come under the court's protection. While section 5A is a laudable addition to the law, a fundamental problem with the Protection Order relates to the impact of the orders on a child or young person who, by traditional norms, is tied to or dependent on the family and the family's sense of cohesion. Thus, while the Protection Orders may be deemed effective in having brought young girls under the court's protection, a necessary and perhaps unexplored part of this 'success' story is the longer-term impact of the orders on the lives of those affected. We flag this not to diminish the contributions made by these Protection Orders, but to again highlight the complex nature of the problem of FGC and the sometimes Janus-faced nature of reform.

The BHRC also recommended that the categories of protected girls should be extended in line with the United Nations Convention on the Rights of the Child, 1989 (Recommendation 2). Therefore, it became a criminal offence to assist in the genital cutting abroad of girls who are UK residents, that is, 'habitually resident' in the UK (sections 3 and 6 of 2003 Act, as amended by the SCA). The BHRC further called for the creation of a central 'anti-FGM unit' to monitor trends in female genital cutting and provide a center of experience and knowledge (Recommendation 3). An FGM unit located at the Home Office has been created to coordinate efforts across government and to provide community outreach.

### Amendments to the UK FGM law

The SCA marked a legislative sea change in the UK's approach to FGC. Its roots are complicated. It was in large part the result of constant campaigning over years by survivor groups, NGOs, and human rights organizations that had again and again sought to sensitize government to FGC as a living reality across the UK. One of the principal concerns of engaged civil society groups has been the lack

---

the efficacy of the UK's response to FGM, and has concluded that the UK has been in breach of its international law obligations to protect young women and girls from mutilation. During the period of the UK's breach, thousands of British girls and young women have been unnecessarily exposed to the risk of mutilation and have suffered irreparable physical and emotional damage. Many could – and should – have been saved. This constitutes a serious breach of the state's duty of care. Immediate remedial action must be taken". The scale of the number of girls at risk of FGC or affected by it was based on research from Julie Bindel and the 'New Culture Forum' and from the research the BHRC conducted itself, speaking to affected communities, frontline workers and survivors.

104 Serious Crimes Act, 2015, c. 9.

of prosecutions. Up until 2015 there was not a single prosecution in the UK for any FGC-related offence. The reasons are complicated. However, one of the chief problems lies in the nature of the victim and her relationship to those who arrange and execute the cutting, which, as we discuss more fully below, makes it difficult for a child to come forward and make a disclosure. The SCA duly amended the 2003 Act to prohibit the publication of any information that is likely to lead to the identification of a person who has made a complaint of FGC. Once a complaint has been made, the anonymity of the complainant will last for the rest of her life.[105] However, the court has a discretionary power to dispense with the prohibition on publication. If it can be established that the defence of the accused is substantially prejudiced by the prohibition on publication, then the court can lift the restriction. Further, if there is an overriding public interest in publication, the court can do the same.

Beyond the grant of anonymity, the criminal courts have an array of other adaptations to the conventional trial process that can be ordered to encourage the active participation of the complainant. This is part of the "Overriding Objective" of the criminal justice system to ensure that the case is dealt with "justly"; this includes ensuring that the guilty are convicted and the innocent' acquitted by, *inter alia*, the court receiving the best evidence.[106] To achieve this aim, the court is expected to take "every reasonable step" to enable witnesses to "give their best evidence".[107] Thus, there is the possibility of the complainant-witness giving evidence behind a "screen", that is, shielded from the defendant and the public. Further, it is possible for a video link to be used, whereby the complainant need not actually be in the courtroom. If the witness is considered "vulnerable" (an assessment to be made by the judge considering all the circumstances), the court is to impose "ground rules".[108] Following a ground rules hearing, a court can impose serious restrictions on the length of defence questioning, the form of the questions, and how challenges are put to the witness. For a girl coming forward to make a complaint of FGC, these "special measures", as they are called, may provide some comfort in making the court proceedings less daunting. However, other obstacles to making and persevering with a disclosure plainly remain and are considered below.

Where the pressure on a complainant becomes overwhelming and she wishes to withdraw from cooperating with the prosecution, the prosecuting authority, the Crown Prosecution Service, will consider whether there is sufficient evidence to proceed without her. In some cases, there may be. This is one of the arguments in favor of creating a duty of mandatory reporting, which we discuss below. It would provide corroborative evidence that the child had been cut. Further, the courts can receive "first complaint" evidence to support the prosecution's case; and if the court is satisfied that the witness has become 'unavailable' to testify at

---

105  Schedule 1, 2003 Act (as amended).
106  Criminal Procedure Rules, 2015 ('CPR'), Rule 1 (UK).
107  Criminal Practice Direction, 2015, EWCA, Crim 1567, 3D.2 (UK).
108  CPR, *supra*, 3.9(7)(b).

trial due to fear, it may order that the statement be read to the jury. Notwithstanding this, a complainant who has had a change of heart may be compelled to testify by a number of compulsive powers of the court, such as witness summons to attend and/or warrant for arrest if the witness fails to do so.

Recognizing these stubborn and persistent problems in the securing of complainant evidence, the BHRC, along with other NGOs and interest groups, recommended to Parliament that there should be mandatory reporting of FGC by frontline professionals (Recommendation 4). This was one of the most hotly contested recommendations in the parliamentary passage of the new law. Concerns were expressed – and indeed continue to be expressed – that mandatory reporting obligations have counterproductive effects: eroding trust between patient and healthcare provider or pupil and teacher; leading to vulnerable girls not receiving necessary medical treatment; and driving the practice of FGC further underground. These are difficult judgments. However, the alternative was that regulated and responsible professionals who came across clear cases of FGC would have no enforceable professional duty to report such crimes to the police. That was considered by the BHRC and others to be an indefensible position, particularly given the vulnerable nature of the victims and the structural, social, and cultural impediments to their coming forward. Further, as explained earlier, such professionals may provide invaluable supportive evidence.

Mandatory reporting became the law on 31 October 2015. The SCA inserted a new section 5B into the 2003 Act. It created a duty to report cases of FGC to the police by people working in regulated professions. The obligation arises in situations where the girl involved is under 18 and the professional is a healthcare professional, teacher, or social care worker (the last in Wales). The 'discovery' of FGC can be by one of two routes: first, if the girl informs the professional that FGC has been carried out on her; second, if the person observes clear physical signs of FGC and there is no reason to believe it was connected to legitimate protected surgery.

Consequently, failure to report FGC is now a matter of serious professional misconduct for regulated health and social care professionals and teachers in England and Wales. FGC in the UK is deemed a form of child abuse, and the failure to report known instances of such abuse is to be regarded as a commensurate breach of duty. In cases where such professionals believe a child is at serious or imminent risk of FGC, other safeguarding protocols apply, such as Working Together to Safeguard Children as well as multi-agency guidance on FGC.

Following the pressure on state authorities to recognize and exercise the state's safeguarding duties in respect of FGC, the first case came to trial in January 2015. There were two defendants. One was Dr. Dhanuson Dharmasena, aged 32, a junior registrar at the Whittington Hospital in London.[109] An adult woman who had undergone an FGC procedure when she was six years of age was admitted to

---

109 A second man, 41-year-old Hasan Mohamed, was charged with aiding or abetting the offence and with intentionally encouraging and assisting in the commission of the offence: *Doctor 'Performed FGM on New Mother in Hospital'*, www.bbc.com/news/uk-30886077.

hospital for an emergency procedure related to pregnancy. The woman began to bleed and the doctor re-infibulated her, replacing the stitching she had received as a child. When the doctor later consulted a more senior colleague, he was advised of another way to stop the bleeding. Once the prosecuting authority decided to charge the doctor under the 2003 Act, the woman in question refused to testify against the defendant. The jury acquitted Dr. Dharamasena in 30 minutes.

In the aftermath of the verdict, public and legal opinion was sharply divided about whether this was an appropriate case to prosecute. The Director of Public Prosecutions (DPP), Alison Saunders, defended the decision, stating that, on three occasions, the trial judge had been invited to dismiss the charges and stop the case, and on each occasion, ruled that there was sufficient evidence to go before the jury.[110] The NGO Equality Now, which campaigns against FGC, stated that the case was an "enormous step forward" and communicated "not only that FGM is against the law, but that the law will be implemented".[111] While we note that a defendant's acquittal does not of itself invalidate the prosecutorial decision to press and proceed with charges, it is important to equally acknowledge the sharp divisions in opinion about the DPP's exercise of its prosecutorial discretion in this case – an issue which, as has been acknowledged in Chapter 2 and elsewhere,[112] can certainly arise with a problem-specific law, such as a law on FGC.

### Female Genital Cosmetic Surgery (FGSC) and the UK FGM Act

The existence of Female Genital Cosmetic Surgery (FGCS), which is not criminalized in the UK, juxtaposed with the criminalized practice of female genital cutting, goes to the heart of the moral conundrum that often besets discourses on the universalism of human rights as well as on the objectives of feminist legal theory. It has been known for a considerable period that FGCS is "an increasingly popular form of surgery".[113] The Parliamentary Inquiry found that there has been a fivefold increase in labiaplasty, the most common form of such surgery, in the previous decade. Since most of such procedures occur in the private sector, they are not subject to the same degree of scrutiny and vigilance as in the National Health Service. Interestingly, section 1 of the 2003 Act allows for surgery necessary for a girl's "physical or mental health",[114] thus giving room to the argument that the law implicitly creates an exception for FGCS. The various police representative organizations have pointed to this "double standard", a form of institutionalized hypocrisy acutely felt by minority ethnic communities.[115]

---

110 BBC, "The Prosecutors" (March 9, 2016), available at www.bbc.co.uk/programmes/b072wyvj.
111 Ibid.
112 Iyioha, "Public Health, Cultural Norms and the Criminal Law", *supra*.
113 Parliamentary Inquiry Report at 39 and 89.
114 S. 1, FGM Act, 2003.
115 Ibid.

The UK government has taken the position that there is no ambiguity in the law around FGCS. While there is no explicit exemption for FGCS in the 2003 Act and section 1 can at best be assumed to be an implicit exception, the evidence received by the Home Affairs Select Committee (HASC) from police, midwives, and campaign groups suggested a pressing need for greater clarity about the status of FGCS. On this, the HASC stated that, "[W]e cannot tell communities in Sierra Leone and Somalia to stop a practice that is freely permitted in Harley Street [the centre of exclusive private medical clinics]".[116] Thus, the Committee recommended that the government change the 2003 Act to clarify that FGCS would be a criminal offence.

This sense of grievance felt by some members of affected communities is reinforced by the fact that it is emphasized in the 2003 Act that in considering medically justified surgery, "it is immaterial whether the girl or any other person believes that the operation is required as a matter of custom or ritual".[117] Contrast this with various forms of non-therapeutic cosmetic surgery that *is* indeed or *proves* to be harmful. Certainly, those who have worked with affected communities regularly encounter this charge: that the UK embraces this chronic double standard, one that is racially and ethnically skewed. This double standard reifies our discussion of the challenges with feminist legal theory and human rights' moralistic stances, in the case of some culturally situated practices at the core of popular advocacy. It remains to be seen whether, and in what way, this serious credibility problem for the national fight against FGC is resolved.

## Substantive legal effectiveness and the UK's FGM Act

Substantive Legal Effectiveness (SLE), which provides the most thorough exploration of legislative objectives and the diversity of societal responses, thus emerges as the most appropriate theory of legal effectiveness in determining which laws, in practice, actually work towards achieving the core goals of supporting women's rights and improving women's lives.

As a concept addressing gaps in the ways law's effect is otherwise understood, theorized and measured, SLE offers both a theory for understanding why law may be ineffective and a three-part standard for measuring law's effectiveness. In this, SLE aims to further the realization of substantive equality. Case law examined in Chapter 2 demonstrates how judicial misconceptions of the true effect of certain legal provisions or statutes on women's lives result in decisions that defeat equality claims filed by women, and thereby deny women the opportunity to succeed on a truly substantive understanding of equality. As a Canadian scholar has noted, the Supreme Court of Canada must come to an understanding of how detrimental the effects of otherwise neutral law can be to women if they are to

---

116 *Female Genital Mutilation: Follow-Up*, on 14 March 2015, Home Affairs Select Committee.
117 S. 1(5), FGM Act, 2003.

truly uphold a version of equality that is substantive rather than formal.[118] The same arguments transported into the context of a gender-based issue-specific law, such as a law on FGC, raises differentiable but substantively similar concerns: what are the determinative factors underlying the effects of such laws and that account for their limitations in furthering the objectives they were designed to achieve?

We offer an answer to this question in the context of FGC by first asking: what is SLE? The idea central to SLE is that law's effectiveness and limits are grounded in the symmetry of certain normative conditions that are structural, contextual, and principle based. Based on a threefold tenet, and drawing upon the analysis in interconnecting discourses, these conditions and their sub-concerns are alignment or symmetry of a law's composition and substance with its objectives (objectives/composition/content and subject's identity/needs/context); alignment of a law's structural components and its administration (language/interpretation/social facts);[119] and alignment of a law's prescriptions and perceptions regarding its subject matter (correctness/reception/compliance).[120] These three points of analysis within the SLE theory vividly capture the major problems with the UK law identified above. To recapitulate, the core problems include victims' reluctance to speak up about their experiences; social and economic factors discouraging reports from disapproving witnesses; health professionals' uncertainty regarding the significance of the practice and the interpretation of the law; lack of "criminal propensity" and "criminal intent"[121] to commit the act; and legislative gaps. We assess these problems against the SLE theory in three steps below.

## Socio-economic factors impeding UK victims' complaints and testimony

### SLE (objectives, composition and content) – statutory objectives and recognition of the identity, needs, and contexts of legal subjects

SLE recognizes the importance of a connection between law's purpose and its content, highlighting the necessity for particular attention to the needs and contexts of the existence of law's diverse subjects. Thus, its first rule is for an alignment of the content or substance of a law and its intended goals or objectives, supported with knowledge of the identity and needs of those who will be affected by the law, as well as with knowledge of the particular contexts of their lived experiences. In the case of FGC, a substantive theory of legal effectiveness recognizes the interrelations between societal pressures, cultural expectations, and the law – and how these combinatorial factors can generate differences in how different

---

118 See generally Beverley Baines, "Constitutionalizing Women's Equality Rights: There Is Always Room for Improvement" (2015/2016) 37.2:1 *Atlantis*.
119 Denoted as internal elements and internal limits: see Iyioha, Chapter 2 of this volume.
120 Denoted as external elements and external limits: see ibid.
121 See Iyioha, "Public Health, Cultural Norms and the Criminal Law", *supra*.

population groups respond to the same law. For example, the individualism in Western social culture in its striking difference from the communal, co-existing culture of African and Middle Eastern communities can influence the response to a criminal law that is framed along the lines of the UK law on FGC. Thus, a victim raised within such a close-knit cultural setting in which the actions of one is said to have an indelible impact on the rest of the members of the family would be less likely to report her experience of the procedure due to the above intersecting factors.

Formalistic analyses of laws' (in)effectiveness that do not account for such socio-cultural backdrops fail to recognize the implicit barriers for victims of FGC that prevent them from coming forward. There are two routes to the prosecution of those responsible for being complicit in the genital cutting of children and young women. The first is that young victims – who are in law 'children' – speak against their families and communities.[122] This presents immense difficulties, as is evident from other fields where crimes are committed within the family or close kinship group, such as Child Sexual Abuse (CSA). There is the obvious and inevitable acute conflict of loyalties: fear of loss of love, position within the family; loss or destruction of the family itself – another reason that victims of intra-familial CSA frequently offer for the lack of disclosure. One cannot ignore the extensive literature on attachment, and the psychological benefits and costs of ending an even dysfunctional attachment relationship. Thus, while the SCA has taken steps to address this by amending the 2003 Act to prohibit the publication of information that is likely to lead to the identification of a complainant, the court's discretionary power to dispense with the prohibition remains problematic, and can discourage victims from speaking out. An additional problem regarding the prohibition on publication of complainant's identity is whether it can effectively prevent a close-knit family or even an averagely close family from identifying or guessing the identity of the person who has disclosed information about the occurrence of FGC.

Further problems obstructing the disclosure and prosecution of FGC are that the cutting procedures are often initiated and arranged by the victim's family members or wider kinship group. If the actual "cutters" are not directly related, they are generally individuals who possess social capital and influence within the community, and sometimes, such as within the Sierra Leone diaspora, are cloaked in a hereditary cult-like mystique.[123] During the parliamentary debates leading to the 2015 Act, Baroness Smith stated in the House of Lords:

> Many activists tell us that pressures from others in the community on parents can become too difficult to resist, even when they have no wish to cut their daughters. Affected communities often retain a strong hierarchical structure, and encouragement or admonishment from elders can carry enormous

---

122 Hannah Summers, "Those Involved in FGM Will Find Ways to Evade UK Law", *The Guardian* (7 March 2018), available at www.theguardian.com.
123 Dias et al., "10 Reasons Why Our FGM Law Has Failed", *supra*.

weight. Not only are parents told that their daughters will never get married, but whole families can be ostracised and isolated as unclean. We need to support those who are seeking to change the culture in affected communities and send the message that the practice is breaking the law. We know from research by the Bar Human Rights Committee and others that there is still significant support among affected communities in Britain for sunna: that is, type 1 and type 2 FGM.[124] The process by which FGM occurs is complex, and sometimes encouragement takes place in small gatherings and in informal settings behind the scenes, where it is difficult to intervene.[125]

This is a heavy burden for anyone to bear, particularly someone who is likely a child or adolescent, someone who is a member of a migrant population in a new state, and/or someone who belongs to a strict patriarchal and gerontocratic cultural community.

Some members of the practicing communities offer strong cultural arguments in support of FGC. There are arguments around tradition, social stability, respect for cultural norms, and fear of ostracism. Girls who are not cut in certain communities are shunned or have difficulties marrying, or there can be an impact on the wider social status of the family or even kinship group. Further, from the perspective of the cutter, there is a powerful socio-economic incentive for performance of the procedure, as income earned by excisors or "cutters" serves to supplement or can constitute the only source of income for a family. Thus, an excisor's recognition of the moral problems associated with FGC may not necessarily deter her from the practice, due to the financial costs of ending what she has found to be a profitable profession.[126] SLE recognizes how these types of contextual factors, whether they are socio-economic or religious, feed into responses to and compliance with law.

Against such considerations, it was emphasized by the BHRC in its submission to the Parliamentary Inquiry that there is an international law requirement for those party states that have ratified CEDAW to take positive steps to combat harmful traditional practices. The basis of this approach is grounded in prevailing international law norms. One of the historic difficulties in combating FGC has been the anxiety about challenging cultural or traditional practices. However, in a General Resolution in 2007,[127] the UN emphasized that custom, tradition, or

---

124 Sunna is considered one of the less severe forms of FGC, in which some blood is drawn from the girl's genitalia: Newell-Jones, Katy, The Orchid Project, "Empowering Communities to Collectively Abandon FGMC in Somaliland", available at https://orchidproject. org/wp-content/uploads/2016/07/AA-Empowering-communities-to-collectively-aban don-FGMC-in-Somaliland.pdf.

125 UK, HL, "Serious Crime Bill [*Lords*]", Session 2014–15 in *Public Bill Committee Debates* (2015), available at www.publications.parliament.uk/pa/cm201415/cmpublic/serio uscrime/150120/am/150120s01.htm.

126 Iyioha, "Public Health, Cultural Norms and the Criminal Law", *supra*.

127 United Nations General Assembly Resolution 61/143: Intensification of Efforts to Eliminate all Forms of Violence against Women, available at www.un.org/ga/search/view_doc. asp?symbol=A/RES/61/143&Lang=E.

religious beliefs cannot be used as excuses for avoiding the obligation to eliminate violence against women and girls. This important clarification must be combined with the recognition that it is legitimate, necessary, and desirable for a state to intervene to modify social and cultural patterns of conduct that result in discrimination against women.[128]

Finally, on this first principle, SLE highlights the importance of considering the particular needs of legal subjects or of beneficiaries of the law, the larger, extended impact of the law on their well-being, and how the demands the law makes can defeat the very goals sought to be achieved in their favor. In the context of FGC, we ask: What is the expected reaction to a law offering a steep penalty for an offence if the outcome of a successful realization of its goal (i.e., successful prosecution) is the separation of a minor from her benefactors, estrangement from parental authorities, and possibly the placement of the minor in the wardship of the state in the absence of familial guardianship? What consideration did the drafters give to these concerns and, if any, what arrangements are in place to address them? It is in this light that we have questioned the overall impact of 'FGM Protection Orders' – which, while they seek to protect the child victim, expose them to the possibility of other social, emotional, and psychological problems, among others, arising from separation from family.

### UK health professionals' uncertainties about legal guidelines

*SLE's internal elements of law (structure and administration/ application) – legal language, interpretation and social facts and the creation of legislative and interpretive loopholes*

SLE's second tenet identifies as inherent in law's constitutive elements – that is, its unique, specialized language and the social facts (economic, cultural, political, religious, etc.) that it often mirrors[129] – the very ingredients that limit its capacity to deliver on its promises. Law's technical language, when ambiguous or vaguely constructed, impedes women's access to healthcare[130] and infringes on the effective enforcement of legal rules, specifically in the case of prohibitive laws, such as those criminalizing FGC. Legal uncertainties arising from the choice of diction or the form of composition of prescriptive provisions have paved the way for healthcare professionals and administrators to make healthcare decisions that defeat the goals of the relevant law. This is evident in the number of claims now brought before international human rights committees challenging state conduct with regard to denying women access to needed reproductive health services.[131]

---

128 CEDAW, art. 5.
129 See Iyioha, Chapter 2 of this volume; see also Iyioha, "Public Health, Cultural Norms and the Criminal Law", *supra*.
130 See Iyioha, Chapter 2 of this volume.
131 Iyioha, "Public Health, Cultural Norms and the Criminal Law", *supra*. See also Joanna N. Erdman, "The Procedural Turn: Abortion at the European Court of Human Rights",

Indeed, it is not unusual to find physicians denying authorization to procedures due, as Erdman has observed, "to legitimate fears in the face of an uncertain law".[132] As part of an integral theory of the nature of law and why law fails, SLE embodies the understanding that "vague and broadly written legal grounds" allow women to be "denied services to which they are *formally* entitled".[133]

In the context of the UK's FGC law, activists have noted that healthcare professionals, who are not equipped to interpret the law, may not appreciate the nature of the problem of FGC or understand the exact requirements of the law. The 2015 not-guilty verdict in the case of Dr. Dhanuson Dharmasena, a UK registrar in obstetrics and gynecology charged with FGM following what was defined as "re-infibulation" may be demonstrative of the problems of interpretation.[134] Some activists have also observed that in some cases, even clearly outlined guidelines on how a law is to be implemented within an institutional setting may still fail to address the broader problems around an interpretive exercise. For example, according to Dias et al. writing on the reasons for the apparent ineffectiveness of UK's FGC law, "despite clear guidelines, many frontline professionals (GPs, midwives, teachers, healthcare visitors, social workers) are not trained" and "do not understand the law"; and combined with their uncertainty about the "significance of "cultural" or "traditional" values",[135] practitioners understandably wary of professional malpractice would prioritize their personal interest in decision-making on matters arising from the law.

### Lack of criminal propensity/intent

*SLE's external elements of law – moral, factual and scientific correctness and its impact on reception of and compliance with law*

SLE's third tenet recognizes that, where proscriptions of a practice or prescriptive norms reflect the common ethos of the target population, it aids compliance with law. Thus, SLE proposes the necessity for perceptions about law to be factored into consideration when assessing the likelihood of compliance with law. Proposing that law has a moral core, or at least aspires towards morality, SLE draws on Alexy's dual nature theory to offer a modified binary theory of law's nature[136] – that law comprises a substantive aspect inclusive of its language of composition, interpretation, and social factors (internal elements) and a moral character that orients towards justice (external elements).

---

in Rebecca J. Cook, Joanna N. Erdman and Bernard M. Dickens, eds., *Abortion Law in Transnational Perspective* (Philadelphia: University of Pennsylvania Press, 2014) at 121 ('Erdman, "The Procedural Turn"').

132  Erdman, "The Procedural Turn" at 121–122.

133  Ibid. at 127. Emphasis is ours.

134  Sandra Laville, *First FGM Prosecution: How the Case Came to Court*, (4 February 2015), available at www.theguardian.com/society/2015/feb/04/first-female-genital-mutilation-prosecution-dhanuson-dharmasena-fgm.

135  Dias et al., "10 Reasons Why Our FGM Law Has Failed", *supra.*

136  For Iyioha's elucidation on this, see Chapter 2 of this volume.

SLE recognizes law's proclivity for moral considerations in lawmaking and interpretation and the centrality of such moral considerations to lawmaking in the area of women's health, especially women's reproductive health. Equally recognizing the innate divergency of morality and its mutative capacity (as we find in the case of China's abortion policies historically), SLE mandates "deliberative negotiation"[137] of the ethics of a given legal prescription, along a broad range of considerations concerning the law's impact on the overall well-being of women and on their fundamental human rights.

Relating this to FGC, we find that, in communities that practice FGC, cutting is viewed as a "purification ritual" which works to ensure that women are virginal, and thus, marriageable.[138] The motive – defensible or not – by parents who often have no criminal history or "criminal propensity"[139] is clearly to adhere to social norms and prevent the rejection of young women from society, not to irreparably harm or kill them.[140] Western feminists would inarguably view the acceptance and practice of FGC as a severe instance of cultural hegemony supporting harmful, patriarchal ideals – a view that is completely antithetical to how these communities view FGC. If the goal is to eradicate the practice of FGC, these perceptions cannot simply be ignored.

Related to this moral viewpoint is the notion that FGC serves what is assumed to be an experientially verifiable purpose: that it curbs the sexual desires of women and protects them from the 'harms' of a life spent alone, unmarried, and repulsed by a brood of otherwise carefully selective, good men. This, of course, erroneous assumption forms the substratum of the strong moral views underlying the practice. Due to these deeply entrenched beliefs about the cultural worthiness of FGC, it is clear that a prescriptive norm on the subject is most likely to obtain the compliance of legal subjects when "fashioned out of an understanding of . . . the importance of [moral] correctness to compliance with [the law]".[141] Thus, a substantive legal effectiveness approach ensures that, while a law may essentially target a marginalized population for the protection of its vulnerable members, they are not alienated by it. SLE's concept of moral and factual correctness recognizes the insidious impact that the above ethically controversial positions can have on the eradication of the practice, and thus highlights the need for prescriptive rules – in their framing, messaging and implementation – to address the problem without alienating target subjects of the law and encouraging clandestine practices.

An associated claim under SLE is that the public's conviction that a practice or norm (social or legal) is scientifically correct can impede the effect of prescriptive rules. In the case of FGC, some advocates of the practice have suggested that concerns around the adverse impact of the procedure can be ameliorated by hospital-based surgical procedures. Such a sanitized process, it is assumed, would

---

137 Ibid.
138 WHO Fact Sheet, *supra.*
139 Dias et al., "10 Reasons Why Our FGM Law Has Failed", *supra.*
140 Iyioha, "Public Health, Cultural Norms and the Criminal Law" at 457.
141 See Iyioha, Chapter 2 of this volume.

displace, on a ground of moral relativism, ethical concerns raised by opposers. These problematic assumptions recognize both the intractable nature of the problem of FGC, as well as the significance of the concept of correctness to discourses about social and legal norms.

In recognizing the law's aspiration towards justice as a definitional component of law, SLE opens the opportunity for further discourses around a notion of correctness that draws on foundational purposes of law as a distinct, authoritative, and ethical field in service of the individual and her needs – and how this notion might transcend the divisive and conflicting perspectives about morality that afflict human rights discourse. In other words, SLE encourages discourses on how law can navigate the matrix of internal and external elements that define its creation and functioning, while retaining its core characteristic of ideological or conceptual independence – to the extent that this is possible – when it matters.

In both the case of uncertainty about the significance and interpretation of the law (discussed under SLE's second tenet) and cases where the law in an otherwise conservative jurisdiction is intentionally riddled with legislative gaps and uncertainties (also fitting within SLE's second tenet), SLE contributes to the ongoing discourse on the effectiveness and/or limits of (human rights) law by clearly identifying the normative link between the law's *composition* (in the case of intentionally restrictive rules) or the *response* to the law (in the case of UK health professionals' uncertainties and wariness) *and* the ethically or morally controversial nature of the practice itself. SLE, in a detour from discourses that pitch the problems of legal uncertainty and vagueness simply as a procedural problem, identifies these problems as normative, placing at their very core the issue of moralistic unease with either the provisions of a law considered 'morally reprehensible' or that of ethical unease with the exact cultural or traditional significance of the practice and the role of a healthcare professional in relation to the act.

In either case, recognition of the normative problem at the core of SLE's third tenet allows for attention to the foundational causes of the problems in the course of recommendations on the ways in which these otherwise procedural or structural gaps can be remedied. And in this, what emerges therefore is (1) the centrality of this normative thread to the SLE theory, which contributes to understanding law's nature, law's constitutive elements and the ways in which that nature and the elements define the very precincts of law's limits; (2) the integral nature of the three tenets proffered under the theory; and (3) the pre-emptive and explanatory character of SLE's propositions, which differ from the non-explanatory, post-legislative assessments within a traditional, formal analysis of effectiveness.

## Conclusion

Problems infringing on human rights are not necessarily easily solved through international law, even when the law is enacted with an eye to effectiveness, due to a broad range of issues, including inherent jurisdictional and enforcement issues. While this chapter has not focused on these latter issues,[142] it has explored the concepts of Western feminist legal theory, the nature of law through philosophical accounts of law, morality, human rights, cultural relativism, and legal effectiveness, and the ways in which all of these interrelate, in the hopes of contributing to a clearer picture of what can and should be done to secure and safeguard women's reproductive health, rights, and autonomy globally.

Although Western human rights activists, including feminists, have utilized international human rights law to "challenge ritualized genital cutting, domestic abuse, and other forms of physical violence" against women, this avenue – as is the case with domestic legislative options – is fraught with challenges. Due to the nature of norms – their "context-dependent oscillation on a moral scale" –[143] it is often the case that nation-states that feel marginalized, misunderstood, or shamed by the language of a treaty have and do exercise the option to refuse to sign or ratify the instrument. This is one of many problems at the heart of the discourse in this chapter. Unfortunately, traditional methods of assessing legal effectiveness have tended to be positivistic and untethered to the foundational and constitutive reasons for law's ineffectiveness. What must take the place of positivistic, formalistic approaches to law and to legal effectiveness, then, is a substantive legal effectiveness approach, which factors into an analysis of effectiveness the interplay and role of moral and social norms in legal compliance, needs-based and contextual nuances, as well as the impact of the structural attributes of law to its effectiveness.

By virtue of the Serious Crime Act 2015, the UK strengthened pre-existing FGC legislation to extend the extraterritorial offences section to include FGC against UK habitual residents inflicted abroad.[144] In addition, it has also been suggested that there is need to invoke international legal norms in the UK to grant refugee status to women and girls at risk of FGC.[145] Though these legal measures undoubtedly have merit, and are compelling suggestions for continuing the push to eradicate FGC worldwide, an approach centred on substantive legal effectiveness, which seeks more representational, collaborative, and pre-legal solutions, may be the avenue which, in actuality, achieves the most success in reaching the goal of greater recognition of women's rights and improved quality of life for women on a global scale. Indeed, the paradigm of social norm change advocated by the UN is one of collective abandonment, with the collaboration, cooperation and meaningful consent of affected communities in the developing world.[146]

---

142  See Iyioha, Chapter 2 of this volume, for a brief coverage of enforcement problems.

143  See ibid.

144  Owen Bowcott, "FGM Law Expanded to Cover Foreign Nationals Habitually Resident in UK", *The Guardian* (4 June 2014), available at www.theguardian.com.

145  Ibid.

146  www.unicef-irc.org/research/pdf/fgm_c_platform_eng.pdf; see also, www.unicef.org/ cbsc/files/UNICEF_FGM_report_July_2013_Hi_res.pdf; https://orchidproject.org/ wp-content/uploads/2016/07/AA-Empowering-communities-to-collectively-aban don-FGMC-in-Somaliland.pdf

That said, the law has the capacity to play an important symbolic and instrumental part in the elimination of FGC. But it must be recognized that its efficacy is limited. One cannot legislate FGC into non-existence. Here is a practice that has existed across many countries, sometimes with prevalence rates higher than 90%, for centuries. In Somaliland, for example, the incidence rate is 99%.[147] There are limits to law. One is confronted by a deeply paradoxical phenomenon: lawyers tend to overestimate the effectiveness of law; those not engaged in it tend to underestimate it. Undoubtedly, the key is to find a way to harness relevant legal powers in intricate and granular ways that are tailored to the specific challenge that FGC presents. This process would also, of necessity, involve a commitment nationally and internationally to work respectfully and imaginatively with affected communities in a way that will foster their willing collective abandonment. This is not an impossible goal. In several regions, the incidence rate of FGC is declining. Although the number of girls being cut is rising, this may be in significant measure attributable to population growth.

In light of the diverse factors that influence legal effectiveness as a whole, SLE positions itself at the existing gap in scholarship, offering an account of legal effectiveness that offers perspectives on the reasons for law's ineffectiveness, grounding these reasons in the inescapable binary attributes of law. SLE recognizes the need for analysis of effectiveness to be prescriptive and thus pre-emptive or forward-looking, while sufficiently grounded in traditional approaches of impact analysis, to offer the tools for a retrospective or backward-looking analysis. SLE also offers the tools for reform of gender- or issue-specific laws such as FGC, as well as for adjudicating and challenging laws such as legislation, which on its face may be composed of neutral terms, but in reality results in a negative impact upon women. In this, the concept of substantive legal effectiveness offers a holistic account of effectiveness allegiant to law and its methods. As the actual lived experiences of women globally is a key concern of modern feminism and feminist legal theory – particularly in the case of global feminist endeavors and projects, as well as in the work of theorizing a "global feminist theory" – the effectiveness of laws which specifically target or drastically affect the lives, well-being, and autonomy of women should be at the forefront of the global discussion. As is illustrated by the UK FGC law, a more nuanced approach to analyzing law and its effect can reveal unintended and unanticipated repercussions that must be addressed if women's rights are to be upheld and safeguarded.

147   https://orchidproject.org/wp-content/uploads/2016/07/AA-Empowering-communities-to-collectively-abandon-FGMC-in-Somaliland.pdf.

# 4 Abortion law in China
## Disempowering women under the liberal regulatory model

*Wei Wei Cao*

## Introduction

The emergence of modern medical and surgical abortion as a safe method of avoiding unplanned or unwanted procreation has tremendously enhanced women's reproductive health and choices. It is therefore considered to be one of the three breakthroughs in the development of reproductive technologies.[1] Access to abortion is also an important consideration for the realization of gender equality and "an emerging human right in international law".[2] There is little doubt that it is essential to satisfy women's healthcare needs, as well as their need to exercise control over their life choices.[3] Yet, in spite of the obvious benefits of women's autonomy, equality and reproductive freedom, women did not have access to safe abortion services for a long time due to the criminalization of abortion.[4] The criminalization of abortion led a large number of women to resort to backstreet providers. This outcome, which gravely impacted women's health and well-being, remains the case today in countries where the right to abortion services is only a life-saving exception in a criminal or penal code criminalizing abortion. As Cook et al. have observed, abortion law survived "several revolutions" and evolved "from placement within criminal or penal codes, to placement within health or public health legislation and eventually to submergence with laws serving goals of human rights".[5] Today, in most regions of the world, abortion has

---

1 Tony Hope, Julian Savulescu and Judith Hendrick, *Medical Ethics and Law: The Core Curriculum* (Edinburgh: Churchill Levingstone, 2003) at 115. The other two are the emergence of various means of assisting conception and prenatal visible technique.
2 Maja Kirilova Eriksson, "Abortion and Reproductive Health: Making International Law More Responsive to Women's Needs", in Kelly Askin and Dorean Koening, eds., *Women and International Human Rights Law* (New York: Transnational Publisher, 2001) at 55.
3 Emily Jackson and Shelley Day Sclater, "Autonomy and Private Life", in Shelley Day Sclater, Fatemeh Ebtehaj, Emily Jackson and Martin Richards, eds., *Regulating Auotnomy: Sex, Reproduction and Family* (Oxford: Hart Publishing, 2009) at 2.
4 Rebecca Cook, Joanna Erdman and Bernard Dickens, eds., *Abortion Law in Transnational Perspective* (Philadelphia: University of Pennsylvania Press, 2014).
5 Ibid.

been liberalized or at least been ostensibly permitted in certain circumstances, for example to save maternal life or health.[6]

The modern regulation of abortion abandons the old oppressive legislative frameworks and moves out from the framework of criminalization, so it appears to be liberal and pro-feminism or autonomy. Thus, the current tendency towards legalizing abortion is considered by some human rights scholars and feminists as a sign that women's right to choose is being recognized and respected.[7] It is widely believed that the removal of legal limits over the performance of abortion effectively promotes women's reproductive health by preventing unsafe abortions. Warriner has noted:

> Broadly speaking, where there is no legal restriction, abortion services are likely to be safe. In these settings, the abortion is performed in a regulated medical setting and the providers are properly trained. In contrast, where abortion laws are highly restrictive, women turn to clandestine providers with a high risk of incurring a serious or life-threatening complication.[8]

In China, the legal limits on when and on what grounds an abortion can be carried out were lifted in the eighties. Technically, termination can be performed lawfully at any gestational stage for a wide range of social reasons. This makes the Chinese abortion law perhaps "the most liberal in the world" and the only law which does not impose any penalties for "having or performing an abortion at any stage of pregnancy".[9] Compared with most jurisdictions where abortion is only allowed on certain medical grounds, such as France[10] and the UK,[11] the Chinese jurisdiction does not require women to prove that their physical or mental health is endangered by the pregnancy or apply for their doctors' permission.[12]

---

6 In about two-thirds of countries in 2013, abortion was permitted when the physical or mental health of the mother was endangered and in half of the countries when the pregnancy resulted from rape or incest or in cases of foetal impairment. About one-third of countries permitted abortion for economic or social reasons or on request. United Nations, Department of Economic and Social Affairs, Population Division (2014). Abortion Policies and Reproductive Health around the World (United Nations publication, Sales No. E.14.XIII.11).

7 R. Cook and B. Dickens, "Human Rights Dynamics of Abortion Law Reform" (2003) 25:1 *Human Rights Quarterly* 1–59.

8 Ina Warriner, "Unsafe Abortion: An Overview of Priorities and Need", in Ina Warriner and Iqbal Shad, eds., *Preventing Unsafe Abortion and Its Consequences* (New York: Guttmacher Institute, 2006) at 2.

9 Susan Rigdon, "Abortion Law and Practice in China: An Overview with Comparisons to the United States" (1996) 42:4 *Social Science & Medicine* 543–560 at 546.

10 Melanie Latham, *Regulating Reproduction: A Century of Conflict in Britain and France* (Manchester: Manchester University Press, 2002).

11 Sally Sheldon, *Beyond Control: Medical Power and Abortion Law* (London: Pluto, 1997) ('Sheldon, *Beyond Control*').

12 For example, in the UK, the Abortion Act 1967 (applicable in England, Wales and Scotland, but not Northern Ireland) states that there are four legal reasons for terminating a pregnancy: to save the pregnant woman's life; to avoid serious permanent damage to her health; to avoid physical and mental harm to her and her existing children and when a serious foetal

Furthermore, foetuses have not been accorded personhood or any serious moral and legal status that is independent of that of pregnant women.[13] A foetus at any stage of the pregnancy is only considered as part of the pregnant woman culturally and legally in Chinese Confucian society and communist jurisdiction.

According to '五脏论' (literally, the Theory of Five Organs) – one of the earliest and most influential Chinese traditional bioethical works, there is no exact upper limit to ideas of animation or viability, and the whole process of foetal development is regarded as horizontal. The birth is the symbol of completing foetal development, and only after the birth can the foetus be treated as a fully developed person.[14] Legally, in accordance with Article 9 of the General Principles of the Civil Code,[15] a person's civil rights start at birth and end at death. Unlike the legislative counterparts in many other jurisdictions, such as the United States, where abortion provokes strong moral controversy,[16] or Ireland, where the right to life of the unborn child is given constitutional protection,[17] Chinese women do not have to fight for the right to make a choice that is against the so-called right to life[18] of a foetus or unborn child, nor do they have to face social stigma caused by seeking a termination.

Yet, in spite of the above, China's legal regime on abortion remains a very controversial one. For scholars from the outside world, like Aird[19] and Ebenstein,[20] such an unrestrictive regulatory method violates the right to life of the unborn

---

abnormality has been detected. For a discussion of the abortion law in the UK, see for example Sheldon, *Beyond Control, supra*.

13 For an analysis of the moral status of foetuses in China, see for example Jing-bao Nie, *Behind the Silence* (Oxford: Rowman & Littlefield, 2005) and David Mungello, *Drowning Girls in China: Female Infanticide since 1650* (Plymouth: Rowman & Littlefield Publishers, 2008).

14 Qiaochu Wang, Jian Xu and Ehua Zhao, *Naotong wuzang lilunyanjiu yu* linchuangyingyong [The Study of Wuzang Theory and Its Clinical Application] (Shanghai: Shanghai Kexuejishu Press, 2013).

15 General Principles of the Civil Code, 1986 (Effective January 1, 1987).

16 N.E.H. Hull and P.C. Hoffer, *Roe v Wade: The Abortion Rights Controversy in American History*, 2nd ed. (Lawrence: University Press of Kansas, 2010).

17 Ruth Fletcher, "Reproducing Irishness: Race, Gender, and Abortion Law" (2007) 17:2 *Canadian Journal of Women and the Law* 365–404. On May 2018, Ireland had a historic abortion referendum and voted overwhelmingly to repeal the Eighth Amendment by 66.4% to 33.6%. The Eighth Amendment guarantees the unborn the right to life, making the Irish abortion law one of the most restrictive laws in Europe. It only allows abortion when the pregnancy is life-threatening. However, the referendum does not change the decriminalization of abortion in almost all circumstances unless the Oireachtas passes legislation providing otherwise. The timetable for legislation is still unclear. While it is still early to say whether the new legislation will grant women any more substantial decision-making rights, it seems clear from the draft legislation that was published by the government that Ireland is very likely to use the regulatory model centred around English medical professionals and grant doctors the authority to be parallel judges and gatekeepers scrutinizing women's abortion requests.

18 For arguments on the right to life, see, for example, John Finnis, "The Rights and Wrongs of Abortion" (1973) 2:2 *Philosophy and Public Affairs* 117–145.

19 John Aird, *Slaughter of the Innocents: Coercive Birth Control in China* (Washington: American Enterprise Institute Press, 1991).

20 Avraham Ebenstein, "The "Missing Girls" of China and the Unintended Consequences of the One Child Policy (2010) 45 *Journal of Human Resources* 87–115.

and allows for the countless abortions of female foetuses. Inside China, many people blame the unrestrictive access to abortion for encouraging unmarried young women to have premarital sex and giving them an excuse to "make moral mistakes".[21] Indeed, the latest official statistics show that there were about 13 million surgical abortions performed in 2013,[22] over 80% of which were by unmarried women. Notably, this figure means that China performs the most terminations in the world. In terms of quantity, the argument that China has the most liberal abortion law in the world seems to be true. However, recently, the Chinese government expressed its concern about the problem of 'backstreet' abortions and announced that about 10 million terminations had been performed annually by unregistered providers.[23] In addition, as will be discussed later, since the start of the 1980s when abortion as a birth control policy was implemented, there has been a large number of abortions performed 'by order' against women's will.

Compared to abortion as described in the written law, abortions done in reality are much more complicated. The above statistics demonstrate that following the legalization of abortion, there are now three types of terminations in China. First, abortions are performed as described and regulated in the written law. Second, abortions are performed by backstreet providers against the law. Third, political abortions are performed for the state's demographic needs. The written law fails to identify the existence of political abortions; in fact, the law intentionally leaves this loophole so that the state can facilitate its exercise of control over women's fertility. This state of affairs – where there exists a dichotomy between formal abortion rights that are legislatively granted and the actual implications of those rights for women's health – necessitates a close examination of the effectiveness of China's law on abortion within the context of Iyioha's distinction between 'formal' and 'substantive' legal effectiveness.[24]

As will be discussed later, the fact that the modern Chinese law of abortion is enacted by the national legislative organ grants the law the element of 'authoritative issuance'.[25] Given the dramatic increase in registered abortions since the passage of the law, the regulation appears to be largely liberal, efficacious and well accepted. Nevertheless, the emergence of the other two kinds of

21  Zhang Xiao (22 November 2008) 'Mianfei liuchan re zhengyi', available at www.js.chinanews. com.cn/news/2008/1017/2431.html (accessed 20 May 2019).

22  The use of abortion drugs, such as mifepristone and misprotal tablets, is also legal in China. However, because the administration of medical abortion creates less profit than the performance of surgical abortion, the main termination methods recommended and adopted in both public and private medical institutions is still surgical in China. The abortion statistics collected annually by the National Family Planning Research Institution includes surgical abortions only.

23  Yi Zhou and Lan Xiang, Zhongguo meinian rengongliuchan 1,300wan (China has 13 million surgical abortions) *Wangyi News* (26 January 2015), available at http://news.163. com/15/0126/05/AGS5I4SS00014AED.html (accessed 20 May 2019).

24  See Iyioha, Chapter 2 of this volume, for a full discussion of law's limits, as well as of theories of legal effectiveness.

25  For further discussion of "authoritative issuance", see Iyioha, Chapter 2 of this volume.

terminations – backstreet and political abortions – paints a different picture of the supposed effectiveness of China's abortion legislation. A few foundational questions are important to explain the purpose of this discussion: Is the removal of legal restrictions over abortion motivated by the authority's desire to eliminate discriminatory oppression and promote gender equality? Does the formal effectiveness of the abortion law regime in China mean that women's needs for reproductive healthcare and well-being are effectively satisfied? Are women able to autonomously make decisions according to their own preferences under the law?

By examining access to abortion under Chinese law and practice from a feminist standpoint, this chapter first plans to resolve the specific questions posed above. By reflecting on these specific questions, the chapter aims to undertake a more general but clearly more difficult task, to argue that law's effectiveness in promoting women's reproductive decision-making and well-being is not to be measured by the form and appearance of law or through formal statistical data on the outcomes of law, but determined, among other considerations, by 'factual correctness'. The concept of 'factual correctness' as Iyioha has outlined in Chapter 2 and as applied in this chapter, reflects an objective assessment of the scientific or factual correctness of the content of a law.[26] A law, such as the Chinese abortion law, which is superficially liberal, enjoys compliance on formal grounds, and is based on erroneous assumptions about the legitimacy of the law, can cause new and even greater repression against women, particularly women from socio-economically disadvantaged backgrounds.

As Raymond has observed, while modern legislation is superficially claimed to pursue procreative liberty and gender-neutral reproductive rights, it may provide women with "a supposed liberty that requires women to give up more freedom" and "a right to privacy that is more accurately a right to private privilege for men (and some women)".[27] Petchesky's exposition on the case of abortion law in the United States also shows that the liberalization of abortion is "perfectly compatible with a wide range of constraints on abortion access, particularly for poor women, rural women, women of color, and young teenagers".[28] The analysis of Confucian values, the Chinese population policy and the Chinese conception of rights in this chapter is targeted at helping the reader understand how the social and factual inaccuracies about women's status in Chinese society – judged even from an objective insider standpoint – accounts for the law's substantive ineffectiveness.[29]

Second, by exploring the underlying reasons why the Chinese abortion law that is supposedly liberal infringes women's rights in reality, the chapter suggests that the factual incorrectness of the abortion law's content goes to the issue of the actual or substantive effectiveness of the law over women's reproductive health.

26 See ibid. for further examination.
27 Janice Raymond, *Women as Wombs* (Melbourne: Spinifex Press, 1993) at 77.
28 Petchesky Pollack Rosalind, *Abortion and Women's Choice* (Boston: Northeastern University Press, 1984).
29 Iyioha sets out the concept of 'substantive effectiveness' in Chapter 2 of this volume.

This implies that the law, due to its very content, is incapable of addressing the reproductive health challenges that millions of Chinese women face. Law's limits in this area are evident in China's system of control over women's reproductive and sexual health choices through the political use of law, in the incorporation of traditional Confucianism philosophies into legislation (in the case of which law reflects social and other non-legal norms[30]), and through the government's political and policy decisions. These philosophies and policies constitute internal and external dynamics that greatly impact law's capacity to respond to women's health needs.[31]

Framed as internal and external limits to law's capacity for a reformative role in women's health, Iyioha's analysis of the elements of law, which themselves constitute constraints on law's effectiveness, highlights the impact of moral considerations and of politics, culture, economics, religion and other social phenomena on attitudes about law. Through a review of Chinese history, my exposition in this chapter throws light on how these factors, specifically culturally grounded philosophies and government population and economic policies can work hand in hand to limit women's health rights against a backdrop of popular societal support or societal attitudes about law.

As many feminists have observed, law is not an objective and gender-neutral institution which deals with disputes and organizes social relations justly,[32] but one that is "profoundly sexist" and can be "seen to assist in the reproduction of the dominant patriarchal social order".[33] Thus, the message and information included in and conveyed by law may appear to be authoritative and well accepted even in cases where they are in fact morally and factually discriminatory or sexist.

To provide an in-depth and thorough analysis of access to abortion under Chinese law and practice, this chapter discusses the following four issues: the family value system through an exposition on Confucianism and Chinese-style Communist legal system, the Chinese legal system, the family planning system and '权' (*quan* or 'power'/'rights') in China. In the matrix formed by these four related issues, abortion is turned into a patriarchal duty imposed on women, even though the regulatory model of abortion has very limited value for women's reproductive health and autonomy.

Finally, by offering a feminist response to the Chinese law on abortion, this chapter aims for what Iyioha describes as a "feasible pathway" for the realization of law's substantive effectiveness for women[34] while contributing to the development of feminist jurisprudence. Feminist jurisprudence was introduced into

---

30 See ibid. for further discussion of the relationship between law and social norms or social facts.
31 See Iyioha, Chapter 2 of this volume, for further exposition on internal and external limits of law.
32 Ngaire Naffine, *Law and the Sexes: Explorations in Feminist Jurisprudence* (London: Allen & Unwin, 1990) at 11 ('Naffine, *Law and the Sexes*').
33 Carol Smart, *Law, Feminism and Sexuality: Essays in Feminism* (London: Sage Publications, 1994) at 85 ('Smart, *Law, Feminism and Sexuality*').
34 See Iyioha, Chapter 2 of this volume.

China only about 10 years ago and its study is still at the stage of translating and discussing relevant theoretical discourses.[35] The analysis of abortion law in China in this chapter serves as an attempt to apply feminist legal studies to women's health problems in China. It also provides feminists in other jurisdictions with a fresh standpoint from which they can reflect on issues of (in)effectiveness and (in)correctness within the context of the abortion jurisprudence in their national and state/provincial abortion laws.

## Confucianism and Chinese-style communist legal system

In pre-20th-century China, Confucianism dominated Chinese society in both official and informal ways, such as formulating law through codification and governing people's everyday lives. The Chinese legal system was based on the Confucian philosophy of social control over moral education and hierarchical relations. For example, a fundamental principle of Confucian hierarchy is that the emperor rules his subjects, a husband rules his wife and concubines and a father rules his children. Within the Confucian hierarchy, women, particularly those who are comparatively socio-economically disadvantaged, were deeply oppressed.[36] The Confucian principle of 'Three Obedience', which could be traced back to the 11th century BC, was treated as the code of female conduct in the imperial era. The 'Three Obedience' principle was part of the theory of *li*, which can be described as Chinese-style self-controlled order and "the idealised form of appropriate behaviour in human conduct".[37] In accordance with this principle, a virtuous woman is required to obey her father before her marriage, her husband during married life and her eldest son in widowhood.

In imperial China, women were not entitled to exert any power on their procreative choices. During married life, women normally had no say in their (in)fertility because their reproductive preferences had to be subject to the needs of their husbands and in-laws. Therefore, the fact that the imperial authorities did not regulate abortion left the power of decision-making on women's fertility in the hands of the male head of their households.

According to the Confucian division of labour between the sexes, there are two principles governing the universe, namely *yin* and *yang*; the husband is *yang*, which is superior, and the wife is *yin*, which is inferior.[38] Furthermore, Confucianism, both as a religion and a customary law, regards reproduction, especially the production of male offspring, as women's main contribution to their family, community and state. Infertility could be used by husbands as a legally acceptable

---

35 Shu Ma, Woguo nvxingzhuyi faxueyanjiu de huigu yu zhangwang (The Review and Prospects of Chinese Feminist Legal Studies) (2012) 30 *Hebei Law Science* 99–106.
36 Chenyang Li, "Confucianism and Feminist Concerns: Overcoming the Confucian 'Gender Complex'" (2000) 27:2 *Journal of Chinese Philosophy* 187–199.
37 Reinhard May, *Law and Society East and West: Dharma, li and Nomos, Their Contribution to Law and to Life* (Stuttgart: Franz Steiner, 1985) at 56.
38 Li, "Confucianism and Feminist Concerns" at 188.

reason to divorce their wives or concubines, but women could not divorce their infertile husbands. Many Western scholars, therefore, blame the Confucian value system for causing society's preference for sons and the widespread practice of sex-selective abortion.[39] In the pre-20th-century Confucianism-dominated society, reproduction as a main issue in the domestic arena was traditionally decided by the male head of individual households rather than the national legislation.

Since the 20th century, particularly after the Communist party took over China in 1949, modern legislation has gradually replaced the Confucian family codes that regulated domestic issues. The Maoist government (1949–1979) repealed the imperial codes and copied most of the legal system from the former Union of Soviet Socialist Republics, where the regulatory methods were state-centred and coercion-orientated.[40] Thus, similar to the blurry boundary between policies and laws in the former Soviet Union, the line between policy and law in China was significantly unclear in the Maoist era. It is accurate to say that Maoist China was ruled by the state's policies or the party leader: by Mao rather than by law. Although some codes, such as the Constitution of 1954, were made and enacted in the Maoist era, they were more like political than legal documents. These codes were not made by the national legislative organ or through formal legislative procedures. However, this situation – state policies and party norms rather than legal codes serving a function equivalent to that of laws – was not unusual in the Maoist era. In spite of the lack of formal issuance, the policies were readily accepted as the norm because that was the reality the people were familiar with, accustomed to and had come to accept as standard.

The Maoist 'rule of person' method led to the three-year 'Great Leap Forward' (1958–1960)[41] and the 10-year disaster of the 'Cultural Revolution' (1966–

---

39 See, for example, Sharon Hom, 'Female Infanticide in China: The Human Rights Specter and Thoughts Towards (An)Other Vision' (1992) 23:2 *Columbia Human Rights Law Review* 249–314; Zongli Tang, 'Confucianism, Chinese Culture, and Reproductive Behavior' (1995) 16:3 *Population and Environment: A Journal of Interdisciplinary Studies* 269–281; Julian Savulescu, "Sex Selection: The Case For" in Helga Kuhse and Singer Peter, eds., *Bioethics: An Anthology*, 2nd ed. (Oxford: Blackwell, 2006).

40 Jingbao Nie, "Limits of State Intervention in Sex-selective Abortion: The Case of China" (2010) 12:2 *Culture, Health & Sexuality* 205–219 at 210 ('Nie, "Limits of State Intervention in Sex-selective Abortion"').

41 In the Maoist era, various domestic affairs were not regulated by law, but by Mao's speech and the political document issued by the Communist Party of China. The campaign of 'Great Leap Forward' was led by Mao. It did not have a realistic purpose or practical strategies; it only aimed to rapidly transform the country from an agrarian economy into a socialist society through rapid industrialization and collectivization. The campaign is widely considered to have caused the serious famine in the 1960s. From 1959 to 1961, China suffered the most serious famine in the 20th century, which caused an estimated 30 million deaths. The Maoist government blamed the natural drought for the famine, though many overseas scholars believed that the main cause of the famine and the lack of economic and cultural development was the fact that the central government focused on class struggle and set impossible production aims for local authorities. Consequently, in order to avoid punishment, local authorities wildly exaggerated agricultural production and concealed the true facts about the situation. Since the start of the 1980s, post-Maoist governments have gradually uncovered

1976).[42] In these 13 years, China was hesitant and virtually at a standstill: There was no law, no economic growth and no rise in the standard of living. In seeking to redress the problems caused by 'rule of person', the first post-Maoist government started to promote the rule of law and made enormous progress in terms of the construction of a formal and official Chinese-style socialist legal system around the beginning of the 1980s. A large number of normative documents have now been enacted since 1980. Article 62 of the Constitution of 1982 states that the national legislative organ is the National People's Congress (NPC) and its Standing Committee. Against this background, from 1980 to 1989, about 3,000 laws and regulations were enacted.[43]

Nevertheless, the task of building China's legal system is currently "a work in progress".[44] First, lawmaking by the NPC is to some extent still dependent on policymaking by the Central Committee of the Communist Party. As will be discussed later, the regulation of abortion is heavily reliant on the state's population policy. Second, abuse of power by government officials who implement law is a serious and unsolved problem. The case of Feng in the province of Shangxi, which will be discussed later, demonstrates that this phenomenon is particularly severe at the grassroots of administration. Consequently, although the Confucian gender value system has been formally replaced by national legislation that are largely ascertainable and predictable, the government's ineffective implementation of law can lead to gender equality in written law being a false declaration and a mirage. Third, the framework of promoting human rights, especially women's rights, is not well established in the current legal system. The government repeatedly claims that Chinese-style development and protection of human rights has its own characteristics that are better than those in Western jurisdictions.[45]

---

the events of the *Cultural Revolution, Great Leap Forward, Catch up with the United Kingdom than the United States*, etc. See Xianzhi Feng and Chongji Jin, *Mao Zedong zhuan: 1949–1976* (A Biography of Mao Zedong: 1949–1976) (Beijing: Zhongyangwenxian Press, 2003), Xuan Xi and Chunming Jin, *Wenhua Dageming Jianshi* (A Brief History of Cultural Revolution) (Beijing: Zhongyangdangshi Press, 2006), Jishen Yang, "Tongwei Wenti – 'Dayuejin Wushizhounianji' " (The Problem of Tongwei – The 50th anniversary of 'Great Leap Forward') (2008) 10 *The Journal of Yanhuangchunqiu*. Felix Wemheuer, "Dealing with Responsibility for the Great Leap Famine in the People's Republic of China" (2010) 210 *The China Quarterly* 176–194.

42 After the campaign of 'Great Leap Forward', Mao started the 10 years of class struggle to impose his own thoughts as the dominant ideology for governance of the country and to position himself in the centre of political power. For more information on the 'Cultural Revolution', see Xing Lu, *Rhetoric of the Chinese Cultural Revolution: The Impact on Chinese Thought, Culture, and Communication* (Columbia: University of South Carolina Press, 2004).

43 Werner Menski, *Comparative Law in Global Context: The Legal Systems of Asia and Africa*, 2nd ed, (Cambridge: Cambridge University Press, 2006) at 584.

44 Pitman Potter, "Legal Reform in China: Institutions, Culture and Selective Adaptation" (2004) 29:2 *Law & Social inquiry* 465–495 at 486.

45 Jinwen Xue, "Zhongguoteserenquan de duteyouxuexing" (The Special Superiority of Chinese-style Human Rights) *News of the Communist Party of China* (9 February 2015), available at http://theory.people.com.cn/n/2015/0209/c352498-26533565.html (accessed 20 May 2019).

However, as I will discuss, these 'Chinese characteristics'[46] are a major reason why women's reproductive decision-making is subjected to the state's demographic policymaking.

## '权' (*quan* – 'power' and 'rights') in the Chinese jurisdiction

Both the development of human rights thinking and the legal protection of human rights in China have strong Chinese characteristics that can be viewed as a product of Chinese Confucian culture, traditions and history. Understanding these Chinese characteristics is essential to examining the Chinese legislation on abortion and access to abortion in reality. The English terms of 'power' and 'rights' are *quan* in Chinese. In pre-20th-century imperial China, *quan* only referred to the power wielded by rulers: there was no concept of citizens' rights. In pursuit of the goal of developing the modern legal system, *quan* (rights) have since the 1980s been accorded more importance by the subsequent post-Maoist governments.

In brief, there are three characteristics of Chinese conception of *quan* (rights), which is different from the concept of human rights in the Western context. The first disparity is that the conception of rights in the Chinese jurisdiction mainly refers to citizen rights rather than human rights, and it derives from the status of 'citizenship' rather than of humanity. In other words, citizens' exercise of rights is reliant on their fulfilment of relevant obligations.[47] This is from the Confucian understanding of people's rights: People do not have rights naturally and automatically, but have to earn rights by having a duty to act appropriately in relation to others.[48] Second, in the current Chinese political and legal systems, citizens' rights are granted by the state and have "no independent basis in human nature or human conditions".[49] The collective good is always given priority over individual rights and personal interests. Also, the state, the Communist party and the government are used "interchangeably in the official discourse" to represent "the highest interests of China as a country and the Chinese people as a whole".[50] Third, the content of citizens' rights can change depending on the state's needs.

---

46  Randall Perenboom, "What's Wrong with Chinese Rights: Toward a Theory of Rights with Chinese Characteristics" (1993) 6 *Harvard Human Rights Journal* 29–59 at 53.

47  Randle Edwards, Louis Henkin and Andrew Nathan, eds., *Human Rights in Contemporary China* (New York: Columbia University Press, 1986) at 126–128.

48  Reinhard May, *Law and Society East and West: Dharma, li and Nomos, Their Contribution to Law and to Life* (Stuttgart: Franz Steiner, 1985).

49  Mark Savage, "The Law of Abortion in the Union of Soviet Socialist Republics and the People's Republic of China: Women's Rights in Two Socialist Countries" (1988) 40:4 *Stanford Law Review* 1027–1117 at 1088.

50  Jingbao Nie, *Behind the Silence* (Oxford: Rowman & Littlefield Publishers, 2005) ('Nie, *Behind the Silence*').

For example, as will be analyzed below, when the pro-natalist policy[51] was advocated in Maoist China, citizens did not have the right to obtain contraceptive and termination services. After the state implemented birth control programmes, accessing contraception and abortion became a right and even a duty for citizens.

In the beginning of the 1990s, when the Cold War ended and the Soviet Union collapsed, the post-Maoist communist state considerably changed its hostile attitude to capitalist jurisdictions. It attempted to learn lessons from capitalist regulatory experiences and introduced Western human rights thinking.[52] Although not all Western human rights ideas were accepted by the Chinese people, they had positive effects on the development of human rights in China. At the start of the 2000s, the Hu Jintao government (2003–2012) repeatedly emphasized the importance of protecting human rights and claimed that the existing trend in the regulation of citizens' *quan* and the state's *quan* is to protect the former to a maximum degree and stop government officials' abuse of power. In 2004, the NPC passed a constitutional amendment, which provides that the state will respect and protect human rights. It was the first time that the term 'human rights' was written into national legislation in China. However, while confirming the significance of protecting human rights, Article 33 of the Constitution (amended in 2004) also states that all citizens enjoy the rights and must fulfil the duties that are regulated by the Constitution and other laws. Thus, having the term 'human rights' written into the Constitution does not eliminate the state's *quan* to legislate to create, change and limit citizens' rights.

Thus, in the Chinese legal and cultural contexts, the legal protection of women's reproductive rights faces three challenges. First, influenced by the sexist Confucian traditions, women's awareness of procreative rights has been proven to be comparatively weaker than that of their Western sisters. Second, the ideology underlying the current Chinese legal system is statist. While legislation has replaced Confucian family values to regulate domestic issues, this does not change the fact that women's fertility and decision-making are under patriarchal control. Within such a legal framework of 'the state knows best', the state has replaced the male head of individual households under the Confucian system and become women's procreative decision-maker. Furthermore, due to an apparent lack of 'woman-friendly polity'[53] in China, the state is not keen to legislate to give

---

51 After the communist takeover, Mao celebrated large birth numbers as a sign of recovery. He believed that the more people there were, the greater the energy for socialist revolution. So he put forward the slogan of 'strength in numbers' and emphasized that a large population was a great advantage and essential to national economic development. Thus, a pro-natalist policy was advocated by the Maoist government to encourage women to reproduce and maintain a large family. For more analysis of the pro-natallist policy, see Thomas Scharping, *Birth Control in China 1949–2000: Population Policy and Demographic Development* (London: Routledge, 2003).

52 Eric Orts, "The Rule of Law in China" (2001) 34:43 *Vanderbilt Journal of Transnational Law* 115.

53 Kathleen Jones, "Citizenship in A Woman-Friendly Polity" (1990) 15:4 *Signs* 781–812.

women reproductive rights. Empowering women to exercise *quan* in practice is even more difficult even if the state were to legislate to give women the right. As Smart has argued, "once enacted, legislation is in the hands of individuals and agencies far removed from the values and politics of the women's movement".[54]

Furthermore, the analysis of the regulation of abortion and the population policy provided below suggests that the state's *quan* can turn citizens' reproductive rights into procreative duties in order to facilitate the state's control over reproduction and its demographic management. Third, the Chinese abortion legislation clearly values the Confucian conception of rights and does not reflect human rights norms as conventionally understood in Western jurisdictions. In fact, there is still no widespread acceptance of Western rights-based language, as well as of certain 'strong' rights-based concepts such as 'power', 'right', 'choice' and 'control' in the Chinese Confucian society. Chinese citizens, particularly females, do not experience much power, choice, control or even rights in their lives. Citizens' acceptance of Confucian norms over external conceptions of human rights further constrains the capacity of China's abortion law regime to promote women's reproductive autonomy and well-being.

## The law of abortion and the population policy in China

There are concrete differences between the regulation of abortion in the Maoist era (1949–1979) and in the post-Maoist era (1979–present). As has been discussed above, Maoist China was ruled by the party leader, Mao, through the enactment of policies, advocating party norms and giving public speeches. The regulatory sources of abortion were not law made by the legislative organ of the state, but the state's policymaking on population figures. The Maoist government defined abortion as an issue which was closely connected with its population policy and which facilitated the demographic objectives set by the party state.[55] This blurred the boundary between the regulation of abortion and the population policy in the Maoist era. It is also the reason why lawmaking on abortion in the post-Maoist era is significantly reliant on the state's demographic policymaking.

Due to tumultuous decades of famines and wars in the period from 1900 to 1949, the Chinese population was small and the birth rate was relatively low in the early 1950s. The Maoist government transplanted the pro-natalist policy from the former Soviet Union to 'celebrated large birth numbers as a sign of recovery'.[56] Mao believed that the more people there were, the greater the energy

54  Carol Smart, *Feminism and the Power of Law* (London: Routledge, 1989) at 164 ('Smart, *Feminism and the Power of Law*').
55  According to the constitution, the Communist Party is the only party in power. Thus, some scholars put 'party' and 'state' together as there is no clear boundary between them. For example, see Zhiyue Zhao, "From Commercialization to Conglomeration: The Transformation of the Chinese Press Within the Orbit of the Party State" (2006) 50:2 *Journal of Communication* 3–28 and Nie, "Limits of State Intervention in Sex-selective Abortion".
56  Thomas Scharping, *Birth Control in China 1949–2000: Population Policy and Demographic development* (London: Routledge, 2003).

for socialist revolution; so he put forward the slogan '人多力量大' (strength in numbers) and emphasized that a large population was a great advantage and essential to national economic development.[57] Reproduction was considered by the Maoist government as the main contribution of female citizens to the state. For example, women who had more than 10 children would be awarded the designation of 'Glorious Mother' by the government.[58]

To enable women to produce more children, the Maoist government restricted access to abortion and contraception. In accordance with a political document entitled '控制女干部堕胎方法' ('Restricting Access to Abortion') issued by the Ministry of Health in 1950, abortion was only allowed in very strict therapeutic circumstances or for eugenic reasons, which were:

1   The pregnant woman has severe tuberculosis, heart disease, kidney disease or any other serious disease and the continuance of the pregnancy would worsen the disease and threaten her life.
2   The performance of abortion is necessary to save the life of the pregnant woman.
3   The woman has at least one child, but is physically unable to have another one.
4   The pregnant woman has a serious genetic mental disease that would be passed on to the child if born.[59]

Apart from satisfying one of these grounds for abortion, women seeking abortion had to obtain their husband's written consent, as well as convince their doctor that they had a medical reason for requesting abortion, such as a physical inability to complete the gestation. According to a report published in 1956 in '人民日报' (*People's Daily*), the Party's official newspaper, the problem of adopting unsafe termination methods, such as jumping from a height and eating river snails or poisonous herbs, caused high maternal morbidity.[60] While there is no official figure to show how many women died or were permanently injured due to their use of these unsafe methods, the number is reckoned to be huge because a bulletin issued by the Ministry of Health in 1956 noted that the phenomenon of using dangerous methods to terminate pregnancy severely damaged the public health.[61]

The implementation of the pro-natalist policy led to a dramatic increase in the national birth rate and total population.[62] However, in the last 20 years of the Maoist era, as discussed above, the political movements of the 'Great Leap

57 Peiyun Peng, *Zhongguo Jihua Shengyu* (Beijing: China Population Press, 1997) at 289 ('Peng, *Zhongguo Jihua Shengyu*').
58 Yinhe Li, *Shengyu yu Cunluo Wenhuai* (Reproduction and Village Culture) (Beijing: Wenhuayishu Publisher, 2003).
59 For the original text, see Peng, *Zhongguo Jihua Shengyu* at 889. What is set out here is my translation into English.
60 Huilan Zhong, "Bixu Youjihuade Jiezhi Shengyu", *People's Daily* (17 March 1957).
61 Peng, *Zhongguo Jihua Shengyu* at 279.
62 According to the first census, the average births per married woman were about six between 1949 and 1955. According to the second and third national censuses, the population had increased dramatically by 12% in the period from 1954 (601,938,035) to 1964

Forward' and the 'Cultural Revolution' as well as the widespread famine of 1958 to 1962 resulted in a collapsing national economy with domestic production and the living standard in an even poorer state than before the Maoist era began. The dramatic increase in the national population and economic difficulty led to fear in the government of Deng Xiaoping (in power between 1980–1988) that economic production could not keep pace with demographic growth. Thus, the post-Maoist governments replaced the Maoist pro-nationalist policy with a Malthusian and eugenic one. The Deng Xiaoping government claimed that the Maoist implementation of the pro-natalist policy was a 'historic mistake'[63] and that the state would adopt all means, including incentives and coercive methods, to lower the national birth rate and reduce the total population quickly for the collective good and the public interest. In order to bring the national population development back under the party state's control, the first post-Maoist government claimed that this was in the public interest. Deng noted:

> Since the foundation of Communist China, our population has doubled. . . . The large population is a burden. . . . We must treat family planning as a strategic problem and try to reduce the growth rate of population to 0.5%–0.6% in a short time. We must ensure that the total population is no more than 1.2 billion by the end of this century. We must set this goal, otherwise the economic development cannot keep pace with the demographic increase.[64]

To emphasize the significance of reducing the population, the government defined 'family planning' as a fundamental state policy.[65] In 1982, the birth control policy was written into the constitution:

> Article 25: The state carries out family planning in order to make population growth keep place with the national plans of economic production and social development.

The second paragraph, Article 49, states that couples must obey the state's family planning policies. Literally, the statutes above are not directly related to abortion;

---

(723,070,269). By 1982, the total population had increased to 1,160,017,381. See www.stats.gov.cn/tjsj/pcsj (accessed 20 May 2019).

63 The Research Office of the Central Committee of the Communist Party, *Dengxiaoping Sixiang Nianpu: 1975–1997* (The Year Book of Deng Xiaoping's Thoughts: 1975–1997) (Beijing: Zhangyangwenxian Press, 1998) at 189.

64 Ibid.

65 Yafei Hou, "Guoce dao guofa: Zhongguojihuashengyulichenghuigu" (From National Policy to National Legislation: A Review of Chinese Family Planning) (2004) 3 *Expanding Horizons* 8–29. Fundamental state policies are jointly issued by the Central Committee of the Communist Party and the State Council. They are defined as the essential guidelines to be used by the party state to conduct internal and external affairs, such as legislation, administration and diplomacy, etc. For more information on fundamental state policies, see Guangyu Yang and Zelin Xu, "Jibenguoce: Liluntantao he jianyi" (The State's Fundamental Policies: Theory and Suggestion) (1991) 12 *Theoretical Exploration* 32–46.

they only confirm the legitimacy of the state's implementation of birth control policy and citizens' fulfilment of their family planning obligation under national law. However, the state's implementation of birth control policy completely changed the regulation of abortion. The Maoist ban on abortion was removed and abortion has now been officially defined by the state as '补救措施' (a back-up method) which must be adopted when contraception fails in order to avoid '超生' (out-of-quota births).[66] An out-of-quota birth means a birth that has not been approved by the local family planning centre in the couple's residential area.

According to the Act for Collecting and Managing the Social Maintenance Fee, 2002 (the 2002 Act),[67] couples who have out-of-quota birth(s) must pay 'out-of-quota' fines to local family planning centres. The official title of the fines is '社会抚养费' (Social Maintenance Fee) and its standard payment varies slightly from area to area; but it is mainly three times the couple's previous year's income. If the couple's annual income is unclear or they are unemployed, the fines are four to six times the per capita income in the local area. The government's justification for the implementation of this rule is still that an individual must obey the population policy for the good of public interests, the state or the majority.

Articles 1 and 2 of the 2002 Act read as follows:

> Article 1: The rule was enacted to implement the fundamental state policy of birth control, protect all citizens' lawful interests and make the population growth keep pace with economic, social, resource and environmental development.
>
> Article 2: Citizens have the right to reproduce, but are under an obligation to practise family planning and keep their reproductive behaviour consistent with the state's population policy.

The imposition of 'out-of-quota' fines has been used by the state since the 2000s as a softer replacement for forced abortions.[68] In the first two decades after implementing the birth control policy, abortion, as a back-up method, was compulsory if the birth was not authorized. '中国卫生年鉴 2008' (*The China Health Year Book*, 2008) shows that the number of abortions in registered medical institutions increased rapidly from 539,000 in 1979 to 7,856,587 in 2007.[69] While there is no official statistics for annual coercive abortions, the number is estimated to be considerable based on a report on family planning services in Guangdong province, which suggests that in 1982, 80% of 624,000 abortions were carried out 'by order'.[70]

---

66 Family Planning White Paper (1995), available at http://cn.chinagate.cn/whitepapers/2007-02/13/content_2367015.htm (accessed 20 May 2019).
67 Promulgated by Decree No. 357, State Council of the People's Republic of China, August 2, 2002 (Effective September 1, 2002).
68 Hongqing Duan, Zhongguo Jihuashengyu diyian (The First Family Planning Case in China) China Value (10 January 2007), available at www.chinavalue.net/media/Article.aspx?ArticleId=10072&PageId=1.cn (accessed 20 May 2019).
69 China Year Book Committee (2000–9), *China Health Year Book 2008* (Beijing: The Press of China Xiehe Medical University) at 40.
70 Nie, *Behind the Silence* at 51.

Furthermore, '优生政策' (the Eugenic Demographic Policy), along with the birth control policy, was implemented in the post-Maoist era. According to an open letter entitled 'The Question of Controlling the Increase in the National Population' issued by the Central Committee of the Communist Party of China in 1982, the state's main demographic goal in the next 30 years was '少生优生' (literally, 'have fewer and healthier births'). The letter further explains that 'having fewer births' means that married couples are required to have only one child and 'having healthier births' involves 'avoiding the births of defective infants'.[71] In quick succession, the birth control and eugenic polices were written into two pieces of the national legislation: the Code on Maternal and Infant Health Care, 1994[72] (the 1994 Code) and the Code on Population and Family Planning, 2002[73] (the 2002 Code). These two codes provide the regulatory basis for access to abortion in China. While the two-child policy has officially replaced the 36-year-old one-child policy in the beginning of 2016, it does not change the legislation on abortion.[74]

Distinct from abortion law in many other jurisdictions, the 1994 Code and the 2002 Code do not impose any limit on the time when or the grounds on which abortion can be performed. Technically, pregnancies can be terminated lawfully in China at any gestational stage and for a wide range of social and medical reasons, with the exception of non-medical sex selection.[75] However, with the large number of illegal abortions in mind, this representation of Chinese abortion law as liberal should be treated more critically. While the regulation of abortion superficially endows women with the right to terminate, it is in practice used to facilitate the state's imposition of a Malthusian and eugenic duty on women. Under such a regulatory model, the state lawfully replaces husbands (who were the decision-makers under the Maoist model) and becomes the decision-makers on women's fertility.

71 The Central Committee of the Communist Party of China is in charge of convening the National People's Congress and drafting and enacting fundamental state policies. For the original text of 'The Question of Controlling the Increase in the National Population', see http://cpc.people.com.cn (accessed 20 May 2019).

72 Law of the People's Republic of China on Maternal and Infant Health Care (Promulgated by Order No. 33 of the President of the People's Republic of China on October 27, 1994; adopted at the Tenth Meeting of the Standing Committee of the Eighth National People's Congress on October 27, 1994).

73 Population and Family Planning Law of the People's Republic of China (Order of the President No. 63).

74 The two-child policy does not change the context of family planning in China. The government lifted the 'one-child' ban nationwide in 2016 because of a steady decrease in the birth rate and the increasing ageing population. Couples who have more than two children still have to pay fines according to the two-child policy.

75 The Rule of Prohibition of Non-medical Prenatal Sex Diagnosis and Sex Selective Abortion (the 2003 Rule) was issued in 2003 by the Ministry of Health in order to help correct the skewed sex ratio. The 2003 Rule does not aim to limit access to abortion, but to stop the use of prenatal techniques, such as amniocentesis and ultrasonic scans, to identify the sex of the foetus and abort female ones.

## Liberal law, fettered rights

As discussed earlier, the 1994 Code and the 2002 Code do not impose any restrictions on the time when or the statutory reasons on which pregnancy can be terminated. In contrast, in accordance with Article 18 of the 1994 Code, doctors have an obligation to inform women and persuade them to end their pregnancies if foetuses are diagnosed with a serious physical or mental abnormality. The Legal Affairs Office of the State Council issued a document in 1995 to clarify this provision. It explained that a serious abnormality means a genetic and congenital defect that may develop into a disease that completely or partially deprives the child of the ability to live independently. As a eugenic law, Article 18 of the 1994 Code does not serve as statutory grounds for abortion but places a duty on doctors to identify foetuses with undesirable traits and to use their medical knowledge to pressure women to make a decision on abortion. It also imposes a duty on putative parents, particularly mothers, to abort foetuses with abnormalities and to produce healthier citizens.

While abortion is available on demand and Chinese women do not have to wait for doctors' approval, yet this 'liberal' regulation does not treat abortion as a choice that can be freely made by women, but as "a dispensable instrument of the national population control agenda".[76] Although women are allowed to end their unwanted pregnancy under the current regulatory model, they can also be forced to terminate their wanted pregnancy if it is classified as authorized, especially if they cannot afford the fines. In 2012, the case of Feng Jianmei who was forced to abort when she was seven months' pregnant with her second child shocked the outside world and sparked international outrage after her relatives took photographs of her and the stillborn, blood-covered foetus minutes after the forced abortion procedure and posted them online.[77] Feng, a 23-year-old mother of a daughter, became pregnant again without first applying for birth permission from the local family planning centre. Feng and her in-laws were given a specified time by the centre officials to pay the 'out-of-quota' fines. However, they could not afford the fines. After being warned by oral and text messages several times, she was finally kidnapped by three local family planning officials from the county hospital and then had her pregnancy forcefully terminated.[78] The case of Feng suggests that the written law of abortion in China actually infringes women's reproductive rights more severely by imposing a heavy demographic duty, though it superficially looks less restrictive compared to the laws of other national jurisdictions.

To enable citizens to fulfil this duty effectively, the government formed a vertical family planning governance structure in 1981, which involved the creation

---

76 Nie, *Behind the Silence* at 44.
77 Shuang Yang, "Fury over 'Forced Abortion'" *Global Times* (14 June 2012), available at www.globaltimes.cn/content/714855.shtml (accessed 20 May 2019).
78 For more information on the official response to the case of Feng, see http://magazine.caixin.com/2007-07-23/100084880.html (accessed 20 May 2019).

of a family planning centre at every level of governance, from the state to province, city, district (urban) or county (rural), township and the neighbourhood. By the 1990s, there were an estimated 300,000 full-time officials and hundreds of thousands of part-time workers in grassroots family planning centres.[79] Family planning centres at the grassroots level directly guide and supervise individual women's practice of controlling their birth rate. The officials have the power to check and record detailed information about local married women of reproductive age, to enable women to abort unauthorized births, and to persuade or even force married women to use an intrauterine device (IUD) after giving birth to one or two children.[80] Such a vertical structure is designed to keep women under the state's close surveillance and treat the practice of the birth control policy as an exclusively female duty.

The current law of abortion has been intentionally left unrestrictive by subsequent governments in order to ensure that abortion can be used lawfully as the state's strategic tool to impose control over women's fertility. Once the woman's pregnancy is classified as unauthorized or the foetus is diagnosed with undesired trait(s), access to abortion becomes the duty which she has to undertake for her state and for the so-called public interest. Thus, the case of Feng is not rare. Rather, the norm is that stories similar to that of Feng happen quite frequently and have been treated as 'normal', especially in the period between 1980 and 2000 when the methods of implementing the birth control policy were particularly coercive.[81]

---

79　Elina Hemminki, Zhuochun Wu, Guiying Cao and Kirsi Viisainen, "Illegal Births and Legal Abortions: The Case of China" (2005) 2:5 *Reproductive Health* 1–8 at 6.

80　The adoption of IUD after giving birth to one or two children was compulsory before 2000. Since the start of the 2000s, some areas, such as Shanghai, have repealed the policy of the compulsory use of IUD or sterilization. In 2009, He, a deputy of the Guangdong People's Congress made an e-proposal (submitted via internet) to repeal some local family planning policies that promoted the compulsory use of IUDs. The proposal, which was written in Chinese, is available at http://news.163.com/13/0303/05/8P15A5090001124J. html (accessed 20 May 2019). Following the implementation of '全面两孩' Policy (Complete Two Children Policy), the policy of compulsory adoption of IUD has been abolished nationwide.

81　Since the start of the 1980s, subsequent governments have adopted all means, including incentives and coercive methods, to reduce the national population. In the first 30 years after the implementation of the birth control policy, the means were mainly coercive, such as forced abortion and sterilization. Since 2000, coercive methods have been gradually replaced by a combination of incentive-based and financial punishment-based methods, such as imposing out-of-quota fines and awarding the families of a single child with the 'jihuashengyu guangrongzheng' (literally, one-child glorious certificate). The couples who are entitled to the certificate can apply for a small allowance of ¥10–50 per month ($2–10), get 30 days more than the statutory maternal leave (90 days) and have better maternal care. The rewards for having only one child vary from area to area. For example, in Shanghai, 'one-child' mothers will receive ¥30 ($5) per month, have a 120-day maternal leave and get two prenatal blood tests and one ultrasonic check free of charge in their community hospital. For more information on the policy of rewarding one-child families in Shanghai, see http:// wsjkw.sh.gov.cn/xzqr/20180526/47006.html (accessed 2 June 2019). Nevertheless, this

While there is no official record of the exact number of the sterilization and abortions performed against women's free will in order to fulfil the family planning duty, the number is considerably large. According to a survey conducted by Zhang et al. in 1998, 10% of 100 women of reproductive age surveyed were permanently injured due to forced and improper abortions and sterilizations.[82] Furthermore, as discussed earlier, in the Chinese Confucian society, women's rights' consciousness and development have historically been weak, and reproduction is treated as women's responsibility and main contribution to societal progress. In such a culture, as Siegel has argued, women's body never belongs to themselves and bearing and raising children are constructed as women's contribution to others – their husband, community and state.[83]

In this construct of patriarchal culture, women are expected to lead a self-sacrificing life in order to effectively take maternal responsibility for others, while their own personal interests and procreative preferences are marginalized and ignored. Therefore, what Feng and her family suffered did not evoke public sympathies in the country where they lived. Some villagers even expressed their anger and hung a banner saying "痛打卖国贼，驱逐曾家镇" ("Expel the Traitor from Zengjia County") after Feng's husband gave an interview to a German newspaper, even though he rejected $100,000 financial aid from the US embassy. Some villagers interviewed believed that what happened to Feng and her family was very normal. One of them said:

> It [forced abortion] also happened before to those who were pregnant against the state's population policy. The policy is for the good of our society, so they must pay the penalty if they break it. It is 'gongdao' (just and fair), isn't it?[84]

As Raymond has observed, it is a cross-national phenomenon that women are always under the pressure to or not to reproduce. She noted: "It is women who bear the burden of their own and their male partners' infertility in the so-called First World, and their own and their male partners' fertility in the so-called Third World".[85]

---

does not mean that coerced abortions have not existed since after the 20th century. Strategies used by family planning centres to reduce the local birth rate may vary from area to area. In some areas, such as Feng's county, the local family planning authorities can still force pregnant women who are not eligible for birth permission to abort in order to achieve their birth control targets.

82 Xingjie Zhang, *Zhendangzhong De Bianqian* (The Changes in Concussion) (Lanzhou: Lanzhou University Press, 1999) at 114.

83 Reva Siegel, "Reasoning from the Body: A Historical Perspective on Abortion Regulation and Questions of Equal Protection" (1992) 44 *Stanford Law Review* 261–381.

84 Wangyi News, 2 November 2015, "Shangxiyunfu bei qiangzhiyinchanhou de zhesannian" (Three Years after the Shangxi Pregnant Woman's Forced Abortion), available at http://news.163.com/15/1105/22/B7MM65FK00011229.html (accessed 20 May 2019).

85 Janice Raymond, *Women as Wombs* (Melbourne: Spinifex Press, 1993) at xx.

Before the 20th century, when abortion was not regulated, women in the Confucianism-dominated family value system owed their husband a duty to reproduce; and it was a duty they had to undertake in gratitude for not being divorced by their husbands and evicted by their in-laws. In the Maoist and post-Maoist era, while the regulatory methods of abortion are completely different, the spirit behind restricting and liberalizing abortion remains unchanged, namely women must fulfil the duty to produce more or less, as well as produce healthier citizens for the state. To gain the rights derived from citizenship or be treated as a citizen, women must undertake this reproductive duty. Consequently, in the current Chinese family planning context, the written liberal right to access abortion quickly turns into the burden of accomplishing a demographic obligation.

Furthermore, while the state does not place many legal restrictions on performance of abortion services, it does impose limits over public funding for abortion. The national population control programmes, including family planning funding, are mainly targeted at reducing fertility among married couples. Article 21 of the 2002 Code states as follows:

> Article 21: Married couples of reproductive age are entitled to access basic family planning services free of charge for the purpose of practising family planning.[86]

Therefore, unmarried women are not entitled to the government's financial support for abortion services. This does not mean that unmarried women do not have to obey the state's population policy. In the current family planning context, only married women are eligible to apply for birth permission[87] mentioned above. Unmarried women's births are classified as unauthorized even if the woman does not have any existing children. To make her birth authorized, she has to pay the 'out-of-quota' fine. Because of the considerable social stigma and financial punishment, abortion becomes the only 'rational and reasonable' choice for unmarried pregnant women, especially those who are socio-economically disadvantaged and cannot afford the fines. In practice, of about 13 million women who had surgical abortions in 2013, more than 81.5% of them were unmarried.[88]

Culturally, because of Confucian influences, premarital sex and particularly premarital fertility are still considered social taboos in China. According to the Confucian *li*, virtuous women should keep their virginity before marriage and

---

86 Basic family planning services are oral contraception, condoms, abortion, female sterilization and the IUD.
87 To apply for birth permission, the couple has to provide the local family planning centre with a marriage certificate, their ID cards, the household register, a three-month pregnancy medical check report and a letter of reference issued by the couple's neighbourhood committee to prove that they do not have any existing children or have only one child but qualify for having a second one according to the population policy.
88 Tengxun News, 24 November 2014, "Woguo Nianjun 1300renci Rengongliuchan, Meinian Zengzhang Chao7%" (China has 13,000,000 Abortions Annually with an Increase of 7% of the Total Number), available at https://new.qq.com/cmsn/20141124/20141124002667 (accessed 20 May 2019).

remain widowed if their husbands die before them. Premarital sex and fertility are thought of as a shame for both themselves and their families.[89] A survey of the reproductive health of unmarried young women aged between 15 and 25 conducted by Wei in 2008 reveals that while 53% of the 280 respondents had had premarital sex, 95% said that they felt too ashamed to seek contraceptive or abortion information or advice from parents, relatives or local family planning centres.[90] Of the respondents who had had sex, 67% of them had not used contraception or had not used it correctly and 18% had had at least one abortion.[91] This Confucian value system has been projected onto the legislation on abortion. The current regulation which restricts financial support for family planning services to married women assumes that marriage is essential to sexual life and construes premarital sex as a legal taboo for women. By placing limits over abortion public funding, access to abortion becomes a 'privilege' for 'virtuous' women who strictly obey the state's population policy and the traditional code of female conduct.

## Conclusion: beyond the letters of the law

On the first day of 2016, the Xi Jinping government officially started '全面二孩政策' (the 'Complete Two-Children Policy') and ended the 36-year-old 'One-Child Policy'.[92] It was announced that the overpopulation problem has been effectively solved and in the next 10 years the government will work on new demographic plans in order to deal with the problems of an aging population and labour shortage.[93] As access to abortion is traditionally reliant on the state's population

---

89 For more analysis of the Confucian value system on women's sexual and reproductive behaviour, see for example Lifeng Xing and Caixia Liu, *Tianli yu renyu: Chuantong rujiashiyezhongde nvxinghunyin shenghuo* (Heavenly Principles and Human Desires: Women's Married Lives Looked at Through a Traditional Confucian Lens) (Wuhan: Wuhan University Press, 2005).

90 Xiangdong Wei, "Diaocha cheng qingshaonian xingxingwei riyi yanzhong" (The Serious Problem of Premarital Sex and Abortions among Adolescent Girls) *China News* (7 April 2008), available at www.china.com.cn/economic/txt/2008-04/07/content_14413812.htm (accessed 20 May 2019). Li Luo, Sun Wu, Xuan Chen, Ming Li and Paul Thomas, "Induced Abortion among Unmarried Women in Sichuan Province, China" (1995) 51:1 *Contraception* 59–63 at 61.

91 Ibid.

92 Since the start of the 2000s, the state's birth control policy has gradually been relaxed. The relaxation varies from area to area. For example, in many rural areas, if the couple's first child is a girl, they are allowed to have the second child. In urban areas, if the couple themselves are the single child in their original family or one of them is the single child, they are allowed to have a second child. Since 1 January 2016, the complete two-children policy has been implemented, which allows all couples to have a second child.

93 According to 'The Report on the Chinese Aging Problems 2013' issued by the Chinese Academy of Social Sciences, China needs to deal urgently with aging and labour shortage problems because the population aged over 60 years old was about 202 million in 2013 and made up 14.8% of the total population. Meanwhile, since 2011, the population aged between 15 and 60 has presented negative growth. In the period from 2011 to 2014, there was a decrease of 11 million in the labour population. For more information about this report, see https://max.book118.com/html/2018/0311/156872556.shtm (accessed 2 June 2019).

policy in the Chinese family planning context, abortion law reform will probably be made in the near future to meet the state's new demographic needs. Given that women's voices are usually muted and their own needs for reproductive health and freedom are marginalized, the reform is unlikely to solve the problems women face discussed in this chapter and may even limit access to abortion in order to impose new and heavier demographic duties on women.

The analysis of the modern regulation of abortion in China conducted in this chapter suggests that the use of law to replace sexist Confucian values merely codifies a state of affairs that neither promotes women's reproductive autonomy nor improves their well-being. In contrast, women are required to undertake a dual responsibility: taking on the maternal role constructed by Confucian culture and managing their fertility according to nationalist orders. The unrestrictive access to abortion in the Chinese family planning context does not provide women with a right to decide whether or not to reproduce but serves to facilitate the state's imposition of the double duties on women. To keep their citizenship, women have to fulfil state-imposed reproductive duties even if the fulfilment is at the expense of their reproductive health and freedom. Women are compelled to fulfil these duties through financial and physical penalties, especially through fines and forced abortions. The imposition of the duties and penalties is justified by both the Confucian family traditions and the paternalistic legal framework of the state knows best.

Paternalistic and sexist laws are surely not a problem that only exists in China. Law itself, as many feminist scholars such as Smart,[94] Naffine[95] and Lacey[96] have observed, has never really been objective and gender neutral. Even in some Western jurisdictions where people's awareness of gender equality and of reproductive rights are much stronger, regulating reproduction often means an imposition of responsibility on women and freedom for men.[97] Thus, based on the foregoing analysis and on Iyioha's theory on 'effectiveness', it is evident that China's abortion law – defined by the social norms reflected in Confucian values – is formally effective but reflects all the signs of substantive ineffectiveness.[98] As has been argued earlier, a number of factors converge to render China's law substantively

---

94  Smart, *Feminism and the Power of Law* and Smart, *Law, Feminism and Sexuality* at 79.

95  Naffine, *Law and the Sexes* at 11.

96  Nicola Lacey, *Unspeakable Subjects: Feminist Essays in Legal and Social Theory* (Oxford: Hart Publishing, 1998) at 4.

97  Sally Sheldon, "Reproductive Choice: Men's Freedom and Women's Responsibility?" in John Spencer and Autje Bois-Pedain, eds., *Freedom and Responsibility in Reproductive Choice* (Oxford: Hart Publishing, 2007).

98  While the objective of the law may be deemed to be population control rather than women's reproductive autonomy, to the extent that the Chinese abortion law may be touted as a victory for women or as an example of reproductive freedom for women, and to the extent that the law in itself has the façade of being in women's reproductive interest, it can be assessed using the standards of ineffectiveness discussed in this book. Furthermore, given the general theme of this book as it relates to the limits of law's role in improving women's health, a law such as China's abortion law, even when regarded as a population policy rather than a law addressing reproductive healthcare, comes under legitimate scrutiny through the standards herein discussed: see Iyioha, Chapter 2 of this volume.

ineffective for Chinese women: these include the *perceived* moral, political and factual correctness of China's abortion law and the consequential acceptance by a large portion of the Chinese population (based on the preference for Confucian values international human rights norms), the government's ineffective implementation (giving rise to backstreet and political abortions) and the state's political use of abortion as a birth control method. In combination, these factors explain why the law disappoints women in practice while appearing to be favourable to women's reproductive health from a purely formal standpoint.

However, laws should not be left unchallenged. The messages conveyed through law can often be considered by the public as factual and logical even when they are discriminatory and sexist. This is due to the legitimacy that is attached to a law that is formally passed or authoritatively issued. Furthermore, as Iyioha notes in Chapter 2, if the content of laws that are authoritatively passed (or that are at least accepted as legitimate in a procedural sense) are deemed socially, morally and scientifically correct by citizens, such laws are most likely to be accepted and obeyed. In a country like China, where the social and political norm for decades has been the subjugation of women's rights through the instrument of state law, both the form of law and its normative character – reinforcing already established behavioural and social patterns – compel acceptance and obedience.

Having stated the above, I am optimistic that by actively engaging with the law, feminists can challenge the so-called truth and knowledge[99] embodied in the current laws which are apparently gender neutral but are in fact deeply against women's interests. In this respect, I suggest that to challenge the law's construction of access to abortion as the state's means of achieving its demographic goal, a proposal for at least three possible reforms can be made. Following Iyioha's approach through the concept of 'Substantive Effectiveness', each of the suggestions I set out here prioritizes women's particular needs and their agency while recognizing and contextualizing their experiences against the background of their history in a Confucianism-dominated political and social landscape.[100]

First, the legislation on abortion has to be independent from the state's population policy and the state's interest in population control, providing for access to abortion services based on independent criteria that include women's healthcare needs. Second, the law should ensure that the provision of abortion services is subject to women's informed consent so that women's decision-making can be protected from the state's controlling interference. Third, the state's family planning financial support should be equally available to all regardless of marital status.

The success of translating these proposals into law and their effective implementation are both heavily reliant on eliminating the sexist Confucian influences and raising women's awareness of gender equality. This can be achieved by promoting women's education, employment and welfare, and encouraging their participation in political decision-making, which are certainly harder to achieve than the reforms per se.

99 Smart, *Feminism and the Power of Law* at 164.
100 See Iyioha, Chapter 2 of this volume.

# 5 Forced sterilizations

## Addressing limitations of international rights adjudication through an intersectional approach

*Charlotte H. Skeet*

## Introduction

This chapter examines international law's normative role through rights adjudication in relation to women's rights cases on forced sterilization,[1] events which breach a number of different international, regional and national rights protections, and provides an analysis that problematizes the competing understandings of women's rights norms and strategies. The chapter situates this discussion in the context of the broader objectives of this book.

The overall purpose of this book is to examine the limits of law in addressing women's health law and health rights. There is a long-standing feminist critique of the claim that law is neutral and universal.[2] In contemporary times, this has also included a critique of international human rights law, and the often individualist approach to rights adjudication.[3] One of the major obstacles that limits human rights adjudication for gender equality is that even where gendered breaches are recognized, "recommendations and subsequent legal changes do not always manage to confront the deeply embedded social, economic and cultural structures that enable gender inequalities and harms".[4]

In Chapter 2 of this volume, Irehobhude Iyioha addresses reasons for legal ineffectiveness and argues that moral perception and factual correctness affect

1 Involuntary sterilization takes place where informed consent is not given or where consent has been gained through fraud, intimidation or financial or legal incentives.
2 For example, see Katherine Bartlett and Rosanne Kennedy, eds., *Feminist Legal Theory: Readings in Law and Gender* (Westview: Routledge, 1991); Elizabeth Kingdom, *What's Wrong with Rights? Problems for a Feminist Politics of Law* (Edinburgh: Edinburgh University Press, 1991).
3 Ratna Kapur, *Erotic Justice, Law and The New Politics of Postcolonialism* (London: Glasshouse Press, 2005); Christine Chinkin and Hilary Charlesworth, *The Boundaries of International Law: A Feminist Analysis* (Manchester: Manchester University Press, 2000); Charlotte Skeet, "Globalisation of Women's Rights Norms: The Right to Manifest Religion and Orientalism in the Council of Europe" (2009) 4:2 *Public Space* 39 ('Skeet, "Globalisation of Women's Rights Norms"').
4 Sandra Fredman and Beth Goldblatt, *Discussion Paper: Gender Equality and Human Rights* (New York: UN Women, 2015), available at www.unwomen.org/en/digital-library/publications/2015/7/dps-gender-equality-and-human-rights (accessed 4 June 2019) at 37.

both whether the initial framing of law and legal remedies adequately address the needs of diverse groups in society and how differences in the perception of both the morality of law and its factual correctness affect subsequent compliance with law.[5] Human rights are themselves based on inherently moral conceptions of behaviour, the assertion of the equality and equal dignity of all human beings. How we give effect to these is subject to contestation and, particularly in relation to reproductive rights, we can see competing and sometimes flawed approaches to what is entailed in giving effect to human rights and how law should best reflect these understandings.[6]

In the campaigns around forced sterilization, women's rights rhetoric is often used by those seeking to justify occurrences of involuntary sterilization as well as those campaigning against them. In some situations, the former can be explained as a co-option of the language of women's rights by the state or by other groups, for example churches, which may have very different agendas. For example, Sta. Maria's chapter on reproductive health law and practice in the Philippines shows how the Philippine government instrumentalized the historical association of population control and eugenics to justify denying women access to reproductive choice on the basis that it is "protecting them" from state manipulation.[7]

In these situations, it is unsurprising that the articulations and actions in relation to 'rights' fails to meet the expectations of the "diverse identities and diverse needs of those subject to law".[8] In other situations, views about rights norms and rights strategies in relation to forced sterilization may differ because they are based on essentialized notions of gender, or on a paternalistic view of 'what is best' for women, or by promoting a corporate view of women's rights which promotes rights for the greater good of 'women' more generally even if this is at the expense of the autonomy of some women. These positions contrast with engaging with women's rights based on conviction about women's autonomy or their right to choose their own course through life. Since NGOs and other rights activists are crucial in developing articulations of rights norms and in supporting compliance in the international system, their approaches to morality and correctness can be determinative of the outcomes for women's rights. Their responsibility is to ensure that their strategies are not exclusionary and are directed to address the "diverse identities and diverse . . . needs"[9] of all women.[10] Reproductive rights

---

5 See Iyioha, Chapter 2 of this volume.
6 See ibid. for a complete discussion.
7 See Sta. Maria, Chapter 6 of this volume. See also Skeet, "Globalisation of Women's Rights Norms", *supra*.
8 See Iyioha, Chapter 2 of this volume.
9 Ibid.
10 Kristina, Koldinska, "Institutionalizing Intersectionality: A New Path to Equality For New Member States of the EU?" (2009) 11:4 *FJP* 547 at 558, argues NGOs are crucial actors in institutionalization of intersectionality in rights adjudication at both national and international levels.

activism can and should counter social norms that create a differentiated impact for some women because of the wider social context of discrimination.

This chapter argues that the absence of an intersectional understanding of claims by tribunals limits the ability of international law to address rights breaches fully, and that this limitation harms effective standards setting and reduces the meaningfulness and influence of recommendations from human rights forums. In some cases, rights activists have themselves unwittingly contributed to this through their limited presentation of both the legal issues and the suggested remedies.

In making these and related arguments central to this chapter, the discussion continues with an overview of some of the issues arising from the problem of forced and involuntary sterilizations and its connections with the history of eugenics.

The next section offers the theory of intersectionality as a necessary approach to achieving substantive effectiveness[11] in human rights adjudication. Then this thesis is explored through a discussion of cases from the Committee for the Convention on the Elimination of All Forms of Discrimination Against Women (CEDAW), the European Court of Human Rights (ECt.HR), the Inter-American Commission on Human Rights (IACHR) and the Inter-American Court of Human Rights (I/A Court HR) to illustrate how adjudication without due attention to, and application of, the standards set out under the theory of intersectionality produces at best limited outcomes for women, and does not meet the criteria for substantive effectiveness already discussed in Chapter 2.

## Forced and involuntary sterilization and eugenics: some issues arising

The contradictory elements that we see in relation to reproductive rights have been present not only in state actions but also in campaigns for women's access to contraception and reproductive rights from the early 20th century.[12] Marie Stopes is noted for her promotion of contraception and reproductive choice for women.[13] Yet, in her overall strategy, she openly supported eugenics, the pseudo-science aimed at improving the genetic quality of the population.[14] In arguing for married upper- and middle-class women to choose how to space their children and have freedom from the fear of pregnancy, she also argued that other women should have no choice. A clear part of her strategy included compulsory sterilization of those deemed 'unfit' to have children.[15] Eugenics

---

11 See Iyioha, Chapter 2 of this volume.
12 Jane Lewis, "The Ideology and Politics of Birth Control in Inter-War England" (1979) 2:1 *WSIQ* 33.
13 Ibid.
14 Ibid. at 35. Contraception was also argued to be necessary as a social good to prevent what was deemed the "overbreeding of the poor", and since at the time poverty was deemed to be a genetic factor, it was thought that this would eradicate poverty in time.
15 Ibid. at 36. The list of people deemed unfit was broad. It included people with previously difficult births or pregnancies, those with congenital diseases, and people who had a physical

policies and laws were once common across the world under a variety of democracies and regimes.[16] While the movement did not gain traction in the UK, policies were enacted into law in the United States and, very notably, Germany in the 1930s.

Forced, coerced and involuntary sterilization affect both men and women directly, but women are affected as a group disproportionally.[17] Eugenics programmes and population control policies have focused more on the control of women's rather than men's fertility.[18] The ideologies that drive many population policies are themselves gendered and often underpinned by 'dominance competition games' between states or by groups within states, played out through the control of female fertility.[19] Wei Wei Cao's chapter illustrates this wider ideological use of population control as a gendered ideology.[20] Her chapter on abortion in China analyzes how, despite a superficially liberal law which appears to provide women with reproductive autonomy, decisions about reproduction are subsumed under the "state's demographic policy making".[21] Moreover, irrespective of the ideology applied to a state's reproductive health policy, women's contact with healthcare services through pregnancy and childbirth also places them in a vulnerable situation.

Sterilization programs involving men have tended to be carried out through overt population policies, often involving coercion, but these have waned since the International Conference on Population and Development in 1994.[22] In contrast to formal policies, informal policies targeting groups of women for sterilization can be carried out covertly through the opportunities that present themselves when women seek maternity or gynaecological healthcare. In the cases brought before international tribunals, states have even often sought to justify these sterilizations by using a 'women's rights' rhetoric, arguing that they

---

disability or a "mental deficiency". It was also applied to people who had a non-conforming sexuality, or women deemed promiscuous. The eugenics movement also determined people as unfit if they had already had "too many" children, those who were considered to have drunk too much or engaged in crime, and later extended to minorities that might impact on national 'racial purity'.

16 Japan's were still in place until 1996, available at www.theguardian.com/world/2018/jan/30/japanese-woman-sues-government-forced-sterilisation.

17 OHCHR, UN Women, UNAIDS, UNDP, UNFPA, UNICEF and WHO, *Eliminating, Forced, Coercive and otherwise Involuntary Sterilization: An Interagency Statement* (Geneva: WHO, 2014), available at www.who.int/reproductivehealth/publications/gender_rights/eliminating-forced-sterilization/en/ (accessed 4 June 2019) at 3.

18 Elizabeth Spahn, "Feeling Grounded: A Gendered View of Population Control" (2007) 27 *Environmental Law* 1295 at 1301.

19 Ibid. at 1306, quoting Paula Abrahams.

20 See Cao, Chapter 4 of this volume.

21 Ibid. at 15.

22 OHCHR et al., *Eliminating, Forced, Coercive and otherwise Involuntary Sterilization, supra* at 2. Note, however, as Human Rights Watch has observed, some countries do still set targets, available at www.hrw.org/news/2012/07/12/india-target-driven-sterilization-harming-women (accessed 4 June 2019).

are providing 'reproductive choice', or that the operation was necessary to save the patient's life.[23]

Despite the evidence that forced and involuntary sterilizations affect women as a group disproportionally,[24] to look at these claims only in the context of the individual affected or to treat these as gendered from an essentialized perspective without considering which women are being affected and why, is to address those rights breaches only in a partial way. Eugenics movements have now rightly been discredited, yet notions of 'fit' and 'unfit' parents and particularly 'mothers' persist and are underpinned by wider structures of discrimination based on among other social categories, race, ethnicity, gender identity, sexuality, disability and health. These structures can determine whether people believe that laws preventing forced sterilization are 'factually correct' in their equal application to all. Discriminatory structures drive justification for exceptions to the norm of 'freedom from forced sterilization', which in principle is well accepted.

At national levels in some jurisdictions, there still exist some legal provisions for involuntary sterilizations. The three examples I give below have all been stated to be unethical by the International Federation of Gynaecology and Obstetrics (FIGO) Committee for the Ethical Aspects of Human Reproduction and Women's Health[25] and are contrary to international law.[26] The people fall into groups which would have been identified by eugenics policies as people 'unfit' to reproduce. Eugenics arguments are no longer used as justification; instead, arguments for sterilization are presented using a language of rights.

The first example is the use of guardianship powers to give consent to sterilize women who lack capacity. This is widespread. In the United Kingdom, the Court of Protection can make a decision that persons who lack the mental capacity to give consent to sterilization can be sterilized if the Court deems it to be in their 'best interests'.[27] The best interests argument suggests that there is an objective standard that the state can apply in the absence of a person's own capacity to make decisions. Disability rights organizations dispute this 'best interests' argument

---

23 For example, *AS v Hungary* CEDAW/C/36/D/4/2004, submitted 2004, heard August 2006.

24 OHCHR et al., *Eliminating, Forced, Coercive and otherwise Involuntary Sterilization*, *supra* at 3.

25 FIGO, *Ethical Issues in Obstetrics and Gynecology* (London: FIGO, 2012), available at www.figo.org/sites/default/files/uploads/wg-publications/ethics/English%20Ethical%20Issues%20in%20Obstetrics%20and%20Gynecology.pdf (accessed 4 June 2019).

26 Re Disability, see the Convention on Rights of Persons with Disabilities, General Comment 3, 2016 CRPD/C/GC/3 para 10; and the UN Committee on the Convention on the Rights of the Child General Comment 13 (2011) re Art. 19. In relation to transgender persons, see *A.P., Garcon and Nicot v France* ECHR (application nos. 79885/12, 52471/13 and 52596/13).

27 For example, *The Mental Health Trust, Acute Trust & The Council v DD and BC*, Reported as *Re DD (No 4) (Sterilisation)* [2015] EWCOP 4). It is debatable on what basis these types of decisions are justified, and the UN has raised 'guardianship' as a specific problem for women's rights.

and argue that sterilization can never be justified on this basis: it is a clear human rights breach.[28]

A second example relates to a form of coerced sterilization, which has not been found to be illegal under domestic law in the United States. Project Prevent gives money to women who are addicted to crack cocaine in exchange for their 'consent' to be sterilized. The moral justification given is that the women are being saved from the pain of giving birth to a child only to have it removed from their care and that it is immoral to allow a baby to be conceived in a circumstance that means it will become addicted to 'crack' in the womb and be born an addict.[29] It is argued that women, whether addicted or not, have the right to autonomy over their bodies and can contract to be sterilized. Conversely, women's rights activists working with addicted women argue that this intervention does nothing to support women to recover from their addiction; rather, it encourages it. They suggest women will access contraceptive services without being paid to do so if they are freely available. It is also argued that buying sterilization in these circumstances not only dehumanizes drug-addicted women and former addicts, but that it also undermines broader campaigns to ensure marginalized women get access to health services, including contraception, in the United States.[30]

A third, not uncommon example at the national level is a requirement that a transgender person must undergo surgery or sterilization before they are allowed to change their legal status from the sex assigned at birth.[31] In 2011 in *A.P., Garçon and Nicot v. France*, the European Court of Human Rights found this requirement to undergo sterilization to be a human rights breach. Other States which are members of the Council of Europe are now reviewing their laws. In the UK (and elsewhere) the proposal to allow self-identification for trans people is being met with strong resistance from some feminist groups. In contrast to feminists who support transwomen's right to self-identify, other feminists are arguing for an essentialist and binary understanding of who and what a woman is. Moreover, they believe that allowing a transwoman to self-identify as female without undergoing surgery undermines women's rights and security in accessing 'women-only' spaces and services.[32]

---

28 Human Rights Watch, *Sterilization of Girls and Women with Disabilities: A Briefing Paper* (2011), available at www.hrw.org/news/2011/11/10/sterilization-women-and-girls-disabilities (accessed 4 June 2019).

29 See www.projectprevention.org/ (accessed 4 June 2019).

30 Lynn M. Paltrow, "Why Caring Communities Must Oppose C.R.A.C.K./Project Prevention: How C.R.A.C.K. Promotes Dangerous Propaganda and Undermines the Health and Well Being of Children and Families" (2003) 5:11 *JLS* 1–117.

31 In *A.P., Garçon and Nicot v. France, supra*. The ECt.HR ruled this requirement was contrary to Art 8.

32 Gaby Hinsliff, "The Gender Recognition Act is Controversial: Can A Path to Common Ground be Found?" *The Guardian* (10 May 2018). See the discussion of claims to legitimate 'feminist politics' in this area. Alison Phipps, "*Whose Personal is More Political? Experience in Contemporary Feminist Politics*" (2016) 17:3 *Feminist Theory* 303. Note the difference of

The preceding examples of existing exemptions to national law on forced steri-lization show the contested nature of reproductive rights and bodily integrity for these marginalized groups.

## Intersectionality

Despite assertions of the indivisibility of human rights,[33] the construction of human rights frameworks have been limited, first through interpretations by both courts and activists of who are 'rights-holders', and second, through their separation into so-called "generations of rights, and through the segregation and relative isolation of rights institutions dealing with specific conventions".[34] There have been feminist critiques of both the content and applicability of rights instru-ments from 18th-century assertions of rights[35] to current 20th- and 21st-century reformulations and adjudication.[36] These critiques question the role of law and the adjudication of rights in defining rights-holders and particularly in relation to who and what 'women' are and what constitutes a rights breach.[37]

These critiques have been applied to the UN system and to regional and domestic systems; they are even addressed to the very conventions and protocols initially set up to address deficiencies in the universal application of rights. Later conventions, such as the Convention on the Elimination of All Forms of Dis-crimination Against Women (CEDAW) and the Convention on the Elimination of Racial Discrimination (CERD), attempt to address the universal application of human rights by seeking to "accommodate the particular".[38]

Intersectionality theory informs us that even in these formulations, it is often the most disadvantaged groups, those who do not typify the dominant group,

---

approach in relation to rights between campaign groups: (www.stonewall.org.uk/our-work/campaigns/come-out-trans-equality) and the newly formed Fairplay for Women (https://fairplayforwomen.com/about/) and Woman's Place UK (https://womansplaceuk.org/statements) (all accessed 4 June 2019).

33  World Conference on Human Rights, Vienna, *Vienna Declaration and Programme of Action* (1993) 1993, www.ohchr.org/EN/ProfessionalInterest/Pages/Vienna.aspx (accessed 4 June 2019).

34  Szabo Imre, "Historical Foundations of Human Rights and Subsequent Developments", in Karel Vasak, ed., *International Dimensions of Human Rights* (Westport: Greenwood Press, 1982). See also Johanna Bond, "International Intersectionality: A Theoretical and Pragmatic Exploration of Women's International Human Rights Violations" (2003) 52 *Emory Law Journal* 71.

35  Nicola Lacey, "Feminist Theory and the Rights of Women", in Karen Knop, ed., *Gender and Human Rights* (Oxford: Oxford University Press, 2012).

36  Katerina Tomaseveski, *Women and Human Rights* (London: Zed Books, 1995); Joanna Kerr, *Ours By Right: Women's Rights As Human Rights* (London Zed Books, 1993); Knop, *Gender and Human Rights* (Oxford: Oxford University Press, 2012); Kingdom, *What's Wrong with Rights? supra*; Andrea Cornwall and Maxine Molyneux, *The Politics of Rights: Dilemmas for Feminist Praxis* (Abingdon, Routledge, 2008).

37  Charlesworth and Chinkin, *The Boundaries of International Law, supra*.

38  Marie-Bénédicte Dembour, *Who Believes in Human Rights?* (Cambridge: Cambridge University Press, 2006) at 179.

or those whose experience of discrimination is at the intersections of different recognized groups, that are less able to bring successful claims.[39] This is because both courts and/or rights activists view who is a valid rights claimant and what is a valid claim through the experience of the most privileged members of any given group. Such categorization may exclude some women as representative of the group 'women' and may too narrowly circumscribe what claims can be considered to be 'women's rights' claims.[40] Rights activists may unwittingly undermine some claims by favouring strategies that reflect or emphasize the experience of the dominant members of their group.[41] They may themselves even show prejudice in relation to non-dominant group members.[42]

Kimberlé Crenshaw[43] illustrates how institutional discrimination frameworks, which rely on addressing a discrete single axis of discrimination, are narrowly circumscribed.[44] Crenshaw develops intersectionality theory to explain how the most disadvantaged groups – those who may not typify the trope experience of the group, or those whose discrimination crosses more than one category or is based on intersecting grounds – were less likely to be able to bring successful claims. Successful claims may therefore be limited to the "otherwise-privileged members of the group". Sex discrimination claims might be limited to women who are richer, white and nationals of the country they live in with no 'visible' religion: "Race and class privileged women".[45] In relation to race discrimination claims, the ideal claimants may be male and heterosexual: sex and class privileged members of the group.[46]

Although intersectionality has been suggested to be "merely an exhortation to take complexity into account"[47] or a call to reject categories completely, it is rather a call to reconsider the fundamental understandings of groups and categories, and how those constructions relate and contribute to oppression. May argues that merely recognizing that different people are differently

---

39 Bond, "International Intersectionality", *supra*; Kimberlé Crenshaw, "Demarginalizing the Intersection of Race and Sex: A Black Feminist Critique of Anti-Discrimination Doctrine, Feminist Theory and Antiracist Politics" (1989) *University of Chicago Legal Forum* 139 ('Crenshaw, "Demarginalizing the Intersection of Race and Sex"').

40 Crenshaw, "Demarginalizing the Intersection of Race and Sex" at 144.

41 Sherene Razack, *Feminism and the Law: The Women's Legal Education and Action Fund and the Pursuit of Equality* (Toronto: Sumach Press, 1991).

42 Note the example given above of the controversy over self-identification. Even transwomen who do not agree with self-identification believe that the language and approach of the campaign against it discriminates against transwomen.

43 Crenshaw, "Demarginalizing the Intersection of Race and Sex", *supra*.

44 Ibid. at 139.

45 Ibid. at 140.

46 Ibid. at 140.

47 Conaghan Joanne, "Intersectionality and the Feminist Project in Law" in Emily Grabham, Davina Cooper, Jane Krishnadas and Didi Herman, eds., *Intersectionality and Beyond: Law, Power and the Politics of Location* (Abingdon: GlassHouse, 2009) at 29. Angela Harris notes and rebuts similar critiques in "Foreword: The Jurisprudence of Reconstruction" (1994) 82:4 *CLR* at 767–768.

situated without going on to use that analysis to address the social construction of discrimination is not intersectionality.[48] "[T]he point is . . . focus on the process by which they are produced, experienced, reproduced, and resisted in everyday life".[49]

In discussing her development of intersectionality in the legal field, Crenshaw divides intersectional analysis into three principle strands: structural, political and representational.[50] The legal field engages all three. Structural intersectionality helps to identify and map the way that a person's positionality affects their everyday lived experience. This may be because of their economic circumstances, which contribute to oppression, or because of institutional and societal discrimination due to race, gender or some other characteristic. Furthermore, structural intersectionality explains the ways in which lived experience is conditioned and mediated by the application of law or the effect of its absence, particularly on the ability to obtain remedies. A structural intersectional approach therefore assists us in gaining a clear understanding and articulation of the actuality of discrimination and the different ways that people do or do not experience discrimination because of their social situation. For example, Wei Wei Cao explains in her chapter how population policies and forced abortions in China do not affect all women equally. The criteria for 'authorizing' or 'permitting' an out-of-quota pregnancy apply equally to all women, but the policies have a differential impact on poorer women who, because of their economic positioning, cannot afford to pay the 'out-of-quota' fines to keep a pregnancy falling outside those 'authorized' by the state.[51]

The second strand of intersectional analysis is political intersectionality. Political intersectionality[52] refers to situations where a claimant may be positioned within one or more recognized groups pursuing political agendas against discrimination. The individual may not be properly represented by either group because their situation is either unacknowledged by the group or is deemed to conflict with the wider group interests.[53] In relation to political positioning, legal change is often framed through the lobbying of groups that privilege campaigns which suit the dominant members. As Sherene Razack notes, rights litigation strategies are driven by groups who choose the cases that they think will best represent their interests or which may have the best chance of winning.[54]

For example, in the early days of the Women's Legal Education and Action Fund (LEAF) in Canada, the board itself was composed of white women lawyers

48 Vivian M. May, *Pursuing Intersectionality: Unsettling Dominant Imaginaries* (Oxford: Routledge, 2015) at 15.

49 Leslie McCall, "The Complexity of Intersectionality" (2005) 30:3 *Signs* 1721 at 1783.

50 Kimberlé Crenshaw, 'Mapping the Margins: Intersectionality, Identity Politics, and Violence against Women of Colour' (1990/1991) 43:6 SLR 1241 at 1245.

51 See Cao, Chapter 4 of this volume.

52 Crenshaw (1990/1991) at 1245.

53 Crenshaw (1990/1991) at 1252.

54 Razack, *Feminism and the Law, supra.*

from homogenous backgrounds.[55] Although they discussed the need to pick up cases which represented a diversity of women's experiences, the race or sexuality of litigants was gradually 'edited out' when they presented cases to ensure that the cases focused on the issue of equality with men.[56] In this situation, 'editing out' meant focusing only on how claimants' membership in the group 'women' materially affected the issue at hand.[57] To do this, LEAF did not mention or reference other positionalities of the claimants – the fact that they were Indigenous, black or poor – in case this affected the argument that the discrimination was gender based. In this way, therefore, LEAF themselves historically contributed to the narrowing of the discourse around gender and the impact of racialized gender discrimination in Canada.[58]

Emily Snyder's analysis of Indigenous Feminist Legal Theory in Chapter 8, which brings "feminist legal theory, Indigenous feminist theory, and Indigenous legal theory into conversation", amply demonstrates the problems of historical exclusions in law as well as the failure to recognize and appreciate intersectional challenges for Indigenous women in Canada. Without proper recognition of these challenges and the ways in which law, social programs and movements designed to fight inequality can sometimes contribute to the challenges, we are at best left with ineffective laws, legal provisions, and legal outcomes that fall below the ultimate goal of substantive equality.

Political intersectionality can be used as a tool to analyze and address the essentialism in the definitions of group identity and therefore any other form of essentialism, which underlie political movements. Crenshaw, for example, illustrated how assumptions and policy around the users of women's services were based on the experience or priorities of the group that was dominant within the movement. In some cases, this excluded the experiences of people not in the dominant group or actively discriminated against them. Crenshaw uses the example of a Latina woman who was refused entry to a domestic violence shelter with available rooms because she could not prove she was proficient enough in English. They considered she might be isolated within the shelter if her English was not proficient and that she would not be able to benefit from group counselling. In their reasoning, giving her a place would not be in her "best interests" because being unable to participate fully would "re-victimize her".[59] The outcome of this narrowly framed assessment was that without a shelter, she was left to wander the streets and sleep out at night with her son. We can see a further instance of

---

55 Ibid. at 48.
56 Kate Sutherland, "The New Equality Paradigm: The Impact of Charter Equality Principles on Private Law Decisions" in David Schneiderman and Kate Sutherland, eds., *Charting the Consequences: The Impact of Charter Rights on Canadian Law and Politics* (Toronto: University of Toronto Press, 1997) at 254.
57 Razack, *Feminism and the Law* at 25.
58 Lise Gotell, "Litigating Feminist Truth: An Anti-foundational Critique" (1995) 4 *SLS* 99–131 at 117.
59 Crenshaw (1990/1991) at 1263.

political intersectionality in the example used above where transwomen resisting surgical intervention found themselves in conflict with some feminist groups.

The third strand is representational intersectionality. Representations about marginalized groups and the generation of discourses about those groups serve to justify differential treatment and resist efforts to change the status quo. For this reason it is important to see how the representation of any group in relation to their rights matches stereotypical representations, historic or current. This helps to uncover the nature of discrimination, how it is being perpetuated, and how to address it. Law can reflect existing negative representations of claimants and create and recreate representational intersectionality providing another source and justification for these discriminatory representations. It can be used to address negative representations and present a positive discourse which counters discrimination.[60] Some women's claims may be analyzed through women's rights norms, but because of negative constructions the women may be denied status as full rights-holders, or find that women's rights norms are actually used against their claims.[61]

An example of this is the portrayal of visibly Muslim women in the ECt.HR cases claiming freedom to wear religious headscarves. 'Orientalist'[62] discourses which are discriminatory are recreated in the judgements. The court presents these claimants on the one hand as lacking the autonomy necessary to make a claim for freedom of religion or expression;[63] at the same time, the claimants are also classified as dangerous and as holding an 'anti-equality' position for bringing the claims in the first place.[64] In these cases, reference to the principle of women's equality is used as a justification to defeat the women's claims. The ECt.HR then becomes a vehicle for embedding negative stereotypes rather than challenging them.[65] The cases illustrate the disparities between people's lived experience and the vehicles for bringing legal claims. They reveal how the problematic construction of legal claims through fallacies about the nature of categorical discrimination can lead either to the rejection of claims from some of the most disadvantaged groups and individuals, or to those claims only partially being recognized.[66]

A classic example in relation to the latter is famously illustrated by *Abdulaziz, Cabales and Balkandali v The United Kingdom ('A, B, and C v UK')*.[67] In this case, women who had immigrated to the UK from a number of different countries

---

60  Jo Bridgeman and Susan Millns, eds., *Law and the Body Politic: Regulating the Female Body* (Aldershot: Dartmouth, 1997).

61  Skeet, "Globalisation of Women's Rights Norms", *supra*.

62  Edward Said, *Orientalism* (London: Vintage, 1979).

63  Skeet, "Globalisation of Women's Rights Norms", *supra*.

64  Ibid.

65  Alexandra Timmer, "Toward an Anti-Stereotyping Approach for the European Court of Human Rights" (2011) 11:4 *HRLR* 707–738 at 709.

66  CERD 56th session (2000) General Recommendation XXV on Gender Related Dimensions of Racial Discrimination in Report of the Committee on the Elimination of Racial Discrimination 56th and 57th Session a /55/10, see www.un.org/documents/ga/docs/55/a5518.pdf at 152 (accessed 4 June 2019).

67  *Abdulaziz, Cabales and Balkandali v The United Kingdom* (1985) 7 EHRR 471.

and had permanent residence in the UK were not allowed to bring husbands into the UK, whereas men who had come from the same named countries were able to. The applicants argued that the UK government breached both their Article 8 right to family life and their Article 14 right not to be discriminated against on the grounds of sex and race.[68] They advanced evidence that the development of immigration policy in the UK was based on racist ideology.

A minority of the European Commission that first heard the claim and found it admissible also accepted that the background evidence showed very clearly that the UK immigration rules had been motivated by a desire to prevent immigration both from Pakistan and new Commonwealth countries in Africa.[69] The European Court also found in the applicants' favour in relation to a breach of Article 8 along with Article 14 (on the ground of sex), but it did not consider that race had played any part. The court accepted the government's claim that it did not intend to discriminate on racial grounds, but only to stem "immigration" more generally.[70] The consequence of this partial finding in relation to the discrimination experienced by the claimants and the failure to challenge the UK policy on race grounds left it open to the UK to remove the sex discrimination against the women by 'levelling down' immigration provisions so that men from those same countries in the same circumstances as the applicants no longer had the right to bring in their wives. While this satisfied the ruling from the ECt.HR it did not advance equality.

*A, B and C v UK* illustrates that it is not just important in relation to rights claims to determine whether 'any' rights breach has occurred, it is also important to examine how that breach is understood to have taken place and the full extent of all of the rights breached. Narrowing the understanding of any claim category, the disregard of elements of a case or the failure to place a claim in its wider context may lead the court to provide an incomplete analysis of the case and a flawed precedent even where the court appears to find in the claimant's favour as with *A, B and C v UK*. Although it looked as if the women in *A, B and C v UK* had won, they were ultimately unsuccessful in bringing their partners to the UK. As Sherene Razack notes when addressing what counts as a 'winning case' in litigation, "'success' is seldom categorical".[71]

*A, B and C v UK* also shows how crucial international law decisions are for subsequent national policy decisions. An "incomplete analysis affects the remedy or outcome" not only of the case itself but of the impact of international law.[72] A finding on both race and sex discrimination would have required the UK

---

68 In the case of *Cabales*, this was also argued on the ground of 'birth'.
69 Ibid. at para 84.
70 Ibid.
71 Razack, *Feminism and the Law, supra*; see also, in relation to reproductive rights, Ciara O'Connell, "Litigating Reproductive Health Rights in the Inter-American System: What Does a Winning Case Look Like?'" (2014) 16:2 *HHRJ* 116 at 125.
72 Ontario Human Rights Commission, *An Intersectional Approach to Discrimination: Addressing Multiple Grounds in Human Rights Claims* (Discussion Paper October 9, 2001) at 15.

government to extend rights to the women claimants as a remedy and not 'level down' the law to 'remove' the discrimination. Cases like this are also important because they are "used as examples by other states when enacting or amending laws, writing reports under international instruments and applying principles in National Courts".[73] Incomplete analysis may also lead to situations where rights breaches are not recognized at all; for example, compare the understanding of the scope of 'sex' by the UN Human Rights Committee[74] with the narrower understanding by the ECt.HR.[75]

The next section examines cases from three different international forums. In these cases, the judgements either do not reflect an intersectional analysis or the intersectional issues, even when identified, are not reflected in the claimants' remedies.

## International case law on forced sterilizations

Involuntary, forced and coerced sterilization has been found to come within the application of principles on the prohibition of torture[76] and recognized as a means of genocide.[77] It is directly referred to and specifically prohibited under Article 39 of the Istanbul Convention – the Council of Europe Convention on Preventing and Combating Violence Against Women and Domestic Violence,[78] which is the newest Convention on women's right to be free from violence.[79] General Recommendations 19 in 1992 issued by the CEDAW committee, No. 25 by CERD in 2000, ICESR General Comment 5 and ICCPR Committee General Comment 28 also refer explicitly to forced sterilization as a breach of those conventions.[80] Sterilization is also covered but not explicitly referred to in the UN

---

73  Ibid. at 5.
74  *Toonen v Australia* (1994) Human Rights Committee Communication 488/1992.
75  See *Silguero v Portugal,* ECHR application no. 33290/96 [1999] and *Toonen v Australia, supra.*
76  Juan Mendez, *Report of the Special Rapporteur on Torture, other Cruel, Inhuman or Degrading treatment or Punishment,* (2013) UN General Assembly A/HRC/22/53, available at www.ohchr.org/Documents/HRBodies/HRCouncil/Regularsession/Session22/A.HRC.22.53_English.pdf (accessed 4 June 2019).
77  *Convention on the Prevention and Punishment of the Crime of Genocide* 1948, available at https://treaties.un.org/doc/publication/unts/volume%2078/volume-78-i-1021-english.pdf (accessed 4 June 2019), Art 11(d).
78  The Council of Europe Convention on Preventing and Combatting Violence Against Women and Domestic Violence 11.V.2011, available at www.coe.int/fr/web/conventions/full-list/-/conventions/rms/090000168008482e (accessed 4 June 2019).
79  Council of Europe Convention on Preventing and Combating Violence against Women and Domestic Violence. Council of Europe Convention 210, Istanbul 11.V.2011. It is unfortunate that the Istanbul convention does not directly refer to intersectionality in its text, only in the accompanying notes.
80  CEDAW General Recommendation 19 11th Session 1992 Art 22 refers to Arts. 5 and 16 of the Convention; General Recommendation of CERD Committee No. 25 56th Session (2000) Art. 2; ICESR General Comment 5 at 31, moreover General Comment 14,

Declaration on the Elimination of Violence Against Women (DEVAW)[81] and the Inter-American Convention on the Prevention, Punishment and Eradication of Violence Against Women – Belém do Pará.[82]

The right to be free from forced and coerced sterilization is also implicit in rights to choose whether to have children and their spacing, as well as access to information on family planning, as for example in the Protocol to the African Charter on Human and Peoples' Rights on the Rights of Women in Africa (Maputo Protocol).[83] The cover-up of forced and coerced sterilizations or difficulties claimants might have in obtaining redress in national courts also breach a number of different types of general rights provisions, such as the right to freedom of expression, which include the right to receive information, prohibitions on inhuman and degrading treatment, the right to be free to marry and found a family, freedom from racial discrimination, and the right to a fair hearing in court.

## *Committee on the Convention on the Elimination of All Forms of Discrimination Against Women (CEDAW)*

CEDAW and CERD are both conventions intended to give fuller effect to Article 7 of the Universal Declaration of Human Rights[84] and Article 26 of the ICCPR.[85] CEDAW recognizes and references 'race' in its preamble but the text of CEDAW itself has no references to race.[86] Likewise, CERD has no specific reference to gender. Kimberlé Crenshaw, who has acted as rapporteur for the UN Committee on the Elimination of Racial Discrimination, produced a background paper on gender-related aspects of racial discrimination, which led to the issue of the "General Recommendation on the Gender Related Aspects of Race Discrimination to raise awareness on the intersectional relationship between race and gender discrimination". The recommendation is intended to avoid conceptions

---

11 August 2000 refers to sexual and reproductive freedom as an intrinsic aspect of health; ICCPR General Comment 28 CCPR/C/21/Rev.1/Add.10 at 11.

81 Declaration on the Elimination of Violence Against Women A/RES/48/104, available at www.un.org/documents/ga/res/48/a48r104.htm (accessed 4 June 2019).

82 www.oas.org/en/mesecvi/docs/BelemDoPara-ENGLISH.pdf Belém do Pará specifically refers to protection against violence in 'health facilities', Art. 2.

83 See Art. 14(a), (b) and (c), African Charter on Human and Peoples' Rights on the Rights of Women in Africa (Maputo Protocol), 2004, available at www.achpr.org/instruments/women-protocol/ (accessed 4 June 2019). See also the Convention on the Elimination of All Forms of Discrimination against Women, Art. 16(e).

84 "All are equal before the law and are entitled without any discrimination to equal protection of the law".

85 "All persons are equal before the law and are entitled without any discrimination to the equal protection of the law. In this respect, the law shall prohibit any discrimination and guarantee to all persons equal and effective protection against discrimination on any ground such as race, colour, sex, language, religion, political or other opinion, national or social origin, property, birth or other status".

86 Bond, "International Intersectionality", *supra*.

of race discrimination being "sex privileged".[87] Crenshaw provides examples of the ways that race discrimination might manifest itself in different ways in relation to women.

No similar recommendations exist for CEDAW specifically in relation to race.[88] Recommendations do focus on specific intersectional issues such as age, the positioning of women seeking asylum and refuge, and of women who have HIV. The latest recommendation is Recommendation 35,[89] which specifically addresses forced sterilization in Section 18 and in Section 12 reaffirms[90] that "discrimination against women is inextricably linked to other factors" affecting women's lives, while noting case law that has recognized intersecting factors in discrimination.[91] In addition to listing some of these factors, the section footnotes a CEDAW inquiry taken under Article 8 of the Optional Protocol, which allows the Committee to investigate "grave or systematic violations".[92] In this instance, the systematic violations investigated by the enquiry related to the failure of the Canadian State to properly address violence against Indigenous women in Canada.[93] The report was widely considered to reflect an intersectional approach in its investigation.[94]

Harmonized reporting guidelines, which must be followed for the first part of the state Report to the CEDAW Committee, refer to the need for states to address 'multiple discrimination',[95] while treaty-specific guidelines for CEDAW refer to 'multiple discrimination' at E5; yet they only require the actual data to be

---

87 CERD 56th session (2000) General Recommendation XXV on Gender Related Dimensions of Racial Discrimination in Report of the Committee on the Elimination of Racial Discrimination 56th and 57th Session a /55/10, available at www.un.org/documents/ga/docs/55/a5518.pdf at 152 (accessed 4 June 2019).
88 See www.ohchr.org/EN/HRBodies/CEDAW/Pages/Recommendations.aspx (accessed 4 June 2019).
89 Recommendation 35 CEDAW/C/GC/35 26 July 2017, available at www.ohchr.org/EN/HRBodies/CEDAW/Pages/Recommendations.aspx This updates the earlier recommendation 19, which specifically referred to forced sterilization at para 22, available at www.ohchr.org/en/hrbodies/cedaw/pages/recommendations.aspx (accessed 4 June 2019).
90 For example Recommendation 28 CEDAW/C/2010/47/ GG.2, which expands on Article 2 and suggests ways that states can implement CEDAW, available at www.ohchr.org/en/hrbodies/cedaw/pages/recommendations.aspx and Recommendation 33 on Women's Access to Justice, available at www.ohchr.org/en/hrbodies/cedaw/pages/recommendations.aspx (accessed 4 June 2019).
91 See www.ohchr.org/en/hrbodies/cedaw/pages/recommendations.aspx (accessed 4 June 2019).
92 Optional Protocol to CEDAW entered into force December 2000, available at www.ohchr.org/EN/ProfessionalInterest/Pages/OPCEDAW.aspx (accessed 4 June 2019).
93 Report of the inquiry concerning Canada of the Committee on the Elimination of Discrimination against Women under Article 8 of the Optional Protocol to the Convention on the Elimination of All Forms of Discrimination against Women, 1 CEAW/C/OP.8/CAN/1, available at https://undocs.org/CEDAW/C/OP.8/CAN/1 (accessed 4 June 2019).
94 For example Meghan Campbell, "CEDAW and Women's Intersecting Identities: A pioneering Approach to Intersectional Discrimination" (2016) 2:3 *Oxford University Working Paper*.
95 HR1/ GEN/2/Rev 4 sections 51 and 55.

disaggregated by sex,[96] but not by sex along with any other criterion, such as ethnicity or religion. Some case law adjudicated under the Optional Protocol reflects an intersectional focus,[97] as do some concluding comments to state Reports; but these can be highlighted as examples of good practice, not usual practice.[98] Even the most positive academic interpretations of the CEDAW Committee in relation to intersectionality recognize that the Committee does not currently take a consistent approach.[99]

The case of *A.S. v Hungary*,[100] where an intersectional approach was absent, illustrates how the absence of that analysis impacts on the Committee's recommendations. *A.S. v Hungary*[101] was one of the first few cases to be heard after the Optional Protocol to CEDAW[102] came into force. It was the first time an international human rights body held a government to account in an individual case for failing to give a woman "sufficient" information to enable her to give informed consent.[103] Yet it also illustrates the problems for forced/coerced sterilization claims where intersectional issues are not addressed. Ms. A.S. was a Hungarian woman of Roma heritage who had three children at the time she entered hospital in 2001 to have her fourth child. On admission to hospital, she was told that the child had died in her womb and needed to be removed by caesarean section immediately to save her life. She was asked to sign a consent form for this. At the bottom of the form in 'barely legible' handwriting and using the Latin term for sterilization was an addition to the effect that the patient did not wish to give birth again and requested sterilization.[104] The records show that the applicant's admission to hospital, signature on consent form, foetus removal by caesarean section, as well as sterilization were concluded within 17 minutes of arrival.[105] On the way out, Ms. AS asked when "she could try to have another baby?"[106] It was at this point that she was told she had been sterilized.[107]

The case progressed through the Hungarian courts, and the Appeal Court in Hungary found that she had not been given full information, a violation of her right to informed consent under Hungarian law. Despite this, the Appeal Court

---

96 See http://www2.ohchr.org/english/bodies/cedaw/docs/AnnexI.pdf (accessed 4 June 2019), E5 and C5.

97 Ivan Truscan and Joanna Bourke-Martigoni, "'International Human Rights Law and Intersectional Discrimination" (2016) 16 *ERR* 16, 103. See particularly *Kell v Canada* and the cases on pp. 115–125.

98 Ibid. at 130.

99 For example Campbell, *supra*, accepts that the Committee is not currently consistent on this.

100 CEDAW/C/36/D/4/2004 submitted 2004 heard August 2006.

101 Ibid.

102 Optional Protocol to CEDAW entered into force December 2000, available at www.ohchr.org/EN/ProfessionalInterest/Pages/OPCEDAW.aspx (accessed 4 June 2019).

103 Christina Zampas and Adriana Lamackova, "Forced and Coerced Sterilisation of Women in Europe'" (2011) 114 *IJGO* 163 at 165.

104 Ibid. at para 2.2.

105 Ibid. at para 2.3.

106 Ibid.

107 Ibid.

denied her a remedy because they considered that she had not established that the sterilization was a 'lasting and irreversible' procedure.[108]

The CEDAW Committee found in favour of AS. The Committee recognized that her Article 10(h), 12 and 16(1)(e) rights had been breached: respectively rights to receive information on health, to access healthcare, and freedom to choose the number and spacing of children. The Committee asked the Hungarian State to monitor hospitals and ensure that they give 'women' better information and that they obtain consent prior to sterilization.[109] When I presented this case to my Women and Human Rights master's students, they interpreted the comments from the committee as patronizing. In the absence of a focus on the wider discrimination against people of Roma heritage, they read the comments as a suggestion by the Committee that AS needed more help understanding the text of the informed consent document such that the state must try harder to get women to understand these texts if they want informed consent. My students were dismayed that the Committee appeared not to recognize the wider context of these rights breaches.

The Committee asked the Hungarian State to amend their law in relation to medical 'consent' and review its operation.[110] To address non-repetition of the hospital's conduct, they could also have asked for a review of discrimination law and its operation, particularly in the context of the failure of the Legal Defence Bureau for National and Ethnic Minorities to get AS a domestic remedy in the Hungarian courts.[111] The NGO, Centre for Reproductive Rights, that put a third-party intervention/amicus curiae to the CEDAW Committee in *AS v Hungary* did not address the intersectional issues or discuss AS's status as a woman of Roma heritage.[112] This was the first individual case on forced sterilization in an international tribunal and they said their concern was to argue for forced sterilization as a 'women's rights issue'. This effort was successful in one sense since there had been no previous finding of this duty owed to an individual woman by a state. The organization was also successful in arguing that sterilization is an irreversible process, something the Hungary Court had denied. Yet, editing out AS status essentialized her gender by assuming that the absence of race or ethnicity would make the claim more universal.[113] It meant they could not direct the court to the underlying discriminatory structures, and buried the broader 'equality potential' that could have emerged from the judgement.[114] In relation to representational intersectionality it is debateable whether the committee's focus on the supposed lack of 'understanding' by AS rather than on systematic discrimination by the

---

108  Ibid. at para 2.8.
109  Ibid.
110  *AS v Hungary, supra* at para 11.5 II.
111  Ibid. at 2.5.
112  Christina Zampas and Aya Fujimura-Fanselow, "UN Committee on The Elimination of All Forms of Discrimination Against Women, Supplemental Information re A.S. v. Hungary Communication no 4/2004" (2016) *Centre for Reproductive Rights*.
113  Crenshaw, "Demarginalizing the Intersection of Race and Sex".
114  Razack, *Feminism and the Law* at 125.

Hungarian State supports discriminatory representations of women of Roma heritage as being less educated or intelligent.[115]

In the 2013 Concluding Comments to Hungary's Report, the CEDAW Committee refers specifically to the problems Roma women face when accessing sexual and reproductive health services.[116] The Committee does not refer to problems women of Roma heritage face in relation to forced sterilization even though a shadow Report addressed to the Committee in January of 2013 made it clear that "Coercive sterilization remains a concern for Romani women in Hungary".[117] The same Report also records that more than six years after the *AS* decision was issued, Hungary has "failed to fully implement the recommendations by the CEDAW Committee".[118]

## *ECt.HR*

Of all the international tribunals, the European Court of Human Rights has been argued to have the weakest record on gender equality[119] and on substantive understandings of equality,[120] though it is argued that its jurisprudence in relation to substantive equality has been "emerging from the shadows" more recently.[121] Intersectionality is even less evident within the decisions of the European Court of Human Rights (ECt.HR).[122] In *BS v Spain*, the complainant argued she was harassed by police because of a combination of her race and status as a sex worker.[123]

---

115 See the discussion of this particular racist discourse in relation to people of Roma heritage in the case of *DH v Czech Republic* [2007] ECHR 922, where the state used the discourse to justify segregated schooling.
116 Para 33 (a).
117 Alternative report submitted to the UN CEDAW Committee for consideration in relation to the examination of the combined seventh and eighth periodic reports of Hungary (January 2013) by the Hungarian Women's Lobby and the European Roma Rights Centre, available at https://www2.ohchr.org/english/bodies/cedaw/docs/ngos/HWLand ERRC_Hungary_ForTheSession_Hungary_CEDAW54.pdf (accessed 4 June 2019) at 7.
118 Ibid. It should also be noted that the CEDAW Committee's Concluding Comments do address the issue of forced sterilization in relation to women with disabilities: See para 33(b).
119 Dembour, *Who Believes in Human Rights? supra.*
120 Clare Overy and Robin White, *Jacobs and White: European Convention on Human* Rights (Oxford: Oxford University Press, 2002); Sandra Fredman, "Emerging from the Shadows: Substantive Equality and Article 14 of the European Convention on Human Rights" (2016) 16:2 *HRLR* 273–301; Timmer, "Toward an Anti-Stereotyping Approach for the European Court of Human Rights", *supra.*
121 Fredman, "Emerging from the Shadows", *supra.*
122 Though Vakulenko argues the Court moves towards an intersectional perspective in relation to religious dress. I would argue exactly the reverse and critique their judgements from an intersectional perspective for using historic negative constructions of visibly Muslim women to justify the denial of their claims. See Anastasia Vakulenko, "Islamic Headscarves and the European Convention on Human Rights: An Intersectional Perspective" (2007) 16:2 *SLS* 183–199; Skeet, "Globalisation of Women's Rights Norms", *supra.*
123 *Beauty Solomon v Spain* [2012] 47159/08; see also K. Yoshida, "Towards Intersectionality in the European Court of Human Rights: The Case of B.S. v Spain" (2013) 21:2 *Feminist Legal Studies* 195–204.

The court found for her, and through they did not refer to the term intersectionality itself, they clearly engaged with her argument and that of the third-party intervention put in on her behalf by Interrights.[124] The latest Council of Europe Gender Equality Strategy 2018–2023 states that intersectionality is to operate as a transversal issue across all priority areas, but it remains to be seen whether this impacts European Court of Human Rights decisions.[125] As already noted, the Council of Europe Istanbul Convention refers directly to forced sterilization as violence against women. The Council of Europe Committee of Ministers Strasbourg Declaration on Roma also refers to a pan-European duty to "[p]ut in place effective measures to abolish where still in use harmful practices against Roma women's reproductive rights, primarily forced sterilisation [*sic*]".[126]

Article 14 of the European Convention on Human Rights and Fundamental Freedoms is not exhaustive in its grounds for discrimination; the provision, 'or other status', has been used to add in grounds for discrimination that were not anticipated by the drafters in the 1950s. Yet, this in itself is not a solution. Crenshaw is clear that intersectionality does not call for a proliferation of 'categories' but, rather, for an expansion of the understanding and recognition of how discrimination under existing legal heads actually impacts differently on different groups.[127] The emphasis should rather be on de-essentializing existing constructions of race, sex and so forth that ensure that these rights apply to 'otherwise-privileged members of the group' and exclude the least privileged.[128]

An analysis under Article 14 does not guarantee that an intersectional approach will be adopted, but the failure to analyze inequality and develop jurisprudence under this article is problematic. Unfortunately, successive sittings of the ECt.HR have shown a wilful reluctance[129] to develop jurisprudence through Article 14. In fact, the ECt.HR very often declines to address Article 14 at all, arguing that it will add nothing to the case analysis to do so.[130]

---

124  Email to author from Adam Weiss, *Interrights*, 2012.
125  *Council of Europe Gender Equality Strategy 2018-2023* https://rm.coe.int/strategy-en-2018-2023/16807b58eb (accessed 10 August 2019) at paras 21 and 22.
126  Declaration on Roma, 20 October 2010 EM (2010) 133 at para 23.
127  Nira Yuval-Davies, "Intersectionality and Feminist Politics" (2006) 13:3 *EJWS* 193–209 at 195 notes that "Any attempt to essentialize 'Blackness' or 'woman hood' or 'working classness' as specific forms of concrete oppression in additive ways inevitably conflates the narrative of identity politics with descriptions of positionality. . . . Such narratives often reflect hegemonic discourses of identity politics that render invisible experiences of the more marginal members of that specific social category and construct an homogenized right way to be its member".
128  Yet Crenshaw does believe that despite this, there will be times when a new category should be recognized. See Crenshaw, "Demarginalizing the Intersection of Race and Sex".
129  Gay Moon, "The Draft Discrimination Protocol to the European Convention on Human Rights: A Progress Report" (2000) 1 *EHRLR* 49; Rory O'Connell, "Cinderella Comes to the Ball: Art 14 and the Right to Non-discrimination in the ECHR'" (2009) 29:2 *Legal Studies* 211 ('O'Connell, "Cinderella Comes to the Ball"').
130  For instance, note the difference between the House of Lords treatment of *A* v *Home Office* where Article 14 was crucial to the finding of incompatibility and the interpretation of the

In recent years, the Court has started to look separately at Article 14 in relation to cases on gender-based violence, and has found state inaction on domestic violence to be discrimination on the basis of sex.[131] Fredman argues that in this positive development, we may be seeing Article 14 jurisprudence "emerge from the shadows" in the jurisprudence from the E.Ct.HR.[132] This development in the use of Article 14 does not seem to be mirrored where claims of discrimination relate to institutionalized racial discrimination, and *DH* v *Czech Republic*, which found 'special' schooling of children of Roma heritage to be widespread and systematic discrimination by the Czech state, is a high point which has not been repeated.[133]

Several cases on forced sterilization of women with Roma heritage have come before the ECt.HR for determination on their merits but many other claims have been dismissed as inadmissible and will never be heard.[134] The two cases detailed below, *VC v Slovakia*[135] and *NB v Slovakia*,[136] followed from an application by eight women of Roma heritage against a refusal by two hospitals in Slovakia to allow them access to their medical records.[137] The Court found that the women's Article 8 right to 'privacy' and Article 6 right to 'access a court' had been breached by the refusal to allow them to access their records. An earlier hearing on admissibility had deemed consideration of Article 14 inadmissible. For that reason, the application to access records was limited to consideration of its narrow facts and did not examine the wider picture of why access to the medical records was being refused. Evidence of a widespread policy of sterilization of women of Roma heritage and evidence that the hospital was trying to suppress knowledge of this by refusing to let people access records was not deemed relevant. The subsequent individual cases on forced sterilization did highlight this but no determinations were made under Article 14. In the cases below, as with *A.S. v Hungary*, the Court found in the applicants' favour. Yet the judgements and their basis leave much to be desired.

The leading case is *VC v Slovakia*. When VC was admitted to the Presov Hospital in labour, she was placed in a ward with only other Roma women and the words "Patient is of Roma origin" were written in her file.[138] The Director

---

ECHR in *A v UK* where it was not considered at all. Rory O'Connell provides a similar example in relation to *S and Marper* v *Chief Constable of South Yorkshire* [2004] UKHL 39, noting that the House of Lords gave Article 14 detailed consideration while the Grand Chamber (*S and Marper* v *UK* applications 30562/04 and 30566/04) based the finding only on Article 8, see O'Connell, "Cinderella Comes to the Ball", *supra*.

131  For example see *Opuz v Turkey* (33401/02) [2009] ECHR 870.
132  Fredman, "Emerging from the Shadows", *supra*.
133  *DH v Czech Republic* [2007] ECHR 922.
134  It is not known how many cases every year never even reach the admissibility stage but are rejected for incomplete presentation. Morvai, cited by Dembour, argues that the rejection of claims by the European Court and former Commission is in itself a scandal. Dembour, *Who Believes in Human Rights? supra* note 38 at 122–130.
135  *VC v Slovakia* [2009] Application no (18968) ('*VC v Slovakia*').
136  *NB v Slovakia* [2012] Application (29518/10).
137  *KH and Others v Slovakia (32881/04)* 2009.
138  *VC v Slovakia, supra* at paras 17–18.

denied that there were separate "gypsy rooms" at the hospital but said that Roma women often asked to be accommodated together.[139] The reality was that Roma women were segregated and not allowed to use the same bathroom and toilets as women who were not of Roma heritage.[140] The hospital records stated that VC requested a sterilization when she was in pain and well advanced into her labour. Her signature on the 'consent' form for the sterilization was very unsteady.[141] Contrary to the records, VC said she was asked if she wanted to have more children and said 'yes'. She said was unaware that she was signing to have a sterilization and thought that it related to the emergency caesarean section procedure needed for the birth of her child.[142] The circumstances of the procedure and method of obtaining 'consent' breached both the Slovakian law on sterilization and international guidelines.[143] VC suffered from "serious medical and psychological after-effects from the sterilization" and maintained that her subsequent divorce was due to her infertility.[144]

The European Court of Human Rights received evidence of an historic policy to sterilize Roma women in the former Czechoslovakia, and of more recent concerns in Slovakia from agencies such as the European Commission against Racial Intolerance (ECRI) and the Council of Europe Commissioner for Human Rights, as well as CEDAW Committee Concluding Comments to the Slovakia State Periodic Reports that discrimination against Roma women was continuing.[145] The court was unanimous in finding a violation of Article 8 on the right to private life and Article 3 on the right to be free from inhuman and degrading treatment. They were also unanimous in finding no violation of Article 13, which provides a right to a remedy in relation to any substantive rights breaches under the Convention. The Court was also unanimous that there was no need to look separately at Article 12 on the right to marry, and found by a majority that there was no need to examine Article 14 – the right to be free from discrimination.

In *VC v Slovakia* itself, Judge Mijovic in a separate opinion criticized the failure of the court to examine Article 14 and dissented on that point. She argued that finding only a breach of Articles 3 and 8 reduced the case to "the individual level whereas it was obvious that there was a general state policy of sterilization of Roma women under the Communist regime that continued to the . . . present case".[146] In her opinion, this represented the strongest form of discrimination and should have led to a finding of Article 14 interpreted with Articles 3 and 8. If the court had done this they would have been bound to give the full amount of compensation – the 'just satisfaction' – that was claimed but denied by the

139  Ibid. at para 23.
140  Ibid. at para 18.
141  Ibid. at paras 14–16.
142  Ibid. at para 15.
143  Ibid. at paras 63–75.
144  Ibid. at para 19.
145  Ibid. at paras 78, 80 and 84, respectively.
146  Ibid. Separate Opinion of Judge Mijovic at para 46.

Court.[147] It is also clear that it would have sent out a strong message as *DH v Czech* did in relation to segregated education, which would have required the state itself to address discrimination against people of Roma heritage. Instead the court viewed it as a state failure to protect "a member of a vulnerable Roma community".[148]

*NB v Slovakia* and *IG v Slovakia* were heard the following year. The *NB* complaint was from a 17-year-old woman of Roma heritage. As with *VC*, *NB* had been placed in segregated facilities in a 'gypsy room' when admitted to Gelnica Hospital. Typewritten alongside the handwritten notes on her procedure was a statement alleging that she requested a sterilization operation at the same time as the delivery of her child. The typewritten sections stated she had been fully informed of its irreversible nature.[149] The applicant stated that she had only been asked to sign the paper while in labour and after she had received premedication which made her feel intoxicated.[150] She did not know what was in the document but was told that if she did not sign she would die; she therefore signed the document.[151] She only found out she had been sterilized a year later in 2002 when her lawyer accessed her medical records. The sterilization commission at the Gelnica hospital gave retrospective approval for the sterilization.

The applicant filed both civil and criminal complaints and lodged a complaint with the Constitutional Court. She was awarded compensation but her claim that the actions were criminal and that they had breached her Convention rights were not successful in the domestic courts.[152] The hospital maintained that although the operation was not necessary to save NB's life at the time it was carried out, a further pregnancy might have threatened her life. They accepted that there was no informed consent for the procedure. The European Court of Human Rights found that the medical staff acted with "gross disregard for her human freedom",[153] and in view of its serious nature and consequences, as well as the lasting suffering it had caused, they believed the action to be within the scope of Article 3. The Court also found that NB's Article 8 right was breached. The Court declined to look at Article 12, the 'right to marry', separately. They also found that there was no "arguable complaint" in relation to a breach of Article 13.

Finally, they declined to look at Article 14 separately. In relation to this the court used the same reasoning that they had in *VC v Slovakia*: They did not consider that the "medical staff had acted with the 'intention' of illtreating the applicant" in any way.[154] The Court reiterated that "shortcomings in legislation and practice relating to sterilization were liable to particularly affect members of the

---

147 Ibid. Dissenting Opinion of Judge Mijovic at para 46.
148 Ibid. Main judgement at para 179.
149 *NB v Slovakia, supra* at para 9.
150 Ibid. at para 10.
151 Ibid.
152 Ibid. at paras 21–46.
153 Ibid. at para 78.
154 Ibid.

Roma Community", yet did not think it could be established that this amounted to "bad faith" or was part of an "organized policy", or was intentionally racially motivated. They also did not consider that legislative gaps or deliberate statutory omissions typically worsen health outcomes for vulnerable and marginalized groups due, as Iyioha notes in Chapter 2, to other contextual and systemic factors that are part of the lived experiences of such groups.

*IG v Slovakia*,[155] decided in 2012, similarly found 'for' two of the applicants and declined to look at Article 14. The third application in *IG* which was unsuccessful related to a Slovakian woman with Roma heritage who had died following a forced sterilization. The application was brought by her children, but the Court found it inadmissible. Nicolas Bratza, the president of the European Court of Human Rights, set out his dissent in relation to the majority's decision to strike the application out of its list of cases under Article 37 § 1(c) of the Convention. In his opinion:

> Having regard to the disturbing circumstances of the case, the *locus standi* of the third applicant's children should have been accepted. The case-law relied on by the majority is of course correct. However, the respect for the third applicant's human rights should have prevailed and the Court should have examined her application on the merits.[156]

It is clear that the ECt.HR has maintained its usual position on a narrow approach to procedure in relation to forced sterilization cases. This is evident in the number of claims that are found inadmissible, the narrow decisions on admissibility that have excluded Article 14, and the full determinations by the court that have failed to both recognize and address the systematic gendered racial discrimination against women of Roma heritage evident in the individual claims brought before the Court. The failure to address these claims from an intersectional perspective has led to narrow recommendations that are not aimed at addressing the causes of these rights breaches. By failing to address the cases through Article 14, the court neither recognizes nor addresses the gendered racial stereotyping as captured by the concept of 'representational intersectionality'.[157] Alexandra Timmer argues that members of the Court were unable to "move beyond their own prejudices about 'the other' ",[158] and when they failed to challenge the systematic stereotyping, they gave a tacit acceptance of the "cultural imagery"[159] in the representation of women with Roma heritage as "not good mothers".[160]

---

155  *IG v Slovakia* [2012] ECHR 1910. This return to a requirement for 'intention' went against the decision of *DH v Czech Republic, supra*, which had found 'intention' to be an unnecessary test.
156  *IG v Slovakia, supra*: Declaration of Judge Bratza.
157  Crenshaw (1990/1991) at 1282–1295.
158  Timmer, "Toward an Anti-Stereotyping Approach for the European Court of Human Rights", *supra* at 734.
159  Crenshaw (1990/1991) at 1282.
160  Timmer, "Toward an Anti-Stereotyping Approach for the European Court of Human Rights", *supra* at 735.

## The Inter-American system

The Inter-American system has the strongest record of any of the regional rights instruments in establishing women's rights norms.[161] The system developed in response to gross and systematic rights breaches across the region at the time the Inter-American Convention came into force.[162] This is reflected both in the initial structure of the system and in the way the Inter-American Commission and Court have developed an innovative jurisprudence in relation to both the procedures for bringing claims and in relation to the substance of the adjudication and remedies.[163] In particular is the jurisprudence on the Belém do Pará Convention,[164] which until the Istanbul Convention was the only regional instrument that dealt solely with violence against women: this was influential in developing both the jurisprudence of the ECt.HR and the drafting of the Istanbul Convention.[165]

Article 9 of the Belém do Pará Convention, which was adopted in 1994, does not refer to intersectionality directly but it does ask States to take account of the "structural positioning" of women and urges States parties and courts to adopt an intersectional approach. According to Article 9:

> States Parties shall take special account of the vulnerability of women to violence by reason of, among others, their race or ethnic background or their status as migrants, refugees or displaced persons. Similar consideration shall be given to women subjected to violence while pregnant or who are disabled, of minor age, elderly, socioeconomically disadvantaged, affected by armed conflict or deprived of their freedom.[166]

In recognition of the limitations of looking at rights breaches through broad categorizations and the limitations of the Courts' view of 'gender, sexuality, race and ethnicity' as impacting on the success of rights claims, two Inter-American Commissioners set up a symposium on intersectionality in 2013 and invited a

---

161 Compliance with judgements is a problem.
162 Marie-Bénédicte Dembour, *When Humans Become Migrants: A Study of the European Court of Human Rights with an Inter-American Counterpoint* (Oxford: Oxford University Press, 2016) at 12–13.
163 For example, the relaxed principle in relation to standing so that anyone can bring a claim on behalf of someone else. This prevents the state or militia simply killing or making a person disappear in order to prevent a rights claim going ahead.
164 Belém do Pará Inter-American Convention on the Prevention, Punishment, and Eradication of Violence Against Women, available at www.oas.org/juridico/english/treaties/a-61. html (accessed 4 June 2019).
165 See *Opuz v Turkey*, *supra* for the influence of the Inter-American jurisprudence at paras 83–86, 164 and 189–191. For the drafting of the Istanbul Convention, see Ronagh J.A. McQuigg, "What potential does the Council of Europe Convention on Violence against Women hold as Regards Domestic Violence?" (2012) 16:7 *IHJR* 947: She notes that the Convention was drawn based on *Opuz* and the cases that followed it.
166 Ibid., Art. 9.

range of global actors.[167] Their focus was not just how to recognize and present intersectional claims, but also how to craft "appropriate reparations and remedies".[168] The impact of this focus is evident if we compare the two cases on involuntary sterilization heard to date.

*Chavez v Peru*, the first case on forced sterilization, was subject to a "friendly settlement" in 2003.[169] The second, *IV v Bolivia*, was heard in 2016.[170] Maria Mamerita Mestanza Chavez was sterilized as part of Fujimori's population programme in Peru, which was initially funded and supported by the UN.[171] The family had seven children in 1996 when Mrs. Chavez was targeted. Between 1996 and 1998, they were visited several times by health personnel who threatened them with the police and told them that because they had over five children, the law allowed them to be imprisoned and fined.[172] Eventually, in 1998 Mrs. Chavez felt compelled to undergo sterilization. There was no pre-procedure examination, and the following day Mrs. Chavez was sent home even though she was clearly still very ill. Mrs. Chavez did not survive the unlawful procedure and died of sepsis several days later.[173] Despite her worsening symptoms prior to her death, the La Encanada Health Centre did nothing about her condition. After her death, the Centre offered her husband some money in "settlement".[174] He was unable to get proper accountability for his wife's death through the legal system in Peru. A report on the "Friendly Settlement" locates the rights breaches as caused by systematic structural discrimination, recording in the 'Facts' section the petitioners'[175] claim that Ms. Maria Mamerita Mestanza Chavez was

> one more among a large number of cases of women affected by a massive, compulsory, and systematic government policy to stress sterilization as a means for rapidly altering the reproductive behaviour of the population, especially poor, Indian, and rural women.[176]

167  Patricia Hill Collins and Sirma Bilge, Intersectionality (Cambridge: Polity Press, 2016) at 93–95.

168  Ibid. at 95.

169  *Chavez v Peru*, I-A CHR Report No 71/03 Petition 12.191, Friendly Settlement, Maria Mam'erita Mestanza *Chavez v. Peru*, October 22, 2003.

170  *IV v Bolivia* Report 72/14 Case 12.655 Merits I.V. Bolivia August 15, 2014, available at www.oas.org/en/iachr/decisions/court/2015/12655fondoen.pdf (In English) (accessed 4 June 2019).

171  Center for Reproductive Rights (2015) Press Release – Peru Reopens Criminal Investigation into Mass Forced Sterilization, 5.13.15, available at www.reproductiverights.org/press-room/peru-reopens-criminal-investigation-into-mass-forced-sterilizations (accessed 4 June 2019).

172  *Chavez v Peru*, *supra* at paras 9–11.

173  Ibid. at para 11.

174  Ibid. at para 12.

175  Five NGOs – Office for the Defense of Women's Rights (DEMUS), The Latin and Caribbean Committee for the Defense of Women's Rights (CLADEM), the Association Pro Derechos Humanos (APRODEH), The Center for Reproductive Law and Policy (CRLP), and the Center for Justice and International Law (CEJIL) – represented the individuals and families affected.

176  Ibid. at para 9.

Figures given later by the Center for Reproductive Rights estimates that around 350,000 women and 25,000 men were sterilized between 1990 and 2000, and that only 10% of these were by consent.[177] The circumstances around the Chavez claim also highlight an example of political intersectionality in relation to Indigenous women in Peru. International and national women's rights actors were reluctant to critique the Fujimori policies even when it became apparent that Indigenous women were being coerced and targeted for forced sterilizations. For the international organizations, Fujimori's program of "expanded services" was what they had "advocated for decades".[178] They were concerned that highlighting abuses with the programme would compromise their priority of choice for women in accessing contraception even if this choice was not there for Indigenous women. National groups were also divided in their support for the regime. Those who supported Fujimori were "caught in a web of political and financial relationships with the Peruvian State and international population agencies",[179] while feminist groups that did not support Fujimori prioritized the "larger fight against an authoritarian regime" over the problems Indigenous women were experiencing with the specific programme.[180] Fujimori was therefore able to "cloak a traditional population control agenda" limiting women's reproductive freedom by utilizing "international feminist discourses on reproductive health and rights".[181] Notably, Fujimori even spoke at the UN Conference on Women in Beijing in 1995.[182]

This highlights the problem for marginalized women when their experience does not match that of privileged or dominant women who set the priorities for action and who may themselves be prejudiced against marginalized women. It shows the need for feminist groups and advocates to subject their own policies and practices to an intersectional analysis. As Lewis et al. suggest in Chapter 3, such an ideological disagreement on a critical matter of reproductive justice for a marginalized group evinces the sometimes tenuous relationship between some Western feminisms and inconsistent accounts of right and wrong embedded within the non-positivistic approach to lawmaking and adjudication.

The 'facts' section of the settlement recognizes the wider political context that targeted Indigenous women for sterilization, yet the settlement only provides individual reparations for the Chavez family. The state's agreement to investigate the wider issues suggests that responsibility lies with individuals: officials, health

---

177 Center for Reproductive Rights (2015) Press Release – Peru Reopens Criminal Investigation into Mass Forced Sterilization, 5.13.15, available at www.reproductiverights.org/press-room/peru-reopens-criminal-investigation-into-mass-forced-sterilizations (accessed 4 June 2019).
178 Christina Ewig, "Hijacking Global Feminism: Feminists, the Catholic Church, and the Family Planning Debacle in Peru" (2006) 32:3 *Feminist Studies* 632–659 at 648.
179 Ibid.
180 Ibid.
181 Ibid. at 639.
182 Jocelyn E. Getgen, "Untold Truths: The Exclusion of Enforced Sterilizations from the Peruvian Truth Commission's Final Report" (2009) 29:1 *BCTWLJ* 1–34 at 10.

personnel, and people in the public prosecutor's office.[183] The state is therefore allowed to devolve its responsibility to a local level based on decisions made by individuals on an individual level. There is no provision for preventative work to ensure non-repetition or for addressing the violations in a more systemic way. The mass sterilizations in this period were not included in the Peruvian Truth Commission's final report even though a strong case could be made that these acts constituted genocide against the Quechua-speaking people.[184] The facts section of the *Chavez* settlement provides the only 'legal' recognition of this atrocity anywhere to date. So the failure of the *Chavez* settlement to address the case more fully holds an added significance. In 2014, the I-ACHR prosecutor found that Peru had not even fulfilled the very limited agreement in *Chavez* to 'investigate'.[185]

Judgement on the more recent case of *IV v Bolivia* was delivered in 2016.[186] The case concerned a Peruvian refugee in Bolivia who, at the time she was sterilized, was admitted to hospital for a planned caesarean section. The state claimed that the procedure was necessary to save *IV*'s life and that she had agreed to it orally.[187] She did not find out until several days later and was shocked to learn about it. Even if consent had been given orally, this would not have been sufficient to meet the standards of Bolivia's informed consent law or international standards.[188] A criminal action was brought against the doctor who performed the sterilization, but the prolonged nature of the proceedings and numerous appeals on different points caused a time-lapse in the criminal proceedings.[189] The Court and Commission found *IV*'s rights, under the Inter-American Convention and the Belém do Pará Convention were breached in a number of areas, including the right to be free from violence and the rights to privacy, dignity, non-discrimination and to access justice.[190]

Both the Commission and Court reports for *IV* referred to intersectionality directly. The Commission referred to the importance of context and considered that the words of the UN Special Rapporteur on Violence Against Women were relevant to this case. According to the UN Special Rapporteur on Violence Against Women:

183  *Supra* at para 14: "Third: Investigation and Punishment".

184  Getgen, "Untold Truths", *supra* at 25.

185  Center for Reproductive Rights (2015) Press Release – Peru Reopens Criminal Investigation into Mass Forced Sterilisation, 5.13.15: www.reproductiverights.org/press-room/peru-reopens-criminal-investigation-into-mass-forced-sterilizations.

186  Corte InterAmericana De Derechos Humanos *I.V. VS. BOLIVIA* Sentencia De 30 de Noviembre (Excepciones Preliminares, Fondo, Reparaciones y Costas), available at www.corteidh.or.cr/docs/casos/articulos/seriec_329_esp.pdf (in Spanish only) (accessed 4 June 2019). The case was earlier found to be admissible on its merits in 2014, Report 72/14 Case 12.655 *Merits I.V. Bolivia supra*.

187  Ibid. at paras 4 and 24.

188  Ibid. at para 65.

189  Ibid. at paras 42 and 184.

190  Ibid.

Discrimination based on race, ethnicity, national origin, ability, socio-economic class, sexual orientation, gender identity, religion, culture, tradition and other realities often intensifies [*sic*] acts of violence against women. The acknowledgement of structural aspects and factors of discrimination is necessary for achieving non-discrimination and equality.[191]

The Inter-American Commission translated this into a call to contextualize even individual reparations and noted in relation to the breach of *IV*'s right to fair trial and judicial protection[192] that a "timely and exhaustive investigation . . . would have constituted for *IV* a form of reparation with a chance of transforming the context of discrimination against women – as well as gender stereotypes – that facilitated *IV*'s sterilization without her consent".[193]

As a female migrant with low economic status, *IV* would be forced into using certain services against her personal preferences, and would be more likely to be discriminated against as a user.[194] The failure to get redress through the Bolivian state was a part of this discrimination. At paragraph 75, the Convention of Belém do Pará recognizes the importance of women's access to appropriate judicial protections in order for them to successfully fight the wider discrimination against them that leads to individual acts of violence. In their final Recommendations, the Commission referred at VII(5) to the "particular needs of persons in a vulnerable situation due to intersection of factors such as sex, or race, economic position, or status condition as migrant, among others".[195] This seems ambivalent and could be interpreted, as in the case of *AS v Hungary*, as suggesting that the problem is caused by the qualities or characteristics of the 'vulnerable people' and not the discriminatory treatment meted out to them. However, read along with the earlier paragraphs, the recommendation is clearly addressing discrimination stemming from structural positioning. The Inter-American Court was more specific on this and required the Bolivian state to produce legislation, public policy and programmes to address discrimination,[196] to design and publish guidance on informed consent and human rights for patients and staff alike,[197] and to train medical students and professional staff to respect all healthcare users.[198]

Yet it has been suggested that while these were positive recommendations, the case also represented a missed opportunity to really think through what an intersectional approach to reparations and non-repetition protections needs to

191 Rashida Manjoo, "Report of the Special Rapporteur on violence against women, its causes and consequences" (Geneva, UN 2011) at 67, cited in *IV v Bolivia, supra* at para 160.
192 *IV v Bolivia, supra.*
193 Ibid. at para 171.
194 Ibid. at paras 161–162.
195 Ibid. at 187 VII(5).
196 Corte Inter Americana De Derechos Humanos I.V. VS. BOLIVIA Sentencia De 30 de Noviembre (Excepciones Preliminares, Fondo, Reparaciones y Costas), available at www.cor teidh.or.cr/docs/casos/articulos/seriec_329_esp.pdf (accessed 4 June 2019) at para 337.
197 Ibid. at 341.
198 Ibid. at 342.

encompass. For example, Daniela Alaattinoglu suggests that rather than focusing only on training medical staff, the entire state and public should have been directed to learn about and confront discrimination.[199]

## Conclusion

This chapter has explored how the construction of legal categories and the form of legal analysis in women's rights cases can limit the ability of international law to address rights breaches. Emily Snyder amplifies the problems associated with law and legal analysis for Indigenous women in Canada in Chapter 8 of this volume, where she underscores the importance of an intersectional approach to making indigenous laws and state laws more effective for women.[200] Similarly, the illustrations in this chapter show that the absence of an intersectional approach can affect the understanding of the context, scope and impact of rights breaches. The specific case examples employed relate to intersections between race and ethnicity, poverty and gender; however, intersectionality theory is not exclusionary. Recently an intersectional approach has been used to address forced sterilizations against women with HIV. The response by the African Commission on Human and Peoples Rights and the Inter-American Commission and the UN to these involuntary sterilizations of HIV women was to recognize the significance of the women's status as HIV-positive people and to address wider structural discrimination on that basis.[201] This institutional response and the interagency statement on forced sterilization launched by WHO show the positive impact of institutional collaboration in developing rights norms and non-repetition remedies.[202] It is to be hoped that the European Court of Human Rights will also be included in UN collaborations in the future.

There is a need for further reflection also from rights activists as well as from rights institutions. Human rights arose through social movement activity,[203] and as the example of Fujimori population control policy shows, that the support from social movements is critical and its absence can be disadvantageous. In the

199  Daniella Alaattinoglu, "Gender-Sensitive Reparations in the I.V. v. Bolivia Case: A Missed Opportunity?" (2017) *INTLAWGRRLS*, available at https://ilg2.org/2017/03/24/gender-sensitive-reparations-in-the-i-v-v-bolivia-case-a-missed-opportunity/ (accessed 4 June 2019).

200  There is a similar acknowledgement of the significant impact of legal analysis on women's rights in Sta. Maria's analysis of reproductive health laws in the Philippines in Chapter 6 of this volume, and in Irehobhude Iyioha's work on the need for a substantive theory of effectiveness in Chapter 2 of this volume.

201  See Joint Statement by UN human rights experts, the Rapporteur on the Rights of Women of the Inter-American Commission on Human Rights and the Special Rapporteurs on the Rights of Women and Human Rights Defenders of the African Commission on Human and Peoples' Rights, www.achpr.org/news/2015/09/d192/ (accessed 4 June 2019).

202  WHO (2014) *Eliminating, Forced, Coercive and otherwise Involuntary Sterilization: An Interagency Statement*, www.who.int/reproductivehealth/publications/gender_rights/eliminating-forced-sterilization/en/ (accessed 4 June 2019).

203  Neil Stammers, *Human Rights and Social Movements* (London: Pluto Press, 2009).

struggle to apply an intersectional approach to forced sterilization, intersectionality needs to be addressed in all its manifestations – structural, political and representational. Collins and Bilge note that human rights frameworks can assist greatly by providing "ethical protection" and possible remedies for social injustices, but warn that they also lend themselves to an over-emphasis by activists on the judicial processes themselves and a tendency to 'individualize' rather than view social injustice as a 'collective' phenomenon.[204]

Rights activists need to be wary not to essentialize claims or edit out the social context of the claims they campaign for or present for adjudication. This delimitation has sometimes occurred because human rights actors have tried to mirror what they perceive to be the appropriate legal frameworks. Actors also hold their own prejudices, blind spots and their own moral understandings of what are appropriate aims and to what extent pragmatism in achieving aims should outweigh concerns about specific outcomes. These feed into the strategies and priorities put into practice and may unwittingly or otherwise exclude or even work against the interests of marginalized groups. When jurists, activists and academics discuss rights from an intersectional approach and recognize the current limitations of law and the fact that their own perspectives may be influenced or limited by a privileged perspective, they perform a valuable step in addressing the limitations of law and legal strategies.[205]

The aim, is first to recognize intersectional discrimination and then to craft strategies to address it and eradicate injustice.[206] In the context of human rights, this entails, amongst other things, such steps as recognizing the failure of previous remedies and crafting context specific non-repetition remedies. The latter might include duties on States to take positive action to counter and combat discrimination through educational programmes and by promoting positive representation of marginalized groups as the Inter-American Court recommended in *IV v Bolivia*.

The use of law is inherently limited and legal strategies should only ever be a part of wider political mobilization to address discrimination and to secure positive rights to reproductive health and services.[207] Whether engaged in wider political activity or used as a legal strategy, an intersectional approach by rights activists and rights institutions is essential to ensure that legal strategies work effectively to dismantle structural discrimination and to ensure that adjudication does not reinforce negative representations and discriminatory structures.

---

204 Collins and Bilge, *supra* at 97.
205 Ibid. at 98.
206 Ibid. at 91.
207 Cornwall and Molyneux, *The Politics of Rights, supra* and Elizabeth Schneider, "Perspectives from the Women's Movement" in Bartlett and Kennedy, *Feminist Legal Theory, supra*.

# 6 Tilted interpretations

## Reproductive health law and practice in the Philippines

*Amparita Sta. Maria*

## Introduction

The journey towards realizing the goal of having a national law on reproductive health has been highly divisive in the Philippines and its implementation, even at present, continues to be contentious. Generally, health as a human right is not as developed a concept in the country when compared to the civil and political rights found in the Bill of Rights of the Philippine Constitution. The latter have been informed and enriched by jurisprudence over a considerable period of time. Even if one were to assume that the discourse on health as a human right is well entrenched in the legal and policy frameworks of the Philippines, reproductive and sexual health, specifically relating to access to modern contraception, does not enjoy priority as a health need, much less as a health right; in fact, it does not enjoy any priority at all. The enactment of the Magna Carta of Women (MCW) into law in 2009 gave hope that reproductive health would follow soon in the legislative agenda of the lawmakers and the executive department. However, even the passage of both the MCW and the eventual Reproductive Health Law have not translated into full and free realization of the right to reproductive and sexual health in the Philippines.

As background, the passage of laws in the Philippines starts with the elected national and local representatives in the Senate and House of Representatives, collectively known as the Congress.[1] The members of congress sponsor or draft bills for legislative action and, after three readings and much debate, vote on their enactment.[2] There are no guidelines for voting, and members of Congress have full discretion to vote either for or against the enactment of a bill. The bill becomes a law upon signing by the president of the Philippines, after having been approved by both houses.

In 2009, the Republic Act (R.A. 9710)[3] was signed into law. It was initially introduced in the Senate as Senate Bill No. 2396 on 11 June 2008. The bill was prepared by the Senate's Committee on Youth, Women, and Family Relations.

---

1 Ph. Const., art. VI, secs. 2, 5(1).
2 Ph. Const., art. VI, sec. 26(2).
3 R.A. No. 9710.

After more than a year of debate and re-drafting in Congress, the enrolled bill was transmitted to then President Arroyo, who signed it into law on 14 August 2009.[4] The discussion and debates in Congress were relatively uneventful, and the bill itself generated little controversy. The R.A. 9710 substantially incorporated the provisions of the United Nations Convention on the Elimination of All Forms of Discrimination Against Women (CEDAW), which entered into force for the Philippines on 4 September 1981.[5]

More commonly known as the Magna Carta of Women (MCW), the Act lays down a general framework for the protection and promotion of women's rights, beginning with a Declaration of Policy, General Principles of Human Rights, and Definition of Terms (Secs. 2–4). It also makes provisions for the duties (recognition, respect, and promotion) related to the human rights of women owed by the state, private sector, society, and all individuals (Secs. 5–6). The MCW further provides for women's rights and empowerment (Secs. 8–19), the rights and empowerment of marginalized sectors, including women in especially difficult circumstances (Secs. 8–34), and finally the institutional mechanisms for the law's implementation (Secs. 36–42).

Section 3 of the MCW, which articulates the principles of women's human rights, affirms that no one "should suffer discrimination on the basis of ethnicity, gender, age, language, sexual orientation, race, colour, religion, political, or other opinion, national, social, or geographical origin, disability, property, birth, or other status as established by human rights standards". The section also confirms that human rights are universal, inalienable, indivisible, interrelated, interdependent, and cross-cutting – as they relate to civil, cultural, economic, political, or social issues. The section further mentions with particularity the use of a rights-based approach in relation to the participatory rights of women.

> SEC. 3. Principles of Human Rights of Women—
>
> All people have the rights to participate in and access information relating to the decision-making processes that affect their lives and well-being. Rights-based approaches require a high degree of participation by communities, civil society, minorities, women, young people, indigenous peoples, and other identified groups.
>
> States and other duty-bearers are answerable for the observance of human rights. They have to comply with the legal norms and standards enshrined in international human rights instruments in accordance with the Philippine Constitution. Where they fail to do so, aggrieved rights-holders are entitled to institute proceedings for appropriate redress before a competent court or other adjudicator in accordance with the rules and procedures provided by law.

4 Senate of the Philippines (n.d.), *Legislative History of the Magna Carta of Women*, available at www.senate.gov.ph/lis/bill_res.aspx?congress=14&q=SBN-2396 (accessed 20 May 2019).
5 Bayefsky. (n.d.), *Ratification History of the Philippines,* available at www.bayefsky.com//pdf/philippines_t1_ratifications.pdf (accessed 20 May 2019).

Relating this to women's right to health, subsections 17(a) and (b) of the MCW respectively guarantee the provision of comprehensive health services and comprehensive health information and education to women. One of the health services identified in the section is access to "[r]esponsible, ethical, legal, safe, and effective methods of family planning". The law also specifically states that the said services shall be culture-sensitive and gender-responsive. A further qualification to these services is that

> due respect shall be accorded to women's religious convictions, the rights of the spouses to found a family in accordance with their religious convictions and the demands of responsible parenthood, and the right of women to protection from hazardous drugs, devices, interventions, and substances.

The comprehensive health information and education to be provided to women by government through education and training programs shall be "appropriate, timely, complete, and accurate". This provision is qualified by:

1   The natural and primary right and duty of parents in the rearing of the youth and the development of moral character and the right of children to be brought up in an atmosphere of morality and rectitude for the enrichment and strengthening of character;
2   The formation of a person's sexuality that affirms human dignity; and
3   Ethical, legal, safe, and effective family planning methods including fertility awareness. (s. 17(b)).

The MCW is largely framed as general declarations that aim to empower women and recognize their rights. It does not actually express specific duties and obligations which women can immediately demand from the government as right-holders, and which would entail the use of resources. It is largely meant to inform further legislation and set the policy direction for Congress to enact laws that enforce the rights recognized by the MCW. Thus, the passing of the R.A. 10354 – otherwise known as the Responsible Parenthood and Reproductive Health Act of 2012 (RH Law) – three years after the MCW would seem a continuation of the work started by the latter. While the MCW was passed without much controversy, the same cannot be said for the RH Law. In contrast to the relatively quick passing of the MCW, the RH Law languished for 14 years in Congress amidst strong opposition from pro-life groups and the Catholic Church.[6] Members of Congress also had much to say about the various provisions of the then RH Bill, pointing out how the bill allegedly conflicted with deeply held Filipino cultural values, religious beliefs, and traditions.

These three factors – culture, religion, and tradition (CRT) – all played major roles in the laborious task of passing the RH Law. While the RH Law was intended

---

6 World Health Organization (WHO), 2013.

to serve the interests of women by providing for comprehensive health services for women, both the passage and, subsequently, the implementation and interpretation of the law have been colored by political and social dynamics embedded in Philippine culture and governance. Evident in attempts at implementation, especially at the local government level, is the imprint of the deeply held moral considerations that permeate the Philippine legal landscape. This has had implications for the interpretation of the RH Law, leading to skewed interpretations of provisions for comprehensive health services for women – an outcome that challenges the foundations of the concept of women's reproductive autonomy.

Against this background, this chapter examines the role of cultural, religious, and traditional norms in the lawmaking process, as well as in the implementation and interpretation of the RH Law in Philippines. Through a close analysis of the processes that led to the passage of the RH Law, the constitutional challenges against the law and decision of the Philippine Supreme Court, and the flawed attempts at implementation at the local level, the chapter provides an exposé on the contextual role of culture, religion, and tradition in informing and influencing the content – and thereby the utility – of a law protecting women's health. These factors fall within Iyioha's constitutive elements of law, with particular regard to the internalized influences that can act upon, shape, and thereby determine the level of effectiveness of a piece of legislation purportedly created to improve women's health.[7] In expanding this thesis, the chapter applies empirical example drawn from the city of Sorsogon, where there has been an attempt to skew the interpretation of the RH Law to achieve a meaning counter to the underlying goal of improving women's health.

In 2015, the mayor of Sorsogon enacted an ordinance[8] declaring the city as "Pro-Life", citing the Magna Carta of Women as the basis for this decision. A local organization found that on the basis of such ordinance, the local government removed reproductive health services not deemed "pro-life" from local health facilities. The case of Sorsogon City illustrates the disconnect between national law and policy, and local implementation. It shows how the sociocultural landscape of the Philippines enables heads of government units, such as the mayor of a city, to make their personal conviction the determinative policy of an entire constituency. It shows how law can be interpreted differently and used to deprive women of access to reproductive health in the guise of 'protecting women'. To date, the Philippines still faces the dilemma caused by the blurring of lines between secular purpose and personal belief.

In setting out the thesis of this chapter regarding CRT's influence in the collective legislative process and in the interpretation and implementation of the RH law, excerpts of the parliamentary deliberations over the RH Law, which transpired during sessions in both the Senate and the House, provide an ideal starting point for analysis.

---

7 See Iyioha, Chapter 2 of this volume.
8 An Executive Order Declaring Sorsogon City as a Pro-Life City, Executive Order No. 3, Series of 2015, February 2, 2015.

## Congressional deliberations: the role of CRT in lawmaking

As stated earlier, the development of reproductive health in the Philippines has faced various challenges from its introduction to its implementation. Aside from its 14-year struggle in Congress amidst strong opposition from pro-life groups and the Catholic Church,[9] the law was also challenged on constitutional grounds before the Philippine Supreme Court.[10] It is vital to have an understanding of the underlying factors that influence the behavior and decision-making of institutions and individuals wielding considerable authority on reproductive health implementation both at the legislative and policy levels. Despite the clear mandate of the law on providing access to reproductive health services, local governments like Sorsogon City impeded the full implementation of the law through executive ordinances.[11] Thus, to understand the status of reproductive health in the Philippines, it is necessary to identify the societal and individual factors that influence the country's position on reproductive health.

The relationship between the individual and the society is a key subject of interest among sociological scholars. To understand the dynamics of a given society, the two-way relationship between the individual and the society naturally forms part of the discourse. Individuals are influenced by society as much as the broader social environment influences the individual.[12] Individuals, as members of society, are influenced by dominant institutions of socialization, including religious, cultural, educational, and political institutions. The pedagogical influences of these institutions, as well as the individual attachment overtime to acquired or learned views and beliefs, can and do have a significant effect on both individual morality and broader societal ethos.[13] In the context of the Philippines, this symbiotic relationship between citizen and society has created special affinities for particular causes or matters and made them issues for impassioned national debate. For the Philippine society, the subject of reproductive health is one such issue. Both strongly divisive and intractable, it permeates the cultural, religious, and political spheres, blurring the lines between church and state.

In order to fully appreciate the philosophies and attitudes about the subject of reproductive health in the Philippines, it is necessary to understand that the socio-political landscape of the country, where policymakers and local government

---

9 World Health Organization (7 January 2013), *The Philippines Passes Reproductive Health Law* (accessed 10 June 2016 from The Partnership for Maternal, Newborn, & Child Health: www.who.int/pmnch/media/news/2013/20130107_philippines_reproductive_health_law/en/ (accessed 20 May 2019).

10 *James M. Imbong et al. vs. Hon. Paquito N. Ochoa*, G.R. No. 204819 (Supreme Court of the Philippines April 8, 2014) ('*Imbong v Ochoa*').

11 Commission on Human Rights (8 April 2016), *CHR Probes Violations of RH Law*, available at http://chr.gov.ph/chr-probes-violations-of-rh-law/ (accessed 2 June 2019).

12 M. Larkin, *Social Aspects of Health, Illness, and Healthcare* (New York: Open University Press, 2011).

13 Ibid.

leaders hold considerable influence over the implementation of laws regarding women's reproductive health, is deeply intertwined with the cultural and the religious.[14] The extent to which culture, religion, and tradition permeated the parliamentary debates on Philippine's Reproductive Health Law provides context and useful insights into the role of these factors in shaping laws on women's health. Parliamentarians on both ends of the RH Law debate invoked CRT in one way or another. However, it was primarily those who opposed the law who relied heavily on CRT to support their arguments. In the interest of achieving clarity on the centrality of CRT to the discussions around the very existence and content of the RH Law, it is important to review the parliamentary arguments proffered by opponents to the law.

One argument, strongly advocated by Senator Vicente "Tito" Sotto III (Sotto) – a staunch opponent of the RH Law – draws an ideological line between CRT values in the Philippines and foreign philosophies, and exhorts the state to stay out of the right of citizens and their families to make their own reproductive health decisions. Senator Sotto was, however, only one of the many who claimed that the then RH bill should not be passed because family planning and the use of contraceptives were allegedly not in line with Filipino culture and traditions. In his first *turno en contra* speech, which he delivered on 13 August 2012, he stated:

> Today, we will define ourselves again, Mr. President, as we decide whether we shall adopt a measure that is dictated by outside cultures, forces and philosophies, or we shall be true to our Filipino reverence for human life, the solidarity of the family, and the right of parents to determine their family size without interference from the State.[15]

Continuing his speech two days later, Senator Sotto added:

> The fact that other countries are doing it does not mean that we have to do the same. We have to remember that we have different cultures, history, and traditions, and most importantly, needs. Who are they to dictate on us [*sic*]? We are not like them in terms of valuing family unity and human life. Other countries have a different attitude.[16]

Beyond drawing on nationalistic sentiments in his 'us-versus-them' iterations, Senator Sotto also tried to establish that dissemination of information on family planning and the use of contraceptives were part of a greater plan to get rid of supposed "weaker" members of the population. In other words, the RH bill, he argued, was part of "eugenics". He tried to do this by making a supposedly

---

14 Like in most Western democracies, the political system is composed of the executive, legislative, and judiciary branches of government: The Constitution of the Republic of the Philippines, 1987, Arts. VI, VII, VIII ('Philippine Constitution').
15 Senate of the Philippines, (2012) – Record, August 13, 2012 (p. 14).
16 Ibid.

logical jump, from the fact that Margaret Sanger, founder of the International Planned Parenthood Federation, one of the most active international organizations advocating family planning, is also an alleged advocate of eugenics.

The connection between this form of argument and the influence of culture, religion, and traditions in women's reproductive health rights and well-being in the Philippines became more evident as his speech progressed from Planned Parenthood and eugenics to a narrative about an alleged meeting between Margaret Sanger and Mahatma Gandhi. He said Gandhi firmly stood by his belief that the spiritual bonds of marriage are strengthened by sexual abstinence. On this basis, he completely rejected Sanger's plea for contraception as a tool to control population growth, fearing it would lead to an increase in non-procreative sex, which he viewed as immoral lust. Senator Sotto narrated that Gandhi's general attitude was that

> Persons who use contraceptives will never learn the value of self-restraint. They will not need it. Self-indulgence with contraceptives may prevent the coming of children but will sap the vitality of both men and women, perhaps more of men than of women. It is unmanly to refuse battle with the devil.
>
> Between a person who had been actively promoting free sex, eugenics and birth control and a person like Gandhi who was an advocate of nonviolence, discipline, chastity, control of the palate, who should we believe? Whose footsteps should we follow? Whose teachings are more in line with Filipino traditions and beliefs? It is very clear; the question is easy to answer.[17]

When another senator, Ralph Recto, proposed an amendment to the bill to prohibit minors from accessing modern methods of family planning without written consent from their parents or guardians, Senator Sotto agreed with it, drawing his own parallel between the amendment and the requirement in the country's Family Code for those persons aged 18 to 21 who wish to get married to obtain parental consent. From this comparison, Senator Sotto concluded that allowing minors access to modern methods of family planning without parental consent would be tantamount to the State sanctioning premarital sex. From these conclusions, it is evident that Senator Sotto, and perhaps others who held the same position as him, were primarily concerned with the issue of morality, in this case the notion of the immorality of premarital sex, as opposed to the more fundamental issue of the preservation of the health of minors who engage in such. This emphasis on sex only within marriage is rooted in the Catholic/Christian teaching that sex should only be allowed within marriage, and should only be done for procreation. More evidence of this perspective came later when Senator Sotto introduced another amendment to the RH bill to include faith-based organizations in the definition of an NGO. In his words:

17 Ibid.

I believe we should include the views of religious groups such as Muslims, Iglesia ni Cristo, Buddhist, Seventh-Day Adventist, Methodist, Christians, Roman Catholics and other religious organizations of what constitutes reproductive health to them and their views on population and development policies, plans and programs [*sic*]. So, the inclusion of faith-based organizations is necessary.[18]

Another argument used by opponents of the bill was that the RH Bill promotes abortion because it does not consider fertilization as the point of conception when life allegedly begins.[19] Senator Sotto argued vehemently and tried to demonstrate that conception, and therefore life, begins at fertilization by citing local and foreign medical authorities.[20] As Iyioha highlights in her discussion on law, normative limits, and women's health, this strategy – which is a mainstay of pro-lifers – is similar to that employed by pro-life groups in Canada's Prince Edward Island in their successful struggle in the eighties to make the province a 'pro-life province'.[21] Specifically, as Iyioha argues, this tactic draws on local and foreign 'scientific' evidence to counter the narrative regarding the social and medical utility of abortion rights, thereby using an expectation regarding law – that is, law's expected congruence with logically or scientifically correct phenomena – to further their goal of limiting the application of abortion rights in the province.[22] In the case of the Philippines, the goal at this early stage of the legal process was to scuttle any such rights before the passage of the law.

Later in the process, during the period of amendments, another senator, Juan Ponce Enrile, tried to insert an amendment in the bill's definition of terms where conception (and therefore life) is defined as beginning from fertilization.[23] The proposed amendment read as follows:

(E) CONCEPTION – refers to the successful penetration of an ovum by spermatozoa in the fallopian tube, otherwise known as fertilization, when a new life begins to form in the mother's womb.

The sponsors of the bill argued against this amendment pointing out that science, its experts, and those in the medical field, have not been able to determine exactly when life begins, and that it was beyond the power of lawmakers to legislate on the same.[24] Senator Defensor-Santiago argued that the suggested

---

18 Senate of the Philippines (2012) – Record, September 5, 2012 (p. 42).
19 Senate, Republic of the Philippines (22 August 2011). Session No. 11. *Senate Journal*, pp. 163–188.
20 Ibid.
21 See Iyioha, Chapter 2 of this volume.
22 Ibid.
23 Senate of the Philippines, 2012.
24 Ibid.

definition could not be accepted as there is disagreement among philosophers, theologians, scientists, and so forth as to when life begins.[25] She further argued that current medical knowledge has not as yet determined when life begins, though scientific evidence points out that pregnancy starts at implantation.[26]

It is interesting to observe the introduction of science into the discourse when the intended goal was *denying* or *limiting* a right, even though debates around the *grant* of reproductive health rights were generally focused, not on the scientific evidence supporting the grant of rights, but on the cultural, religious and traditional reasons for a denial of those rights. Nonetheless, in spite of the transitory debate on the scientific evidence (or lack thereof) on when life begins, religion was the most obvious "theme" of the oppositionist arguments during the debates in Congress.

Arguments based on culture and tradition would also surface as significant factors that the parliamentarians wanted to apply to determine the conceptual framework of the RH Law. For example, parliamentary discussion on whether or not the "right to [a] safe and satisfying sex life" should be recognized and embodied in the law, highlights the influence that the perceived "Filipino culture" has on even the simplest details like what words or language – which Iyioha identifies as a key 'internal' limit to law's effectiveness[27] – should be used in the law. In two separate instances, heated debates ensued when certain senators insisted that the law be amended to recognize only "safe sex/a safe sex life". Senator Sotto adamantly insisted that he would have no part in a law that explicitly mentions the phrase "safe and *satisfying* sex life" because, in his own words, "*masagwang tingnan eh* (It is lewd.)" Senators Francis "Chiz" Escudero and Jose "Jinggoy" Ejercito-Estrada Jr. also voiced their discomfort in using the phrase in question. To these concerns, Senator Alan Peter Cayetano responded:

> What is the discomfort with that phrase? Is it because we are prude, meaning, *hindi lamang natin gustong ilagay iyong language na iyan kasi pagkamalan tayong malaswa tayo*? (We do not want to include that language because we might appear lewd?) Or is there something inherently wrong with a safe and satisfying love life and sex life? I do believe that many here are also arguing from religious points of view. The Bible does say that we should not deny our body to the other except during times of prayer. Sex life is part of a relationship.
>
> It does not sound *malaswa* (lewd). So, if we are saying that the English term is *malaswa*, then let us find another term. But, if we are just saying we are uncomfortable because we are more prude and we are more conservative, do we sacrifice the substance of that paragraph just to satisfy our being prude?[28]

25 Ibid.
26 Senate of the Philippines, 2012 at 14.
27 See Iyioha, Chapter 2 of this volume.
28 Senate of the Philippines, 2012 at 42.

During the December 17 hearing, the same controversy arose. The use of the phrase "safe and satisfying sex life" was again put in issue. Senator Sotto took the opportunity to clarify his stand. To wit:

> The reason I wanted to remove the whole phrase originally, Mr. President, is that I believe that reproductive health, in the context of a true Filipina, does not pertain to "safe and *satisfying* sex". When a true Filipina speaks of reproductive health, she means family, marriage and responsible parenthood, nurturing and rearing her children, the health of the mother. I want to take into consideration our culture as Filipinos. There are things that are acceptable to our culture but not to others. There are things which are unique to our culture.[29]

Clearly, pre-conceived notions of Filipino culture, as well as ideas of what a "true Filipina" is, became a factor during the deliberations. To the RH opponents, the bill was conceptually antithetical to Filipino culture and traditions. This thinking carried on well past the debates up to the voting, when some Senators repeated their sentiments regarding the bill and the Filipino culture. Senators Ejercito-Estrada and Ramon "Bong" Revilla Jr., for instance, explained their votes respectively as follows:

> Now, the most compelling reason being forwarded by anti-RH proponents is on moral grounds, that this measure is anti-family and anti-life, and that it effectively tramples on and despoils Filipino culture and family values. It is on this issue that I feel most strongly about. I believe that our morality will deteriorate and our culture and tradition will lose their worth, when we should cherish them [Senator Ejercito-Estrada].
>
> What we need is a law attuned to our unique culture. It is wrong to follow the lead of our neighboring countries if it is contrary to our customs and beliefs as a nation, which values responsible parenthood within the sacred institution of marriage [Senator Revilla].[30]

Other senators, like Recto, also argued against the RH bill on the bases of culture, religion, and tradition. During one interpellation, he noted that as far as he knows, there is no Barangay (the smallest political unit or a basic political unit, municipality, or city in the Philippines) which celebrates infertility, and that community celebrations are often associated with pregnancy, or at least fertility. This statement was immediately affirmed by Senator Sotto, confirming that Filipinos treat children as gifts or blessings from God. He further stated that

> Apparently, when you look at the history of reproductive health – I am not saying that it will happen in the Philippines – but the aforementioned eastern

29 Senate, Republic of the Philippines (17 December 2012). Session No. 44, Fifteenth Congress, Third Regular Session. *Senate Journal*, pp. 1272–1311 ('Senate, Republic of the Philippines').
30 Ibid.

tradition of celebrating life does not arise from the western concept of reproductive health. We have feasts to celebrate life, right? I do not know of any
feast to celebrate death, right? All right.[31]

The use of the contextual factors of culture, religion, and tradition as instruments to shape the making of the RH Law was not limited to those who opposed
the provisions of the then RH Bill. Legislators who supported the bill were not
insulated from the influence of CRT. While he voted for the passage of the RH
bill, Senator Arroyo noted that "there are statements of policy equating human
life with mere economic value that are obnoxious to Christian morals [and that]
[t]here are provisions that violate religious conscience and establish secular
humanism as supreme over all other belief systems".[32] Even the principal sponsor
herself, Senator Pia Cayetano, in one of the interpellations, noted that Filipino
culture played a role in the formulation of certain provisions.

In explaining the provision requiring health service providers to provide
humane and compassionate treatment for women suffering from complications
arising from abortions, the senator said:

> As we know, Mr. President, Filipinos are known to espouse a culture of
> kindness and empathy. In fact, we are world-class nurses and caregivers. We
> uphold the tradition of reaching out and extending genuine care and health-
> care, in particular, to those in need both in our country and out of the coun-
> try, more so, for women who are pregnant and in need of special care at this
> time. And that is the reason for this provision.[33]

## Opposition against the RH Bill: five common grounds

Debates in both the lower and upper houses of Congress showed indications
of the kind of role CRT plays in defining national policies and crafting laws. To
better understand the dynamics of the legislative process with all the nuances
introduced by CRT, it is useful to examine the five common grounds of opposition that permeated the discussion in both the House of Representatives and the
Senate. These grounds are:

1  The tendency to equate one's personal beliefs and values with the public
   interest or general welfare.
2  The emphatic and continuous references to the pro-life stance of the Catholic Church.
3  The perception that the RH bill was a threat to the preservation of Filipino
   culture and traditions.

---

31  Ibid.
32  *Record*, September 5, 2012, 15th Session, Third Regular Session, Fifteenth Congress, Senate
    of the Philippines, p. 80.
33  Ibid. at 42.

4   The alleged need to protect women from "harmful" reproductive health methods.
5   The redundancy of the RH Bill due to existing laws and measures protecting and promoting women's right to health.

### *The tendency to equate one's personal beliefs and values with the public interest or general welfare*

First, in the context of the RH bill, the wide discretion given representatives in making their decisions proved to be a challenge, which needed to be overcome. While the guiding principle for all public officers is to ensure the general welfare of the public, in the case of the RH Bill, opponents often equated the fulfillment of their own personal agendas and beliefs with the fulfillment of general welfare. During the deliberations on the RH Bill in Congress, it was not uncommon for representatives to cite personal beliefs and their "conscience" as basis for their opposition.

In the second reading of the RH Bill in the House of Representatives for example, Saranggani Representative and internationally renowned boxer, Emmanuel "Manny" Pacquiao, voted 'no' to the bill's passage, stating: "*Ang buhay ay sagrado, . . . hindi kailangan dapat ilagay sa kamay ng kanyang kapwa tao, tanging ang Diyos ang may karapatan dito*" (Life is sacred . . . It should not be put in the hands of humans, only God has the right over it).[34] Pampanga Representative, Aurelio Gonzalez, also voted against the bill because it was the dying wish of his mother.[35] Representative Jun Alcover Jr. of the Alliance for Nationalism and Democracy (ANAD) Party-List also voted against the bill's passing, stating: "[W]e consider this Bill an evil one and the target of this Bill is the Catholic Church. ANAD Party-List will follow the Church. We will not follow the dictates of Malacañang (the seat of the presidency)".[36] The representative further stated that the bill was a product of "godless elements" and asked God to forgive those "elements".[37] Another representative declared that "[t]he legislature has no business interfering with [the] natural law and the law of God unless one is an atheist".[38]

It was actually ironic when one senator justified his vote as not influenced by religion, but at the same time admitted that his vote was rooted in his personal belief. In his own words: "[L]et it not be said that my vote today is

---

34  Jess Diaz, *Pacquiao, Other Celebrity House Members Voted 'No' on RH*, PHILSTAR, available at www.philstar.com/headlines/2012/12/14/885816/pacquiao-other-celebrity-house-members-voted-no-rh (accessed 2 June 2019). Pampanga Representative, Aurelio Gonzalez, also voted against the bill because it was the dying wish of his parents.
35  Ibid.
36  House of Representatives (2012), 15th Congress, Third Regular Session. *Congressional Record, 2* (40), 1–49 ('House of Representatives, 2012').
37  Ibid.
38  Ibid.

Church-influenced or politically motivated. This is my own personal stand".[39] Another senator also declared: "[T]hese are my considerations: my faith, my conscience and my notion of what is in the long-term interest of this country that impelled me to cast the vote of NO on the bill [*sic*]".[40]

### Continuous references to the pro-life stance of the Catholic Church

Second, emphatic and continuous references to the Catholic Church's pro-life stance pervaded the deliberations of the RH Law. This was manifest in legislative debates in both the Senate and the House of Representatives on the definition of "conception" or the beginning of life. There were prolonged discussions as to whether or not certain contraceptive methods were "abortifacients" or result in the termination of a fertilized ovum. In her response in a Senate session, Senator Pia Cayetano stated that the debate on the RH Bill is "based mostly on the opinions of peoples with different backgrounds", but emphasized that her mandate, as a senator, was to come to a decision that will be applicable to every Filipino, not to a particular religion.[41] There were also anti-RH legislators who even prayed for the forgiveness of God in the event that the bill was passed into law.[42]

The influence of religion on the RH Bill proceedings was so pervasive that those who voted in favor of the RH Bill felt the need to defend their votes against perceptions that they were godless or "evil". House Representative Arlene "Kaka" Bag-Ao, for example, explained that her affirmative vote for the RH Bill was "not just a question of religion or of faith, but of integrity". She also acknowledged the authority of Church leadership but maintained that Congress should listen to the voice of the people.[43] Another senator invoked the Church's teachings on "conscience" and how such teachings were not against the RH Bill.[44]

### The RH Bill as a threat to the preservation of Filipino culture and traditions

A third common ground that generated much discussion at the debates was the continued influence of what is perceived as Filipino culture. One house representative voted against the bill on the conviction "that the RH Bill [was] not right for this nation because it [went] against *the moral grain that the Filipino family is made of*".[45]

To be fair, references to religion, culture and tradition are not by themselves inherently problematic. Even the Committee on the International Covenant on

---

39 Senate, Republic of the Philippines, 2012.
40 Ibid.
41 Senate, Republic of the Philippines, 2011.
42 Senate, Republic of the Philippines, 2012.
43 House of Representatives, 2012.
44 Senate, Republic of the Philippines, 2012.
45 House of Representatives, 2012. Emphasis supplied.

Economic, Social and Cultural Rights in General Comment No. 14 (The Right to the Highest Attainable Standard of Health)[46] has emphasized that "health services should be culturally appropriate, taking into account traditional preventive care, healing practices and medicines".[47] Thus, the critique by one representative – who said that the bill is not "culturally sensitive in handling the sexuality education of youths, especially those in provinces where youths are not as sexually awakened as those in highly urbanized areas due to the influence of foreign and local media, dysfunctional families, and peer pressure" – deserves further attention.[48] While that is beyond the scope of this chapter, there is no reason why there should be a blanket denial of reproductive health services to women based on incompatibilities between reproductive health rights and the personal moral convictions of some elected officials.

Promiscuity was also a recurring issue in the debates, and legislators opposed the RH Bill on the ground that it seemingly encouraged promiscuity and pre-marital sex among youths. This argument, however, was also used in support of the RH Bill. During the vote for the RH Bill, a senator acknowledged that sex is a taboo subject in the Philippines, but through the RH Bill, citizens will be more informed of "how to best deal with their bodies and physical health".[49]

### A protectionist approach over women and their right to health

References to religion and the Catholic Church pervaded the discussion of the RH Bill in both the Senate and the House of Representatives. The rhetoric translated to the "protection" of women from contraceptive methods that anti-RH proponents link to chronic illnesses and diseases. The bill was also challenged as being an affront to women's health due to its endorsement of contraceptives and sterilization[50] and for allegedly "sacrificing the well-being of women and the unborn children in their wombs".[51] In a personal narrative, one senator alleged that the death of his unborn child was due to a complication caused by the use of contraceptive pills.[52]

### The redundancy of the RH Bill due to existing laws and measures

Anti-RH legislators also used existing laws on women's rights as reason to brand the bill as unnecessary and redundant. The existence of the Magna Carta for Women and the domestic implementation of CEDAW were used as reasons to block the progress of the RH Bill. This is obviously absurd because the Magna

---

46  See Article 12.
47  Ibid. at para 27.
48  House of Representatives, 2012.
49  Senate, Republic of the Philippines, 2012.
50  House of Representatives, 2012.
51  Senate, Republic of the Philippines, 2012.
52  Ibid.

Carta for Women provides for measures for women's right to health while the RH Bill seeks to expand this right to health.

As an explanation to his vote against the bill, Senator Antonio "Sonny" Trillanes IV explained:

> I have reviewed our existing laws on reproductive health and family planning and I have discovered that there are in fact more than twenty laws and executive issuances dealing with these issues. These laws and executive orders provide an adequate policy framework or platform. . . . In short, the RH Bill is not necessary and indispensable [*sic*].[53]

There were also extensive discussions comparing the RH Bill to existing laws to illustrate its redundancies. Apart from the Magna Carta of Women, the laws and measures that were deemed sufficient in providing for a reproductive health framework were the executive orders on maternal and neonatal mortality, Republic Act No. 7875 (the National Health Insurance Act of 1995), Republic Act No. 9502 (the Cheaper Medicines Act), programs of the Department of Health, and Philippine Health Insurance Corporation circulars, policies, and regulations, among others.[54]

### CRT and the adjudication process: the challenge before the Supreme Court

Once passed, the constitutionality of the law was immediately challenged by fourteen petitioners and two intervenors, representing various groups opposing modern contraceptive methods.[55] The constitutional challenge to the RH Law is relevant to the foregoing analysis because it further emphasizes the primacy of the role of CRT in the legal process. As we would see in the following discussion, CRT formed the basis of the constitutional challenge to the law and constituted major elements in the court's adjudication and decision.

Three main areas of the law were contested by petitioners/intervenors. First, the petitioners alleged that the RH law violated the constitutional protection given to the life and health of the unborn child because it allows access to, and use of, "abortifacients" such as contraceptives that accordingly "[result] in abortion as they operate to kill the fertilized ovum which already has life". Petitioners argued that the RH Law contravenes Article II, section 12 of the Philippine Constitution, which provides:

---

53 Senate, Republic of the Philippines (22 August 2011), Session No. 11, *Senate Journal*, pp. 163–188. Senate, Republic of the Philippines (17 December 2011). Senate, Republic of the Philippines, 2012, *supra*.

54 Senate, Republic of the Philippines (22 August 2011), *supra*.

55 *Imbong v Ochoa*, *supra*. In the Philippines, as is the case in the United States and other societies, these challengers are known as the "pro-life" faction. At the other end of the ideological divide are those in favor of the RH-bill, the "pro-choice" group.

The State recognizes the sanctity of family life and shall protect and strengthen the family as a basic autonomous social institution. It shall equally protect the life of the mother and the life of the unborn from conception. The natural and primary right and duty of parents in the rearing of the youth for civic efficiency and the development of moral character shall receive the support of the Government.[56]

In resolving this issue, the court first dealt with the question of when life begins. Based on the deliberations of the 1987 constitutional convention, medical literature, and the position paper by the Philippine Medical Association, it ruled that the moment of conception, as articulated in the Constitution begins from fertilization. It also found that the RH law did not violate the relevant section of the Constitution since it only allows access to reproductive health services and supplies that are "non-abortifacient".[57] Under the law, the term "abortifacient" "refers to any drug or device that induces abortion or the destruction of a fetus inside the mother's womb or the prevention of the fertilized ovum to reach and be implanted in the mother's womb upon determination of the FDA [*sic*]".[58]

However, the court struck down two provisions in the law's Implementing Rules and Regulations (IRR), which qualified the meaning of "abortifacients" and "contraceptives" with the word "primarily". In other words, in the IRR, a drug or device is considered an abortifacient if its purpose is to *primarily* induce abortion, destroy a fetus, or prevent the implantation of a fertilized ovum.[59] In the opinion of the court, in the absence of a qualifying word in the main law, the Implementing Rules and Regulation cannot qualify abortifacients as only those that primarily induce abortion; for, even if the drug has a secondary effect of inducing abortion, it is still an abortifacient. The IRR defined a contraceptive as:

(j) . . . [a]ny safe, legal, effective and scientifically proven modern family planning method, device, or health product, whether natural or artificial, that prevents pregnancy but does not primarily destroy a fertilized ovum or prevent a fertilized ovum from being implanted in the mother's womb in doses of its approved indication as determined by the Food and Drug Administration (FDA).

The court emphasized that adding the word *primarily* "[would] pave the way for the approval of contraceptives which may harm or destroy the life of the unborn from conception/fertilization" since "a contraceptive will only be considered as an 'abortifacient' if its sole known effect is abortion or, as pertinent here, the prevention of the implantation of the fertilized ovum".[60] It added that

---

56 *Imbong v Ochoa, supra.*
57 Section 3 [d].
58 Sec. 4[a]; FDA – Food and Drug Administration.
59 Sec. 301[a].
60 *Imbong v Ochoa, supra.*

for contraceptives to be allowed, they must also not have "the secondary action of acting the same way". Thus, the court considered these two provisions of the IRR violative of the constitution.

The second area objected to by the petitioners involved the issue of consent – both concerning parental and marital consent – to reproductive health services. The legal question was whether the consent provisions of the RH Law, which extended decision-making powers to spouses and parents of women and minors respectively interested in reproductive health services violated the Philippine Constitution. Section 7, paragraph 2 of the RH Law, which addresses parental consent, provides:

> No person shall be denied information and access to family planning services, whether natural or artificial, provided that minors will not be allowed access to modern methods of family planning without written consent from their parents or guardian/s except when the minor is already a parent or has had a miscarriage.

The court found this section in contravention of the constitutional mandate "to protect and strengthen the family as an inviolable social institution". It also stated that it was "deplorable" for the provision to prevent a parent from participating in the decision-making process of a minor with regard to family planning just because the minor already suffered a miscarriage or is a parent herself. The only exceptions where parental consent is no longer required are in cases of emergency procedures and elective procedures "where the parent or the person exercising parental authority is the respondent, accused or convicted perpetrator as certified by the proper prosecutorial office of the court".[61]

Another area of legal contention was the RH Law provision on marital consent. The RH Law imposed a penalty on healthcare providers, both public and private, who refuse to "perform legal and medically-safe reproductive health procedures on any person of legal age on the ground of lack of [s]pousal consent in case of married persons: Provided that in case of disagreement, the decision of the one undergoing the procedure shall prevail".[62] To this provision, the court ruled that except in life-threatening cases, decisions on reproductive health procedures involve the mutual consent of husband and wife as they relate to the right to found a family. Citing Article XV, section 3(1) of the Constitution mandating the state to defend the right of spouses to found a family, the court said that founding a family is a shared right and decisions involving reproductive health procedures such as tubal ligation and vasectomy belong to both spouses, not to just one of them. The court further said:

> The RH Law cannot be allowed to infringe upon this mutual decision-making. By giving absolute authority to the spouse who would undergo a

61  Sec. 23(a) [2.ii].
62  Sec. 23(a) [2.i].

procedure and barring the other spouse from participating in the decision would drive a wedge between the husband and wife, possibly result in bitter animosity, and endanger the marriage and the family, all for the sake of reducing the population. This would be a marked departure from the policy of the State to protect marriage as an inviolable social institution.[63]

The third issue objected to by the petitioners dealt with penalties for breaches of duties and obligations imposed under the RH Law. Petitioners claimed that the duties and obligations violated their religious freedom and threatened their right to conscientious objection. The court agreed with the petitioners and found no compelling state interest "to justify the infringement of the conscientious objector's religious freedom". It is important to set out in some detail the ruling of the court:

> The Court is of the view that the obligation to refer imposed by the RH Law violates the religious belief and conviction of a conscientious objector. Once the medical practitioner, against his will, refers a patient seeking information on modern reproductive health products, services, procedures and methods, his conscience is immediately burdened as he has been compelled to perform an act against his beliefs.
>
> Though it has been said that the act of referral is an opt-out clause, it is, however, a false compromise because it makes pro-life health providers complicit in the performance of an act that they find morally repugnant or offensive. They cannot, in conscience, do indirectly what they cannot do directly. One may not be the principal, but he is equally guilty if he abets the offensive act by indirect participation.
>
> Moreover, the guarantee of religious freedom is necessarily intertwined with the right to free speech, it being an externalization of one's thought and conscience. This in turn includes the right to be silent. With the constitutional guarantee of religious freedom follows the protection that should be afforded to individuals in communicating their beliefs to others as well as the protection for simply being silent. The Bill of Rights guarantees the liberty of the individual to utter what is in his mind and the liberty not to utter what is not in his mind (citing the separate opinion of Justice Cruz in *Ebralinag v. Division Superintendent of Schools* G.R. No. 95770, March 1, 1993). While the RH Law seeks to provide freedom of choice through informed consent, freedom of choice guarantees the liberty of the religious conscience and prohibits any degree of compulsion or burden, whether direct or indirect, in the practice of one's religion (citing *Estrada v. Escritor*, A.M. No. P-02–1651, August 4, 2003).
>
> In case of conflict between the religious beliefs and moral convictions of individuals, on one hand, and the interest of the State, on the other, to provide access and information on reproductive health products, services,

---

63 Citing Art. XV, sec. 2, Philippine Constitution.

procedures and methods to enable the people to determine the timing, number and spacing of the birth of their children, the Court is of the strong view that the religious freedom of health providers, whether public or private, should be accorded primacy. Accordingly, a conscientious objector should be exempt from compliance with the mandates of the RH Law. If he would be compelled to act contrary to his religious belief and conviction, it would be violative of "the principle of non-coercion" enshrined in the constitutional right to free exercise of religion.

In upholding the petitioners' freedom of religion and their standing as conscientious objectors, the Supreme Court struck down the penal provisions regarding both the referral system and any act manifesting a refusal to support the reproductive health programs under the law. Overall, while declaring Law "R.A. No. 10354 as [n]ot unconstitutional", the court declared unconstitutional the following provisions of the law:

> 2) Section 23(a)(1) and the corresponding provision in the RH-IRR, particularly Section 5.24 thereof, insofar as they punish any healthcare service provider who fails and or refuses to disseminate information regarding programs and services on reproductive health regardless of his or her religious beliefs.
>
> . . .
>
> 5) Section 23(a)(3) and the corresponding provision in the RH-IRR, particularly Section 5.24 thereof, insofar as they punish any healthcare service provider who fails and/or refuses to refer a patient not in an emergency or life-threatening case, as defined under Republic Act No. 8344, to another health care service provider within the same facility or one which is conveniently accessible regardless of his or her religious beliefs;
>
> 6) Section 23(b) and the corresponding provision in the RH-IRR, particularly Section 5.24 thereof, insofar as they punish any public officer who refuses to support reproductive health programs or shall do any act that hinders the full implementation of a reproductive health program, regardless of his or her religious beliefs;
>
> 7) Section 17 and the corresponding provision in the RH-IRR regarding the rendering of pro bono reproductive health service in so far as they affect the conscientious objector in securing PhilHealth[64] accreditation.

As can be seen above, conscientious objection was sustained not only because the provision guaranteed and sustained the right of conscientious objectors to refuse patients access to "modern" reproductive health services but also because the provisions could not be used to compel conscientious objectors to refer patients to other healthcare providers who would be willing to perform such services. Furthermore, since the penalties were ruled out by the court on

---

64 Acronym for the Philippine Health Insurance Corporation.

constitutional grounds, an objector, whether he or she belongs to the public or private sector, would have the right to withhold information to a patient whose preference for reproductive service is against the objectors' religious beliefs. It should also be noted that under Section 23(b) of the law, no penalty can be imposed on public officers who shall refuse "to support reproductive health programs; or shall do any act that hinders the full implementation of a reproductive health program" (Sec. 23(b)). Save for giving misinformation about modern reproductive healthcare, a public officer can manifest his or her non-support and interference in the implementation of the law without suffering any penalty for doing so. It can be said, therefore, that in balancing the freedom of religion of the provider against the right to health of the patient, the former is clearly considered paramount as far as reproductive health is concerned.

## CRT and the implementation process: hurdling the challenges of RH implementation

The RH Bill finally passed the halls of Congress despite staunch opposition on 21 December 2012. However, this has not translated into smooth implementation of the law. Obstacles to the full implementation of the RH Law persisted at the level of the local government to a point that the Commission on Human Rights had to launch an inquiry on violations of the RH Law. The inquiry was prompted by various reports of local government units passing ordinances and other policies "that impact upon women's access to reproductive health services".[65]

At the level of Congress, once again, the budget allocation for contraceptives was removed during the deliberations of the Senate and House Bicameral Conference Committee. This will undoubtedly have a huge impact on the operations of the Department of Health, which is mandated by the RH Law to "procure, distribute to local government units, and monitor the usage of family planning supplies for the whole country.[66]

### Earlier obstacles to reproductive health implementation in general (the case of the Barangay Ayala Alabang)

Prior to the enactment of the RH Law, other legal mechanisms existed to provide for access to reproductive health, although not in the specific manner provided for in the RH law. The Department of Health had existing programs on

65 Commission on Human Rights of the Philippines (8 April 2016), *CHR Probes Violations of RH Law*, available at http://chr.gov.ph/chr-probes-violations-of-rh-law (accessed 2 June 2019).

66 J.Y. Geronimo, *What Happened to the 2016 Budget for Contraceptives?* (7 January 2016), available at www.rappler.com/nation/118239-explanation-no-2016-budget-contraceptives (accessed 20 May 2019). See also the Republic of the Philippines, *RH Law Implementation Continues Despite Budget Cut* (14 January 2016), Official Gazette of the Republic of the Philippines, available at www.officialgazette.gov.ph/2016/01/14/reproductive-health-law-continues/ (accessed 2 June 2019).

reproductive health and family planning. However, these measures were further impeded by the issuance and implementation of ordinances limiting access to reproductive health.

One such instance is in Barangay Ayala Alabang, in the city of Muntinlupa, wherein a Barangay Ordinance was enacted to "provide for the safety and protection of the unborn child within the territorial jurisdiction of Barangay Ayala Alabang".[67] In the Declaration of Barangay Policies in the Ordinance, the Sanggunian[68] Barangay of Ayala Alabang stated that they support the State's recognition (in the Constitution) of the "role of women in nation-building". The ordinance also "*protects*" the rights of women, particularly –

> The BARANGAY as well (a) endorses the view that contraceptives and the IUD may kill children and injure the health of women who use them; (b) condemns the irresponsible and indiscriminate use of contraceptives as they undermine the solidarity of families by promoting premarital sex, giving rise to more fatherless children, more single mothers, more poverty, and more abortions when the contraceptives fail to prevent conception, and by causing a decline of legitimate marriages, and (c) denounces the use of condoms as far as they promote and sanction immoral sexual congresses among the unmarried and especially among the young, thereby contradicting the Constitutional injunction that the State "shall promote and protect . . . the physical, moral, spiritual, intellectual and social well-being" of the youth.[69]

To fulfill the objectives of the ordinance, the Sanggunian Barangay focused on natural family planning for married couples and those engaged to be married because "it strengthens rather than weakens the marriage bond".[70] The ordinance also encouraged "legal", moral, and healthy sexual relationships pursuant to the laws of the country as well as to religious convictions.[71] The Barangay Health Unit, in charge of health service delivery, was also enjoined to use safe, ethical, effective, legal, and non-abortifacient medicines or drugs, or machines, devices, or methods. The definition for abortifacients, apart from medicine and methods that endanger or cause the expulsion of the fetus, included intrauterine devices and hormonal contraceptives. A prescription was also required for the purchase of any medicine containing abortive or anti-conceptional substances, and required that such purchase must also be recorded in a separate register book

---

67  Sanggunian Barangay of Ayala Alabang (3 January 2011). An Ordinance Providing for the Safety and Protection of the Unborn Child within the Territorial Jurisdiction of Barangay Ayala Alabang. *Barangay Ordinance No. 01, Series of 2011* (Muntinlupa City) ('*Barangay Ordinance No. 01, Series of 2011*').
68  The "Sanggunian" is the Council of the Barangay, the smallest political unit.
69  *Barangay Ordinance No. 01, Series of 2011, supra.*
70  Ibid.
71  *Barangay Ordinance No. 01, Series of 2011, supra.*

for abortives and anti-conceptionals.[72] In practice, this resulted in the requirement of a prescription to buy a condom or birth control pill. Injectables were
also banned in the Barangay. This was in stark contrast to other pharmacies in the
Philippines, where condoms and pills are available over the counter.[73] According
to the spokesperson of the Barangay, the Barangay Council passed the ordinance
because "they wanted to be proactive in their pro-life stance". The Catholic
Church parish in the Barangay was apparently active in opposing the passing into
law of the RH Bill.[74]

The Philippines also gained international criticism when an executive order,
which restricted access to reproductive health, was passed in Manila. Executive
Order (E.O.) No. 003, issued by former Manila Mayor Jose L. Atienza, affirmed
the sanctity of life and protection of the life of the mother and the unborn, and
declared that the City of Manila would take an "affirmative stand on pro-life issues
and responsible parenthood".[75] The executive order also promoted natural family planning and discouraged the use of artificial methods of contraception like
condoms, pills, intrauterine devices, and surgical sterilization, amongst others.[76]

The CEDAW Committee indicated in its report on the order that while E.O.
No. 003 did not expressly prohibit the use of modern contraceptives, "its continued implementation in practice severely limited women's access to sexual and
reproductive health services and effectively resulted in a ban of modern contraceptives in the City of Manila".[77] A subsequent Executive Order No. 30 was also
issued, which "allegedly imposed a funding ban on modern contraception".[78]

The committee found that the Philippines was in violation of rights under
CEDAW. As a state party to the convention, it was bound to respect, protect, and
fulfill women's rights to non-discrimination, which it had failed to do under the
circumstances because prohibiting women's access to reproductive health services
was discriminatory. The committee found that the "women in the City of Manila
primarily bore the consequences of, and were disproportionately disadvantaged
by, the inability to access and use the full range of reproductive health services".[79]

---

72 Ibid.
73 C. Montenegro, *Barangay Ayala Alabang Requires Prescription to Buy Condoms* (24 February 2011), GMA News Online, available at www.gmanetwork.com/news/story/213863/
   news/nation/barangay-ayala-alabang-requires-prescription-to-buy-condoms (accessed
   20 May 2019).
74 Ibid.
75 See http://tbinternet.ohchr.org/Treaties/CEDAW/Shared%20Documents/PHL/CEDAW_
   C_OP-8_PHL_1_7679_E.pdf (accessed 20 May 2019).
76 United Nations, Committee on the Elimination of Discrimination against Women (2014
   August). Summary of the inquiry concerning the Philippines under article 8 of the Optional
   Protocol to the Convention on the Elimination of All Forms of Discrimination against Women
   ('Committee on the Elimination of Discrimination against Women, Article 8 (2014 August)').
77 Ibid.
78 Committee on the Elimination of Discrimination against Women, Article 8 (2014 August).
79 Ibid.

The committee further observed the influence of the Catholic Church in the determination of reproductive health services:

> The Committee notes that while the 1987 Philippine Constitution provides for the separation of the Church and the State by proclaiming in Section 6 of the Directive Principles that "[t]he separation of Church and State shall be inviolable", the Church has considerable influence on public policy making in the State party. Religion has been relied on as a basis for sexual and reproductive health policies, including at the level of LGUs, as under Article 2 Section 12 of the Constitution. The State party is required to "equally protect the life of the mother and the life of the unborn from [the time of] conception".[80]

Prior to the enactment of the RH Law, similar ordinances protecting the life of the unborn child were also enacted in other Barangays in the Philippines.[81] The passage of the RH Law should have rendered such ordinances illegal and invalid; however, the law has not prevented subsequent local action against access to reproductive health.[82]

### The city of Sorsogon

On 2 February 2015, Mayor Sally A. Lee of Sorsogon City issued Executive Order (E.O.) No. 3, "An Executive Order Declaring Sorsogon City . . . a Pro-Life City". This meant that the mayor intended Sorsogon City to solely implement reproductive health programs which involve the use and practice of natural family planning. The executive order cited the Constitution's provisions on the protection of the sanctity of the family and the rights of children. It also mentioned the Universal Declaration of Human Rights as well as the Magna Carta for Women, specifically its provisions on comprehensive health services.

The executive order cites the Magna Carta for Women as follows:

> Whereas, under the Magna Carta of Women (RA 9710), the state shall at all times provide for comprehensive, culture-sensitive, and gender responsive health services and programs covering all stages of a woman's life cycle . . .

None of these instruments or documents, however, justifies the city's sole preference for implementing reproductive health programs using only natural family planning methods.

---

80 Ibid.
81 T. Orejas, Bataan Villages Backed on Pro-life Ordinances (12 September 2011), *Inquirer. net*, available at http://newsinfo.inquirer.net/57187/bataan-villages-backed-on-prolife-ordinances (accessed 20 May 2019).
82 Since the passage of the Local Government Code of 1991, health care and services have been devolved to local governments under Sections 16 and 17 of the Code. Thus, the type of reproductive health services and facilities that women could access depended on the programs and policies promoted by their local government.

The executive order did not have any guidelines, although a draft was proposed,[83] which cited E.O. No. 3 and added the following pertinent clauses:

> WHEREAS, in his account, Pope Benedict XVI wrote that "he joined all those marching for life from afar, and prayed that political leaders will protect the unborn and promote a culture of life. That "every unborn child, though unjustly condemned to be aborted, has the face of the Lord".
>
> WHEREAS, in the apostolic exhortation *Evangelii Gaudium*, Pope Francis wrote, "that a human being is always sacred and inviolable, in any situation and at every stage of development".

The draft guidelines also regulated acts with regard to "abortifacient contraceptives". Accordingly, the following acts are regulated under Section 4:

a   Officers and employees of the City Government of Sorsogon shall not purchase and accept abortifacient contraceptives and other related medicines. Officers of Health offices, Barangay Health Centers, and other private clinics and hospitals are also prohibited from dispensing, giving, donating, selling, delivering, and recommending any of the abortifacient contraceptives.
b   All local offices and other agencies of the Government of the city of Sorsogon are mandated to conduct pro-life missions by encouraging modern natural family planning method.
c   All 64 Barangays of the City Government of Sorsogon shall include, in their Appropriation Ordinance, Annual Investment Plan, 5-year Investment Plan, and Annual Procurement Plan, the conduct of activities to defend and care for human life.
d   All drug stores and pharmacists in the City of Sorsogon are hereby enjoined to support this pro-life program and they are strictly prohibited from selling, dispensing, and promoting abortifacient contraceptives, drugs, and related medicines.

Despite the absence of guidelines for implementation, the local government has proceeded to implement the executive order. In practice, contraceptives were pulled out from health centers in Sorsogon, effectively depriving women of reproductive health services.[84] Women were also denied free contraceptives in public health clinics and health workers were forbidden from administering or dispensing modern birth control.[85] The ordinance allegedly formed part of the city's *moral recovery program*, which is part of the mayor's political

---

83  Hon. Emmanuel D. Diolata is the proponent of E.O. No. 3.
84  R. N. Araja, RH Law Violations Rampant; Probe Set, *The Standard* (2 March 2016), available at http://thestandard.com.ph/mobile/article/200708 (accessed 20 May 2019).
85  A. P. Santos, Probe into RH Law Implementation Starts April 1, *Rappler* (31 March 2016), available at www.rappler.com/views/imho/127679-chr-implementation-rh-law (accessed 20 May 2019).

platform.[86] Finally, on 27 June 2017, the Philippine Commission on Human Rights (PCHR), acting on the letter-complaint filed by Likhaan Center for Women's Health, found the executive order in violation of the CEDAW, the Magna Carta of Women, and the RH Law, for denying women access to the full range of family planning information, methods and services; and effectively banning artificial contraceptives.[87] Mayor Sally A. Lee has filed a Motion for Reconsideration of the PCHR's resolution.

### Temporary restraining order on certain contraceptives

The DOH has also found itself embroiled in a legal battle in its very implementation of the RH Law. In 2015, the Supreme Court of the Philippines issued a temporary restraining order prohibiting the DOH from (1) granting any and all pending applications for reproductive products and supplies, including contraceptive drugs and devices; and (2) procuring, selling, distributing, dispensing or administering, advertising, and promoting the hormonal contraceptive "Implanon" and "Implanon NXT".[88]

The temporary restraining order is an outcome of a petition from the Alliance for the Family Foundation, Inc., which claimed that the implants have an "abortifacient" character.[89] Regrettably, the restraining order was also used as one of the justifications why the budget for contraceptives worth one billion pesos, was cut from the budget of the DOH by Congress.[90]

## CRT in the medical-legal arena: implications for law and policy

In law and policymaking in the Philippines, personal beliefs play a significant role in decisions over the reproductive health of women, and this was evident in the

---

86 F. J. Epineda, I Invested in Our People – Mayor Sally Lee, *Bicol Today* (21 December 2015), available at http://bicoltoday.com/2015/12/21/i-invested-on-our-people-mayor-sally-lee/ (accessed 20 May 2019).

87 Commission on Human Rights Resolution Case No. 2015–0411, titled *In the Matter of the Issuance by Mayor Sally Lee of Executive Order No. 003, Declaring Sorsogon City a "Pro-Life City", the alleged effects thereof, and the Violation of the Women's Right to Reproductive Health*, dated June 27, 2017.

88 Alliance for the Family Foundation Philippines, Inc. (ALFI) and Atty. Maria Concepcion S. Noche, in her own behalf as President of ALFI, et al. v. Dr. Janette L. Garin, Secretary-Designate of the Department of Health, et al., G.R. No. 217872 (Temporary Restraining Order) (Supreme Court of the Philippines 2015 17-June).

89 T. Quismundo (4 July 2015). *High Court Stops DOH Contraceptive Implants*, available at http://newsinfo.inquirer.net/702730/high-court-stops-doh-contraceptive-implants (accessed 22 May 2019). On 10 November 2017, the FDA issued Advisory #302 certifying 51 contraceptive products are non-abortifacient, including the contested implants. This effectively lifted the restraining order by the Supreme Court.

90 J.Y. Geronimo, *What happened to the 2016 budget for contraceptives?* (7 January 2016), available at www.rappler.com/nation/118239-explanation-no-2016-budget-contraceptives (accessed 22 May 2019).

decisions taken by individual members of Congress on the RH Bill. As the foregoing discussion has shown, a significant number of legislators, in both the Senate and the House of Representatives voted against the RH Bill on the dictates of
their conscience. One legislator even declared that his vote against the RH Bill is
an affirmation of his "faith in God".[91] In the case of Sorsogon city, the mayor as
primary proponent of the pro-life ordinance has contended that the ordinance is
for the protection of women against the negative effects of using artificial contraceptive methods. It does not appear, however, that her conclusion is backed by
sufficient evidence. Despite the investigation conducted by the Commission on
Human Rights, she continues to deny women access to artificial contraceptives.[92]

It is important to acknowledge that there were congressional members who
prudently separated their "conscience" from the "will of the people". Thus, in
some instances, representatives voted against their personal conscience in support of the RH Bill. Representative Wilfrido Enverga, for example, explained
that he was born and raised as a Catholic and voted against the RH Bill during
the second reading. But in the final reading of the Bill, he voted for the RH Bill
because upon consultation with his constituents, "not a single Barangay health
worker told [him] not to support the measure".[93] Overwhelming support for the
RH Bill prompted the legislator to vote "yes" for the bill, although with an allegedly heavy heart. Another legislator, Representative Victoria Sy-Alvarado, also
originally opposed the bill, but after consultations with her constituents, voted in
affirmation of the bill. In her explanation, she mentioned that she changed her
vote because her solemn oath to serve the people and to follow their will implies
that she, as an elected official, had to raise the people's voices and will to the
national consciousness.[94]

Despite the mandate of legislators to "represent" the people who elected them,
legislators who opposed the RH Bill do not seem to have delineated what is good
for their constituents and what is "conscionable" for them. Inherent in their
arguments is the assumption that as long as the bill is contrary to their personal
beliefs, then it cannot be for the general good of the people. As explained at the
outset, different institutions have also contributed to the formation of personal
beliefs, and legislators cited these institutions when explaining their votes. References to Catholic Church teachings, of man and woman's role to procreate, the

91 House of Representatives, 2012.
92 Dona Z. Pazzibugan, 14 November 2016, *CHR: Sorsogon City Depriving Women of Artificial Contraceptives: Prolife City Mayor stands firm despite DOH and CHR warning*, available
at https://newsinfo.inquirer.net/843981/chr-sorsogon-city-depriving-women-of-artificial-
contraceptives (accessed 2 June 2019).
93 House of Representatives, 2012.
94 Ibid. This perspective is not limited to issues of reproductive health. Representatives have
also used religion to substantiate their positions on other issues, such as the death penalty.
For example, Senator Manny Pacquiao supported the death penalty (and by hanging) on the
opinion that the Bible allows the punishment of death penalty: See ABS-CBN News (20 May
2016). *Pacquiao: Death Penalty in Accordance with Bible Teachings,* available at http://
news.abs-cbn.com/sports/05/19/16/pacquiao-death-penalty-in-accordance-with-bible-
teachings (accessed 22 May 2019).

sanctity of life, and the hard stance against abortion (or anything remotely similar to it) expose the influence and authority of the Catholic Church in Philippine politics and society.

To reiterate, the principal institution influencing the formulation and implementation of reproductive health measures in the Philippines is the Catholic Church. As a predominantly Catholic country, the Catholic Church has actively lobbied against the RH Law. According to the School of Economics at the University of the Philippines:

> The Catholic Church hierarchy has maintained its traditional stance against modern family planning . . ., [and while] the State acknowledges the difficulties posed for development by rapid population growth . . ., it has been immobilized from effectively addressing the issue by the Catholic hierarchy's hard-line stance, as well as the tendency of some politicians to cater to the demands of well-organised and impassioned single-issue groups for the sake of expediency".[95]

The church has also been unafraid to exercise retribution against those who support reproductive health measures. During the election period of 2013, a local diocese put up two tarpaulins to indicate Team "Buhay" (Life) – with the names of candidates opposing the RH Bill and Team "Patay" (Death) – with the names of candidates in favor of the bill. These signs were meant to caution the electing public against candidates who supported the RH Bill and to vote their conscience. The local officer for Commission on Elections issued a Notice to Remove Campaign Materials, stating that the materials were outside the size limitations for campaign materials. The church questioned this notice and cited the right to free speech. The case eventually reached the Supreme Court, which upheld the right of the diocese to free speech.[96]

At the peak of the RH Law deliberations, it was reported that "[p]riests denied communion to community health workers, campaigned against politicians supportive of the bill, and even threatened President Benigno Aquino III with excommunication".[97] It is this kind of socio-political climate that enables the predominance of the exercise of individual conscience over the general welfare of the

95 UP School of Economics, *Population, Poverty, Politics, and the Reproductive Health Bill* (February 2011), available at www.econ.upd.edu.ph/dp/index.php/dp/article/viewFile/670/132 (accessed 22 May 2019).
96 The Diocese of Bacolod, represented by the Most Rev. Bishop Vicente M. Navarra and the Bishop himself in his personal capacity v. Commission on Elections and the Election Officer of Bacolod City, Atty. Mavil V. Majarucon, G.R. No. 205728 (Supreme Court of the Philippines 21 January 2015); T. Torres-Tupas (21 January 2015), *SC Rules in Favor of Bacolod Diocese on "Team Patay", Team Buhay posters*, available at http://newsinfo.inquirer.net/667048/sc-rules-in-favor-of-bacolod-diocese-on-team-patay-team-buhay-posters (accessed 22 May 2019).
97 BBC, *Is the Catholic Church's Influence in Philippines Fading?* (25 May 2014), available at www.bbc.com/news/world-asia-27537943 (accessed 22 May 2019).

populace, allowing lawmakers and local leaders to create or implement measures against reproductive health with little or no liability. Society also encourages local leaders to act "with conscience" and not in consideration of their constituents.

It is also noteworthy that the discourse on reproductive health, especially in the making of a law for women, has been dominated by men who were concerned more with issues of morality and the declared philosophies of Filipino culture and tradition rather than with matters pertaining to the implications of the bill for women's health, including the benefits as well as possibility of harm, if any, to women and their bodies.

The dominant rhetoric on the value of culture, religion and tradition as the lens through which the reproductive health bill and indeed matters of reproductive and sexual health in the Philippines are to be assessed is also reinforced by the weak appreciation of international instruments and commitments, specifically the CEDAW and its domestic articulation, the MCW, and the International Conference on Population and Development (ICPD). It is clear that the declarations and provisions of the MCW have not resonated with the lawmakers. What is noticeably missing from the debates is the attention to women's rights as human rights, women's right to non-discrimination, and the use of rights-based approach in achieving gender equality and non-discrimination. These ought to be reformative legal tools. They are tools designed to reverse women's experiences with discrimination and poor health expectations. But, they are also tools that can, and have been, severely weakened by the context within which they are sought to be implemented.

The MCW has been viewed in isolation from its significance as an integral norm-setting tool and as a rights-based framework for subsequent law and policy reforms for women. This has resulted in skewed perceptions or interpretations of the objectives sought to be achieved by the law. The random citing of the MCW has not been to support the RH Law but to prove that the latter is either redundant or that the MCW allows the enactment of an ordinance which totally replaces women's rational agency by dictating what kind of services and treatment they should get. Even the Supreme Court's decision on the RH Law[98] has considerably enervated the significance of having a Magna Carta for Women. Addressing the evolution of the use of modern family planning methods "from being a component of demographic management, to one centered on the promotion of public health, particularly, reproductive health", the court said that despite the intended paradigm shift brought about by the enactment of laws and measures to promote women's rights and health and the well-being of the family as a whole, the national program has always been based on the "principle of no-abortion" and the "principle of non-coercion", because of the Constitutional protection granted to life and religious freedom.[99] The Court was also of the

98  *Imbong v. Ochoa, supra.*
99  Ibid.

opinion that existing laws, including the MCW already "amply cater to the needs of women in relation to health services and programs".[100]

The parliamentary debate on the right to a safe and satisfying sex life further highlights the lack of awareness of the lawmakers on the commitment that the country has made during the ICPD and its subsequent participation in its follow-up conferences.[101] As revealed in the congressional discussions above, senators who argued the point had a totally different take on the phrase "safe and satisfying sex life" because they were not aware that such phrase is actually articulated in an international document, which has a broader context. It is evident from Paragraph 7.2 of Chapter VII of the ICPD Programme of Action that this phrase alluded more to the freedom from fear of unplanned pregnancies.[102]

## Conclusion

The development of reproductive health in the Philippines has slowly but surely progressed over the past few years. With the enactment of the RH Law, the country finally has, what is in theory at least, a definitive framework for the promotion, protection and fulfillment of women's right to health in all stages of development.

Unfortunately, the promotion, protection, and fulfillment of women's right to reproductive health have yet to resonate in Philippine society. Despite the presence of the RH Law, the opposition mounted by various executive bodies and a group of policymakers continue to hamper the implementation of the law through anti-RH strategies, especially through the issuance of ordinances or the filing of cases in courts. Skewed interpretations of both the MCW and the RH Law have also contributed to the latter's weak implementation. Perhaps this can be avoided by having definitive language that categorically defines usages and legislative intent in law and policy documents. In line with Iyioha's analysis in Chapter 2, clear use of language in definitions and outlines of legislative purpose will go a long way towards addressing the problems associated with language as an internal limit on law's effectiveness.

100 Ibid.
101 International Conference on Population and Development (18 October 1994), *Report of the International Conference on Population and Development,* available at www.un.org/popin/icpd/conference/offeng/poa.html (22 May 2019).
102 According to paragraph 7.2 of Chapter VII of the ICPD Programme of Action, "Reproductive health is a state of complete physical, mental and social well-being, and not merely the absence of disease or infirmity, in all matters relating to the reproductive system and to its functions and processes. Reproductive health therefore implies that people are able to have a satisfying and safe sex life and that they have the capability to reproduce and the freedom to decide if, when and how often to do so. Implicit in this last condition is the right of men and women to be informed and to have access to safe, effective, affordable and acceptable methods of family planning of their choice, as well as other methods of their choice for regulation of fertility which are not against the law, and the right of access to appropriate healthcare services that will enable women to go safely through pregnancy and childbirth and provide couples with the best chance of having a healthy infant".

These drawbacks have also been made possible by an environment where strong reliance on personal beliefs pervades public and state discourses. This is complicated by a weak appreciation of the enabling laws for women (specifically the MCW which espouses a human rights-based approach to women's rights) and little awareness of the country's commitments and obligations under international treaties and other international instruments for the promotion of reproductive health. This lack of awareness among legislators creates a dissonance, evident in the oppositions in parliament, between the goals and aspirations of international human rights law and local ideals and practices.

The end goal of most rights-based reproductive health agenda is to have reproductive and sexual health programs that are comprehensive, available and accessible to all who need them. It is important that women's access to such programs be free from discrimination and recrimination. The journey towards obtaining full access and experiencing healthier lives must, of necessity, begin with questioning the man-made boundaries that CRT-based values have constructed around law.

# 7 Economics and the limits of law

## An international analysis of persistent gaps in women's reproductive health

*Karen A. Grépin, Jeni Klugman and Matthew Moore*[χ]

## Introduction

Gender equality has moved to the forefront of development debates. The United Nations General Assembly adopted gender equality as one of the 17 stand-alone Sustainable Development Goals (SDGs) that are the cornerstone of the post-2015 development framework.[1] This prominence is consistent with the key message of the World Bank's 2012 World Development Report (WDR2012) – that gender equality is a core development outcome in its own right – since greater gender equality can enhance productivity, improve development outcomes for future generations, and make institutions function better.[2]

Addressing women's reproductive health needs is a prerequisite to achieving gender equality. But despite international commitments, progress on this front has been slow and major gaps persist. Millions of women still have no say over whether, when, and how many children to have, and lack the means to prevent unwanted pregnancies or to prevent and address the complications of childbirth. Pregnancy and the consequences of childbirth remain the leading causes of death and disability among women of reproductive age in developing countries.[3] Many teenage girls are heavily affected; complications from pregnancy and childbirth are the leading cause of death among girls aged 15 to 19 in developing countries.[4]

As shown in Figure 7.1, while there has been some progress in tackling maternal mortality since 1990, the risks remain unacceptably high in poor countries.

χ The authors wish to thank Jill Sheffield and Louise Dunn for encouragement and feedback, Miranda Berry, Sarah Haddock, Samia Khan, and Jing Dong for their assistance with background research, and the Women and Public Policy Program, Harvard Kennedy School, for the support.

1 United Nations Women, "SDG 5: Achieve Gender Equality and Empower All Women and Girls", available at UN Women www.unwomen.org.
2 World Bank, *World Development Report 2012: Gender Equality and Development* (Washington, DC: World Bank, 2011) ('World Bank, *World Development Report 2012*').
3 Rafael Lozano et al., "Global and Regional Mortality From 235 Causes of Death for 20 Age Groups in 1990 and 2010: A Systematic Analysis for the Global Burden of Disease Study 2010" (2012) 380 *Lancet* 2095.
4 World Health Organization, "Adolescent Pregnancy" (2018), available at World Health Organization, www.who.int/en/news-room/fact-sheets/detail/adolescent-pregnancy.

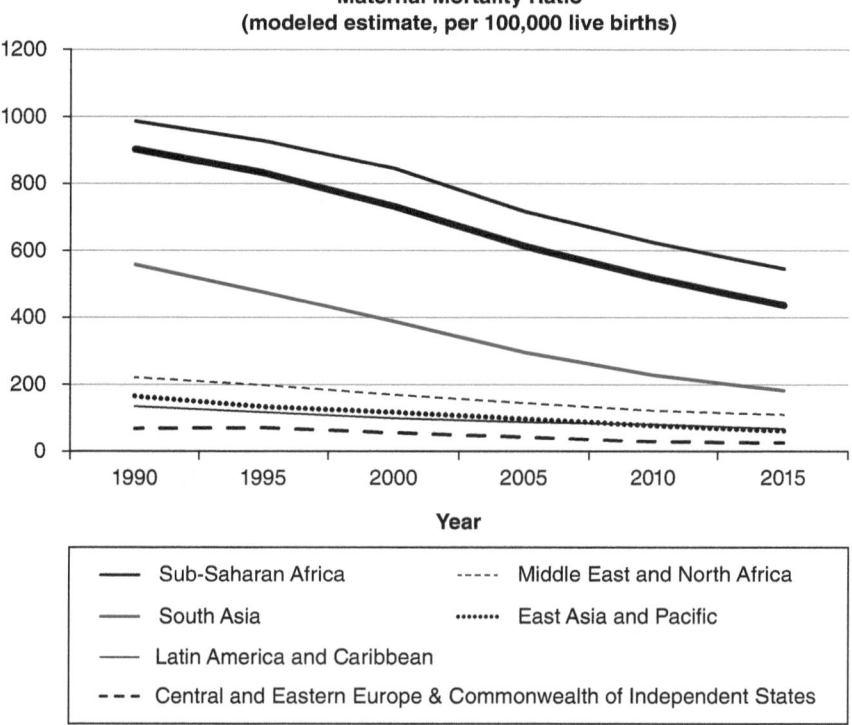

*Figure 7.1* Trends in Maternal Mortality and Attended Births

Note: Modeled estimate, per 100,000 live births.

Source: Maternal Mortality Estimation Inter-Agency Group.[5]

In 2015, there were an estimated 303,000 maternal deaths – an average of more than 800 every day – almost all of which occurred in developing countries.[6]

The Maternal Mortality Ratio (MMR) in the least developed countries (436 deaths per 100,000 live births) is more than 30 times higher than in developed countries.[7] This gap has long been described as the "widest disparity in all statistics of public health".[8] In high-income countries, estimated lifetime risk of maternal mortality is 1 in 3,300, but in low-income countries, lifetime risk is 1 in 41.[9] In Sierra Leone and Chad, 1 in 17 and 1 in 18 women, respectively, will die of

5  Ibid.
6  Maternal Mortality Estimation Inter-Agency Group, *Trends in Estimates of Maternal Mortality Ratio: 1990 to 2015* (2015), United Nations Children's Fund, available at http://data.unicef.org.
7  Ibid.
8  Halfdan Mahler, "The Safe Motherhood Initiative: A Call to Action" (1987) 329 *Lancet* 668.
9  Ibid.

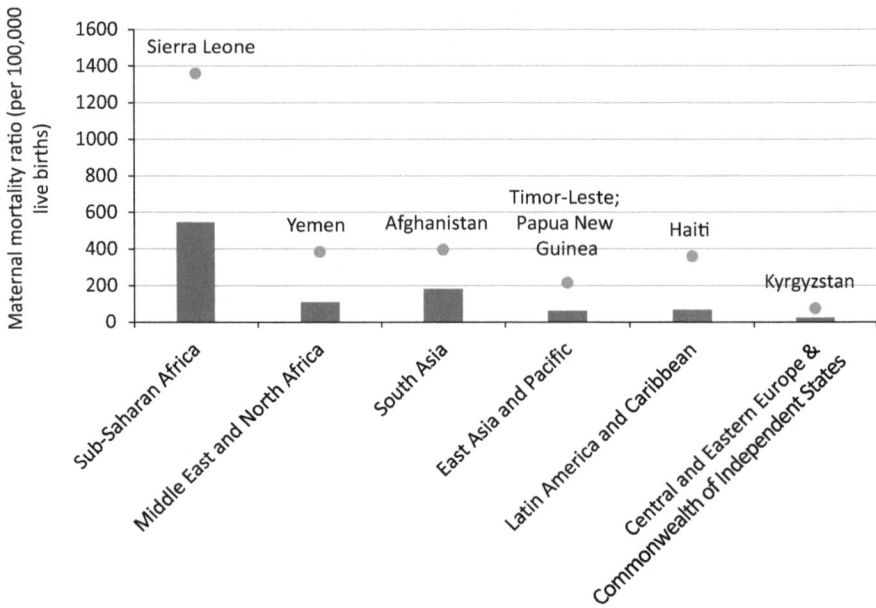

*Figure 7.2* Maternal Mortality: Regional Averages and Country Outliers, 2015
Source: Maternal Mortality Estimation Inter-Agency Group.

complications during childbirth.[10] In all low-income countries, 1 in 41 women will die a maternal death.[11]

Figure 7.2 shows the variation in regional averages, highlighting that there are large differences across regions and important outliers within every region. In sub-Saharan Africa, which has by far the highest regional average, there are more than a dozen countries above the average. Sierra Leone is the region's highest and world's worst, followed by Central African Republic, Chad, Nigeria, South Sudan, Somalia, Liberia, Burundi, The Gambia, Democratic Republic of Congo, and Guinea.[12] Moreover, maternal mortality is just the tip of the iceberg: for every woman who dies, another 30 suffer long-lasting injury or illness.[13]

Why do such gaps in poor reproductive health outcomes persist in spite of existing domestic laws and international conventions protecting women's reproductive health rights, and what can be done to address them? This chapter makes

10  Ibid.
11  Ibid.
12  Ibid.
13  M.A. Koblinsky, "Beyond Maternal Mortality – Magnitude, Interrelationship and Consequences of Women's Health, Pregnancy-Related Complications and Nutritional Status on Pregnancy Outcomes" (1995) 48 *International Journal of Gynecology & Obstetrics* S21.

three important contributions towards addressing these questions. First, we bring together the evidence highlighting the impact of poor economic status on women's reproductive health in order to emphasize the instrumental importance of economic factors to better reproductive health outcomes, as well as how better reproductive health is good for the economy. Second, building on the insights of the analytical framework put forth in the WDR2012, we synthesize the micro-level economic evidence on the factors that contribute to poor reproductive health. Drawing on Iyioha's theory of Substantive Effectiveness,[14] we conceptualize these factors as "external limits" on the actualization of rights-based frameworks in relevant jurisdictions. As Iyioha shows, the effectiveness of reproductive health laws is often enabled or constrained by "external limits" on the law itself. Our contributions highlight how economic factors form one such external limit. Third, we review robust evidence about key policy levers and programs that can accelerate reproductive health improvements in developing countries.

## The relationship between economic factors and reproductive health

In this section, we examine the interaction of reproductive health with economic factors. We focus on two issues: (1) labor supply and productivity and (2) out-of-pocket spending. Although these are not the only economic factors that impact reproductive health, they demonstrate that this interaction runs both ways: economic factors can lead to improved reproductive health outcomes and, at the same time, better reproductive health creates economic benefits. Throughout, we emphasize that non-economic factors, such as social norms and government policies, shape how economic factors impact reproductive health. This interaction is influenced in important ways by a country's educational system, labor market, provision of public healthcare, and cultural custom, among other non-economic factors.

### *Labor supply and productivity*

It is well known that poor health reduces labor supply and contributes to lost wages.[15] Not surprisingly, poor reproductive health outcomes also likely reduce the labor supply and productivity of affected women. This could have major repercussions for total global productivity, since women are important contributors to the global economy: about 40% of the global labor force and more than 60% of agricultural workers in sub-Saharan Africa, for example, are women.[16]

---

14 See Iyioha, Chapter 2 of this volume.
15 Paul Gertler and Jonathan Gruber, "Insuring Consumption Against Illness" (2002) 92 *American Economic Review* 51; William Jack, "The Promise of Health: Evidence of the Impact of Health on Income and Well-Being" in Sherry Glied and Peter C Smith, eds., *The Oxford Handbook of Health Economics* (Oxford: Oxford University Press, 2010).
16 World Bank, Food and Agriculture Organization, International Fund for Agriculture Development, *Gender in Agriculture Sourcebook* (Washington, DC: World Bank, 2009).

Labor losses may result from maternal deaths, but many more women suffer maternal morbidities that can also negatively affect labor supply and productivity, especially in developing countries.[17]

Empirical evidence documenting the effects of maternal mortality and morbidity on productivity is available for several countries. In Bangladesh, one study found lower productivity among women with adverse pregnancy outcomes, in particular from severe complications of pregnancy.[18] Poor maternal health outcomes may mean that other family members need to take up the work done by women, lowering overall household productivity.[19]

High fertility can also affect female labor supply, since having children adds to women's domestic responsibilities, given prevailing gender roles.[20] In studies of female labor supply, labor participation is generally negatively associated with the individual's number of children.[21] For example, in Latin America and the Caribbean over the past decade, the total fertility rate fell by almost 11% while female labor force participation rates simultaneously surged by some 15%.[22] Another channel of effects on labor productivity is via the links between delayed fertility and human capital accumulation. If girls and women are better able to control their fertility through, for example, access to contraception, then they can also stay in school longer and accumulate more skills.

The relationship between fertility, schooling, and economic opportunities is mutually reinforcing. Not only does lower fertility potentially improve economic outcomes, but better economic opportunities can also reduce fertility rates through increased opportunity costs. This is illustrated by a randomized experiment in India that helped young women enter the call center industry, which led to fewer women getting married and to more women reporting wanting fewer children.[23] Another study found that the expansion of the information technology sector in India led to an increase in primary schooling in the areas exposed to the new economic opportunities.[24] These findings were corroborated

17  Lale Say and Rosalind Raine, "A Systematic Review of Inequalities in the Use of Maternal Health Care in Developing Countries: Examining the Scale of the Problem and the Importance of Context" (2007) 85 *Bulletin of the World Health Organization* 812.

18  Mohammad Enamul Hoque et al., "Costs of Maternal Health-Related Complications in Bangladesh" (2012) 30 *Journal of Health Population & Nutrition* 205.

19  Fang Ye et al., "The Immediate Economic Impact of Maternal Deaths on Rural Chinese Households" (2012) 7 *PLoS ONE* e38467.

20  World Bank, *supra* note 2.

21  Martin Browning, "Children and Household Economic Behavior" (1992) 30 *Journal of Economic Literature* 1434.

22  World Bank, *Latin America and the Caribbean Poverty and Labor Brief* (Washington, DC: World Bank, 2012).

23  Robert Jensen, "Do Labor Market Opportunities Affect Young Women's Work and Family Decisions? Experimental Evidence from India" (2012) 127 *Quarterly Journal of Economics* 753 ('Jensen, "Do Labor Market Opportunities Affect Young Women's Work and Family Decisions?"').

24  Emily Oster and Bryce Millett Steinberg, "Do IT Service Centers Promote School Enrollment? Evidence from India" (2013) 104 *Journal of Development Economics* 123.

in Bangladesh, where the expansion of the garment manufacturing industry has been associated with girls delaying marriage and childbirth, and increased educational and economic opportunities for girls who had the opportunity to work in the industry.[25]

### Increased out-of-pocket health spending

It is well established that catastrophic health care costs can impoverish families in developing countries – households frequently report having to borrow or sell assets to pay for health services.[26] Even in countries where health services are free in public clinics, many women report financial challenges in paying for maternity care.[27] This is because transport may be relatively expensive,[28] they may be forced to turn to the private sector for services that are not available or are of poor quality in the public sector,[29] or may be required to pay for additional medical supplies.[30]

However, when complications arise during pregnancy and delivery, households usually have to bear ever higher, and usually unexpected, out-of-pocket health expenditures. In Benin and Ghana, the costs associated with delivery complications were estimated to be more than 15 times higher than routine deliveries, and represented more than one-third of the annual household cash expenditures.[31] In Burkina Faso, women with severe obstetric complications reported a more frequent sale of assets, more borrowing, and slower repayment of debt in the following year.[32] In rural China, households experiencing a maternal death also experienced greatly increased out-of-pocket expenditures for non-health-related

25 Rachel Heath and A. Mushfiq Mobarak, "Manufacturing Growth and the Lives of Bangladeshi Women" (2015) 115 *Journal of Developmental Economics* 1 ('Heath and Mobarak, "Manufacturing Growth and the Lives of Bangladeshi Women"').

26 Margaret E. Kruk, Emily Goldmann and Sandro Galea, "Borrowing and Selling to Pay for Health Care in Low- and Middle-Income Countries" (2009) 28 *Health Affairs* 1056; Ke Xu et al., "Household Catastrophic Health Expenditure: A Multicountry Analysis" (2003) 362 *Lancet* 111.

27 Justin Oliver Parkhurst et al., "Health Systems Factors Influencing Maternal Health Services: A Four-Country Comparison" (2005) 73 *Health Policy* 127.

28 Emma Sacks et al., "Factors Influencing Modes of Transport and Travel Time for Obstetric Care: A Mixed Methods Study in Zambia and Uganda" (2016) 31 *Health Policy & Planning* 3.

29 Margaret E. Kruk et al., "User Fee Exemptions Are Not Enough: Out-of-Pocket Payments for 'Free' Delivery Services in Rural Tanzania" (2008) 13 *Tropical Medicine & International Health* 1442.

30 V. Gohou et al., "Responsiveness to Life-Threatening Obstetric Emergencies in Two Hospitals in Abidjan, Cote d'Ivoire" (2004) 9 *Tropical Medicine & International Health* 406; Justin Oliver Parkhurst and Syed Azizur Rahman, "Life Saving or Money Wasting?" (2007) 80 *Health Policy* 392.

31 Jospehine Borghi et al., "Costs of Near-Miss Obstetric Complications for Women and Their Families in Benin and Ghana" (2003) 18 *Health Policy and Planning* 383.

32 Katerini Storeng et al., "Paying the Price: The Cost and Consequences of Emergency Obstetric Care in Burkina Faso" 66 *Social Science and Medicine* 545.

expenses, mostly associated with newborn care.[33] A detailed study in Bangladesh documents large increases in health expenditures as a direct result of maternal illness.[34] Families reported having to borrow and sell assets to pay for these unexpected maternity costs.

## Understanding gaps in reproductive health: examining external limits to law

Despite the manifest health benefits and intrinsic value of reproductive health, alongside the potential economic gains, progress in addressing reproductive health needs has been slow. We now investigate the factors underlying the persistent gaps, beginning with limits on the agency of women and girls and proceeding to examine overlapping constraints. Our analysis highlights the intersection of these factors with key economic factors, such as poverty and wealth inequality, that impact gaps in reproductive health, and shows how these factors constitute 'external limits' on the law. As Iyioha observes, non-legal factors shape the context within which reproductive health legislation is implemented and whether it is effective.[35] 'External limits' on the law, as we understand them, constitute factors exogenous to the law (as opposed to internal factors, such as law's formal elements), which set an upper bound on law's ability to achieve its objectives. Culture, politics, religion, and tradition, for example, all influence how particular laws are interpreted, whether they are regarded as authoritative, and if sufficient resources are made available for their effective enforcement. Our chapter contributes to this picture by showing how economic factors similarly enable or constrain reproductive health laws.

### *Women's agency*

Agency – or the lack thereof – appears to be a very important part of the reasons for persistent gaps in women's reproductive health. In the capabilities approach, as conceived and developed by Nobel Prize–winning economist Amartya Sen, agency is the ability to pursue goals that one values and has reason to value,[36] and an agent is "someone who acts and brings about change".[37] The concern is with both *processes* (intrinsic) and *outcomes* (instrumental). Increasing women's agency has both significant intrinsic and instrumental benefits in the domain of sexual and reproductive health and rights.

33  Haijun Wang et al., "Economic Impact of Maternal Death on Households in Rural China: A Prospective Cohort Study" (2013) 8 *PLoS ONE* e76624.
34  Timothy Powell-Jackson and Mohammad Enamul Hoque, "Economic Consequences of Maternal Illness in Rural Bangladesh" (2012) 21 *Health Economics* 796.
35  See Iyioha, Chapter 2 of this volume.
36  Amartya Sen, "Development as Capability Expansion", in Keith B. Griffin and John B. Knight, eds., *Human Development and the International Development Strategy for the 1990s* (London: Palgrave Macmillan, 1990).
37  Amartya Sen, *Reason Before Identity* (New York: Oxford University Press, 1999).

Economic conditions influence the level and shape of women's agency. Poverty and income inequality, especially, drive whether women are able to exercise control over sexual and reproductive decisions.[38] At the same time, economic factors are not the only cause of agency deprivations, nor are they necessarily the most important. The factors impacting women's agency – such as education, poverty, and wealth inequality – are interrelated and mutually reinforcing.[39] As explored below, legal norms, government policy, and social norms shape the context in which economic limits interact with reproductive health.[40] Thus, public policy can influence how binding the economic limits on reproductive health are.

The WDR2012 highlighted women's voice and agency as a critical area in which progress over time has been especially slow – and underlined the critical links between agency and reproductive health. More recent analysis presented in Klugman et al. (2014) investigated the extent and nature of agency deprivations across a large number (54) of developing countries.[41] The study empirically investigated various types of constraints, including a lack of sexual autonomy (not being able to refuse sex), not being able to ask a partner to use a condom, and not being able to make own health decisions.

Table 7.1 shows selected deprivations, averaged for country groups, using World Bank income thresholds and nationally representative samples of women aged 15–49.[42] The headlines are striking: large percentages of women in all countries face these deprivations, and the association between the extent of deprivation and the level of per capita gross domestic product (GDP) is in the expected direction. Agency deprivations are especially severe in some of the least developed countries. In Mali, 82% of women responded that they had no say in their own healthcare, and in Niger 89% of women responded that they could not ask their partners to use a condom. However, there are some interesting exceptions. For example, there is no difference between low- and lower-middle-income countries in the percentage of women that is unable to ask their partner to use a condom.

The United Nations Population Fund (UNFPA) has underlined the strong relationship between poverty and wealth inequality – both between and within countries – and women's lack of agency over their own reproductive health.[43] Within countries, the study found that women in the poorest quintile within a country, regardless of the country's income grouping, have lower access to family

---

38 Jeni Klugman et al., *Voice and Agency: Empowering Women and Girls for Shared Prosperity* (Washington, DC: World Bank, 2014) ('Klugman et al., *Voice and Agency*').

39 Lucia Hanmer and Jeni Klugman, "Expanding Women's Agency and Empowerment in Developing Countries: Where Do We Stand?" (2016) 22 *Feminist Economics* 237 ('Hanmer and Klugman, "Expanding Women's Agency and Empowerment in Developing Countries"').

40 See Wei Wei Cao, Chapter 4 in this volume, for an exploration of the impact of Chinese cultural norms and history on the implementation of China's formally liberal abortion law.

41 Klugman et al., *Voice and Agency, supra*.

42 Hanmer and Klugman, "Expanding Women's Agency and Empowerment in Developing Countries", *supra*.

43 United Nations Population Fund, *Worlds Apart: Reproductive Health and Rights in an Age of Inequality* (2017), available at UNFPA, www.unfpa.org.

*Table 7.1* Selected Agency Deprivations in Developing Countries

| | Low Income | Lower-Middle Income | Upper-Middle Income | All |
|---|---|---|---|---|
| **Movement restricted** | 46% (11) | 28% (13) | 52% (5) | 31% (29) |
| **Cannot ask use of condom** | 45% (19) | 45% (14) | 17% (4) | 44% (37) |
| **Cannot refuse sex** | 35% (19) | 32% (14) | 11% (4) | 33% (37) |
| **No say in own healthcare** | 39% (21) | 33% (23) | 18% (9) | 34% (53) |

Notes: Numbers in brackets show the number of countries; population-weighted averages. *Movement restricted* = her husband limits her contact with girlfriends or family, or insists on knowing where she is.

Source: Hanmer and Klugman (2016).

planning across a range of indicators. And between countries, the study confirmed that the rate of "unmet demand" for family planning is higher in low-income countries. Similarly, married women in the least developed countries experience more deprivation than married women in other low-income countries.[44] The UNFPA concluded that, while the relationship between economic inequality and women's health is "complex", it is clear that "[t]he poorest women have the least access to sexual and reproductive health [and] are least able to exercise their reproductive rights".[45]

Among the observed correlates of these outcomes, (lack of) education stands out. This is illustrated in Figure 7.3, which shows that, across a range of countries and regions, much higher percentages of women with primary education or less lack sexual autonomy. The analysis of 54 developing countries presented in Klugman et al. found that while 9 out of 10 university graduates say they can refuse sex, only about 7 out of 10 women with only a primary education can do so.[46] In Mozambique, Cameroon, and Côte d'Ivoire, we find that up to four-fifths of women with no education lack sexual autonomy.

Multivariate analysis of the correlates of these outcomes – controlling for the woman's own characteristics, husband's education, household characteristics, and country-fixed effects – suggests that education plays a positive role, although the effects are especially marked for secondary education and above.[47] Completing at least secondary education improves a woman's sexual autonomy two to threefold over having no education. The husband's education also increases the likelihood of his partner having sexual autonomy, albeit to a lesser extent.

Child marriage – defined as before the woman's 18th birthday – emerges as a significant negative correlate of various agency outcomes in Hanmer and

44  Ibid.
45  Ibid.
46  Klugman et al., *Voice and Agency*, *supra*.
47  Hanmer and Klugman, "Expanding Women's Agency and Empowerment in Developing Countries", *supra*.

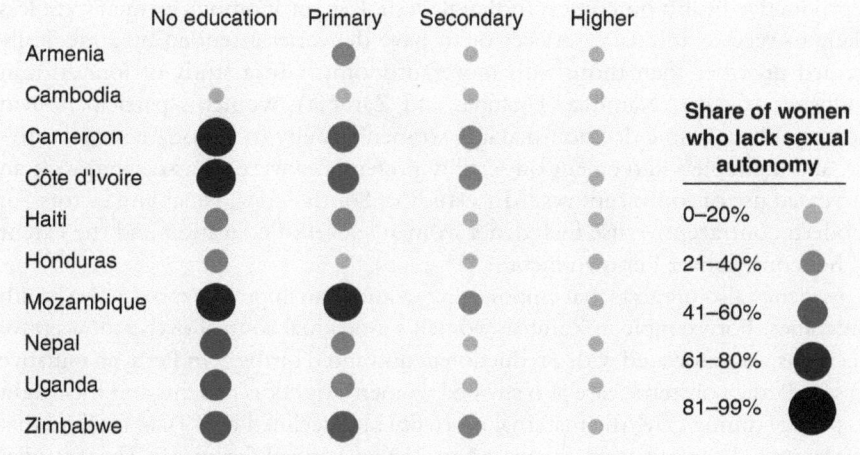

*Figure 7.3* Relationship between Education and Share of Women Who Lack Sexual Autonomy

Source: Klugman, Jeni, Lucia Hanmer, Sarah Twigg, Tazeen Hasan, Jennifer McCleary-Sills, and Julieth Santamaria. 2014. Voice and Agency: Empowering Women and Girls for Shared Prosperity. Washington, DC: World Bank. doi:10.1596/978-1-4648-0359-8. License: Creative Commons Attribution CC BY 3.0 IGO.

Klugman,[48] including sexual autonomy and contraceptive use. This is consistent with more detailed analysis in India, for example, where rates of child marriage are very high. Among women aged 20–24, child marriage is significantly associated with the lower use of contraceptives prior to the birth of the first child, high fertility (three or more births), multiple unwanted pregnancies, and short birth spacing.[49] The high prevalence of child marriage and its association with high fertility reflects the crucial need to expand comprehensive sexual and reproductive health services that reach married adolescents.

The impact of child marriage again highlights the role of economic conditions in limiting women's reproductive agency and health. Poverty and economic considerations often precipitate child marriage, which are undertaken to obtain a dowry, to settle debts, or to announce an economic alliance.[50] Again, however, the relationship between economics and deprivations is not straightforward: non-economic factors, such as a belief that child marriage will protect premarital virginity, also play a role.[51]

---

48  Ibid.
49  Anita Raj et al., "Prevalence of Child Marriage and Its Effect on Fertility and Fertility-Control Outcomes of Young Women in India: A Cross-Sectional, Observational Study" (2009) 373 *Lancet* 1883.
50  UNPF, *Marrying Too Young: End Child Marriage* (2012), available at UNFPA http://unfpa.org.
51  Ann Starrs et al., "Accelerate Progress – Sexual and Reproductive Health and Rights for All: Report of the Guttmacher – Lancet Commission" (2018) 391 *Lancet* 2642 ('Starrs et al., "Accelerate Progress"').

Recent studies using micro-level data confirm the importance of agency in reproductive health outcomes. In Bangladesh, less autonomous women were less likely to receive antenatal services or to have deliveries attended by a medically trained provider than those with more autonomy.[52] In a study of four African countries (Ghana, Namibia, Uganda, and Zambia), women's participation in household economic decision-making, women's ability to negotiate sexual activity, and a couple's agreement on fertility preferences were all associated with an increased use of contraceptives.[53] In a study of South Africa, "enabling factors" of modern contraceptive use included a woman's level of education and the extent of her control over her own income.[54]

Evidence also suggests that empowering women can improve reproductive health outcomes. For example in Zambia, women's individual control over contraceptive decisions was associated with a reduction in unwanted births.[55] In Peru, an initiative to standardize obstetric care also stressed women's rights as patients and their right to privacy during care; the maternal mortality rate declined by 49% in facilities that implemented the initiative, compared to 25% in control facilities.[56] These studies suggest that policies and programs that promote women's awareness, knowledge, and autonomy – especially when linked to efforts to promote economic opportunities – can be crucial to improving reproductive health outcomes. A 2017 study conducted by the *Lancet* and the Guttmacher Institute concluded that among the most impactful reforms in the area of sexual and reproductive health are those that "give women greater control over their bodies and lives".[57]

### Mutually reinforcing constraints

Figure 7.4, adapted from the WDR2012, illustrates how good reproductive health outcomes result from the interplay of a number of factors. Key dimensions of gender equality – in terms of endowments, agency, and opportunities – are related, and are influenced by the interaction of markets, formal institutions (e.g., public health systems and legal systems), and informal institutions (influenced by prevailing norms and attitudes), as well as decision-making within the household. This dynamic explains why formally valid legislation on women's

---

52  Syed Emdadul Haque et al., "Reproductive Health Care Utilization Among Young Mothers in Bangladesh: Does Autonomy Matter?" (2012) 22 *Women's Health Issues* e171.

53  Mai Do and Nami Kurimoto, "Women's Empowerment and Choice of Contraceptive Methods in Selected African Countries" (2012) 38 *International Perspectives on Sexual and Reproductive Health* 23.

54  Rob Stephenson, Andy Beke and Delphin Tsihbangu, "Contextual Influences on Contraceptive Use in the Eastern Cape, South Africa" (2008) 14 *Health & Place* 839.

55  Nava Ashraf, Erica Field, and Jean Lee, "Household Bargaining and Excess Fertility: An Experimental Study in Zambia" (2014) 104 *American Economic Review* 2210 ('Ashraf et al. "Household Bargaining and Excess Fertility"').

56  Elisabeth Rottach, Sidney Ruth Schuler, and Karen Hardee, *Gender Perspectives Improve Reproductive Health Outcomes: New Evidence* (2009), available at Population Reference Bureau, www.prb.org/Publications/Reports/2010/genderperspectives.aspx.

57  Starrs et al., "Accelerate Progress", *supra*.

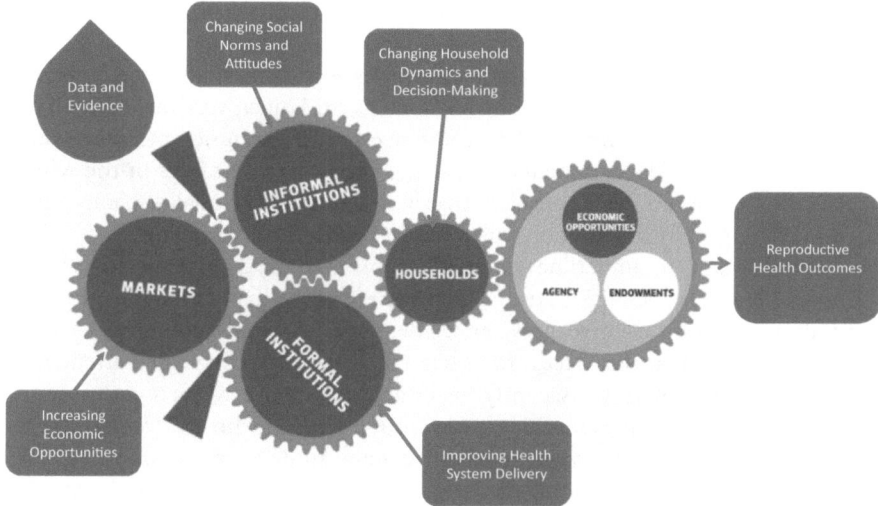

*Figure 7.4* Limited Progress in Reproductive Health Is Explained by Mutually Reinforcing Constraints

Source: Adapted from World Bank, World Development Report (2012).

health may fail to attain its goals. In line with Iyioha's theory of substantive effectiveness, the economic context in which laws operate can constrain "law's ability to deliver on its mandate".[58] For example, recent court decisions in India, discussed below, established a legal right to maternal health under India's Constitution. However, progress in India on maternal health has been slow, especially among the poorest segments of the population, suggesting the significant role of wealth in determining individual maternal health. Notwithstanding India's formally valid laws, attainment of the goal of the law (improved reproductive health outcomes) remains highly circumscribed by economic factors.

Thus, notwithstanding the (admittedly incomplete) progress with respect to laws on women's rights around the world in recent decades, poor women continue to have lower access to high-quality healthcare services than wealthier women,[59] while the low quality of public health services (i.e., the functioning of formal institutions) often deters utilization.[60]

---

58  See Iyioha, Chapter 2 of this volume.
59  Sarah Barber, Stefano Bertozzi, and Paul Gertler "Variations in Prenatal Care Quality for the Rural Poor in Mexico" (2007) 26 *Health Affairs* w310; Manju Rani, Sekhar Bonu, and Steve Harvey, "Differentials in the Quality of Antenatal Care in India" (2008) 20 *Int'l Journal for Quality Healthcare* 62; C. G. Victora et al., "Socio-Economic and Ethnic Group Inequities in Antenatal Care Quality in the Public and Private Sector in Brazil" (2010) 25 *Health Policy & Planning* 253.
60  Jean Christophe Fotso and Carol Mukiira, "Perceived Quality of and Access to Care Among Poor Urban Women in Kenya and Their Utilization of Delivery Care: Harnessing the

Sometimes these factors move in the wrong direction and vicious cycles can impede progress – as in Niger, for example. This country is a global outlier in terms of fertility, maternal mortality, and poverty – with very adverse gender norms documented in recent qualitative analysis – and has made little progress in the past 20 years.[61] In some countries, such as Sri Lanka, virtuous cycles have been initiated that have improved reproductive health, alongside other key outcomes, with positive developments reinforcing each other. The cogs-in-the-wheel visualization in Figure 7.4 emphasizes that women often face dual or compounding disadvantages, in which poor reproductive health is one element.

It is important to underline the large gaps in reproductive health within countries. The 2017 UNFPA study[62] highlighted these gaps in relation to four key indicators: contraceptive prevalence; demand for family planning satisfied through modern methods; access to antenatal care; and use of skilled attendants during childbirth – with consistently lower access for poor women with respect to each. Contraceptive prevalence is lower among women who are "poorer, rural, or less educated". The poorest quintile of women in developing countries have the least access to modern family planning. Similarly, women in the poorest 20% of households have the least access to antenatal care and are substantially more likely to give birth without a skilled attendant. These findings accord with Wagstaff, Bredenkamp, and Buisman,[63] who confirmed the persistence of inequality in both access and outcomes across a range of health indicators, including maternal mortality.[64]

As highlighted above, the way in which economic limits impact reproductive health is itself shaped by factors such as norms, government policy, and adherence to rule of law.[65] In Thailand, a low-income country, contraceptive prevalence is actually *higher* among the poorest 20% of the population than the richest 20%, due in large part to proactive government policy for universal family planning.[66] Domestic tax and spending policy also has a role to play. In countries where tax policy is oriented toward providing social protection for all, the poor are less likely to rely solely on out-of-pocket spending to cover reproductive healthcare costs.[67]

---

Potential of Private Clinics?" (2012) 27 *Health Policy & Planning* 505; L. Nikiema et al., "Quality of Antenatal Care and Obstetrical Coverage in Rural Burkina Faso" (2010) 28 *Journal of Health, Population & Nutrition* 67.

61 World Bank, *Voices of Men and Women Regarding Social Norms in Niger* (Washington, DC: World Bank, 2014).

62 United Nations Population Fund, *supra*.

63 Adam Wagstaff, Caryn Bredenkamp, and Leander Buisman, "Progress on Global Health Goals: Are the Poor Being Left Behind?" 29 *World Bank Research Observer* lku008.

64 Ibid.

65 *See* Angela Pinzon-Rondon et al., "Association of Rule of Law and Health Outcomes: An Ecological Study" (2015) 5 *BMJ Open* e007004 (finding adherence to rule of law is a "foundational determinant" of health, including with respect to maternal health indicators). For further discussion of the impact of the rule of law on women's health, see Snyder, Chapter 8 of this volume.

66 United Nations Population Fund, *supra*.

67 Starrs et al., "Accelerate Progress", *supra*.

External funding assistance is also crucial in the area of reproductive health, as government spending on healthcare in low-income countries is projected to fall below international targets.[68] Thus, economic limits on reproductive health are themselves constrained by a constellation of factors including government policy, tax and spending, external assistance for reproductive health programs, and adherence to the rule of law.

Women disadvantaged by class, caste, location, and ethnicity experience far worse reproductive health outcomes than other women.[69] In Afghanistan, for example, maternal mortality ratios in the remote Ragh district are four times greater than in urban Kabul.[70] In Latin America and the Caribbean, Indigenous women have less access to modern contraception, antenatal care, and skilled birth attendants.[71] In China, a study of Sichuan province found ethnic minority counties experienced higher maternal mortality ratios than non-minority counties, although this gap has narrowed in recent years.[72] In Western China, women from minority ethnic groups had lower utilization of maternal healthcare than women from the Han majority group.[73] In Vietnam, 60% of women from ethnic minorities give birth without prenatal care, twice the rate as that for the majority Kinh women.[74] However, this issue is not restricted to developing countries: in the United States, African American women and non-citizens have less access to prenatal care due to discrimination and immigration status.[75] Thus, even where a state seems to provide an array of modern health services for its citizens, particular groups of people defined by disparate economic levels, ethnicities, needs, and contexts often experience a formal, otherwise effective system differently than those not similarly situated and similarly identified.

Formal institutions affect access to reproductive health services. Robust public healthcare institutions, social insurance, and governmental budgetary support – or the lack of these institutional factors – all influence whether individuals can afford the services they need, such as skilled birth attendants, to attain an adequate standard of maternal health. According to UNICEF, only 68% of births

68 Ibid.
69 Paul Adamson et al., "Are Marginalized Women Being Left Behind? A Population-Based Study of Institutional Deliveries in Karnataka, India" (2012) 12 *BMC Public Health* 30; Victora et al., *supra* note 59; Cuntong Wang, "Trends in Contraceptive Use and Determinants of Choice in China: 1980–2010" (2012) 85 *Contraception* 570.
70 Linda Bartlett et al., "Progress and Inequities in Maternal Mortality in Afghanistan (RAMOS-II): A Retrospective Observational Study" (2017) 5 *Lancet Global Health* e545.
71 Marilia Mesenburg et al., "Ethnic Group Inequalities in Coverage with Reproductive, Maternal and Child Health Interventions: Cross-Sectional Analyses of National Surveys in 16 Latin American and Caribbean countries" (2018) 6 *Lancet Global Health* e902.
72 Starrs et al., "Accelerate Progress", *supra*.
73 Huang et al., "Ethnicity and Maternal and Child Health Outcomes and Service Coverage in Western China: A Systematic Review and Meta-analysis" (2017) 6 *Lancet Global Health* e39.
74 World Bank, *supra*.
75 Center for Reproductive Rights, *Reproductive Injustice: Racial and Gender Discrimination in U.S. Healthcare* (New York: Center for Reproductive Rights, 2014).

globally and 47% in Africa had skilled birth attendants in 2013.[76] In Nepal, only 44% of pregnant women received antenatal care and fewer than 1 in 5 gave birth with the assistance of skilled health personnel.[77] Here, as elsewhere, there are major differences across the distribution – in India, nearly 9 out of 10 women in the richest quintile have assistance during delivery, while only 2 out of 10 in the poorest quintile do.[78]

Barriers in accessing healthcare vary across countries and regions, but both demand and supply factors appear to matter. On the demand side, financial and physical barriers, inadequate transportation options, low-quality health services, and a lack of knowledge are all frequently cited as reasons for not seeking care.[79] In Cambodia, 3 out of 4 women cited unaffordability as a factor hindering access to maternal healthcare. In Burkina Faso, 46% of women cited long distances as a main barrier to accessing healthcare, and another 40% cited lack of transportation.[80]

On the supply side, part of the institutional challenge is the lack of resources, in particular human resources, in the health system. In a cross-section of countries, a low density of health human resources has been found to be correlated with high levels of maternal mortality.[81] Sierra Leone, for example, currently the country with the highest MMR, has only 0.20 nurses/midwives per 1,000 people.[82] Poor coverage can be exacerbated by the low quality of care from healthcare providers and high rates of absenteeism.[83]

The impact of these factors on reproductive health outcomes again shows the importance of context to the efficacy of reproductive health laws.[84] Just

76 United Nations Children's Fund, "Delivery Care" (2014), available at UNICEF http://data.unicef.org/maternal-health/delivery-care.
77 World Bank, *Population & Reproductive Health – Reproductive Health Country Profiles*, available at World Bank http://go.worldbank.org/6DZC2ITCQ0.
78 Ibid.
79 Josephine Borghi et al., "Financial Implications of Skilled Attendance at Delivery in Nepal" (2006) 11 *Tropical Medicine & Int'l Health* 228; Sabine Gabrysch, Virginia Simushi and Oona Campbell, "Availability and Distribution of, and Geographic Access to Emergency Obstetric Care in Zambia" (2011) 114 *Int'l Journal of Gynecology & Obstetrics* 174; Amy Kesterton et al., "Institutional Delivery in Rural India: the Relative Importance of Accessibility and Economic Status" (2010) 10 *BMC Pregnancy & Childbirth* 30; Christina R. Titaley et al., "Why Don't Some Women Attend Antenatal and Postnatal Care Services? A Qualitative Study of Community Members' Perspectives in Garut, Sukabumi and Ciamis Districts of West Java Province, Indonesia" (2010) 10 *BMC Pregnancy & Childbirth* 61.
80 World Bank, *supra*.
81 Sudhir Anand and Till Bärnighausen, "Human Resources and Health Outcomes: Cross-Country Econometric Study" (2004) 364 *Lancet* 1603.
82 World Bank, "Nurses and Midwives (Per 1,000 People)" available at World Bank http://data.worldbank.org/indicator/SH.MED.NUMW.P3.
83 Nazmul Chaudhury et al., "Missing in Action: Teacher and Health Worker Absence in Developing Countries" (2006) 20 *Journal of Economic Perspectives* 91; Jishnu Das et al., "In Urban and Rural India, a Standardized Patient Study Showed Low Levels of Provider Training and Huge Quality Gaps" (2012) 31 *Health Affairs* 2774.
84 See Iyioha, Chapter 2 of this volume.

as contextual elements such as religion and socio-cultural norms affect how a law is implemented,[85] institutional and economic factors act as a limit on the law. No matter how comprehensive a formal law on reproductive health is, resource constraints and institutional challenges may defeat the objective of the policy or legislation. This dynamic was sharply observed by the United Nations Special Rapporteur on the right to health, in reporting on maternal mortality in India, who remarked that "[t]here is a yawning gulf between India's commendable mortality policies and their urgent, focused, sustained, systematic and effective implementation. For the most part, maternal mortality reduction is still not a priority in India".[86] This "gulf" between laudable reproductive health laws and effective implementation persists in many countries, and highlights that "formally effective" laws may lack sufficient institutional and political support to achieve their objectives.[87] The case of India, where recent jurisprudence has recognized the right to maternal health but progress is slow, is emblematic.

## Limited accountability

Poor-quality services are endemic in the health sector.[88] As the World Development Report 2004 persuasively argued, the lack of provider accountability helps explain poor services. Part of this story is the paucity of quality data with which to measure, monitor, and track maternal health. A recent report found that only 11 of 75 high-priority maternal and child health countries have data on 11 core maternal and child health indicators, and many have no data at all.[89] Thus, without reliable and regular data, accountability is likely to be lacking.[90] The WDR2012 suggested that better data and evidence can be the oil to help grease the wheels of both the administrative and political systems, to help achieve better outcomes. In Sri Lanka, the government prioritized the collection of high-quality data on maternal mortality and good monitoring and evaluation of its programs; thus we are able to learn from the country's success. Administrative data on maternal mortality in Sri Lanka during the 1940s exceeds the quality of data available in many developing countries today.

85 See Sta. Maria, Chapter 6 in this volume, for an exposition of the impact of religion and culture on reproductive health legislation in the Philippines.
86 *Report of the Special Rapporteur on the right of everyone to the enjoyment of the highest attainable standard of health*, UNHRC, 14th Sess, UN Doc A/HRC/14/20Add.2 (15 April 2010).
87 See Iyioha, Chapter 2 of this volume.
88 Jorge Coarasa, Jishnu Das, and Jeffrey Hammer, "Private vs. Public" (2014) 51 *Fin & Dev* 34.
89 Independent Expert Review Group (iERG) on Information and Accountability for Women's and Children's Health, *Every Woman, Every Child: From Commitments to Action* (Geneva: World Health Organization, 2012).
90 Alain B. Labrique et al., "Pregnancy Registration Systems Can Enhance Health Systems, Increase Accountability and Reduce Mortality" (2012) 20 *Reproductive Health Matters* 113.

# Moving forward: policies to improve reproductive health outcomes

A number of policies have been shown to be effective in improving reproductive health outcomes. Below we review some of the most promising policy options for initiating more virtuous cycles in reproductive health outcomes and enhancing the substantive effectiveness of sexual and reproductive health laws. We group these interventions into those that expand women's agency and those that target improvements in the health sector.

## *Measures to expand agency*

Expanding women's and girls' agency (i.e., their power to make decisions) could have major ramifications on their reproductive health. Sometimes this comes through expanding educational, work, or other economic opportunities, or through increased awareness, knowledge, and aspirations. Evidence is accumulating about how well-designed policies and programs, appropriated to the local context, have improved reproductive health. We highlight some examples in this subsection.

There is also accumulating evidence that educating girls can directly improve their maternal health outcomes. In Turkey, an increase in primary education has been linked to lower fertility and increased use of contraception.[91] Similarly, the introduction of universal primary education in Nigeria in the 1970s led to lower fertility among women exposed to the policy.[92]

The impact of secondary education has also been investigated. An expansion of compulsory schooling from sixth to ninth grade in Mexico has been linked to an increased use of contraception.[93] In Kenya, an experiment reducing the costs of education for adolescent girls found that increased school attendance was associated with lower adolescent pregnancy.[94] Similarly, a conditional cash transfer program that incentivized teenage girls in Malawi to stay in school was associated with lower rates of pregnancy.[95]

Some countries appear to be explicitly implementing policies via the education system with the goal of reducing fertility. In Peru, conditional cash transfers for

---

91 Mehmet Dinçer, Neeraj Kaushal, and Michael Grossman, "Women's Education: Harbinger of Another Spring? Evidence from a Natural Experiment in Turkey" (2014) 64 *World Development* 243; Pinar Gunes, "The Role of Maternal Education in Child Health: Evidence From a Compulsory Schooling Law" (2015) 47 *Economics of Education Review* 1.

92 Una Osili and Bridget Long, "Does Female Schooling Reduce Fertility? Evidence from Nigeria" (2008) 87 *Journal of Development Economics* 57.

93 Mabel Andalón, Jenny Williams, and Michael Grossman, "Empowering Women: The Effect of Schooling on Young Women's Knowledge and Use of Contraception" (2014), available at National Bureau of Economic Research, www.nber.org.

94 Esther Duflo, Pascaline Dupas, and Michael Kremer, "Education, HIV, and Early Fertility: Experimental Evidence From Kenya" (2015) 105 *American Economic Review* 2757.

95 Sarah Baird, Craig McIntosh, and Berk Özler, "Cash or Condition? Evidence from a Cash Transfer Experiment" (2011) 126 *Quarterly Journal of Economics* 1709.

increased school attendance were identified as a mechanism for reducing fertility among beneficiaries,[96] and in Chile extended school-hours programs were found to reduce teen pregnancy.[97] Meanwhile, evidence from Bogota, Colombia, suggests that performance-based incentives were critical to the success of a conditional cash transfer program in reducing teen pregnancy.[98] The study found that the *Subsidio Educativo* program, conditioned on the teen female beneficiary being enrolled in the following year, caused a sizeable reduction in teenage pregnancy, while the *Familias en Accion* program, which does not contain a performance condition, had no effect.

There is a growing consensus that high school education might be particularly important in helping to delay the birth of a woman's first child. Following independence, Zimbabwe implemented policies that greatly increased access to secondary school for black girls. Exploiting age-specific exposures to the program, one study found that an additional year of education was associated with important delays in the age of sexual debut, age of marriage, and age of first birth.[99] Women who benefited from the policy also had lower desired fertility and demonstrated evidence of increased economic opportunities. Importantly, children born to women who went on to secondary school due to these policy reforms were 20% less likely to die prematurely than children born to mothers who had been slightly too old to benefit from these institutional changes. This is consistent with recent analysis using data from 54 developing countries, which found that having completed at least secondary education was an especially important correlate of greater sexual autonomy.[100] This points to the potential for tremendous future gains, since, as illustrated by Figure 7.5, rates of girls' secondary enrollment are below 80% in all developing regions except Europe and Central Asia, and still below half in South Asia and sub-Saharan Africa.[101]

Girls' aspirations, their anticipated economic returns on education, and family and social attitudes are important factors that also affect teen pregnancy rates.[102]

---

96 Joao Azevedo et al., *Teenage Pregnancy and Opportunities in Latin America and the Caribbean* (Washington, DC: World Bank, 2012).

97 Mathias Berthelon and Diana Kruger, "Risky Behavior Among Youth: Incapacitation Effects of School on Adolescent Motherhood and Crime in Chile" (2011) 95 *Journal of Public Economics* 41.

98 Darwin Cortés, Juan Gallego, and Dario Maldonado, *On the Design of Education Conditional Cash Transfer Programs and Non Education Outcomes: the Case of Teenage Pregnancy* (Munich: CESifo Working Paper Series, 2011).

99 Karen Grépin and Prashant Bharadwaj, "Maternal Education and Child Mortality in Zimbabwe" (2015) 44 *Journal of Health Economics* 97.

100 Hanmer and Klugman, "Expanding Women's Agency and Empowerment in Developing Countries", *supra*.

101 Esther Duflo, "Women Empowerment and Economic Development" (2012) 50 *Journal of Economic Literature* 1051.

102 Kate McQueston, Rachel Silverman, and Amanda Glassman, "Adolescent Fertility in Low- and Middle-Income Countries: Effects and Solutions – Working Paper 295" (2012), available at Center for Global Development, www.cgdev.org/content/publications/detail/1426175.

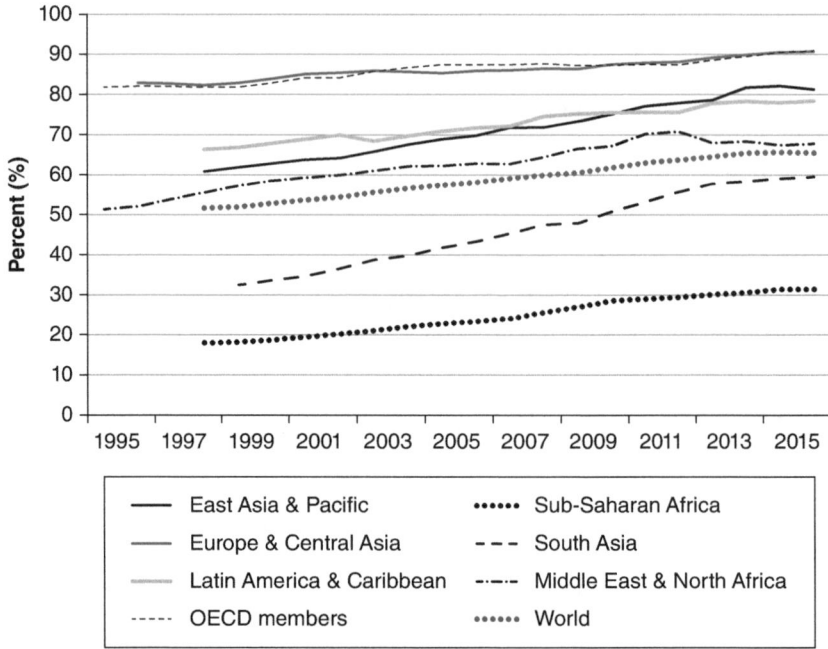

*Figure 7.5* Trends in Girls' Net Secondary Enrollment by Region, 1995–2016
Source: World Development Indicators.

A sexual education program targeting teenage girls in Kenyan high schools that provided information on the riskiness of contracting HIV with different sexual partners reduced teenage pregnancy rates and risky sexual behavior, while a program based on abstinence messages had no impact on sexual behavior.[103] A female empowerment program in Uganda that provided teenage girls with vocational training and information on sex and marriage led to a 26% decline in teenage pregnancy rates.[104]

Greater economic opportunities can alter traditional definitions of gender roles, duties, and responsibilities as well as girls' and women's aspirations, as was described in the case of the Indian call centers noted above.[105] In Bangladesh, the expansion of job opportunities for women in the garment sector was associated with a rapid increase in girls' schooling: Between 1983 and 2000,

103 Pascaline Dupas, "Do Teenagers Respond to HIV Risk Information? Evidence from a Field Experiment in Kenya" (2010) 3 *American Economic Journal: Applied Economics* 1.
104 Oriana Bandiera et al., *Women's Empowerment in Action: Evidence from a Randomized Control Trial in Africa* (Washington, DC: World Bank, 2017).
105 Jensen, "Do Labor Market Opportunities Affect Young Women's Work and Family Decisions?" *supra*.

villages within commuting distance to garment factories saw a 27% increase in girls' school enrollment rates.[106] Similarly, reforms to inheritance laws in India, which gave women greater economic power, resulted in delays in marriage for girls, an 11%–25% increase in years of schooling, and lower dowry payments.[107]

In many developing countries, women's lack of agency is also associated with discrimination under the formal legal system. The World Bank has documented how this limits women's economic opportunities.[108] Measuring indicators such as access to institutions, property laws, and restrictions on women's labor market participation, among others, the World Bank shows that laws in these areas are important determinants of women's access to economic opportunity. Notably, nearly 90% of the 143 economies surveyed have at least one legal restriction on women's access to economic opportunities.[109] The same is true in the health sphere. Even in the 21st century, legal barriers – such as laws requiring parental notification of their daughters' intended abortion or that allow husbands or partners to veto wives' or girlfriends' use of contraception – can contribute to delays in accessing (or exclusion from) essential maternal health services.[110] For example, as highlighted by Sta. Maria in this volume, the issue of parental and marital consent to reproductive health services was in contention in a recent legal challenge to reproductive health legislation in the Philippines.[111]

Legal reforms can play an important role in improving reproductive health outcomes, particularly with respect to access to abortion services. Nearly 22 million unsafe abortions occurred globally in 2008, many of them in developing countries. Over half of all abortions in developing countries are unsafe, compared with just 6% of those in developed countries.[112] While highly restrictive abortion laws do not tend to lower abortion rates, they do typically make it unsafe. The 82 countries with the most restrictive abortion legislation are also those with the highest incidence of unsafe abortions and abortion mortality rates.[113] By contrast,

106 Heath and Mobarak, "Manufacturing Growth and the Lives of Bangladeshi Women", *supra*.

107 Sanchari Roy, "Empowering Women: Inheritance Rights and Female Education in India" (2015) *Journal of Development Economics* 233.

108 World Bank, *Women, Business and the Law 2014 – Removing Restrictions to Enhance Gender Equality* (Washington, DC: World Bank, 2014), available at World Bank http://wbl. worldbank.org/reports; Mary Hallward-Driemeier, Tazeen Hasan, and Anca Bogdana Rusu, *Women's Legal Rights Over 50 Years: What Is the Impact of Reform?* World Bank Policy Research Working Paper (Washington, DC: World Bank, 2013).

109 World Bank, *supra*.

110 Rodolfo Carvalho Pacagnella et al., "The Role of Delays in Severe Maternal Morbidity and Mortality: Expanding the Conceptual Framework" (2012) 20 *Reproductive Health Matters* 155.

111 See Sta. Maria, Chapter 6 of this volume.

112 World Health Organization, *Unsafe Abortion: Global and Regional Estimates of the Incidence of Unsafe Abortion and Associated Mortality in 2008* (Geneva: World Health Organization, 2011).

113 Marge Berer, "National Laws and Unsafe Abortion: The Parameters of Change" (2004) 12 *Reproductive Health Matters* 1.

where abortion is permitted on broad legal grounds, it is generally safer.[114] Abortion policy liberalization, coupled with the implementation of safe abortion services and other reproductive health interventions, can lead to dramatic declines in abortion-related mortality.[115] In Romania, following policy reform in 1989, the abortion-related mortality ratio dropped from 148 deaths per 100,000 live births in 1989 to five deaths per 100,000 in 2006.[116] Similarly, in Bangladesh, there was more than a 50% reduction in the share of maternal deaths due to abortion, from 24% in 1976–1985 to 11% in 1996–2005, in areas receiving specific interventions in addition to legal liberalization.

### Reducing financial barriers within the health sector

Over the past decade, many governments have sought to reduce the financial barriers women face in accessing maternal health services. Three types of interventions are common: vouchers to cover pregnancy services,[117] exemptions from user fees for specific services or for pregnant women,[118] and direct financial payments conditioned on the use of certain services.[119] These approaches are likely to be most effective where demand-side factors are the most important bottlenecks to increased utilization.

Several countries – including Bangladesh, Cambodia, Kenya, Pakistan, Tanzania, and Uganda – have implemented voucher-based programs to encourage the use of maternal and reproductive health services, which evaluations have generally found to be effective.[120] In Bangladesh, women who gave birth in areas

114  Gilda Sedgh et al., "Induced Abortion: Incidence and Trends Worldwide From 1995 to 2008" (2012) 379 *Lancet* 625.
115  See Cao, Chapter 4 of this volume.
116  Janie Benson, Kathryn Andersen, and Ghazaleh Samandari, "Reductions in Abortion-Related Mortality Following Policy Reform: Evidence from Romania, South Africa and Bangladesh" (2011) 8 *Reproductive Health* 39.
117  Nicole M. Bellows, Ben W. Bellows, and Charlotte Warren, "Systematic Review: The Use of Vouchers for Reproductive Health Services in Developing Countries: Systematic Review" (2011) 16 *Tropical Medicine & Int'l Health* 84 ('Bellows et al., "Systematic Review"'); Ha T.H. Nguyen et al., "Encouraging Maternal Health Service Utilization: an Evaluation of the Bangladesh Voucher Program" (2012) 74 *Sociacl Science & Medicine* 989 ('Nguyen et al., "Encouraging Maternal Health Service Utilization"').
118  Valéry Ridde and Florence Morestin, "A Scoping Review of the Literature on the Abolition of User Fees in Health Care Services in Africa" (2011) 26 *Health Policy & Planning* 1; Sophie Witter et al., "The National Free Delivery and Caesarean Policy in Senegal: Evaluating Process and Outcomes" (2010) 25 *Health Policy & Planning* 384; Sophie Witter et al., "The Experience of Ghana in Implementing a User Fee Exemption Policy to Provide Free Delivery Care" (2007) 15 *Reproductive Health Matters* 61.
119  Stephen Lim et al., "India's Janani Suraksha Yojana, a Conditional Cash Transfer Programme to Increase Births in Health Facilities: an Impact Evaluation" (2010) 375 *Lancet* 2009 ('Lim et al., "India's Janani Suraksha Yojana"'); Timothy Powell-Jackson and Kara Hanson, "Financial Incentives for Maternal Health: Impact of a National Programme in Nepal" (2012) 31 *Journal of Health Economics* 271.
120  Bellows et al., "Systematic Review", *supra*.

targeted by the vouchers were more likely to use an accredited provider and were 13% more likely to give birth in a facility than those in comparison areas.[121] In rural Kenya, women living in voucher areas were also more likely to give birth in health facilities and with skilled healthcare providers.[122] Similar results were obtained among women in Nairobi.[123] However, none of these voucher programs was randomly assigned, and most also included substantial supply-side interventions. Nonetheless, a randomized evaluation of maternity vouchers delivered via mobile phones in Western Kenya demonstrated a large positive impact on facility deliveries.[124]

Other countries, in response to concerns about the regressive impact of user fees, have exempted women from paying for certain maternity services. Such policies have been introduced in Ghana, Senegal, Mali, Morocco, Sierra Leone, and elsewhere.[125] While evaluations have generally concluded that these policies can increase the coverage of maternal health services, weakness in the study designs suggest that there is not yet sufficient evidence to conclude that these policies have been effective.[126] Some qualitative research has found that some of these programs were ill conceived or poorly implemented, which may have limited their impact.[127]

Another approach is to provide cash payments to women conditional upon their use of maternal services. The most rigorously evaluated conditional cash transfer (CCT) program, the Progress/*Oportunidades* program in Mexico, targeted the health-seeking behavior of poor households.[128] Women exposed to the program, especially younger mothers, were more likely to both access antenatal

121  Nguyen et al., "Encouraging Maternal Health Service Utilization", *supra*.
122  Francis Obare et al., "Community-Level Impact of the Reproductive Health Vouchers Programme on Service Utilization in Kenya" (2013) 28 *Health Policy & Planning* 165.
123  Ben Bellows et al., "Increase in Facility-Based Deliveries Associated with a Maternal Health Voucher Programme in Informal Settlements in Nairobi, Kenya" (2013) 28 *Health Policy & Planning* 134.
124  Karen Grépin, James Habyarimana, and William Jack, "Cash on Delivery: Results of a randomized experiment to promote maternal health care in Kenya" (2019) 65 *Journal of Health Economics* 15.
125  Issam Bennis and Vincent De Brouwere, "Fee Exemption for Caesarean Section in Morocco" (2012) 70 *Archives of Public Health* 3; Frédérique Ponsar et al., "Abolishing User Fees for Children and Pregnant Women Trebled Uptake of Malaria-Related Interventions in Kangaba, Mali" (2011) 26 *Health Policy & Planning* ii72; Wairagala Wakabi, "Mothers and Infants to Get Free Health Care in Sierra Leone" (2010) 375 *Lancet* 882; Sophie Witter et al. (2010), *supra* note 118; Sophie Witter et al. (2007), *supra* note 118.
126  Susie Dzakpasu, Timothy Powell-Jackson, and Oona Campbell, "Impact of User Fees on Maternal Health Service Utilization and Related Health Outcomes: a Systematic Review" (2013) 29 *Health Policy & Planning* 137.
127  Mary Hadley, "Does Increase in Utilisation Rates Alone Indicate the Success of a User Fee Removal Policy? A Qualitative Case Study From Zambia" 103 *Health Policy* 244; Manassé Nimpagaritse and Maria Paola Bertone, "The Sudden Removal of User Fees: The Perspective of a Frontline Manager in Burundi" 26 *Health Policy & Planning* ii63.
128  Paul Gertler, "Do Conditional Cash Transfers Improve Child Health? Evidence from PROGRESA's Control Randomized Experiment" (2004) 94 *American Economic Review* 336.

care and utilize skilled healthcare providers for delivery.[129] India has also recently introduced the *Janani Suraksha Yojania* program, a CCT to promote the use of maternal health services through financial incentives for women to deliver in healthcare facilities. A recent evaluation found that the program increased rates of institutional delivery,[130] although there is minimal evidence to date that it has improved the quality of care delivered or mortality rates.[131] Nonetheless, the evidence generally suggests that CCT programs can be an effective route to increase the utilization of maternal health services.

Some countries have introduced reforms that target the supply side: providers. These schemes have been generally referred to as performance-based financing or performance-based incentive schemes. Some of these programs have specifically targeted maternal and reproductive health outcomes, and at least nine of the country case examples available have been evaluated for effectiveness in increasing service utilization and quality.[132] Although the studies vary in terms of quality, most of the evaluations generally find that the schemes do lead to increases in key maternal health indicators, in particular institutional deliveries. For example, result-based financing schemes have been tried in several countries. In Rwanda, small incentives were paid to providers conditional on ensuring that their patients received the prescribed maternal and child health services.[133] After two years, a 23% increase in institutional deliveries and increases in the quality of prenatal care were evident. In Zimbabwe, a similar scheme provides subsidies to rural health clinics and hospitals based on their performance in delivering a package of free health services to pregnant women and young children. Initial results from the program were positive: the number of women who had four or more prenatal visits increased by 65% over the year before.[134]

Efforts to scale up the availability of human resources, in particular less qualified health workers who can be more rapidly trained and more easily deployed into rural communities, hold promise but require more evaluation. Ethiopia, a large and mostly rural country with one of the lowest ratios of physicians to population in the world, undertook a massive expansion of health human resources

---

129  Sarah Barber and Paul Gertler, "Empowering Women to Obtain High Quality Care: Evidence From an Evaluation of Mexico's Conditional Cash Transfer Programme" (2009) 24 *Health Policy & Planning* 18; Sandra Sosa-Rubí et al., "Learning Effect of a Conditional Cash Transfer Programme on Poor Rural Women's Selection of Delivery Care in Mexico" (2011) 26 *Health Policy & Planning* 496.

130  Lim et al., "India's Janani Suraksha Yojana", *supra*.

131  Stephen Lim et al., "India's Janani Suraksha Yojana: Further Review Needed – Authors' Reply" (2011) 377 *Lancet* 296.

132  Rena Eichler et al., "Performance-Based Incentives to Improve Health Status of Mothers and Newborns: What Does the Evidence Show?" (2015) 31 *Journal of Health, Population, & Nutrition* S36.

133  Paulin Basinga et al., "Effect on Maternal and Child Health Services in Rwanda of Payment to Primary Health-Care Providers for Performance: An Impact Evaluation" (2011) 377 *Lancet* 1421.

134  World Bank, "In Rural Zimbabwe, No Fees, Better Care for Women and Children" (12 November 2012), available at World Bank, www.worldbank.org/en/news/2012/11/30/in-rural-zimbabwe-no-fees-better-care-for-women-children.

by scaling up health extension workers in rural regions. Some studies have shown that the program has been well received by women, and suggested that the use of family planning and antenatal care have increased.[135] However, other evaluations have found that the Ethiopian project has had only a limited impact on maternal health indicators such as provision of most prenatal and postnatal services.[136] Evaluations suggest that in rural Pakistan, the Lady Health Worker program – which briefly trains local female residents to deliver a range of health services from immunizations to family planning in order to provide basic health education and to identify and refer more complicated cases – has led to national increases in the use of contraceptives.[137]

Fewer than 2 out of 3 women globally are using modern contraception. Regional rates of contraceptive prevalence range from about 80% in East Asia and the Pacific and North America to 24% in sub-Saharan Africa.[138] Estimates of the unmet need for contraception are correspondingly large – and suggest that there is scope to expand these programs. In sub-Saharan Africa, a quarter of women report an unmet need for family planning, and this rate has remained relatively constant since the early 1990s.[139] However, studies also underline the importance of understanding household preferences and the constraints on female autonomy when designing family planning programs. A randomized controlled trial in Zambia found that a program was effective at reducing unwanted pregnancies when women were able to access family planning services without their husbands present.[140] In Ethiopia, a lack of high-quality, concealable forms of contraception was thought to be a reason why a randomized intervention to increase the uptake of family planning programs failed to increase utilization.[141] Recent work in Peru suggests that where machismo, or a strong male-dominated culture, is present, reaching out to men can be a prerequisite for programs targeted at women's contraceptive use.[142]

At the same time, it is unlikely that any single intervention will be sufficient to make significant improvements in reproductive health outcomes. In Sri Lanka,

135 Marge Koblinsky et al., "Responding to the Maternal Health Care Challenge: The Ethiopian Health Extension Program" (2010) 24 *Ethiopian Journal of Health Development* 105; Araya Medhanyie et al., "The Role of Health Extension Workers in Improving Utilization of Maternal Health Services in Rural Areas in Ethiopia: a Cross Sectional Study" 12 *BMC Health Services Research* 352.
136 Assefa Admassie, Degnet Abebaw, and Andinet Woldemichael, "Impact Evaluation of the Ethiopian Health Services Extension Programme" (2009) 1 *Journal of Development Effectiveness* 430.
137 Megan Douthwaite and Patrick Ward, "Increasing Contraceptive Use in Rural Pakistan: an Evaluation of the Lady Health Worker Programme" (2005) 20 *Health Policy & Planning* 117.
138 See Figure 7.6.
139 Alex Ezeh, John Bongaarts, and Blessing Mberu, "Global Population Trends and Policy Options" (2012) 380 *Lancet* 142.
140 Ashraf et al. "Household Bargaining and Excess Fertility", *supra*.
141 Jaikishan Desai and Alessandro Tarozzi, "Microcredit, Family Planning Programs, and Contraceptive Behavior: Evidence from a Field Experiment in Ethiopia" (2011) 48 *Demography* 749.
142 World Bank, *The Third Asset: Improving Development Outcomes Through Agency* (Washington, DC: World Bank, 2012).

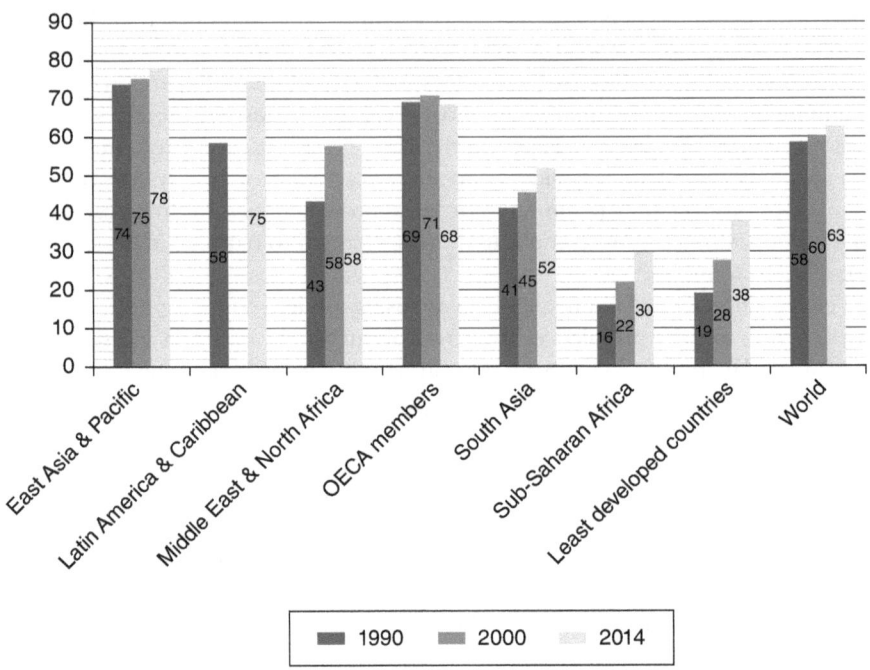

*Figure 7.6* Trends in Contraceptive Prevalence by Region, 1990–2014

Note: Contraceptive prevalence rate is the percentage of women married or in-union aged 15 to 49 who are practicing, or whose sexual partners are practicing, any form of contraception.

Source: UNICEF's State of the World's Children and Childinfo, United Nations Population Division's World Contraceptive Use, household surveys including Demographic and Health Surveys and Multiple Indicator Cluster Surveys.

where a rapid decline in maternal mortality was documented in the 1940s through the 1960s, several health system improvements were implemented.[143] More recently, the Saving Mothers, Giving Life program has piloted a "whole of health systems" approach to reducing maternal mortality in eight districts in Zambia and Uganda.[144] While the program is believed to have reduced maternal mortality in targeted districts, concerns have been raised about its long-term sustainability.

143 Seema Jayachandran and Adriana Lleras-Muney, "Life Expectancy and Human Capital Investments: Evidence From Maternal Mortality Declines" (2009) 124 *Quarterly Journal of Economics* 349.
144 Margaret Kruk et al., "'Big Push' to Reduce Maternal Mortality in Uganda and Zambia Enhanced Health Systems but Lacked a Sustainability Plan" (2014) 33 *Health Affairs* 1058.

*Improving accountability for reproductive health outcomes*

Increasing provider accountability to patients can help improve health service delivery and health outcomes.[145] Options include creating community participation mechanisms,[146] enhancing the quality of health information for consumers, establishing community groups to empower consumers to take action, and including non-governmental organizations to expand access to care.[147] Information, dialogue, and negotiation have been widely identified as important elements of accountability mechanisms that address problems and foster better service provision. But power relations (and the social contexts within which they are applied) must be taken into account when determining how accountability mechanisms should be used.[148] Social accountability mechanisms can also help empower marginalized groups when they are encouraged to be active participants in such measures. This was reportedly the case among Sangha women in Andhra Pradesh, India, who were given training on gender, health, and social action as part of a pilot project to make the health system more accountable by improving interactions between providers and lower caste women.[149]

Some evidence from Uganda suggests that introducing a local accountability mechanism, which included efforts to stimulate beneficiary control alongside provision of information about staff performance, can lead to significant improvements in maternal health outcomes. Treated communities had 21% fewer births over the period 2006–2009 and a drop in the rate of stillbirths of almost 1%.[150] By contrast, if a community lacked information about staff performance, the same type of intervention had no measurable impact on the quality or uptake in the use of medical care.[151] Accountability can thus play an important role in improving provision of primary healthcare and health outcomes.

145 David Berlan and Jeremy Shiffman, "Holding Health Providers in Developing Countries Accountable to Consumers: A Synthesis of Relevant Scholarship" (2011) 27 *Health Policy & Planning* 271 ('Berlan and Shiffman, "Holding Health Providers in Developing Countries Accountable to Consumers"').

146 Martina Björkman and Jakob Svensson, "Power to the People: Evidence from a Randomized Field Experiment of a Community-Based Monitoring Project in Uganda" (2009) 124 *Quarterly Journal of Economics* 735 ('Bjorkman and Svensson, "Power to the People"').

147 Berlan and Shiffman, "Holding Health Providers in Developing Countries Accountable to Consumers", *supra*.

148 Asha George, "Using Accountability to Improve Reproductive Health Care" (2003) 11 *Reproductive Health Matters* 161 ('George, "Using Accountability to Improve Reproductive Health Care"'); Ranjani Murthy and Barbara Klugman, "Service Accountability and Community Participation in the Context of Health Sector Reforms in Asia: Implications for Sexual and Reproductive Health Services" (2004) 19 *Health Policy & Planning* i78.

149 George, ibid.

150 Bjorkman and Svensson, "Power to the People", *supra*.

151 Martina Björkman, Damien de Walque, and Jakob Svensson, *Information Is Power: Experimental Evidence of the Long Run Impact of Community Based Monitoring* (Washington, DC: World Bank, 2014).

Peru is an interesting case where improved reproductive health outcomes were associated with expanding entitlements and a strengthening public sector.[152] In the early 2000s, rates of perinatal and maternal mortality in Peru were high by regional standards, and institutional deliveries had plateaued nationally at about 70%; in addition, less than half of rural births were in a clinic or hospital. As part of a broader set of health sector reforms, the government targeted institutional delivery rates as a key indicator. From 2002, poor households were exempted from health user fees and entitled to specific services for particular health conditions.

The Ministry of Health also attempted to address non-financial barriers by developing and promoting culturally informed birth practices in government facilities. On the supply side, facilities and human resources were strengthened to provide more and higher-quality health services, especially in previously under-served regions. A new standards process was created to inform monitoring, and the performance-based budget was contingent on meeting certain institutional birth targets. Although these efforts have not yet been rigorously evaluated, there have been significant gains in access. Institutional delivery rates among women in the bottom income quintile rose by more than half from 2005 to 2009 (32% to 48% of all births).

Recent work from Orissa, India, identifies three processes underpinning effective social accountability: generating demand for rights and better services, leveraging intermediaries to legitimize the demands of poor and marginalized women, and sensitizing leaders and health providers to women's needs. In this context, social accountability mechanisms such as public hearings provide new ways for women to collectively voice their concerns and demands in a supportive environment. These demands are then reinforced and legitimized by intermediary partners such as local elected officials and the media, leading to increased receptivity to women's needs.[153]

Technology is also creating ways to help strengthen accountability chains between healthcare providers and their patients. A good example of this comes from Uttar Pradesh, India, where a grassroots women's organization, SAHAYOG, launched the My Health, My Voice program in 2012. Using a mobile phone application, women have been encouraged to report any illicit informal fees demanded of them by healthcare providers when they deliver in public clinics that should normally be free to users.[154] While the program has not been rigorously evaluated, over a thousand reports have been logged, women report positive

---

152 World Bank, "Peru – Recurso Programmatic AAA – Phase IV: Improving Health Outcomes by Strengthening Users' Entitlements and Reinforcing Public Sector Management" (4 February 2011), available at World Bank, https://openknowledge.worldbank.org/handle/10986/2739.

153 Susan Papp, Aparajita Gogoi, and Catherine Campbell, "Improving Maternal Health Through Social Accountability: a Case Study From Orissa, India" (2012) 8 *Global Public Health* 449.

154 Averting Maternal Disability and Death and SAHAYOG, "Using Mobile Phones to Report Informal Fees Requested for Maternal Health Care" (2014), available at Maternal Health Task Force, www.mhtf.org/2014/05/05/using-mobile-phones-to-report-informal-fees-requested-for-maternal-health-care.

satisfaction with the program, and the information has been shared with health managers.

Similar systems have been implemented in other countries, such as the U-Report system in Uganda. Since its launch, over 290,000 citizens – including every member of parliament – have voluntarily signed up to become "U-reporters". Every week, U-reporters are polled on issues of public importance, including those related to health service delivery, and the data from these polls are aggregated at the district level and made available to interested parties. Data collected from the program frequently makes it into the national newspapers and has led to discussions among policymakers. UNICEF is currently supporting the rollout of a similar system in other African countries.

Finally, legal and quasi-legal mechanisms facilitate accountability by allowing poor and disempowered people to enforce their reproductive rights. Both international treaties and domestic laws create legal obligations on governments with respect to reproductive health. For example, the right to sexual and reproductive health is a central component of the "right to the highest attainable standard of physical and mental health" guaranteed by the International Covenant on Economic, Social and Cultural Rights (ICECSR).[155] The International Convention on the Elimination of All Forms of Discrimination Against Women (CEDAW) requires non-discrimination with respect to the provision of family planning and that women are provided appropriate services in connection with pregnancy.[156] In some countries, the national constitution or legislation may also create duties on the government regarding reproductive health.

Broadly, the mechanisms that enforce these rights fall into three categories: (1) national courts and institutions; (2) regional human rights bodies; and (3) international mechanisms, such as the UN human rights treaty monitoring bodies. At the national level, litigation in domestic courts is one way in which governments have been held accountable. Two recent cases in India involving reproductive health highlight this trend. In 2011, the Delhi High Court ruled in the consolidated cases of *Laxmi Mandal v. Deen Dayal Harinagar Hospital & Others* and *Jaitun v. Maternal Home MCD, Jangpura & Others*, which involved the denial of maternal care to impoverished women from scheduled caste communities. The court found violations of reproductive rights in both cases and held that under CEDAW and ICECSR, "no woman, more so a pregnant woman should be denied the facility of treatment at any stage irrespective of her social and economic background".[157] In the opinion of the court, "[t]his is where the inalienable right to health which is so inherent in the right to life gets enforced".[158]

155 International Covenant on Economic, Social, and Cultural Rights, 19 December 1966, 993 UNTS 3, art 7.

156 Convention on the Elimination of All Forms of Discrimination against Women, 18 December 1979, 1249 UNTS 13, art 12.

157 Ibid.

158 Consolidated Decision, *Laxmi Mandal v Deen Dayal Harinagar Hospital & Others*, W.P. (C) No. 8853/2008 and *Jaitun v Maternal Home MCD, Jangpura & Others*, W.P. (C) 8853/2008 & 10700/2009, Delhi High Court (2010).

In 2012, the High Court of Madhya Pradesh held that "the inability of women to survive pregnancy and child birth violates her fundamental right to live as guaranteed under Article 21 of the Constitution of India", and that "it is the primary duty of the government to ensure that every woman survives pregnancy and child birth".[159]

Regional bodies also provide a mechanism through which to enforce reproductive rights. In *Xákmok v. Paraguay*, the Inter-American Court of Human Rights rebuked Paraguay for its failure to ensure adequate maternal healthcare to Indigenous women and required the state to establish certain procedures, such as the training of skilled birth attendants.[160]

Accountability for violations of reproductive rights may also be sought through international mechanisms, such as the UN human rights treaty monitoring bodies. In 2011, the Committee on the Elimination of Discrimination Against Women, the UN body that monitors state compliance with CEDAW, issued two major rulings in this area. The first ruling, in *Pimentel v. Brazil*, represents the first decision in a maternal death case issued by an international human rights body. The committee found that states have an obligation under CEDAW to ensure the provision of adequate maternal care to all women and to reduce preventable maternal deaths under a national action plan.[161] In the second case, *L.C. v. Peru*, the committee concluded that states are required to ensure access to abortion when a woman's physical or mental health is at risk and to decriminalize abortion when pregnancy results from rape.[162] Both *Pimentel* and *L.C.* demonstrate the role of international human rights treaties and treaty monitoring bodies in upholding the reproductive rights of women. Of course, legal mechanisms do not always work effectively for women. Charlotte Skeet's chapter in this volume insightfully shows how, in some cases, courts fail to grasp the true nature of a claimant's case, thereby defeating the claims.[163]

Efforts to increase the ability of women in developing countries to use and understand the law (known in the scholarly literature as 'legal empowerment' activities) can also increase accountability and women's agency.[164] In Nepal, a USAID-backed legal literacy program increased participants' willingness to pursue change around issues such as domestic violence and household decision-making.[165] In Honduras, legal literacy and advocacy programs were successful

---

159 *Sandesh Bansal v Union of India* W.P. (C) 9061/2008, High Court of Madhya Pradesh (2012).

160 *Case of the Xákmok Kasek Indigenous Community v Paraguay* (2012), Judgment, Inter-Am Ct HR (Ser C) at para 233.

161 Committee on the Elimination of Discrimination against Women, *Views on Communication No. 17/2008*, CEDAW, 49th Sess, CEDAW/C/49/D/17/2008 (2011).

162 Committee on the Elimination of Discrimination against Women, *Views on Communication No. 22/2009*, CEDAW, 50th Sess, CEDAW/C/50/D/22/2009 (2011).

163 See Skeet, Chapter 5 of this volume.

164 Laura Goodwin and Vivek Maru, "What Do We Know about Legal Empowerment? Mapping the Evidence" (2017) 9 *Hague Journal on the Rule of Law* 157.

165 Raju Dhakal and Misbah Sheikh, "Breaking Barriers, Building Bridges: A Case Study of USAID/Nepal's SO3 Women's Empowerment Program" (Washington, DC: Asia Foundation, 1997).

in increasing agency for women working in textile factories on issues such as women's rights and labor rights.[166]

## Conclusion

Improving the reproductive health of women around the world is vitally important for the health benefits that will ensue. Discussions about improving reproductive health outcomes have tended to focus on making improvements from within the health sector. Our survey and analysis complements more recent work, including the WDR2012 and discussions around SDG 5, and suggests that measures of gender inequality are important predictors of poor reproductive health, and therefore addressing these economic and related sources of inequality is critical to improving reproductive health outcomes.[167]

Proven policy options are available to realize those gains, although what does and does not work will be very much driven by each country's institutional, political, and cultural context. Context matters, not only because of how it shapes the technical and financial possibilities, but also because of the complicating influence of social norms and attitudes in policymaking and implementation. More broadly, the recognition of gender inequalities in agency underlines the need to engage both women and men in reproductive health interventions. All of this underlines the importance of both "internal" and "external" limits in constraining the effectiveness of reproductive health laws.

There are important implications for policy. In many developing contexts, alongside the need to actively consider the technical interventions that have been shown to work,[168] poverty and constraints on the agency of women and girls need to be addressed in order to be able to realize gains in reproductive health.

166 Juan-Carlos Arita, "A Life with Dignity: Honduran Women Raising Voices to Improve Labor Standards" (2018), available at Oxfam, https://policy-practice.oxfam.org.uk/publications/a-life-with-dignity-honduran-women-raising-voices-to-improve-labour-standards-120557.

167 United Nations General Assembly, *The Road to Dignity by 2030: Ending Poverty, Transforming All Lives and Protecting the Planet*, UNGA, 66th Sess, UN Doc A/69/700 (2014).

168 Oona Campbell, Wendy Graham and Lancet Maternal Survival Series Steering Group, "Strategies for Reducing Maternal Mortality: Getting on with What Works" (2006) 368 *Lancet* 1284.

# 8 Indigenous feminist legal theory

## A multi-juridical analysis of the limits of law on Indigenous women's health in relation to HIV in Canada

*Emily Snyder*

## Introduction

Indigenous women in Canada experience stark health disparities compared to non-Indigenous people, as well as pronounced differences compared to Indigenous men.[1] While law aspires to challenge social problems and ought to resist rather than contribute to those inequalities, difficult questions remain about the limits and effectiveness of law in supporting Indigenous women's health. For example, the Canadian legal system, as discussed in this chapter, is born of colonial and heteropatriarchal structures, and Canadian law has historically functioned, and continues to operate, as an institutional tool that works to entrench the Canadian state as a legitimate authority over Indigenous peoples. As D'Arcy Vermette emphasizes, "Aboriginal people continue to be faced with the inability to define their own world within the confines of Canadian law".[2]

"Law" in Canada is typically imagined (especially by settlers) as state laws, yet multiple Indigenous legal orders have existed and continue to exist in this territory. It is vital then in this chapter's assessment of the limits of law to center the following question: whose laws are we talking about when we are examining legal effectiveness and limits in relation to Indigenous women's health? I take up this question through an examination of law as a social determinant of health in order

---

1 See: Vivian O'Donnell and Susan Wallace, "First Nations, Métis and Inuit Women" in Statistics Canada, *Women in Canada: A Gender-based Statistical Report,* 6th ed. (July 2011), available at https://www.150.statcan.gc.ca/n1/en/pub/89-503-x/2010001/article/11442-eng.pdf?st=18Jy2Yev at 43–46; Carrie Bourassa, Kim McKay-McNabb and Mary Hampton, "Racism, Sexism, and Colonialism: The Impact on the Health of Aboriginal Women in Canada" (2004) 24:1 *Canadian Woman Studies* 23 ('Bourassa et al., "Racism, Sexism, and Colonialism"'); Native Women's Association of Canada, "Social Determinants of Health and Canada's Aboriginal Women" (4 June 2007), available at www.nwac.ca/wp-content/uploads/2015/05/2007-Social-Determinants-of-Health-and-Canada%E2%80%99s-Aboriginal-Women-NWAC-Submission-to-WHO-Commission.pdf. In this chapter, I use the term "Indigenous" to speak to First Nations, Métis, and Inuit people. At times quotes use "Aboriginal" and refer to the same groups of people.

2 D'Arcy Vermette, "Colonialism and the Suppression of Aboriginal Voice" (2008) 40:2 *Ottawa Law Review* 225 at 230 ('Vermette, "Colonialism and the Suppression of Aboriginal Voice"').

to create an approach that analyzes law not only as rules, but to also examine legal orders more broadly in terms of how they are shaped by social norms and are intimately woven into social problems (for example, by creating or perpetuating conditions that make people unwell or by failing to respond to harm or support responses that promote well-being).

Towards this objective, this chapter analyzes how Canadian law has been, and continues to be, a central mechanism that reproduces and operationalizes gendered colonial ideologies that work against Indigenous women's health. State law has been a negative determinant of health for Indigenous women and has supported toxic social conditions that undermine their well-being. A common response to the failure of Canadian law in relation to Indigenous women's health has been to call for reform to Canadian law and health policies. While these are important discussions, and the power of Canadian law cannot be ignored, Indigenous legal responses also need to be central in discussions on the relationship between law and Indigenous women's health. Indigenous laws evoke sets of legal norms and practices grounded in Indigenous communities and can be much more productive for supporting Indigenous health, compared to state laws.

However, as I argue, a practical and critical approach to understanding Indigenous laws as a determinant of health must be one that *also* engages with the limits of Indigenous law. As Irehobhude O. Iyioha's chapter in this collection cogently demonstrates, there are limits inherent to any legal order, as humans attempt to articulate, interpret, challenge, and use law.[3] Indigenous laws too often are idealized as having no limits or are characterized through colonial tropes as backwards, inferior, and deeply limited. In relation to women's health, this dichotomy frames Indigenous laws as either fully supportive of Indigenous women (or as a wholly positive determinant) or as sexist and unsafe for Indigenous women's well-being. Drawing on Indigenous feminist legal theory, I work in between these extremes to illustrate why gendered power dynamics and considerations of limits need to be more complexly engaged in relation to Indigenous laws and women's health. I ground this discussion about state laws and Indigenous laws in relation to available research on health and legal issues faced by Indigenous women who are HIV-positive.

## State law as a social determinant of health

Indigenous people experience health in ways that are distinct from non-Indigenous people in Canada. As Yvonne Boyer outlines:

> [D]isparities in health status typically arise from social, political, cultural, and economic determinants, which lie largely outside the health realm. Certain disparities inevitably have an impact on individuals, their communities, and their nations. These determinants also have an impact across generations.

3 See Iyioha, Chapter 2 of this volume.

Determinants affect the health of both the individual and the communities in which they live.[4]

These impacts are especially felt by Indigenous women. Heteropatriarchy, racism, and colonialism do not operate in isolation – there are particular ways that colonialism is operationalized against Indigenous women's bodies. For example, Indigenous women have faced, and are facing, issues such as alarmingly high rates of gendered violence, state regulation of midwifery/birthing practices in Indigenous communities, and coerced sterilization in Canadian hospitals.[5] These are identifiable "women's health" issues, though it is imperative to also understand how gendered colonial oppression operates through seemingly "gender-neutral" Indigenous health issues as well. Sexism is rampant in settler society, and is also a significant problem in Indigenous communities;[6] thus, it is pertinent to examine the ways that gender discrimination, alongside other forms of oppression, shape well-being. Further, Indigenous people who are 2LGBTQI can deal with challenging issues, including lack of access to inclusive medical care and treatments, legal barriers, increased vulnerability to violence, disproportionate mental health issues, high suicide rates, and struggles with addictions.[7]

Social determinants of health are one way of engaging in contextual analyses of well-being.[8] They refer to social environmental realities that impact health. While determinants such as healthcare services, education, and employment status are often focused on, it is imperative to also take a broader approach that reads these through deeper analyses of social structures or what are referred to by some as "distal determinants". As Karina Czyzewski explains, distal determinants encourage macro level analyses that examine "the *causes of causes*" regarding the uneven ways that groups of people experience privilege and oppression.[9] She (and

---

4 Yvonne Boyer, *Moving Aboriginal Health Forward: Discarding Canada's Legal Barriers* (Saskatoon: Purich Publishing Limited, 2014) at 166 ('Boyer, *Moving Aboriginal Health Forward*').

5 Regarding gendered violence, see Amnesty International "No More Stolen Sisters" (2009), available at www.amnesty.ca/sites/amnesty/files/amr200122009en.pdf. Regarding midwifery, see Boyer, *supra* at 77–79. Regarding sterilization, see Boyer, *supra* at 83–86; Karen Stote, *An Act of Genocide: Colonialism and the Sterilization of Aboriginal Women* (Winnipeg: Fernwood Publishing, 2015).

6 For discussions about this, see Joyce Green, ed., *Making Space for Indigenous Feminism*, 2nd ed. (Winnipeg: Fernwood Publishing, 2017).

7 Two-spirit, lesbian, gay, bi, trans, queer, intersex. See First Nations Centre, "Suicide Prevention and Two-Spirited People" (Ottawa: National Aboriginal Health Organization, 2012).

8 There are many ways to engage in contextual analyses of law and well-being. There is much important literature that examines how colonialism is gendered and how state policies and laws create harms for Indigenous women (see, for example, work by Sarah Hunt, Sarah Deer, Sherene Razack). In this chapter, I am focusing only on social determinants of health literature, though it is evident that people working in this area could benefit from drawing on decolonial feminist legal literature.

9 Karina Czyzewski, "Colonialism as a Broader Social Determinant of Health" (2011) 2:1 *The International Indigenous Policy Journal*, article 5, 1 at 4 [emphasis in original] ('Czyzewski, "Colonialism as a Broader Social Determinant of Health"').

others) argues for the importance of understanding colonialism as a distal determinant that has impacted Indigenous well-being historically and today.[10] From this perspective, approaching law as a determinant of health entails examining not only how specific laws, legal interpretations, and justice practices are impacting Indigenous women, but also how colonialism, racism, and heteropatriarchy are shaping those very laws, interpretations, and practices.

Similarly, Naomi Adelson argues that Indigenous health needs to be understood in relation to "the direct and indirect present-day symptoms of a history of loss of lands and autonomy and the results of the political, cultural, economic and social disenfranchisement that ensued".[11] While it has long been clear to Indigenous people (and repeatedly publicly expressed by Indigenous communities and political organizations) that colonialism negatively impacts their well-being, it has only somewhat recently appeared in broader scholarly and policy analyses of determinants of health. In addition to the determinants of health literature overlooking colonialism, law has regularly been overlooked as a determinant of health.[12] Richard Horton reflects that "[p]ublic health advocates do not typically see the law as a critical influence on health" and declares, "[t]hey are wrong".[13] Law can be a site through which rights are protected or restricted and specific laws and policies can shape the administration of and access to healthcare. As well, laws not directly related to health can impact well-being because of the ways that a legal climate can reproduce difficult social circumstances for some, and privileges for others.

State law is a social determinant of health for all people, but in very predictable gendered, racialized, classed ways, Canadian law upholds and empowers the well-being of some, while utterly compromising and impeding the well-being of others. Of the sparse literature that examines law as a determinant of health, most of it centers on Western approaches to law.[14] For instance, Angela Maria Pinzon-Rondon et al. conceptualize that "the rule of law is overlooked as a cross-cutting 'determinant of determinants' ".[15] Horton also focuses on the rule of law, noting that

> law does not mean only the statutes passed by a legislature. The idea of law is far more important than that. The "rule of law" is a quality of the prevailing political culture, one that puts great weight on notions of good governance,

---

10  Ibid. at 4.
11  Naomi Adelson, "The Embodiment of Inequity: Health Disparities in Aboriginal Canada" (2005) 96:2 *Canadian Journal of Public Health* S45 at S59.
12  See Boyer, *Moving Aboriginal Health Forward, supra*, generally; Richard Horton, "Offline: The Rule of Law – an Invisible Determinant of Health" (2016) 387:10025 *The Lancet* 1260 ('Horton, "Offline" '); Angela Maria Pinzon-Rondon, Amir Attaran, Juan Carlos Botero, and Angela Maria Ruiz-Stemberg, "Association of Rule of Law and Health Outcomes: An Ecological Study" (2015) 5 *BMJ Open* 1 ('Pinzon-Rondon et al., "Association of Rule of Law and Health Outcomes" ').
13  Horton, ibid. [no page numbers].
14  Ibid.; Pinzon-Rondon et al., "Association of Rule of Law and Health Outcomes", *supra*; OBK Dingake, "The Rule of Law as a Social Determinant of Health" (2017) 19:2 *Health Human Rights* 295 ('Dingake, "The Rule of Law as a Social Determinant of Health" ').
15  Pinzon-Rondon et al., "Association of Rule of Law and Health Outcomes", *supra* at 1–2.

independent accountability, and respect for certain rights. The most basic right of all is the right to liberty.[16]

Interestingly, Dingake speaks to the importance of Indigenous laws for supporting improved access to health for women and girls, though that discussion, which is framed through the language of traditional justice, is unfortunately very brief and overlooks colonialism.[17]

Few scholars bring together work on colonialism as a determinant of health and law as a determinant of health, to examine state laws as a colonial institution that undermines Indigenous well-being.[18] An exception to this is Boyer who, in her book-length analysis of state laws as a determinant of health, emphasizes how law has operated to bolster the creation of a settler state through "mechanisms of law, institutions, and public policies" such as the Indian Act and residential schools.[19] Colonial legal regulation of Indigenous health includes denying Indigenous legal authority to fully regulate health within one's society. For instance, Boyer writes about various ways (e.g., through criminal law, the Indian Act, and regulatory bodies that oversee medical practice) that settler laws regulate the use of traditional medicine and reflects that "Canadian laws may at times criminalize actions that are positive and normal in an Aboriginal context".[20] She shows how Indigenous people have been denied access to their own health practices *and* equal access to the settler health system.[21] Inevitably Indigenous people will be unwell in such circumstances and state laws sanction these harms onto Indigenous bodies, rather than prevent them. Boyer shows how Indigenous ill-health has been racialized and constructed as an inherent deficiency of Indigenous people instead of settlers examining the social structures that have acted as barriers to Indigenous well-being.[22]

Intimately related to the problems with the right to traditional health practices, Indigenous peoples do not have full access to their own legal orders *or* full access to leveraging state laws. As Vermette explains more generally of Canadian law:

16  Horton, "Offline", *supra* [no page numbers].
17  Dingake, "The Rule of Law as a Social Determinant of Health", *supra* [no page numbers].
18  For exceptions, see Boyer, *Moving Aboriginal Health Forward, supra,* generally; Richard Matthews, "The Cultural Erosion of Indigenous People in Health Care" (2017) 189 *CMAJ* E78 ('Matthews, "The Cultural Erosion of Indigenous People in Health Care"').
19  Boyer, *Moving Aboriginal Health Forward* at 22.
20  Ibid. at 92.
21  Full access to settler health care would not then solve everything. As Matthews cautions, "a modern industrial health care system can be a determinant of *ill*-health, especially when it is culturally unsafe" (Matthews, "The Cultural Erosion of Indigenous People in Health Care", *supra* at E78 [emphasis in original]).
22  Boyer, *Moving Aboriginal Health Forward* at 90. It should be noted that in emphasizing structural barriers, I am not intending to suggest that Indigenous health would have then been perfect prior to contact, as Boyer tends to suggest in her book. This issue of Boyer romanticizing Indigenous health practices is discussed later in the chapter.

The colonizer's ability to frame disputes with the colonized within colonial law is a key process in perpetuating the norms of colonialism. This action involves removing disputes from Aboriginal peoples, communities and ways, and into an arena and discourse where the colonizer has a monopoly on the interpretation of Aboriginal peoples' existence. Colonial law provides the colonizer with the ability to exclude and with the exclusive power to interpret. Aboriginal rights discourse shows us that the colonizer can completely dominate the debate. This domination is displayed in the colonizer's ability to create the laws, interpret the laws, and force Aboriginal people into the courts.[23]

Writing more specifically about health, Richard Matthews states:

Indigenous peoples were tricked out of, robbed of or pushed off their traditional lands, with the consequent erosion of their own complex system of spirituality, law, trade, governance and health. Health law and policy in Canada is part of this unilateral assertion of governance, and thus, despite the technical excellence or best intentions of individual practitioners, is *a priori* systemically racist.[24]

While I disagree with the language of trickery to characterize the forced imposition of Canadian law onto Indigenous people, Matthews nonetheless makes important connections between the colonial nature of Canadian law, the attempted denial of Indigenous legal agency, and ill-health. These challenges of well-being are further intensified for Indigenous women who have little authority within state law, and whose voices have also been pushed to the margins in Indigenous politics and in discussions about Indigenous law.[25]

There is excellent and expanding literature on Indigenous women's health, though decolonial intersectional analyses that *conceptualize* state laws as a *gendered colonial determinant of health* are notably absent.[26] Indigenous women's health experiences are too often ignored when "Indigenous health" is broadly spoken of, yet Indigenous women have distinct health experiences and socio-legal realities. One way to examine how state laws contribute to poor health for

23 Vermette, "Colonialism and the Suppression of Aboriginal Voice" at 257.
24 Matthews, "The Cultural Erosion of Indigenous People in Health Care" at E78–E79. Italics added for clarity.
25 Regarding state laws, see Bourassa et al., "Racism, Sexism, and Colonialism", *supra*. Regarding Indigenous politics, see Isabel Altamirano-Jiménez, "Nunavut: Whose Homeland, Whose Voices?" (2008) 26:3,4 *Canadian Woman Studies* 128; Emily Snyder, *Gender, Power, and Representations of Cree Law* (Vancouver: UBC Press, 2018) ('Snyder, *Gender, Power, and Representations*').
26 For an exception, see Bourassa et al., "Racism, Sexism, and Colonialism", *supra*. Boyer does engage with gender in her book, though engages with gender in relation to different women's issues, rather than taking up a gendered analysis (see Boyer, *Moving Aboriginal Health Forward, supra*, generally).

Indigenous women is by drawing on research on Indigenous women's experiences with HIV.

Indigenous people are overrepresented in HIV statistics. While Indigenous people make up 4.9% of the population in Canada,[27] a 2016 study by the Public Health Agency of Canada estimated that Indigenous people represented 11.3% of new HIV cases and 9.6% of the overall number of people living with HIV.[28] HIV rates in the province of Saskatchewan are particularly troubling. The national rates for HIV overall in 2016 were 6.4 per 100,000, whereas the rates in Saskatchewan were 14.5 per 100,000, which is more than double the national average.[29] Indigenous people in Saskatchewan represented 79% of all new HIV cases in that province in 2017,[30] despite representing about 16% of the provincial population.[31] Further, Indigenous women represented 92% of the 62 female cases in Saskatchewan in 2017, whereas Indigenous men represented 72% of the 115 male cases.[32]

The Canadian Aboriginal AIDS Network (CAAN) has raised concerns that despite this problem of the overrepresentation of Indigenous women in HIV statistics, "there continues to be a startling lack of gender specific, Aboriginal specific delivery models or programs for Aboriginal women" and that "most services have not been designed with the needs of women in mind".[33] Indigenous women's health and experiences with HIV are shaped by many factors. For example, poverty and housing are common issues that are noted in the research.[34]

---

27  Statistics Canada, "Aboriginal Peoples in Canada: Key Results From the 2016 Census", available at https://www150.statcan.gc.ca/n1/daily-quotidien/171025/dq171025a-eng.htm.

28  Public Health Agency of Canada, "Summary: Estimates of HIV Incidence, Prevalence and Canada's Progress on Meeting the 90–90–90 HIV Targets, 2016" (Ottawa, July 2018), available at www.canada.ca/en/public-health/services/publications/diseases-conditions/summary-estimates-hiv-incidence-prevalence-canadas-progress-90–90–90.html#t1.

29  National averages for 2017 are not available, however the 2017 provincial rate increased to 15.1% in 2017. Ministry of Health, Population Health Branch, "HIV Prevention and Control Report 2017" Government of Saskatchewan, available at http://publications.gov.sk.ca/documents/13/108029-2017-Saskatchewan-HIV-Prevention-and-Control-Report.pdf at 7 ('Ministry of Health, "HIV Prevention and Control Report 2017"').

30  Ministry of Health, ibid. at 15.

31  Number based on 2016 census. Saskatchewan Bureau of Statistics, "Saskatchewan Aboriginal Peoples: 2016 Census" available at http://publications.gov.sk.ca/documents/15/104388-2016%20Census%20Aboriginal.pdf at 1.

32  Ministry of Health, "HIV Prevention and Control Report 2017" at 15.

33  Canadian Aboriginal AIDS Network, "FACT Sheet: Aboriginal Women and Girls" (2011), available at http://caan.ca/wp-content/uploads/2012/05/Womens-Fact-Sheet-EN.pdf at 1 ('CAAN, "Fact Sheet"').

34  Canadian HIV/AIDS Legal Network, "Indigenous Women, HIV and Gender-Based Violence" (2017) available at www.aidslaw.ca/site/indigenous-women-hiv-and-gender-based-violence/?lang=en at 6 ('Legal Network, "Indigenous Women"'); Kimberly Hawkins, Charlotte Reading and Kevin Barlow, "Our Search for Safe Spaces: A Qualitative Study of the Role of Sexual Violence in the Lives of Aboriginal Women Living with HIV/AIDS" (Canadian Aboriginal AIDS Network, 2009) available at www.caan.ca/wp-content/uploads/2012/05/Sexual-Violence-Document-ENGLISH1.pdf at 27 ('Hawkins et al., "Our Search for Safe Spaces"'); Emily Snyder, "The Impacts of the Criminalization of HIV

As the Canadian HIV/AIDS Legal Network (hereinafter "the Legal Network") explains:

> Women without stable housing are at higher risk for chronic and infectious diseases, including HIV. This is because housing instability, homelessness and transience compromise access to adequate health care and appropriate and effective social supports. For Indigenous women, these barriers are exacerbated by individual and institutional discrimination, and disadvantages on the basis of race, gender and class.[35]

Other factors that impact HIV-positive Indigenous women's well-being can include lower educational training;[36] low employment rates;[37] vulnerabilities and legal barriers for those involved in sex work;[38] addictions;[39] stereotyping and discrimination from service providers, including those in the healthcare system[40] and child protection services;[41] isolation;[42] and poor sexual well-being.[43] It is crucial to understand how colonialism and sexism, including intergenerational trauma, have produced the social conditions for these issues to manifest.[44]

All of these factors intersect with Canadian law in complex ways. For example, Indigenous women who are HIV-positive can face challenging health and legal issues related to violence. In a report authored by Kimberly Hawkins, Charlotte Reading, and Kevin Barlow for a national research project done by CAAN, they explain a multitude of ways that Indigenous women who are HIV-positive have been exposed to violence at some point in their lives. Of the people interviewed, "[a]lmost all told of various forms of abuse and trauma experienced from a relatively young age".[45] Part of the vulnerabilities experienced by Indigenous women

---

Non-Disclosure on Indigenous People: A Case Study of Regina" (All Nations Hope Network, 2018), available at http://allnationshope.ca/userdata/files/187/HIV%20Non%20Disclosure%20Project/HIV%20Non-Disclosure%20Report%20-%20ESnyder.pdf at 9 ('Snyder, "The Impacts of the Criminalization of HIV Non-Disclosure"').
35 Legal Network, "Indigenous Women", ibid.
36 Ibid.; Hawkins et al., "Our Search for Safe Spaces", *supra*.
37 Legal Network, "Indigenous Women", *supra*.
38 Ibid. at 7–8; Hawkins et al., "Our Search for Safe Spaces" at 34.
39 Legal Network, "Indigenous Women" at 9–10; Hawkins et al., "Our Search for Safe Spaces" at 34.
40 Hawkins et al., "Our Search for Safe Spaces" at 18; Snyder, "The Impacts of the Criminalization of HIV Non-Disclosure" at 16.
41 Canadian HIV/AIDS Legal Network & Canadian Aboriginal AIDS Network, "Summary of Legal Needs Assessment" (2016) at 4 ('Legal Network, "Summary"').
42 Hawkins et al., "Our Search for Safe Spaces" at 44; Snyder, "The Impacts of the Criminalization of HIV Non-Disclosure" at 6–7.
43 Allison Carter et al., "Supporting the Sexual Rights of Women Living With HIV: A Critical Analysis of Sexual Satisfaction and Pleasure Across Five Relationship Types" (2018) 1; Snyder, ibid. at 11.
44 CAAN, "Fact Sheet", *supra*; Hawkins et al., "Our Search for Safe Spaces", *supra*, generally; Legal Network, "Indigenous Women", *supra*, generally; Snyder, ibid., generally.
45 Hawkins et al., "Our Search for Safe Spaces" at 25. See also Snyder, ibid.

included fear of men and a lack of control in relationships with men.[46] The Legal Network explains that gender-based violence increases the risk of HIV transmission *and* being HIV-positive increases risks of experiencing violence.[47] For example, for someone who is not HIV-positive, sexual abuse and assault can put one at risk of HIV transmission, and for someone who is positive, they could be vulnerable to violence, for instance, if a partner discovers their HIV status or where a partner who already knows about their HIV status chooses to manipulate them.[48] Thus for Indigenous women who are HIV-positive, they are faced with the problem of high rates of violence against Indigenous women intersecting with the problem of violence against women who are HIV-positive. All of this needs to be understood, as the Legal Network emphasizes, "within the context of historical and ongoing colonial violence".[49] The said context is also one in which violence against Indigenous women has not been taken seriously and state legal agents, such as police and courts, have reinscribed gendered colonial violence and contributed to worsening Indigenous women's well-being.[50]

Additionally, Indigenous women who are HIV-positive are criminalized through Canadian law in particular ways. Regarding criminal charges related to HIV non-disclosure, the Legal Network found that "[o]f the women charged between 1989 and 2016 whose ethnicities were known, 42 per cent were Indigenous" and noted that "[t]his disproportionate use of the criminal law against Indigenous women is particularly troubling given the connection between gender-based violence and HIV".[51] It is also troubling because of other complexities, for example, that Indigenous women who are HIV-positive might be exposed to increased racialized and gendered police surveillance and abuse leading to incarceration,[52] and because Indigenous women are already over-incarcerated.[53] Beyond the Canadian criminal justice system, Indigenous women who are HIV-positive are still implicitly criminalized; for example, by being stereotyped as involved in sex work (and targeted as spreading HIV), and being criminalized as mothers, for example through coerced sterilization or having one's children taken away by child protection services.[54] All of these challenges make clear that if

46  Hawkins et al., "Our Search for Safe Spaces" at 29–30.
47  Legal Network, "Indigenous Women" at 10–11.
48  Ibid. at 10.
49  Ibid. at 3.
50  There are unfortunately numerous examples in Canada that illustrate this problem. See, for example, discussions as they relate to violence against Indigenous women and girls such as Helen Betty Osborne, Pamela George, Cindy Gladue, Angela Cardinal, and Tina Fontaine: These are a small number among many instances of violence that have been poorly dealt with by the Canadian criminal justice system.
51  AIDSLAW, "Indigenous Communities and HIV: Resilience, Strength and Solidarity" (Canadian HIV/AIDS Legal Network, 21 June 2017), available at www.aidslaw.ca/site/indigenous-communities-and-hiv-resilience-strength-and-solidarity/?lang=en.
52  Snyder, "The Impacts of the Criminalization of HIV Non-Disclosure" at 12–13; Hawkins et al., "Our Search for Safe Spaces" at 48.
53  Legal Network, "Indigenous Women" at 8, 9.
54  Snyder, "The Impacts of the Criminalization of HIV Non-Disclosure" at 8, 12.

one does not consider law, colonialism, and gender when examining Indigenous health issues around HIV, much would be missing from the analysis.

In their research on the rule of law as a determinant of health, Pinzon-Rondon et al. employed a method of examining the relationship between disease statistics and the Rule of Law Index in multiple countries (including Canada and several other settler states).[55] After examining their data, they concluded, "the more that a country adheres to the rule of law, the more likely it is that it has a healthy population".[56] Such an assertion makes good sense if thinking generally about a legal order that is consensually adhered to, has productive mechanisms for working with conflicts, and is inclusively deployed to protect the rights of all citizens. However, much more realistically, their conclusion grossly overlooks power relations and legal pluralism.

The rule of law within the Canadian legal system has not ensured equality and supported well-being for Indigenous women (or people) as a group. In fact, the inverse is true – the more that Canada adheres to the rule of law, as it is dominantly conceptualized within that settler legal order, the more likely it is that Indigenous women will continue to face socio-legal challenges that foster poor health. Although many of the examples above, for instance the criminalization of Indigenous women who are HIV-positive, highlight what some might characterize as misuse or abuse of Canadian law, it is worth reiterating that these uses of state law are not anomalies: they are the predictable outcomes of a legal system that has historically and currently reproduces gendered colonial oppression that targets Indigenous women's bodies for erasure.[57]

Overall, Canadian law has been and continues to be intimately tied up with sustaining the social conditions that negatively impact Indigenous women's well-being. Canadian law can be deployed to produce the very structures that have been shown to harm Indigenous people and peoples (e.g., prisons, child welfare policies, laws around HIV non-disclosure), and other times contributes to the worsening of health outcomes by not being used to respond to glaring inequalities and injustices. When the Canadian state is complicit in gendered colonial violence, disallows Indigenous women's legal agency and bodily self-determination, and carries on with various iterations of laws, policies, and practices that cause Indigenous women to be physically, mentally, emotionally, and spiritually unwell, it is perpetuating a politics of erasure that has been, and continues to be core to assimilation and white settler supremacy. Can state law then ever be a productive determinant of health for Indigenous women who are HIV-positive or for Indigenous women more generally?

55 Pinzon-Rondon et al., "Association of Rule of Law and Health Outcomes" at 2.
56 Ibid. at 5.
57 This has occurred (and occurs) through many areas of law. Other chapters in this collection show, for example, that discrimination or adverse legislative outcomes are the products of criminal law itself in terms of how it is constructed in ways that do not account for women's experiences. See, for example, Iyioha (Chapter 2), Lewis et al. (Chapter 3), and Shah et al. (Chapter 10), all in this volume.

## Indigenous law as a social determinant of health

In a report on violence against Indigenous women who are HIV-positive, the Legal Network makes many recommendations for change, which cover Canadian law reform involving changes to criminal law in relation to non-disclosure, sex work, and mandatory minimums; addressing sexism, racism, and HIV stigma as they are perpetuated through policing and the justice system; prison reform; increased and improved programs and services for survivors; and fostering broader structural change to challenge inequality.[58] Although the focus of their recommendations is on changing settler legal approaches, they also note the importance of alternatives to incarceration and the need for funding to support Indigenous community-based responses to wrongdoing.[59]

When examining the suggestions made by Czyzewski, Boyer, and Matthews for improving Indigenous health, the limits of law are constructed in ways that concentrate on Canadian law. Czyzewski, for example, advocates for deep structural change that challenges colonialism by "restoring respectful relationships, nation-to-nation relations . . ., the return of lands and allowing for self-determination" as ways for fostering Indigenous well-being.[60] Boyer is similarly focused on nation-to-nation relations for advocating for Indigenous health. In particular, she approaches the issue through a constitutional lens and examines whether Indigenous and treaty rights to health exist, if they have been breached, and if the state has a legitimate justification for such a breach.[61] She argues that Indigenous and treaty rights to health do exist and that the actions of the state in breaching these rights are not justified.[62] Further, Matthews suggests that healthcare professionals should adhere to the Truth and Reconciliation Commission of Canada's *Calls to Action*[63] and should:

> [E]ngage with Indigenous healers and elders; pay them well and include them in policy-making; provide ongoing antiracism education; build,

---

58  Legal Network, "Indigenous Women" at 15–20.
59  Ibid. at 18. Hawkins, Reading & Barlow also make several policy recommendations in their report, though they are broader recommendations aimed at services and supports (see Hawkins et al., "Our Search for Safe Spaces", *supra*, generally).
60  Czyzewski, "Colonialism as a Broader Social Determinant of Health" at 9.
61  Boyer, *Moving Aboriginal Health Forward* at 127. The language of "Aboriginal rights" in the Canadian context refers to state laws.
62  Though she notes, "[t]he Government of Canada has always maintained that the provision of health services to First Nations and Inuit peoples is done as a matter of policy and not through any legal obligation" (Boyer, ibid. at 150).
63  Specifically, he cites: "[R]ecognize the indigenous health care rights enshrined in international and national law; dialogue with indigenous peoples to identify and eliminate health care inequities; acknowledge, respect and address the distinct health needs of Métis, Inuit, and off-reserve First Nations people; provide sustainable funding for existing and new Aboriginal healing centres to address the harms cause by residential schools; in collaboration with indigenous healers and elders, recognize as medically legitimate the value of traditional healing practices; hire and retain indigenous health care professionals, as well as ensure that

maintain and adequately staff sweat lodges, where appropriate; advocate for change to harmful policies like those of the Non-Insured Health Benefits to make them consistent with superior provincial healthcare norms; advocate for transformation of health law; and perhaps most importantly, support Indigenous sovereignty and the treaty relationships – especially as they relate to healthcare.[64]

Gender intersects with all of these recommendations in different ways, though is not acknowledged.[65] While each of the recommendations implies the existence of Indigenous laws through self-determination, nation-to-nation relations, and discussions about tradition and health, the limits of law are explicated only for state laws and, as is often the case in the scholarship, not for Indigenous laws.

In other words, the ways that legal limits are constructed often create a simple binary in which state laws are framed as inherently bad and Indigenous laws as inherently good. This binary gets perpetuated, for instance, in Earl Nowgesic's article on HIV and determinants of health for Indigenous people. He conveys findings assessing that the Aboriginal Healing Foundation's community initiatives that were the most successful "included use of Elders, traditional ceremonies, individual counseling, and western healing strategies used in conjunction with Aboriginal cultural practices".[66] He states "that 'culture is good medicine' " and that "whereas colonialism, residential schools and poverty are negative determinants of health, Aboriginal culture and self-determination are key determinants positively affecting the health of Aboriginal populations".[67]

There *is* something unsettling about using only state laws to try and improve Indigenous health, as there are numerous ways that Canadian law has been absolutely ineffective and at times unequivocally violent towards Indigenous well-being. However, a problem also arises in these discussions where the limits of state law are discussed and engaged while Indigenous laws are only ever mentioned in passing or are spoken of indirectly through the language of "culture".[68]

---

all staff have cultural competency training" (Matthews, "The Cultural Erosion of Indigenous People in Health Care" at E79).

64 Ibid. at E79.

65 For example, ensuring that women and two-spirit Elders are listened to in policy discussions; approaching antiracism education intersectionally so as to grapple with gendered colonialism; and understanding that Non-Insured Health Benefits, while an impediment to Indigenous health generally, can be experienced differently for Indigenous women who might have difficulties accessing services and dealing with claims because of childcare responsibilities, employment restrictions, the need to travel for health services, and vulnerabilities related to safety and travel.

66 Earl Nowgesic, "Addressing HIV/AIDS among Aboriginal People using a Health Status, Health Determinants and Health Care Framework: A Literature Review and Conceptual Analysis" (2010) 3 *Canadian Journal of Aboriginal Community-based HIV/AIDS Research* 35 at 39.

67 Ibid.

68 Hadley Friedland argues that it is important to shift from asking only questions about culture and what is culturally appropriate, to directly asking questions about law in Indigenous legal

The complexities of Indigenous laws are undermined when their limits are under-theorized. I am not suggesting that the limits of state law for Indigenous well-being are the same as limits that can happen within Indigenous laws. The problem is that the latter is not being analyzed in the literature, and this lack of analysis risks oversimplifying Indigenous laws and people. It is important not to lose the complexities of self-determination, law, and culture. As John Borrows cautions more generally regarding the need to embrace complexity:

> Ambiguity and uncertainty can lead us to lose our will to fight for "the cause" – because it is so complicated. This is a problem that fundamentalist and unified approaches attempt to solve. They strive for certainty. As a result, essentialized viewpoints often seem more compelling because they are easy to grasp in the abstract. For instance, we are told we shall overcome our sub-jugation when we become more traditional, authentic, culturally connected, educated, spiritual, economically self-sufficient, or in touch with ourselves and the Earth. Of course, cultivating these attributes may improve our lives. They may deepen our relationships and enhance freedom. At the same time, our diversity means that they may not; there is no one true foundation on which to base action when dealing with Indigenous issues.[69]

Theorizing the limits of Indigenous laws is not meant to suggest that they are invaluable or inferior; rather this approach upholds Indigenous laws as valuable, dynamic resources. As Val Napoleon and Hadley Friedland emphasize, "if people cannot reason with [Indigenous law] and apply it to the messy and mundane, then it will continue to be talked about only in an idealized way or as a rhetorical critique of Canadian law".[70] The lack of in-depth engagement with Indigenous laws, for example, risks important issues such as gender and power becoming overlooked. Indigenous feminist legal theory is useful here for critically engaging with Indigenous laws.

## Indigenous feminist legal theory

Indigenous feminist legal theory is an approach for directly engaging with Indigenous laws and gender.[71] I have articulated and used this framework not as an

---

analyses. See Hadley Friedland, "Reflective Frameworks: Methods for Accessing, Under-
standing and Applying Indigenous Laws" (2012) 11:1 *Indigenous Law Journal* 1 at 29.
For further discussion about culture and pluralistic legal systems, see Odunsi and Adewole
(Chapter 9) and Shah et al. (Chapter 10), both in this volume.

69  John Borrows, *Freedom and Indigenous Constitutionalism* (Toronto: University of Toronto
Press, 2016) at 103–104 ('Borrows, *Freedom and Indigenous Constitutionalism*').

70  Val Napoleon and Hadley Friedland, "An Inside Job: Engaging with Indigenous Legal Traditions through Stories" (2016) 61:4 *McGill Law Journal* 725 at 741.

71  Emily Snyder, "Indigenous Feminist Legal Theory" (2014) 26:2 *Canadian Journal of
Women and the Law* 365; Snyder, *Gender, Power, and Representations, supra.* I first heard
the term "Indigenous feminist legal theory" used by Val Napoleon while in a class that

assertion of identity politics but rather as an analytic tool that has been useful for deconstructing the ways that state law asserts itself in the singular, and for taking a critical and inclusive approach when learning about and engaging with Indigenous laws. This framework is useful to me as a white settler cisgender woman for holding myself accountable to decolonial feminist analysis and engagement with law. In the short discussion that follows, I introduce core tenets of Indigenous feminist legal theory to identify areas where there are potential legal limits in relation to Indigenous laws and gender. There is a need for research on Indigenous legal responses to HIV and HIV-related health and legal issues and so my discussion is preliminary in nature rather than emerging from substantive analysis of a particular legal order's engagement with HIV. Also, it is noteworthy that the lack of published research in this area in the standard academic sense does not mean that Indigenous people are not using their laws in complex and practical ways to respond to HIV issues.

Indigenous feminist legal theory treats gender, sex, and sexuality as complex and plural. Gender is not singular and when it is treated as such, difference and dissent can end up being silenced and unproductive binaries can become entrenched. For example, in their work on supporting Indigenous women who are HIV-positive, CAAN emphasizes the plurality of gender and gendered experiences:

> [I]t is important to recognize and honour the diversity of the women's community in our response inclusive of two-spirit women, heterosexual women, [transgender] women, women who are in prison, women who have sex with women, women who are involved in survival sex, women who use substances, women who are involved in gangs and for all women involved in high risk behaviours.[72]

---

she was teaching. I have detailed and articulated a framework for this concept elsewhere by bringing feminist legal theory, Indigenous feminist theory, and Indigenous legal theory into conversation. Feminist legal theory offers important insights regarding the relationship between gender, power, and law, though too often this field naturalizes state laws as "the law", with little consideration of Indigenous legal orders. While intersectionality is an important contemporary goal of feminist legal theory, and is critically engaged by some scholars, there is still significant work to do in deeply practicing intersectionality in feminist legal studies, particularly in relation to race and colonialism [See Rakhi Ruperalia, "Legal Feminism and the Post-racism Fantasy" (2014) 26:1 *Canadian Journal of Women and the Law* 81; Twila L. Perry, "Family Law, Feminist Legal Theory, and the Problem of Racial Hierarchy" in Martha Albertson Fineman, ed., *Transcending the Boundaries of Law: Generations of Feminism and Legal Theory* (New York: Routledge, 2011) at 243]. Indigenous feminist theory clearly addresses those oversights by producing analyses that center gender, indigeneity, power, and decolonization, though Indigenous feminist work on law tends to focus on state law and there is a need for more engagement with Indigenous laws (for exceptions, see for example the work of Val Napoleon and Isabel Altamirano-Jiménez). Indigenous legal theory is invaluable for centering Indigenous laws, though work in this field would benefit from engagement with feminist theories, as gender is under-addressed in the literature on Indigenous legal theory.

72 CAAN, "Fact Sheet" at 1. It is important to point out that high-risk behaviour is framed in relation to vulnerabilities created by social structures, rather than more common approaches that individualize and blame Indigenous women for "choosing" high-risk "lifestyles".

Concerns have been raised by Indigenous feminists that Indigenous laws too often only work well for, or are accessible to, Indigenous women who align with normative expectations about gender (e.g., women who wear skirts), rather than using Indigenous laws in ways that work for people of all genders, with a plurality of experiences.[73] Indigenous legal responses to HIV and HIV-related health issues then, need to ensure, that Indigenous laws are accessible to all citizens within a legal order.

An intersectional approach is also core to Indigenous feminist legal theory because gender cannot be separated out from Indigenous people's (or other people's) identities and experiences. By extension, Indigenous feminist legal theory treats Indigenous societies and laws as gendered. This tenet is based on the idea that all societies have gender norms and that law as a social entity is not exempt from the influence of them. Seemingly "gender neutral" approaches can end up universalizing maleness and men's legal experiences as "Indigenous experiences" more broadly, given the contemporary power dynamics in Indigenous communities wherein Indigenous men have been afforded more power than people of other genders.[74] Patriarchal gender norms have been imposed on Indigenous societies through colonialism and have had a significant impact on Indigenous gender norms,[75] and thus also on Indigenous legal interpretation and practices.

However, some scholars have cautioned on the need to be conscientious of how gendered power dynamics also shaped Indigenous laws prior to contact. Napoleon, for example, states that "there was no golden age – hardship, wars, violence, sexism, prejudices, repression, and homophobia existed for many Aboriginal nations as in the rest of the world".[76] Others might argue that Indigenous feminist legal theory is unnecessary because gender roles and gender complementarity are central to the social, cultural, political, economic, and legal structures of Indigenous societies. However, in describing Indigenous law as gendered, the purpose is not to focus on gender roles; rather it is to examine how gendered power dynamics can shape legal decisions, processes, and interpretations of Indigenous law.

In her advocacy work for Indigenous women who are HIV-positive, Tracey Prentice has emphasized that programs have to address sexism and gendered violence.[77] She explains:

---

73 See, for example, Emma LaRocque, "Métis and Feminist: Ethical Reflections on Feminism, Human Rights, and Decolonization", in Joyce Green, ed., *Making Space for Indigenous Feminism* (Winnipeg: Fernwood, 2007) 53; Darcy Lindberg, *kihcitwâw kîkway meskocipayiwin (sacred changes): Transforming Gendered Protocols in Cree Ceremonies through Cree Law* (Master of Laws Thesis, University of Victoria, 2017); Zoe Todd, "Moon Lodge This Way" (2016), available at https://zoeandthecity.wordpress.com/2016/03/10/moon-lodge-this-way/.

74 See Snyder, *Gender, Power, and Representations, supra.*

75 See, for example, Kiera L. Ladner, "Gendering Decolonisation, Decolonising Gender" (2009) 13:1 *Australian Indigenous Law Review* 62.

76 Val Napoleon, "Raven's Garden: A Discussion about Aboriginal Sexual Orientation and Transgender Issues" (2002) 17:2 *Canadian Journal of Law and Society* 149 at 153.

77 Tracey Prentice, "Alarming Rates of HIV/AIDS for Canada's Aboriginal Women" (2005) 8:1/2 *Canadian Women's Health Network* ('Prentice, "Alarming Rates of HIV/AIDS"').

HIV prevention efforts for Aboriginal women must also begin to address the imbalance of power that is often a feature of intimate relationships. Prevention and education must target Aboriginal heterosexual men as well as women, and prevention efforts must address domestic and sexual violence against women.[78]

While Indigenous women can experience domestic and sexual violence from Indigenous and non-Indigenous men, it is still important to center these realities in Indigenous legal responses. It is crucial to be explicit about gendered power dynamics to recognize the particular legal and social experiences of Indigenous women. It is clear from the discussion in the previous section that Indigenous women who are HIV-positive are experiencing HIV in particular ways because of their gender, and it would be remiss to overlook these realities in Indigenous legal responses and misguided to think that discrimination cannot be perpetuated through Indigenous laws. If a person misunderstands HIV, for instance, myths and stigma could end up being taken up in legal interpretations and responses in Indigenous laws, as they also have in Canadian laws.[79] These misconceptions are especially pronounced for Indigenous women who are HIV-positive as they can end up being labeled as sex workers, treated as "diseased", be perceived as irresponsible mothers, and be blamed in particular gendered ways for not being more responsible with their health (for example, as caregivers, women should "know better").[80] While these myths are pronounced in settler legal practices, Indigenous communities too can take up myths and misunderstandings about Indigenous women who are HIV-positive.[81]

It is important to recognize that while discrimination can sometimes be perpetuated through the interpretation and use of Indigenous laws, there would also be legal resources within Indigenous legal orders for challenging sexism, gendered violence, and also HIV stigma.[82] For instance, in her work on the contemporary application of Cree legal principles as they relate to conflict, violence, and harm, Friedland emphasizes that

> because violence and vulnerability are issues all societies face, logic alone dictates Indigenous societies had ways to deal with these issues prior to the arrival of Europeans. Logically, these legal traditions must have provided principled ways to address social problems and order human affairs. These legal traditions, like all legal traditions, also provide a specific way of not

---

78  Ibid.
79  Regarding this problem with Canadian law see, for example, Alison Symington, "Injustice Amplified by HIV Non-Disclosure Ruling" (2013) 63:3 *University of Toronto Law Journal* 486.
80  Snyder, "The Impacts of the Criminalization of HIV Non-Disclosure" at 7–8.
81  For a discussion about these issues, see Snyder, ibid., generally.
82  Regarding sexism and gendered violence, see Emily Snyder, Val Napoleon and John Borrows, "Gender and Violence: Drawing on Indigenous Legal Resources" (2015) 48:2 *UBC Law Review* 593 ('Snyder et al., "Gender and Violence"').

just solving, *but articulating and reasoning through social problems* in the first place.[83]

While gendered violence and health issues are different now for Indigenous women – and HIV specifically is a recent health phenomenon – Friedland's work, among others, still highlights that Indigenous legal resources exist and are adaptable for contemporary application.[84] Borrows also emphasizes the importance of treating Indigenous peoples "as contemporary, flexible, and fluid societies. It shows that we are capable of resisting and adapting to change according to our practical needs and desires".[85] Part of treating Indigenous laws as dynamic includes recognizing both the possibilities and limits of Indigenous laws. To reiterate, acknowledging limits is not to suggest that Indigenous laws, broadly speaking, are not useable; rather, an engagement with limits gets to the heart of the difficulties of law: how people interpret and use law, and how it could be used differently if it is causing harm instead of challenging harm. This issue is reflected in Iyioha's discussion of Substantive Legal Effectiveness in Chapter 2, where she observes that the very construction of law and the interpretative exercise have an impact on law's effectiveness for women's health.

Friedland's focus on reasoning and Borrows' pushback against stereotypes that construct Indigenous people as "intellectually stagnant"[86] are significant because they challenge approaches to law that rely on static notions of culture and tradition. Central to Indigenous feminist legal theory is deconstructing rigid representations of law and tradition, which can be especially problematic for Indigenous women if tradition is deployed to pressure Indigenous women to act in certain ways that they might otherwise be uncomfortable with. More than 20 years ago, Emma LaRocque raised concerns about the ways that "[t]erms such as 'traditional' or 'culturally appropriate' appear as a matter of course in discussions on Aboriginal governance, or . . . any community-oriented programs related to justice, violence, women, and 'healing' ".[87] For example, there has been much disagreement over programming at Hollow Water (an Anishinaabe community), which is described as using traditional approaches to respond to sexual abuse. LaRocque has raised concerns that Indigenous women at Hollow Water are at risk of being coerced because it is difficult to speak out in a context of uneven gendered power dynamics. Further, she highlights that there are challenging identity politics wherein speaking out against programming that places tradition

---

83  Hadley Louise Friedland, *Reclaiming the Language of Law: The Contemporary Articulation and Application of Cree Legal Principles in Canada* (Doctor of Philosophy Thesis, University of Alberta, 2016) at 328.

84  See also Val Napoleon, *Ayook: Gitksan Legal Order, Law, and Legal Theory* (Doctor of Philosophy Thesis, University of Victoria, 2009).

85  Borrows, *Freedom and Indigenous Constitutionalism* at 17–18.

86  Ibid. at 22.

87  Emma LaRocque, "Re-Examining Culturally Appropriate Models in Criminal Justice Applications", in John Borrows and Leonard Rotman, eds., *Aboriginal Legal Issues: Cases, Materials, and Commentary*, 2nd ed. (Markham: LexisNexis Butterworths, 2003/essay originally published 1997) 966 at 967.

and healing at its core could be perceived as being inauthentic, misguided, or colonized.[88] Similarly, Sarah Deer has raised concerns that Indigenous societies are not exempt from oppression operating through Indigenous approaches to law and that "there is a tendency to over-romanticize the peacemaking process as one that can 'foster good relations' and heal victims".[89]

I have argued elsewhere, with Napoleon and Borrows, that Indigenous laws can be resources for responding to gendered violence, though as we, as well as LaRocque and Deer have argued, the ways that sexism can operate through law have to be kept at the forefront.[90] Some might argue that if tradition is used in ways that are sexist, that it is not actually tradition or a valid use of Indigenous law; and while this might be accurate in some ways, such an approach also risks creating a narrative wherein Indigenous laws are flawless or conflated with legal ideals, instead of examining laws as messy in practice and as socially embedded.

It is crucial to recognize and support the legal agency of Indigenous women in choosing the legal responses that they are most comfortable with (including if Indigenous women who are HIV-positive want to use state laws to advocate for their well-being). Sexism and other forms of discrimination create constraints, but Indigenous women still have legal agency, and approaches to Indigenous law should work to support that agency. I have noted many challenges that Indigenous women who are HIV-positive deal with – including introducing the idea of Indigenous law as a potential site of gender struggle. Yet as Prentice notes:

> Aboriginal women, and Aboriginal HIV positive women are speaking out in record numbers, offering their experiences to others as learning tools, telling their stories, breaking down stereotypes, acting as role-models, and changing the way we think about Aboriginal women living with HIV/AIDS. For this they may be applauded. For this, they must be respected. In this, they must be supported.[91]

A related aspect of Indigenous feminist legal theory is to deconstruct romanticized approaches to gender and Indigenous laws, as they undermine the usability of law and the actual diverse lived realities of Indigenous people. Boyer's book, for example, makes an important contribution for thinking about state laws as a determinant of health for Indigenous peoples, but is limited by romanticized conceptualizations of the past. She frames Indigenous health issues as starting at the point of contact:

> Aboriginal people enjoyed a relatively disease-free society and practiced medical and health ceremonies with a detailed and self-sustaining pharmacopeia of medicines and treatments for prevention of disease and treatment

---

88 See ibid., generally.
89 Sarah Deer, "Decolonizing Rape Law: A Native Feminist Synthesis of Safety and Sovereignty" (2009) 24:2 *Wicazo Sa Review* 149 at 157.
90 Snyder et al., "Gender and Violence", *supra*.
91 Prentice, "Alarming Rates of HIV/AIDS", *supra*.

of medical conditions. Beginning at European contact, a degradation of the state of health began.[92]

Without a doubt, Indigenous health changed *significantly* because of colonialism – for example, epidemics (and government policies that enabled epidemics to worsen), starvation and nutritional issues (also enabled through government policies), and impacts of gendered colonial violence.[93] However, in her efforts to validate Indigenous health practices as legitimate, Boyer creates a confusing narrative in which few ailments occurred in Indigenous societies, yet sophisticated medicinal responses existed. Complex approaches to medicine existed in Indigenous societies arguably because Indigenous people would have indeed experienced illness, and not because people were always healthy. Likewise, Indigenous laws existed because Indigenous societies dealt with conflicts prior to contact – not because everyone always harmoniously got along.[94]

There are many intricate challenges with romanticization that arise in relation to health, indigeneity, gender, and law that need to be addressed in a number of ways: recognizing the harm of state laws on Indigenous people and Indigenous laws but then not treating Indigenous laws as flawless; understanding the terrible historical and ongoing damage of colonialism on Indigenous health and health practices but then not depicting Indigenous health as pristine prior to contact; and being able to recognize the harm done to Indigenous gender relations while not treating Indigenous gender norms as though they were historically uncontested or without conflict. Indigenous feminist legal theory encourages working with such nuances when considering the effectiveness and limits of law on Indigenous women's health.

## Conclusion

The discussion in this chapter is preliminary. There is a need for more specific discussion related to particular Indigenous legal orders and in relation to specific health issues. What is evident though is that when examining the complex relationship between law and health, it is vital to take a multi-juridical approach to accurately reflect plural legal realities and to take a gendered approach that seriously engages with the ways that power dynamics and gendered norms operate not only in relation to state laws but in relation to Indigenous laws as well. I have argued that state laws have been detrimental for Indigenous women's health, and while it is vital for Indigenous legal responses and self-determination to be central in future discussions, that work also needs to recognize limits of Indigenous laws in order to be productive for Indigenous women's well-being. As with

---

92  Boyer, *Moving Aboriginal Health Forward* at 126.
93  See ibid. at ch. 3 regarding settler policies related to epidemics and starvation.
94  See Val Napoleon and Hadley Friedland, "Indigenous Legal Traditions: Roots to Renaissance" in Markus D Dubber and Tatjana Hörnle, eds., *The Oxford Handbook on Criminal Law* (Oxford: Oxford University Press, 2014) at 255.

intersectionality, which – as Charlotte Skeet explains in Chapter 5 – is a "necessary approach to achieving substantive effectiveness", Indigenous feminist legal theory offers critical insights towards ensuring law is effective for Indigenous women.[95] Indigenous feminist legal theory requires us to listen to women's experiences, voices, community-based knowledge, and multiple critical theories about women's health so as to deepen analyses about the complexities of women's legal agency and aspirations.

---

95 See Skeet, Chapter 5 of this volume.

# 9 Domestication and reception of international reproductive health law and the limits of law

Perspectives from Nigeria and South Africa

*Babafemi Odunsi and Oluwayemisi A. Adewole*

## Introduction: the concept of reproductive health

Reproductive health refers to a state where an individual has a safe and satisfying sex life and a healthy capability to reproduce, as well as control over when to do so. It is a state of complete physical, mental and social well-being, and not merely the absence of disease or infirmity, in all matters related to the reproductive system and to its functions and processes.[1] Its determination benefits from a life-cycle approach involving an assessment of the factors that affect both women and men from infancy to old age. It also involves an understanding of how social and sexual behaviours and relationships affect health and create ill-health.[2]

Although the United Nation's definition of what constitutes reproductive health encompasses women and men, the field of reproductive and sexual health law and discourses about reproductive health are primarily about women. This is the case in Nigeria, where women are the primary subjects in reproductive health

---

1 A. Fadeyi and T. Oduwole, "Effect of Religion on Reproductive Health Issues in Nigeria" (2016) 4:1 *International Journal of Innovative Healthcare and Research* at 20, http://seahipaj. org/journals-ci/mar-2016/IJIHCR/full/IJIHCR-M-3-2016.pdf (accessed 22 May 2019). See also the UN Department of Public Information, *Platform for Action and Beijing Declaration* 1995 at para 94, where Reproductive health was defined as follows: "a state of complete physical, mental and social well-being and not merely the absence of disease or infirmity, in all matters relating to the reproductive system and to its functions and processes. Reproductive health therefore implies that people are able to have a satisfying and safe sex life and that they have the capacity to reproduce and the freedom to decide if, when and how often to do so. Implicit in this last condition are the right of men and women to be informed and to have access to safe, effective, affordable and acceptable methods of family planning of their choice, as well as other methods of their choice for regulation of fertility which are not against the law, and the right of access to appropriate health care services that will enable women to go safely through pregnancy and childbirth and provide couples with the best chance of having a healthy infant". See further paras 7.2 and 7.3, ICPD Programme of Action, 1994.

2 O. Olomola, "Revisiting State Responsibility for Women's Right to Reproductive Health Care Services in Nigeria – Maternal Death Rate Threatens MDGs" (2011) 2 *University of Benin Journal of Private and Property Law* at 70.

matters. Hence, the majority of the instruments fostering reproductive health in Nigeria tend to be protective of women. Nonetheless, reproductive health has to be understood within the context of relationships between men and women, as well as between communities and societies, since sexual and reproductive behaviours are governed by complex biological, cultural and psychosocial factors.[3] In our discussion of the limits of women's reproductive health rights within the context of the reception of international reproductive health laws in Nigeria, we return to the unique understanding of reproductive health in the African context and the notion of the interconnectedness of biological, cultural and societal factors as determinants of women's reproductive health.

As we further discuss below, these interconnections and unique understanding of reproductive health in the country, and other significant factors complicate the implementation of international reproductive health laws in local jurisdictions, such as Nigeria. Indeed, while many member states have made legislative attempts to fulfill the right of every woman to accessible services, as well as accurate information on sexual, reproductive, and contraceptive methods to maintain safe sexual and reproductive health,[4] a close reading of some legislation purportedly promulgated to protect women reveals complicating factors inherent in the law itself which, as Iyioha discusses in Chapter 2, are often evident in the language and framing of rights or entitlements.

Beyond legislation, formalities around the reception of international reproductive health laws within the domestic legal system also hinder the utility of international conventions domestically. This chapter focuses on this critical issue, exploring how local reception and implementation of international reproductive health laws limit the effects of such laws in member states. Drawing on insights from the theory of substantive effectiveness outlined in Chapter 2 – specifically its discourse on internal and external limits to effectiveness and on the influence of the perception of correctness on effectiveness –we argue that the influence of received English law on Nigeria's dual legal system and the dualist approach to the reception and domestication of treaties and other international reproductive health obligations applicable in the country have, among other factors, greatly

---

3 Ibid.
4 The 1969 Declaration on Social Progress and Development Adopted by the General Assembly in resolution 2542 affirmed the Tehran Proclamation of the International Conference on Human Rights, Tehran, Republic of Iran, held on 22 April to 13 May 1968; it urged Governments to provide couples not only the 'education' but also the "means necessary to enable them to exercise their right to determine freely and responsibly the number and spacing of their children". See UN General Assembly Resolution 2542, U.N. Doc. A/7630. The Tehran Proclamation in paragraph 3 stated that: "couples have a basic human right to decide freely and responsibly on the number and spacing of their children and a right to adequate education and information in this respect". See Resolution XVIII: Human Rights Aspects of Family Planning, Final Act of the International Conference on Human Rights. U.N. Doc. A/CONF. 32/41, p. 15. See www.un.org/en/development/desa/population/theme/rights/ (accessed 22 May 2019).

impeded the effectiveness of international reproductive health law in the regulation of reproductive health.

We further argue that the influence of the dual legal system as well as the dualist approach to the reception of international reproductive health laws, coupled with the attendant socio-cultural issues affecting the domestication of international reproductive health law constitute internal and external limits to the effectiveness of these laws for the reproductive health of Nigerians.[5] We explore the dimensions to these limits by examining some socio-cultural issues and religious predilections which have affected the will of members of the executive and the legislature to ensure the domestication of international reproductive health laws. In this discussion, we note that socio-cultural and religious issues have largely affected the willingness of the Nigerian people to demand for the domestication of these laws, and may likely affect the willingness of citizens to comply with the laws if they are eventually domesticated. We conclude by examining some of the effects of these internal and external limits for the reproductive health of Nigerians and proffer some solutions to the problems identified.

## *The Nigerian reproductive health policy*

The National Reproductive Health Policy and National Strategic Framework and Plan (November 2002–2006), which was launched in 2002 in Nigeria[6] sets the goals for the country's reproductive health strategy and plan. The country's Reproductive Health Policy is set within the framework of the National Health Policy, which upholds primary healthcare as the key to improving the health of men, women, adolescents and children at all levels. Primary healthcare, as envisioned in the country aims to help every individual in Nigeria to live an acceptable quality of life that positively contributes to national development. Therefore, essential reproductive healthcare ought to be integrated and accessible to every citizen, inclusive of those in rural areas.

The Reproductive Health Policy aims to achieve several objectives, some of which include the reduction of maternal morbidity and mortality, reduction of the level of unwanted pregnancies in all women of reproductive age (15–49 years), while reducing the prevalence of infertility and the elimination of all forms of gender-based violence and practices harmful to the health of women and children, such as female genital mutilation. The 2017 National Reproductive Health Policy incorporates the aims of the 2002–2006 policy. The policy was launched alongside training manuals on post-abortion care, as well as documents on the integration of reproductive health and HIV services.[7]

---

5  See Iyioha, Chapter 2 of this volume.
6  See the National Reproductive Health Strategic Framework and Plan 2002–2006, available at www.policyproject.com/pubs/countryreports/NIG_RHStrat.pdf (accessed 2 June 2019).
7  Other documents launched include Guidelines on Medical Management of Victims of Violence, Post-Abortion Care Training Manual, National Training Manual on Integration of Reproductive Health and HIV Services, and National Family Planning/Reproductive Health Service Protocol. See www.dailytrust.com.ng/fg-launches-reproductive-health-policy.html (accessed 2 June 2019).

## Reproductive healthcare in Nigeria: law, policy and socio-cultural perspectives

Reproductive health is a much-contested area of studies, especially in terms of the inordinate attention accorded to lawmaking on women's health and bodies in the public and private domain. This is no different in Nigeria, where a woman's reproductive health is negatively impacted by a number of factors, such as the pluralistic legal systems as well as social, cultural and political factors. For example, women's reproductive health is hugely affected by the cultural norms of marriage in given communities, some of which might include early marriage[8] and tender age at first delivery. Other challenges of a socio-cultural nature might include the orientation that women ought to bear as many children as possible, cultural preferences for some forms of healthcare services and facilities over others as evident, for example, in the patronage of traditional birth attendants, perception of maternity-related illnesses as supernatural and gender inequality that is buoyed up by traditional beliefs regarding the status of the sexes. Thus, the reproductive health problems of African women are often related to pregnancy, delivery and harmful cultural practices associated with sexuality and marriage.[9] It is, therefore, not surprising that maternal mortality in African countries is significantly higher for women under 18 years[10] compared with other parts of the world, as child and teen marriages are rampant in African countries, including Nigeria.

Besides these non-legal norms, reproductive health in Nigeria is governed and thereby impacted by a number of laws and policies. Over the years, the country has adopted different legal and policy measures to address reproductive health challenges in the country. These measures encompass international reproductive health instruments as well as domestic laws. The international instruments provide for obligations and specific actions to be undertaken by the country, following ratification, to ensure the progressive realization of the components of reproductive health rights. Domestic laws on reproductive health rights, on the other hand, indicate endorsements of the spirit of international reproductive health laws. In discussing the overall impact of law, legal systems and non-legal norms on women's health in Nigeria, it is important to start with the impact of the country's dual legal systems on women's healthcare before examining limits to the implementation of the multitude of domestic and international laws on

---

8 This is also very rampant in the northern region of Nigeria, where female children 10 years of age or younger are given out in marriage. The situation is not at all helped by the Constitution of Nigeria in Section 29(4)(b), which presumes maturity for any married woman, age notwithstanding.

9 See D. Cooper et al., "Coming of Age? Women's Sexual and Reproductive Health after Twenty-One Years of Democracy in South Africa" (2016) 24:48 *Reproductive Health Matters* at 79–80, available at www.tandfonline.com/doi/full/10.1016/j.rhm.2016.11.010 (accessed 22 May 2019) ('Cooper et al., "Coming of Age?"').

10 N. Mashalaba, "Commentary on the Causes and Consequences of Unwanted Pregnancy from an African Perspective" (1989) 3 *International Journal of Gynecology and Obstetrics* at 15–19.

women's healthcare. Finally, we examine the reasons for the limited effectiveness of these international reproductive health laws in the regulation of reproductive health in Nigeria and conclude by offering suggestions to address the situation.

## Impact of Nigeria's dual legal systems

The duality of the Nigerian legal system is an important feature to be considered in our discourse.[11] The Nigerian legal system is made up of two broad systems of laws – English law and customary law.[12] English law comprises the received English law, which is made up of Common Law, Doctrines of Equity, Statutes of General Application[13] and subsidiary legislation on specified matters.[14]According to Okeke:

> [T]he central legacy bequeathed to Nigeria by her British colonizers is the common law system combined with the doctrines of equity and statutes of general application, enacted in England on January 1, 1900. . . . At its independence, Nigeria still had a substantial connection with the British under the 1960 Independence Constitution, and it was not until 1963 that it officially detached itself from the colonial grip.[15]

The strong historical link between Nigeria and the British legal system referred to above has occasioned a conflict between the English common law system and the indigenous laws to which the citizens were accustomed before the colonization of the entity now known as Nigeria. The plural nature of the Nigerian society has also compounded the conflict of laws as native societies consider English law to be alien to their ways of life and an imposition by the colonialists. Indeed, in the words of Okeke, there is no other area in which the clash of legal cultures is more manifest than the interaction of common law and customary law in post-colonial African states.[16]

Despite this recognition of customary law as one of the sources of law in Nigeria, it is regarded by the Evidence Act as a "fact" which needs to be proved

---

11 Opinions of scholars now differ as to whether Nigeria actually operates a dual legal system or a tripartite legal system. The reason for this, among others, is that many are of the view that Islamic/Sharia law does not constitute part of customary law because it came into operation in Nigeria as a result of an external influence – the Jihad of Usman Dan Fodio of 1804–1808, unlike customary law which evolved from the indigenous cultural practices of the natives of the entity now known as Nigeria.

12 See *Folarin v. Durojaiye* (1988) 1 NWLR 351.

13 These are statutes that were in force in England as at 1 January 1900.

14 Y. Dina, J. Akintayo and F. Ekundayo (2015) *Guide to Nigerian Legal Information*, available at www.nyulawglobal.org/globalex/Nigeria1.html (accessed 22 May 2019).

15 C. Okeke, "The Use of International Law in the Domestic Courts of Ghana and Nigeria" (2015) 32 *Arizona Journal of International & Comparative Law*372 at 384 ('Okeke, "The Use of International Law"').

16 Ibid.

before the court, except such a custom has been judicially noticed.[17] According to Okeke:

> In Nigeria, there seems to be only one area where the legal system, though structured in accordance with the common law system, has given recognition to the traditional institutions of the indigenous people. This is in the area of criminal law administration in Northern Nigeria. Thus, the Penal Code that applies to the North enunciates more of the religious tradition of the North through its recognition of some Muslim offenses, like adultery, insult to the chastity of a woman, and drunkenness. It is not surprising then why some courts, in their decisions, appear to be influenced by the traditional background of the North.[18]

Shah, Akintola and Iyioha make similar observations in their exploration of the claims that positivism makes about law and the validity of these claims in the Nigerian context. The significant foreign influence of the English common law and Sharia law on the Nigerian legal system makes it unlikely that Nigeria will be able to harmonize her legal system into one that works seamlessly throughout the whole country.

Rules embodied within the Islamic customary law are derived from the Quran.[19] Most of these rules have been codified through the Nigerian Penal Code, which is applicable in northern Nigeria. In the south, the Criminal Code applies. Thus, the country has had different standards for similar acts or omissions that ultimately constitute different offences in different parts of the country. Nigerians from these different parts of the country who are raised and/or educated according to standards of customs obtainable in their places of birth are later elected into the National Assembly with their predilections for and prejudices against certain practices, and these preferences and biases would, in turn, inform the sort of bills they would sponsor or the type of conventions that would be domesticated in Nigeria.

An example of this judicial crisis can be seen in the prescription of death-bystoning as punishment for unlawful sexual intercourse in northern Nigeria. Introduced under the Muslim Sharia Code in some parts of northern Nigeria in 1999,[20] the sentence of deathbystoning is a practice that is rooted in the Maliki

---

17 See Sections 68, 73 and 122(2)(l) of the Evidence Act, CAP E14, 2011.
18 Okeke, "The Use of International Law" at 385.
19 In *Sidi v. Sha'Aban* (1992) 4 NWLR 113, the Court of Appeal held that the injunction of Allah in the Quran is that he who adjudicates in a way that is not in accordance with the injunctions of Allah is a sinner.
20 See R. Uzoma, "Religious Pluralism, Cultural Differences, and Social Stability in Nigeria"(2004)*Brigham Young University Law Review* at 651, cited in Okeke, "The Use of International Law" at 403. The introduction of Sharia criminal law in northern Nigeria provoked the Christians in the region, who felt marginalized. Many also felt their human rights were abused. This led to a conflict that resulted in loss of lives and property. See ibid.

School of jurisprudence among Muslim advocates.[21] From the perspective of international law, this sort of administration of criminal justice is incompatible with Nigeria's obligations under a number of international treaties, such as the International Covenant on Civil and Political Rights,[22] the Convention Against Torture and Other Cruel, Inhuman and Degrading Treatment or Punishment[23] and the African Charter.[24]

The implication of the foregoing is that the dual nature of the Nigerian legal system coupled with the plural nature of the Nigerian society has negatively affected the reproductive health of women in the country. Those in the rural areas are deeply mired in their customary ways of thinking and seem disconnected from the reality of the country's obligations under various international instruments concerning women's health and rights. In northern Nigeria, for example, child marriage and polygyny are very rampant and people from the area, including the elites, have accepted these phenomena as their traditional ways of life, regardless of what Nigeria's obligations are under international law. Women are often considered to have no say in important matters, including those matters in which they have a personal interest. Such a way of thinking has, over the years, affected the will of those in government saddled with the domestication and implementation of the various international instruments on the reproductive health of women, as we further discuss below.

## Reception and domestication of international reproductive health laws in Nigeria

### Domestic laws and policies and international reproductive health laws

The Constitution of the Federal Republic of Nigeria, 1999, which is the highest law in the land, contains provisions under Chapters 2 and 4 that are relevant for

---

21  See Okeke, "The Use of International Law" at 403.

22  For example, Article 6(2) allows countries that are yet to abolish the death penalty to impose death sentence only in respect of the most serious crimes, and in accordance with the Covenant. It has been argued – and rightly too – that although the ICCPR does not define what constitutes "most serious crimes", the General Comment of the UN Human Rights Committee and the position of the UN Commission on Human Rights that limit " 'most serious crimes' " to " 'intentional crimes with lethal or extremely grave consequences and . . . not [to] non-violent acts such as . . . [s]exual relations between consenting adults' ", suggests that adultery does not amount to "most serious crimes", and therefore the sentence of death-by-stoning as a punishment for adultery as provided under the Sharia Code violates the ICCPR. See Press Release, Amnesty International, Nigeria: Death by stoning upheld in the case of Amina Lawal (August 19, 2002), availableatwww.amnesty.org.uk/press-releases/nigeria-death-stoning-upheld-case-amina-lawal (accessed 2 June 2019). In addition, death by stoning violates Article 7 of the ICCPR, which prohibits torture or cruel, inhumane, or degrading treatment or punishment. See also Okeke, "The Use of International Law" at 403, footnote 208.

23  Articles 1, 2 and 16.

24  Articles 4 and 5.

the promotion and protection of reproductive health and rights in Nigeria. In addition, Section 54 of the Nigerian Labour Act[25] provides for maternity leave for pregnant female employees and prohibits wrongful dismissal of employees during the maternity leave. Section 18 of the Marriage Act provides for parental consent to marriage of minors and Section 3 of the Matrimonial Causes Act provides that a marriage is void where the consent obtained is not a real consent or where either of the parties is not of marriageable age.[26] The National Health Act, 2014 also contains provisions on ensuring that all Nigerians have access to the basic minimum standard of healthcare, which includes reproductive health. The Violence Against Persons (Prohibition) Act, 2015 contains provisions prohibiting all forms of violence against all persons, including women; it also prohibits all harmful cultural practices, prominent among which is female genital mutilation.

Notably, the provisions of the National Reproductive Health Policy and Strategy of 2002 and a host of other policies, including the National Policy on the Elimination of Female Genital Mutilation (1998 and 2002), the National Adolescent Health Policy (1995), National Policy on Maternal and Child Health, 1994, and the National Reproductive Health Policies (2010 and 2017), among others,[27] constitute the key policy frameworks governing the provision of reproductive and sexual health services for all Nigerians.[28]

Nigeria became a member of the United Nations on 7 October 1960[29] and is also a member of the African Union. It has, therefore, ratified a number of international and regional instruments, some of which govern the subject of reproductive health. These include the Protocol on the Rights of Women in Africa,[30] the African Charter on Human and Peoples' Rights,[31] the African Union Charter on the Rights and Welfare of the Child,[32] the UN Convention on the Elimination of All Forms of Discrimination Against Women (CEDAW),[33] the UN Convention on the Rights of the Child (CRC),[34] the UN Convention against Torture

---

25 Chapter 21 and Part 5 of the Criminal Code.
26 Section 3(d) and (e) of the Matrimonial Causes Act.
27 Other policies include the National Policy on HIV/AIDS (2003), The National Health Policy and Strategy (1998 and 2004), National Policy on Women (2000 and 2004), the National Policy on Population for Development, Unity, Progress and Self-Reliance (1998 and 2004).
28 M. Ladan, "Review of Existing Reproductive Health Policies and Legislations in Nigeria", A paper presented at a one-day stakeholders' forum on Reproductive Health in Nigeria, held on 20 April 2006, available at www.gamji.com/article5000/NEWS5997.htm (accessed 22 May 2019) ('Ladan, "Review of Existing Reproductive Health Policies"').
29 See www.un.org/en/member-states/index.html (accessed 22 May 2019).
30 Ratified on 16 December 2004. See www.lawnigeria.com/Treaties/Treaties-Global.php (accessed 22 May 2019). See also Ladan, "Review of Existing Reproductive Health Policies", *supra*.
31 Ratified on 22 June 1983, ibid.
32 Ratified on 23 July 2001, ibid.
33 Ratified on 13 June 1985, ibid.
34 Ratified on 19 April 1991, ibid.

and other cruel, inhuman or degrading treatment or punishment (CAT),[35] the International Covenant on Civil and Political Rights (ICCPR),[36] the International Covenant on Economic, Social and Cultural Rights (ICESCR)[37]and the International Covenant on the Elimination of All Forms of Racial Discrimination (ICERD).[38] The Universal Declaration of Human Rights,[39] though not a treaty, has nevertheless become binding as customary rules of international law and *Jus cogens*, with particular reference to core provisions relevant to reproductive health and rights.

Other instruments and standards relevant to reproductive health and rights in Nigeria include the 1993 Vienna Declaration and Programme of Action, the Programme of Action of the 1993 UN International Conference on Population and Development (ICPD) and the 1995 Beijing Declaration and Platform for Action – UN Fourth World Conference on Women.[40]

## *Reception and domestication: challenges with the implementation of international reproductive health laws in Nigeria*

There are two traditional theoretical approaches on the relationship of international law with national legal systems. These are monism and dualism. Monists regard international and national law as part of a single, legal order.[41] The implication of this is that international law is considered superior to municipal laws, and is thus directly applicable in the national legal order. Based on this, there would be no need for a domesticating legislation; international law will thereby be automatically applicable within the municipal jurisdiction. Municipal laws in such jurisdictions must be consistent with international law, as the latter is considered to be founded on natural law.[42] Monism is practiced in countries like France, the Netherlands, Switzerland, and many Latin American and some Francophone African countries.[43] Accordingly, the process by which international law is municipalized is through the methodology of incorporation, meaning instruments that have been ratified by a state automatically form part of the laws of that state and

---

35 Ratified on 28 June 2001,ibid.
36 Ratified on 29 July 1993,ibid.
37 Ratified on 29 July 1993, ibid.
38 Ratified on 16 October 1967, ibid.
39 10 December 1948, ibid.
40 Ladan, "Review of Existing Reproductive Health Policies", *supra*.
41 See I. Brownlie, *Principles of Public International Law* (Oxford: Oxford University Press, 1990), M. Mwagiru, "From Dualism to Monism: The Structure of Revolution in Kenya's Constitutional Treaty Practice" (2011) 3:1 *Journal of Language, Language, Technology & Entrepreneurship in Africa* at 144–155 ('Mwagiru, "From Dualism to Monism"').
42 See O. Ngara, "Nigerian National Assembly and Domestication of Treaties in Nigeria's Fourth and Fifth Assembly" (2017) 2:2 *Social Scientia Journal of the Social Sciences and Humanities*at60 ('Ngara, "Nigerian National Assembly and Domestication"').
43 F. Bangamwabo, "The Implementation of International and Regional Human Rights Instruments in the Namibian Legal Framework" (2008) *Human Rights and the Rule of Law in Namibia* at 167.

are accordingly binding.[44] Monists are of the view that although the executive is responsible for the ratification of treaties, the parliament is ultimately responsible for scrutinizing the treaties and may either vote for or against the ratification of such treaties by the executive.[45] Once the treaty is signed, however, it becomes law without the need for domestication.

Dualism, on the other hand, has its roots in legal positivism and posits that domestic and international laws exist independently of each other, with each one being competent in its own domain.[46] In essence, dualism posits that international law does not have any superiority over municipal laws and that the latter may not necessarily conform to the former. This position is predicated on the principle of state sovereignty and that states do have a right to decide which international laws they wish to incorporate into their municipal laws. Such incorporation may then be done through domestic legislative measures, which would thereafter transform the given international law into a domestic one.[47] Based on the foregoing and on Section 12(1)–(3) of the constitution, Nigeria is a dualist state. The next subsection examines Section 12(1)–(3) in some depth.

### *The process of domestication*[48]

Section 12 of the Constitution of the Federal Republic of Nigeria, 1999 (as amended) prescribes the requirement of domestication for any international instrument that is to be applied in any Nigerian Court. The section, apparently, was inserted by the drafters of the Constitution in order to protect the country's sovereignty, an intention already expressed in Section 1(1) of the Constitution. According to Section 12(1)–(3):

> (1) No treaty between the federation and any other country shall have the force of law except to the extent to which any such treaty has been enacted into law by the National Assembly;
> (2) The National Assembly may make laws for the Federation or any part thereof with respect to matters not included in the Exclusive Legislative list for the purpose of implementing a treaty; and

44 Mwagiru, "From Dualism to Monism" at 144.
45 Ibid.
46 See Ngara, "Nigerian National Assembly and Domestication", *supra*.
47 Ibid. According to Mwagiru, "The dualist school is supported by the methodology of transformation. In that methodology, treaties do not become automatically binding on states unless they have first been transformed into municipal law. The methodology of transformation requires that the legislature which makes laws domestically, must first of all transform treaties into municipal law. The transformation of treaties into municipal laws entail clothing them domestically, by making them part of the statutes of the country".
48 See generally A. O. Enabulele, "Implementation of Treaties in Nigeria and the Status Question: Whither Nigerian Courts?" (2009) 17 *African Journal of International & Comparative Law* at 326; C. Nwapi, "International Treaties in Nigerian and Canadian Courts" (2011) 19 *African Journal of International & Comparative Law* at 38; and Okeke, "The Use of International Law" at 396.

(3) A bill for an Act of the National Assembly passed pursuant to the provisions of subsection (2) of this section shall not be enacted unless it is ratified by a majority of all the Houses of Assembly in the Federation.

The Supreme Court affirmed the provisions of Section 12(1)–(3) in the case of *Abacha v Fawehimi*,[49] where it was held that

An international treaty entered into by the Government of Nigeria does not become binding until enacted into law by the National Assembly. The court further held that where the treaty is enacted by the National Assembly, as was the case with the African Charter which is incorporated into municipal law by the African Charter on Human and Peoples' Rights (Enforcement and Ratification) Act of 1983, it becomes binding on Nigerian courts to give effect to it like all other laws falling within the judicial powers of the court.

The process of domestication of a treaty is the same as that used to pass a bill into law. The process is initiated by the promotion of the bill, in this case a treaty bill, on the floor of the House of Representatives or the Senate as the case may require. On the receipt of the bill, it is forwarded to the Committee of Rules and Procedure,[50] which assesses the bill against the required standards in its draft and presentation.[51] The bill would, thereafter, be published in the House/Senate Journal[52] and sent to the floor of the House/Senate for the first reading.[53] The bill is debated during the second reading and from there may be allowed to move to the committee stage or be 'negatived'. Where the bill scales the hurdle of the second reading, it is moved to the committee stage where either the committee of the whole house or the standing committee makes critical deliberations on it

---

49 (2000) 6 NWLR (pt 660) 228. See also *MHWUN v Minister of Health & Productivity & Ors* (2005) 17 NWLR (Pt. 953) 120, where the court of appeal held at 155–157 that "there is no evidence . . . that the ILO Convention, even though signed by the Nigerian Government, has been enacted into law by the National Assembly. In so far as the ILO Convention has not been enacted into law by the National Assembly, it has no force of law in Nigeria and it cannot possibly apply. . . . Where, however, the treaty is enacted into law by the National Assembly as was the case with the African Charter which is incorporated into our municipal (i.e. domestic) law by the African Charter on Human and People's Rights (Ratification and Enforcement) Act, Cap. 10, Laws of the Federation of Nigeria 1990, it becomes binding and our courts must give effect to it like all other laws falling within the judicial powers of the Courts".

50 Rules and Business Committee, House of Representatives. See "Federal Republic of Nigeria National Assembly – The Legislative Process", available at https://nass.gov.ng/page/the-legislative-process (accessed 2 June 2019) for detailed information on the process of passing a bill into law.

51 If it fails at this level, it would be forwarded to the legal department for re-drafting and further advice. Ibid.

52 An executive bill must be published in the House/Senate Journal once, while a member's bill must be published three times before being presented for the first reading. See ibid.

53 At this stage, there is no debate on the bill. This is done to merely inform the members of the house that a bill has been received. See ibid.

and report to the plenary with or without amendments. The bill then moves to the third and final reading where the clean copy of the bill will be verified as accurate. It would thereafter be sent for concurrence of the receiving chamber,[54] and lastly, to the president for his or her assent. If the president refuses to assent after 30 days, the bill may be passed by two-thirds majority of the National Assembly.

It is evident, from the foregoing, that the Constitution is the instrument for determining how the national law of a state interacts with international law. Such interaction determines the extent to which individuals can employ international law to enforce their rights within the national legal system.[55] Although international law recognizes the right of states to negotiate treaties on matters which fall within the purview of their national sovereignty, the law and procedure on treaty making capacity, according to Nwabueze,[56] is not documented under the Nigerian Constitution, as what is outlined in the Constitution is treaty implementation.[57] This is unlike the situation in other jurisdictions, such as the United States and the United Kingdom, where the law and procedure on treaty making is well spelt out.

Traditionally, the executive arm of government leads the process of negotiating a treaty through the Ministry of Foreign Affairs, even though constitutionally treaty making is an area where the National Assembly participates in foreign policymaking.[58] This is because the National Assembly plays the decisive role of approving or disapproving a treaty entered into by the executive on behalf of the country and has the power to make changes to the text of a treaty to be domesticated.[59]

It has been said that the provisions of Section 12 of the Constitution were meant to check the powers of the executive when it takes on international obligations on behalf of the federation as is the case with other constitutional provisions that serve as check and balances on the powers of the different arms of

---

54 Meaning either by the House of Assembly to the Senate, or vice versa. See ibid.
55 See Okeke, "The Use of International Law", *supra*. See also F. Onomrerhinor, "A Re-Examination of the Requirement of Domestication of Treaties in Nigeria" (2016) *Nnamdi Azikiwe University Journal of International Law and Jurisprudence* at 17, available at www. ajol.info/index.php/naujilj/article/viewFile/136236/125726 (accessed 22 May 2019) ('Onomrerhinor, "A Re-Examination of the Requirement of Domestication"').
56 Ibid. See also B. Nwabueze, *Federalism in Nigeria under the Presidential Constitution* (London: Sweet & Maxwell, 1985) at 25.
57 The Nigerian Treaties (Making Procedure etc.) Decree No 16 of 1992 classifies treaties into three categories and stipulates the conditions which they must satisfy: (1) lawmaking treaties (which affect or modify existing legislation or powers of the National Assembly),which must be enacted into law; (2) agreements (which impose financial, political and social obligations or have scientific or technological importance), which must be ratified; and (3) those that deal with mutual exchange of cultural and educational facilities and need no ratification by any legal instrument. See ibid. at 256.
58 R.A. Dunmoye, P. Njoku and O. Alubo, eds., *The National Assembly: Pillar of Democracy* (Abuja: The National Secretariat of Nigerian Legislatures, National Assembly, 2007) cited in Onomrerhinor, "A Re-Examination of the Requirement of Domestication", *supra*.
59 See ibid.

government.[60] The section is thus intended to foster cooperation between the executive and the legislature, as the checks and balances envisaged would only be effective in an atmosphere of mutual trust cooperation.[61]

### Challenges with domestication and implementation of international reproductive health laws in Nigeria

According to the UN Committee on Economic and Socio-Cultural Rights, reproductive rights, along with the "element of freedom", embody social entitlements, and the realization of these entitlements depend largely on the government by virtue of its position as the overseer of state resources and the protector of the collective interests of the society.[62] Areas abound where international law and domestic or municipal law are interconnected or pursue the same objectives. Prominent among such areas is human rights,[63] as well as reproductive rights, which are themselves embodied in human rights law. In the case of international obligations, citizens need to rely on an enabling domestic instrument to benefit from or ensure that a state meets its obligation at the international level.[64] Furthermore, relationships and problems that were once domestic, such as economic and environmental matters, have become international in scope; as a result, matters that previously were the exclusive preserve of municipal law are now covered by treaties.

Sometimes, the object of the treaty is the regulation of activities of individuals and private entities within a state, rather than that of changing the behaviour of relevant actors.[65] Regardless of the objective, it is expected that when these treaties are entered into, Nigeria – despite being a dualist state – would incorporate them into the domestic laws of the country in order for them to be applicable in the courts, especially in the wake of globalization in the 21stcentury. This, however, is not the case.

60  These powers include the power of impeachment granted the legislature in Sections 143 and 188; the power to veto acts of parliament granted the president – the head of the executive – which makes him part of the lawmaking body in Section 58; the power granted the judiciary to declare executive actions and laws made by the legislature unconstitutional in Section 6; the legislative endorsement required for some executive acts such as declaration of war in Section 5(4); the legislative endorsement of executive nominees in Sections 147(2), 154, 192(2) and 198 and budgets in Section 81; and the legislative and executive input in the appointment of judges and the exercise of prerogative of mercy in sections 175 and 212 of the Constitution of the Federal Republic of Nigeria 1999 as amended. Onomrerhinor, "A Re-Examination of the Requirement of Domestication" at 22.

61  Ibid.

62  See "The Right to the Highest Attainable Standard of Health", UN Committee on ESCR General Comment, UN Doc. EC/12/2000/4 (General Comment 14'), paras 34–38. See also R. Dixon-Mueller etal., "Towards a Sexual Ethics of Rights and Responsibilities" (2009) 17 *Reproductive Health Matters* at 111.

63  M. Shaw, *International Law*,6th ed. (Cambridge: Cambridge University Press, 2008) at 130.

64  Onomrerhinor, "A Re-Examination of the Requirement of Domestication" at 19.

65  Ibid.

Of all the aforementioned treaties, only the African Charter on Human and Peoples' Rights ('the Charter') has been domesticated as CAP 10, Laws of the Federation of Nigeria, 1990 and applied in cases that have come before Nigerian courts. Having said this, it is also significant that only one out of the more than 60 articles in the treaty makes specific reference to women. The Charter also fails to explicitly define discrimination against women and does not guarantee the right to consent to marriage and equality in marriage. Additionally, it incorporates 'culture' and traditional values and practices into the treaty in a way that seems impervious to the long history of women's deprivation in Africa – a history in which these same practices have impeded the advancement of women's rights in Africa.[66]

Another bold attempt to implement the provisions of the UN Convention on the Rights of the Child (CRC) and African Charter on the Rights and Welfare of the Child, as well as CEDAW in particular was the promulgation of the Child Rights Act, 2003. The Child Rights Act (CRA) defines a child as a person below the age of 18 years and sets 18 as the minimum legal age for all purposes, including marriage, sexual consent, criminal liability, deprivation of liberty, corporal punishment and imprisonment, as well as for subjecting a person to capital punishment and labour. It also prohibits economic and sexual exploitation.[67] The Act, however, failed to protect the girl-child from harmful practices like female genital mutilation. A selective domestic implementation of the provisions of Article 6 of CEDAW on prohibition of trafficking in women and exploitation for prostitution can be found in the Trafficking in Persons (Prohibition) Law Enforcement and Administration Act, 2003.[68] This Act prohibits and prescribes punishment for traffic in persons, particularly women and children, and establishes a national agency (NAPTIP) charged with the responsibility for investigation and prosecution of offenders, as well as the counselling and rehabilitation of trafficked persons. However, a significant number of cases are thrown out of court for want of diligent prosecution. Additionally, there are various logistical handicaps, such as the unavailability of necessary resources and funds needed to combat trafficking.

The Violence Against Persons (Prohibition) Act 2015 (VAPP), which is also an attempt at implementing some of the provisions of CEDAW, criminalizes carrying out, attempting to carry out, inciting, aiding, abetting, or counselling another person to carry out harmful traditional practices, and prescribes a punishment of four years' imprisonment or a fine of 500,000 naira or both for the offence.[69] The Act defines Harmful Traditional Practices (HTP) as all traditional behaviour, attitudes or practices which negatively affect the fundamental rights

---

66 Article 17. According to the provision: (1) Women shall have the right to live in a positive cultural context and to participate at all levels in the determination of cultural policies. (2) States Parties shall take all appropriate measures to enhance the participation of women in the formulation of cultural policies at all levels.

67 Section 277(21)–(34); 221.

68 No. 24, as amended by Act No. 14 of 7 December 2005.

69 Section 20, Violation Against Persons (Prohibition) Act, 2015.

of women, girls or any person and includes harmful widowhood practices, denial of inheritance or succession rights, female genital mutilation or female circumcision, forced marriage and forced isolation from family and friends.[70] Apart from the generic crime of carrying out harmful traditional practices, the Act also specifically prohibits harmful widowhood practices in Section 15 and female genital mutilation in Section 6, prescribing the punishment of a term of imprisonment not exceeding four years or a fine of not more than 200,000 naira or both for the latter, and a term of imprisonment not exceeding two years or to a fine not exceeding 500,000 naira or both for the former. The jurisdictional reach of the Act is, however, limited by Section 47 of the Act, which makes it applicable only in the Federal Capital Territory, Abuja.

The National Health Act, 2014 is another legislation that purports, at least implicitly, to advance health rights already recognized under international law. It was passed to establish a framework for the regulation, development and management of the National Health System and set standards for the regulation of health services,[71] though it failed to create a framework for the implementation of the policies contained therein. Under the Act, all Nigerians are entitled to the "basic minimum package" of health services.[72] Unfortunately, 'basic minimum package' is undefined in the Act. Furthermore, traditional healing practices, which the Act envisages,[73] and which women often seek, are not properly regulated.

An assessment of the above laws against the different theories of legal effectiveness, as well as against the theory of substantive effectiveness brilliantly enunciated by Iyioha in Chapter 2, would indicate that the laws cannot be said to be effective. Under the compliance theory of effectiveness, there must be congruence between the stipulation of the law and the behaviour of the people for a law to be considered effective. A law would be effective only if it commands popular compliance with the stated objective. Thus, for the VAPP Act, for example, effectiveness would be measured by the amount of data received from the Federal Capital Territory indicating a significant number of offenders who have been prosecuted for the contravention of the provisions of the Act or, as Iyioha explains in Chapter 2, from empirical evidence showing a reduction in the number of girls who have undergone female genital mutilation since the promulgation of the Act. The National Health Act would, under the outcomes and compliance theories be said to be effective if everyone who walks into a healthcare facility receives a 'basic minimum health package' or if every Nigerian has access to the National Health Insurance Scheme.[74] Sadly, these outcomes do not capture the complete

---

70 Section 47, ibid. This definition tallies with that given in the Maputo Protocol to the African Charter on Human and Peoples Rights, 2003.

71 Section 1, National Health Act, 2014.

72 Section 3(3), ibid.

73 Section 1(2), which establishes the National Health System, includes traditional and alternative health care providers as part of the system, but fails to establish a framework for the regulation of that branch of medicine.

74 See Article 16(2) of the African Charter, which provides that states shall take necessary steps to ensure that their sick citizens receive medical treatment.

picture of the types of experiences that can and do follow from the prohibitions and provisions in the above laws, making simplistic assessment of progress based on mere numerical outcomes an unproductive exercise.

The Social Legal theory, on the other hand, posits that an effective law is one which is closely constructed to fit societal norms and values. A social legal theorist, therefore, might view favourably the African Charter's provision in Article 17(2) and (3), which guarantees every individual's right to freely take part in the culture of his or her community and charges contracting states to promote the moral traditional values recognized by the community. The social legal theory would seem to validate the conservative stance of the majority of the Nigerian legislature, as is further explained below, which explains their unwillingness to import international laws that are counter to the cultures of the Nigerian people into the country's legal system.

### Primary factors

It has been suggested that the domestication of a treaty is a major challenge to the legislature in Nigeria because the legislators have historically shown little interest in ensuring ratified treaties are domesticated within a reasonable time.[75] This is evident in the fact that 63% of the treaty bills passed by the National Assembly (both Senate and the House of Representatives) between 1999 and 2007 have a gestation period of 150 to 499 days (which is about 5 to 17 months). Only 30% of the treaty bills were passed within 150 days (i.e., within five months from the date of the introduction of the bill).[76]

Akanle[77] has attributed this poor performance to the selfish motives and pecuniary interests of the national legislators, remarking that ulterior motives partly explain why the national legislators frequently increase their salaries and allowances with much ease while they find it difficult to do same for lawmaking and constituency responsibilities. He further argued that "if the relative ease, speed and commitment with which the legislators settle personal benefit [*sic*]are extended into performance of other important roles, they would have made better impacts on the nation".[78]

Akanle's opinion however contrasts with the reason given by national legislators for the non-domestication of treaties. The Senate Order Paper of 2014,[79] for instance, shows that the problem of non-domestication is largely due to the failure of the executive arm to lay treaties, protocols and conventions to which Nigeria

75  W. Alli, "Nigeria's National Assembly and Foreign Policy in a Changing Domestic and External Environment" (2014) 6:1 *Nigerian Journal of Legislative Affairs* at 25–55.
76  See Ngara, "Nigerian National Assembly and Domestication" at 63.
77  O. Akanle, "Legislative Inputs and Good Governance in Nigeria: 1999–2009", in I. Ogundiya, O. Olutayo and J. Amzat, eds., *Assessment of Democratic Trends in Nigeria* (India: Gyan Publisher House, 2011) at 109–126.
78  Ibid. at 120.
79  Senate Order Paper, *The Senate of the Federal Republic of Nigeria, 7th National Assembly Fourth Session, No. 28, Wednesday, 24th September* (Abuja: National Assembly Press, 2014).

is a signatory before the National Assembly. Others[80] have also claimed that the non-domestication of treaties is caused by the unwillingness or reluctance of the executive arm to submit treaties ratified by the executive for legislative action at the National Assembly, and that the National Assembly is not sufficiently carried along in the process of negotiating treaties or international agreements.[81] This gap in communication, they claim, creates a fundamental knowledge gap for the legislators, who may have to engage consultants or conduct public hearings in order to educate members on a specific treaty matter before they can undertake legislative action.[82]

However, one of the challenges with domestication and implementation is deeply stemmed in the cultural orientation of the individuals who make up the executive and the legislative branches of government.[83] Owing to the dualist approach that Nigeria has adopted to international instruments, these two organs of government are pivotal to the operation of any international instrument in the country. As has been observed earlier, many of these legislators have deep-seated bias against some of the stipulations of international reproductive health laws, especially where they relate to child-marriage, cultural practices, abortion, homosexuality and other areas that are traditionally incompatible with the often conservative Nigerian mentality. This bias has resulted in excessive local politicization of these reproductive health issues, causing those who see themselves as stakeholders to exert undue pressure and influence on the National Assembly.

A good example is the Child Rights Act, which was passed in 2003. Nigeria was a signatory to the Convention on the Rights of the Child of 1989 (CRC).[84] The process of domestication of the Act based on the CRC proved extremely difficult due to religious and cultural issues arising from the CRC's definition of a child as a human being below the age of 18 years. The Child Rights Bill was misconstrued particularly in some parts of northern Nigeria as an attempt to impose Western cultural values on them, especially in relation to marriageable age of 13 years under Sharia law.[85] Citing inconsistencies between the bill and Islamic values, majority of the members of the National Assembly from northern Nigeria objected to passage of the bill because Islamic law allows girls to be married out at a much younger age than 18, in which case the consent of the bride is immaterial and she is, in fact, subject to the wishes of her family – a family expectedly

---

80  See Ngara, "Nigerian National Assembly and Domestication" at 63.
81  Ibid.
82  Ibid.
83  This is further discussed below.
84  Signed 20 November 1989.
85  E. Omoregie, "Implementation of Treaties in Nigeria: Constitutional Provisions, Federalism Imperative and the Subsidiarity Principle", *A paper delivered at the International Conference on Public Policy (ICPP)* held on 1–4 July, 2015, Milan, Italy under the auspices of the International Public Policy Association (IPPA), cited in Ngara, "Nigerian National Assembly and Domestication" at 11.

sympathetic to the union.[86] Some religious bodies, such as the Supreme Council for Sharia in Nigeria (SCIAN), not only opposed the bill but also pressured states in northern Nigeria implementing Sharia law to keep their representatives in both the Senate and the House of Representatives from supporting the draft bill.[87]

It should be borne in mind that Section 29(4)(b) of the Nigerian Constitution provides that every married woman shall be presumed to be mature, notwithstanding the age of such a "woman".[88] This provision, it is submitted, is in tandem with the provision of the Sharia law on marriage and therefore constitutes a disadvantage to women since it can be "presumed" under that section that a married 10-year-old is "matured". Hence, the domestication of a treaty, which specifically prohibits the marriage of girls below 18 years, is expectedly problematic for some members of the legislature. Ironically, under Nigerian law, the Child Rights Act would then be open to being declared null and void to the extent of its inconsistency with the provision of the Constitution on maturity.[89] Another area where the bias referred to above is evident is in the prohibition of abortion.[90]

The preference for a lowered maturity age for marriage, as discussed above, is rooted in morality and validated by religious precepts, and therefore, constitutes an example of an external limit to the effectiveness of international reproductive health law. As can be deduced from the subsection on the dual nature of the Nigerian legal system, issues that are considered by the lawmakers to be of a 'moral' nature are usually informed by their cultural upbringing, the tenets of religion and personal preferences – and there is often a blurring of lines between all of these factors. For example, the Same Sex Marriage (Prohibition) Act, 2014 prohibits marriage and all forms of public display of amorous affection by same-sex individuals. Years after the passage of this law, many Nigerians are still in support of the provisions of the Act, the most support coming from religious organizations. Ironically, the law has not reduced the number of gay people in Nigeria. What it has done is to scare them into the shadows and prevent them from openly admitting their sexual orientation. The effect of this is that LBGT individuals in Nigeria cannot come out to receive reproductive healthcare, an outcome contrary to Article 2 of the African Charter. A similar argument can

---

86 U. Emelonye, *Proportionality and Best Interests: Calibrating the Twin Pillars of Child Justice in Nigeria* (Doctoral Thesis presented for public examination by due permission of the Faculty of Law, University of Helsinki in Porthania Hall IV on 28 November 2014).

87 Ibid.

88 The section is contained in Chapter 3 of the Constitution, which makes provisions for citizenship. The said section provides for renunciation of citizenship.

89 See Section 1 of the Constitution of Nigeria, 1999.

90 Other relevant provisions are found in Part 5 of the Criminal Code, which bears the title, "Offences against the Person and Relating to Marriage and Parental Duties and Against the Reputation of Individuals". These offences include infanticide, killing an unborn child and concealment of the birth of children. Section 328 provides that, "Any person who, when a woman is about to be delivered of a child prevents the child from being born alive by any act or omission of such a nature that, if the child had been born alive and had then died, he would be deemed to have unlawfully killed the child, is guilty of a felony, and is liable to imprisonment for life".

also be made for the continued criminalization of abortion except for therapeutic reasons.[91]

In all of the above examples, what emerges is that lawmakers often mistake moral correctness with factual correctness. Whether the target group is same-sex individuals or individuals below 18, legislators have failed to separate their personal views about the morality of the situation from the facts that undergird the circumstances of life of the group – circumstances that entitle the group to the protection of the law and to the necessary healthcare resources to live full and complete lives.

### *Other factors*

Apart from the direct roles of the executive and the legislature in the continued failure to domesticate these international reproductive health laws, there are also secondary factors which affect the willingness of the legislature to domesticate. These factors also affect the willingness of citizens to demand the domestication of international reproductive health laws as well as their willingness to comply with the laws if domesticated.

A major factor is the influence of culture. Culture is a determinant of reproductive health laws, as well as the reproductive and sexual health status of Nigerians, especially as it entrenches many practices that foster gender inequality in societies across the country. The impact of culture commences the day the girl-child is born, when the news of her birth is greeted with less enthusiasm. As the child grows, she may be subjected to less favourable conditions such as nutritional deprivation, unlike the male child who is offered better nutrition, opportunities and resources for proper and adequate growth. Nutritional deprivations may result in inadequate or contracted pelvis later in life, with the potential attendant complications at childbirth. The imposition of cultural practices such as female circumcision,[92] childhood marriages, wife hospitality,[93] widowhood rites and wife inheritance also contribute negatively to women's reproductive and sexual health.[94]

---

91  See Iyioha's examination of 'correctness' and the limits of law in Chapter 2 of this volume.

92  This is usually referred to as Female Genital Mutilation (FGM). FGM is often motivated by beliefs about what is considered acceptable sexual behaviour. It aims to ensure premarital virginity and marital fidelity. FGM is in many communities believed to reduce a woman's libido and therefore believed to help her resist extramarital sexual acts. See O. Olomola, "Unending Harmful Tradition Shrouded in Secrecy: Female Genital Mutilation", in H. O. Nwagwu et al., eds., *Women Issues in Nigeria* (Ibadan: Royal People Limited, 2009) at 66.

93  In some parts of Benue state of Nigeria, as well as in the Ovahimba and Ovazimba tribes in the Kunene and Omusati regions in Northern Namibia, the best form of hospitality a man can offer his male guest is his wife. The said male guest is permitted to use his host's wife in the satisfaction of his sexual desires throughout his stay. The woman has no say in the matter, as she is expected to do as she is told.

94  Some of these cultural practices have been outlawed, but are still very much in operation in the country, especially in rural areas.

There is a general notion that motherhood is the natural, desired and ultimate goal of all 'normal women'. Thus, any woman who denies her maternal instinct is regarded as selfish, peculiar or disturbed. The result of this social construct has been the suppression of women's reproductive health rights and autonomy in the private sphere and control and exclusion of women from the public sphere. In the private sphere, the social construct is responsible for sexual stereotyping or sexual roles in reproductive health decisions.[95] The woman traditionally has the responsibility to guard against pregnancy and, ironically, is not expected to suggest family planning or the use of protection. She often has little or no say in long-term family planning decisions and is legally, culturally and religiously not allowed to abort any unwanted pregnancy, no matter how many children she has already had.[96] She, usually, is the prime suspect where infertility is suspected in a marriage.

According to social and cultural constructs, girls are expected to be chaste, pure and inexperienced as far as sexuality and issues of reproduction are concerned. This expected behaviour affects the seeking of reproductive health services by adolescent girls. Teenage girls are reluctant to share sensitive information for fear that their confidentiality will not be protected. Legislative provisions around parental notification constitute a barrier for adolescents seeking contraceptive advice, thus leading to poor reproductive health outcomes.

Members of the Nigerian legislature as well as the executive have not sufficiently learned to separate their religious or culture-induced prejudices from the interest of the state, and the reproductive health of Nigerians have greatly suffered for it. As has been mentioned earlier, deep-seated cultural bias has greatly affected the political will of the legislature to domesticate international reproductive health laws, especially those in conflict with prevalent cultural norms. Several laws that are presently in force in the country have been tainted with cultural prejudices. For example, a woman's testimony in a case of sexual assault is not by itself credible enough to prove her case, and would still require corroboration. A rape victim is still required to provide corroborated evidence that the rape occurred.[97] Also, domestic violence or Intimate Partner Violence (IPV) is

---

95 O. Olomola, "Gender Equity, Status of Women and the Girl Child: A Legal Perspective" (2010) 1:1 *FIDA: International Federation of Women Lawyers* at 25.

96 Under Nigerian law (as prescribed by the Criminal and Penal Codes), interfering with pregnancy no matter how early this takes place is regarded as criminal, unless such interference is undertaken for therapeutic reasons to preserve the life of the mother. See Sections 228 and 229 of the Criminal Code, which criminalize the conduct of both the woman and the person who aids or attempts the abortion of a woman's pregnancy. Other relevant provisions are found in Part 5 of the Criminal Code, which – as noted above – bears the title "Offences against the Person and Relating to Marriage and Parental Duties and Against the Reputation of Individuals". These offences include infanticide, killing an unborn child and concealment of the birth of children. See also Section 328 of the Criminal Code.

97 A person shall not be convicted of the offences in Sections 218, 221, 223 and 224 of the Criminal Code upon the uncorroborated evidence of one witness. This is the reason many women decide against reporting incidences of sexual assault and rape.

rampant in the society, being a patriarchal one. If a woman walks into a police station to report her husband's assault, she gets laughed at and turned back, with the officer on duty brushing it aside as a 'domestic matter'. This situation is rampant in societies where patriarchy is encouraged and affirmed by custom, legal structures and religious systems.[98] Today, there remains no provision for marital rape in Nigeria, so that when a woman is sexually abused by her husband, it is believed that she voluntarily gave herself up to her husband at marriage, hence *volenti non fit injuria*.[99]

Some laws also expressly discriminate against unmarried pregnant women. One of such is Police Regulation 127 of the Police Act, which states that "an unmarried woman police officer who becomes pregnant shall be discharged from the force, and shall not be re-listed except with the approval of the Inspector-General [*sic*]". Sections 54 and 55 of the Labour Act contain prohibitions on employing women for underground and night work, thereby arming an employer with a legitimate weapon against women or the interest group in question, except that the prohibitions do not apply to women falling within the middle level and high level cadres of employment. Thus, the women affected are those most likely in childbearing age and who, due to systemic and other reasons, are typically in lower levels of employment. Furthermore, the Factories Act Cap. 126, Laws of the Federation of Nigeria 1990, which offers detailed provisions for the health, safety and welfare of workers, does not take into consideration the sensitivity and susceptibility inherent in the state of pregnancy and the need to protect the woman and her unborn from the effect of toxic substances and radioactive materials. These legislative silences, falling within law's internal limits,[100] foster adverse health outcomes or contribute significantly to worsening health outcomes for women.

Religion is yet another strong influence on the sexual and reproductive health indices of Nigerians. Religion is a prominent force in all societies: it is estimated that more than five billion people follow one of the world's religions. In many societies, religious people and institutions promote human rights. However, some use religion to justify violations of human rights or to oppose certain rights, including sexual and reproductive health rights.[101]

---

98  R.E. Dobash and R.P. Dobash, *Violence Against Wives* (New York: Free Press, 1979), cited in O. Olomola, "Pains and Gains of a Gender-Based Law Clinic – The Women's Law Clinic of the Faculty of Law, University of Ibadan as a Case Study" (2016) 4:1 *Akungba Law Journal* at 389. Olomola states, "In many instances during the legal proceedings, several gender stereotypes could becloud the judges' perception of the whole picture of violence. There is an adage in Yoruba which states '*Ile oko ile eko ni*', whose literal meaning is that 'the matrimonial home is a place to learn'. So when the woman complains to her family members about violence . . . from the husband, the answer is usually that she . . . keep(s) enduring since she has gone there to learn".

99  This is the situation as at the time of researching and writing this work.

100 See Iyioha, Chapter 2 of this volume.

101 Interestingly, a member of the Nigerian National Assembly, Senator Ahmed Yerima, married a 13-year-old girl right in the face of the Child's Right Act, citing Islam as his defence.

While the fundamental values of all religions promote the integrity and well-being of all human beings, differences in interpretations and the ways the values are translated into practice can create barriers to sexual and reproductive health. This is especially so for young people seeking to make choices about their sexual and reproductive lives that deviate from common practice. Young people often face contradictions between their religious beliefs, as passed on by religious leaders and institutions, and their life circumstances. Furthermore, religion may operate through a number of other processes, including the establishment of health facilities without health personnel trained or willing to deliver certain healthcare options or procedures deemed morally unacceptable. They may also teach their followers not to access medical help but rather to seek healing through faith, as well as limit their followers' choice of contraception, all of which adversely impact their sexual and reproductive health.[102]

Further challenges arise when sexual and reproductive health policy is viewed through the lens of immorality (or morality as the case may be). Education is an important weapon in the public health armoury. However, doctrinally driven, abstinence-only sexual education programs in schools pose challenges and infringe on educational ethics because their purpose is to withhold critical knowledge with demonstrable effectiveness in protecting against pregnancy and sexually transmitted infections, such as HIV/AIDS. Also, some denominations prohibit outright seeking medical care,[103] blood transfusion,[104] surgeries and so forth. Women in such denominations are left with no choice than to live with their ailments and pray for healing.

The impact of the Nigerian attitude regarding the reception and implementation of reproductive health laws are evident. As Shah et al. show in Chapter 10, Nigeria holds a significantly high record of maternal mortality due to reasons such as the incidence of HIV, lack of quality healthcare, unsafe abortions and early marriage, among other reasons. The non-justiciability of Chapter 2 of the Nigerian Constitution – a section providing for a host of citizen rights to advancement, including social, economic and political – and the lack of a strategy for the implementation of the National Health Act have made it impossible for the average Nigerian to enjoy basic health services. There is continued prevalence of polygyny and child marriages, especially in the rural areas, and harmful cultural practices like female genital mutilation and harmful widowhood practices have not been eradicated, only shrouded in secrecy. In these cases, women, as Iyioha has succinctly surmised, are "offered a right without content – a situation that

---

He defended his act by saying, "[i]f anyone tells me what I have done is against Islam, I'll submit – and I'll do whatever they ask me to do". See www.aljazeera.com/news/africa/2010/05/2010518858453672.html (accessed 22 May 2019).

102 See also L. Omo-Aghoja, "Sexual and Reproductive Health: Concepts and Current Status Among Nigerians" (2013) 2:2 *African Journal of Medical and Health Sciences* at 103–113.

103 As practiced by the Apostolic Faith Church.

104 As practiced by the Jehovah's Witnesses.

continues to prevent millions of women in many parts of the world from using the law and the courts to advance their healthcare entitlements".[105]

## Reception and domestication in the Republic of South Africa (RSA)

According to Section 231(1) of the Constitution of the Republic of South Africa, the signing of treaties is the prerogative of the executive. Subsection 4 of the section provides that such treaties will be applicable to the republic only if they are enacted into law through legislation. The exceptions to this provision are where such treaties are of technical, administrative or executive nature, or where such treaties are self-executory.[106] Section 232 provides that "Customary international law is law in the Republic unless it is inconsistent with the Constitution or an Act of Parliament".[107]

Section 233 requires the court to favour an interpretation of any legislation that is consistent with international law over that which is not. Section 39 of the Constitution provides that courts, in the interpretation of the Bill of Rights, must promote values underlying an open and democratic society based on human dignity, equality and freedom; consider international law, and may consider foreign law. Thus, RSA can be said to operate a mash of monism and dualism.

As opposed to Nigeria, RSA has a more receptive approach to international reproductive health law. For example, South Africa's laws and policies support a rights-based framework for sexual and reproductive health and are aligned with international conference documents and health and development frameworks, such as the 1994 International Conference on Population – 1995 Beijing Fourth Conference on Women,[108] the Millennium Development Goals (MDGs), Sustainable Development Goals (SDGs) and Global Family Planning 2020.[109]

Additionally, the country made a groundbreaking move by the passing of the Choice on Termination of Pregnancy Act of 1996 (CTOPA), with amendments introduced in 2004 and 2008 with the aim of broadening access to abortion services. South Africa's Maternal and Child Health Strategic Plan for 2012–2016[110]

105  See Iyioha, Chapter 2 of this volume.
106  See Section 231(2)–(4) of the Constitution of the Republic of South Africa, 1996. See also E. De Wet et al., *The Implementation of International Law in Germany and South Africa* (Pretoria: Pretoria University Law Press, 2015), available at www.icla.up.ac.za/images/news/2015/The%20implementation%20of%20international%20law%20in%20Germany%20and%20South%20Africa.pdf (accessed 22 May 2019).
107  Section 232 of the Constitution of the Republic of South Africa, 1996.
108  Cooper et al., "Ten Years of Democracy in South Africa: Documenting Transformation in Reproductive Health Policy and Status" (2004) 24:12 *Reproductive Health Matters* at 70–85, cited in Cooper et al., "Coming of Age?", *supra*.
109  United Nations, Millennium Development Goals, available at www.un.org/millennium goals (accessed 22 May 2019).
110  Republic of South Africa, Strategic Plan for Maternal, Newborn, Child and Women's Health (MNCWH) and Nutrition in South Africa, Department of Health, available at

is aligned with the African and UNFPA's Campaign on Accelerated Reduction of Maternal and Child Mortality (CARMMA), which aims to generate political commitment, quality maternal data and best practices.[111]

However, an examination of RSA's reproductive health system under the lens of the theory of substantive legal effectiveness(SLE) discussed by Iyioha in Chapter 2 would reveal that the system is still plagued by external limitations to the effectiveness of international reproductive health laws, particularly in the area of reception and compliance. Drawing from SLE, these laws cannot be said to be achieving their aims. For example, despite the legalization of abortion, girls and young women in South Africa are reportedly seeking unsafe abortion outside institutional settings and are finding it quicker and cheaper.[112] While the law has helped to liberalize the 'legal' stance on abortion, many stakeholders, including citizens and law and policymakers, continue to reject the procedure on moral grounds.[113] With this pressure, the political will to realize the full extent of the law has dissipated over the years. Furthermore, challenges such as inadequate use of healthcare facilities, inadequacy of services and deficient care due to insufficient healthcare provider knowledge and skills have impacted negatively on the goal of eradicating maternal mortality in South Africa. Other challenges include disrespect and abuse of maternal care, lack of privacy and confidentiality, fear of being obligated to test for HIV and difficulties in meeting transport costs to healthcare facilities.[114]

Although South African women have full constitutional equality, cultural factors such as unequal gender power relations continue to undermine women's sexual and reproductive health rights, particularly among teenagers and young women.[115] Teenagers often face criticism and judgement from healthcare providers for being sexually active, despite the legislation stipulating that contraception be provided in the public health system free of charge and on request to any woman or girl aged 12 years and above.[116] This constitutes an external limit (with reference reception and compliance) to the effectiveness of reproductive health laws.

While the South African Constitution commits the government to reproductive health in Section 27 of the Constitution, the government is yet to implement evidence-based sexual violence prevention programmes even though the epidemic

---

https://extranet.who.int/nutrition/gina/en/node/11521 (accessed 22 May 2019), cited in Cooper et al., "Coming of Age?", *supra*.

111 Republic of South Africa, Department of Health, "Campaign on Accelerated Reduction of Maternal and Child Mortality (CARMMA) to Reduce Maternal Mortality in Africa", 2010.

112 Cooper et al., "Coming of Age?", *supra*.

113 See Iyioha's discussion of 'correctness' and the 'limits of law' in Chapter 2 of this volume.

114 Cooper et al., "Coming of Age?", *supra*.

115 Cooper et al., ibid. Initiatives such as the Family Planning 2020 are geared towards improving the sexual and reproductive rights of young people by giving them more control over their futures and eliminating barriers to their sexual and reproductive rights. See www.familyplanning2020.org/about-us#what-we-do (accessed 4 June 2019).

116 Republic of South Africa, The Children's Amendment Act No. 41, 2007.

proportions of sexual violence demand that attention is paid to this problem at a broader societal level. Approximately 150 rapes are reported to the police daily, but fewer than 30 cases are prosecuted and only 10 convictions secured.[117] Given the foregoing, the country has recorded mixed success in advancing measurable sexual and reproductive health outcomes over the last decade.[118]

## Conclusion: Reconsidering domestication rules in relation to international reproductive health laws in Nigeria – some recommendations

It is true that international treaties arguably remain a major source of Nigerian law, especially in the area of reproductive health, in spite of the challenges with domestication and compliance discussed above. The fundamental principle of treaty law is undoubtedly the proposition that treaties are binding upon the parties to them and must be performed in good faith. This rule, known in legal parlance as *pacta sunt servanda*, is arguably the oldest principle in the field of international law. Every state, however, has its own rule on the domestic application of international treaties. While treaty provisions, in some states, automatically acquire the force of law upon ratification, some others insist that a legislative instrument must domesticate a treaty before it becomes enforceable within the municipal legal order, as is the case with Nigeria.[119]

The requirement that a treaty must be enacted as a municipal law before it can be enforced in Nigeria appears to be merely a historical incidence and a colonial relic. As a result of the years of being under the colonial domination of Britain, Nigeria, on independence, automatically adopted the British practice requiring a treaty to be transformed into law before it could apply locally. In the Supreme Court of Nigeria case of *Ibidapo v Lufthansa Airlines*,[120] Wali JSC explained that "Nigeria, like any other Commonwealth country, inherited the English common law rules governing the municipal application of international law".[121] In light of the challenges discussed in this chapter, it is time for Nigeria to live up to her independent status by shedding this unwarranted trace of colonial heritage because continued adherence to these types of rules constitutes a failure to conform to the demands of modern day realities.[122]

The intention of Section 12 of the Constitution, as has been observed, was neither to shield insincerity nor act as a cloak under which a state should hide to avoid discharging an obligation that was voluntarily undertaken. It was not to be

---

117  Cooper et al., "Coming of Age?", *supra*.
118  M. Stevens, *What was done in South Africa and what can be learnt from it* (2007), available at www.who.int/social_determinants/resources/sa_case_study_wgkn_2007.pdf (accessed 22 May 2019).
119  Onomrerhinor, "A Re-Examination of the Requirement of Domestication" at 24.
120  (1997) 4 NWLR (Part 498) 124.
121  Ibid. at 150.
122  Onomrerhinor, "A Re-Examination of the Requirement of Domestication" at 24.

used to deny the average Nigerian the dividends of a truly just and progressive society duly recognized in the international community; instead, it was to be a sword to defend her sovereignty and territorial integrity as enshrined in the principle of the supremacy of the Constitution, something that would still be realized if a better approach is taken towards the matter.[123]

While admitting the need to sustain the preservation of the sovereignty of the entity known as Nigeria, there is need for an amendment of Section 12 or an alteration of the section to take advantage of the benefit of globalization for, in the face of the globalization, no country can afford to stand isolated. While it would be undesirable that Nigeria allows her Constitution and municipal laws to be overrun by international treaties, it would only be fair to allow her citizens benefit from the good inherent in them, particularly as they relate to reproductive health. Given these extremes, it is important to strike a balance for the good of the populace, one that can be achieved through a re-examination of Section 12 of the Nigerian Constitution. As Okeke has noted on this issue, the existence of the two main approaches of monism and dualism constitutes an "impediment" to the application of international law in municipal jurisdictions, and dualism, in particular, runs counter to the notion of universality of international law.[124] According to Okeke –and it is important to set out his arguments in this regard:

> If international law has attained some universality as argued or is at least attaining universality, then the monism-dualism dichotomy seems to be incompatible with international law. The universality of international law would tend to presuppose or require that international law apply automatically in national law. This in turn would imply that dualism would no longer have relevance in the application of international law by states. Ghana and Nigeria, being dualist states, should discard their dualist approach to international law, which accounts for why they have not accorded international law a befitting place in their domestic courts. When Ghana and Nigeria drop their dualism garment, they would be uninhibited in their enforcement of international law.[125]

Given the fact that Section 12 was intended to ensure cooperation between the executive and the legislature as evident in the provision for checks and balances encapsulated therein, there is need for a coordination of efforts between the two arms of government. The signing of a treaty should not be shrouded in secrecy. To that end, it is recommended that where possible, the legislature should be informed before an international instrument is signed. Such advance knowledge will ensure the commitment of the executive arm in enforcing treaty obligations.

Notably, the promulgation of the Constitution of the Federal Republic of Nigeria (Third Alteration) Act, 2010 ushered in a ray of light on the issue of the

123 Ibid.
124 Okeke, "The Use of International Law" at 428.
125 Ibid.

application of international law in a municipal court, in this case the National Industrial Court of Nigeria. The Act has been regarded as a watershed moment in the history of the National Industrial Court of Nigeria because it introduced "a number of radical but positive innovations on the structure, powers, status and jurisdiction of the Court".[126] The Act lists the court among the superior courts of record in Nigeria and confers on it exclusive jurisdiction over matters relating to international best practice in labour and in the application or interpretation of international labour standards. Section 254(c)(2) provides:

> Notwithstanding anything to the contrary in this Constitution, the National Industrial Court shall have the jurisdiction and power to deal with any matter connected with or pertaining to the application of any international convention, treaty or protocol of which Nigeria has ratified relating to labour, employment, workplace, industrial relations or matters connected therewith [*sic*].[127]

This section is so radical in the history of Nigerian legislation that it nullifies the provision of Section 12 of the Constitution in respect of labour matters. Claimants can, by virtue of this provision, invoke before the court relevant provisions of international treaties ratified by Nigeria even when those treaties have not been domesticated by an Act of the National Assembly.

A similar provision such as that cited above should, as a matter of urgency, be made in relation to human rights and reproductive health treaties as well as treaties that foster social and economic rights that are presently unenforceable under the 1999 Constitution as amended. Again, members of the legal profession in Nigeria should be inspired by trends in jurisdictions like Canada where, despite also operating the dualist model, "courts and litigants look to international law to resolve a great range of domestic legal issues".[128] The attitude of members of the legal profession will go a long way in determining the extent to which international laws can be used to enforce the reproductive health rights of Nigerians in domestic/municipal courts.

It is our contention that the Nigerian legal system as a whole should be reviewed and vestiges of Sharia law, which has been codified, should be replaced with neutral provisions.[129] A review of the application of Sharia law as a binding law in the country would take care of a plethora of violations of reproductive rights, such as punishments for adultery, prohibition of abortion, child marriages, suppression of women's agency and many other practices which are rooted in Sharia law. As Okeke has observed:

---

126 B. Atilola, "National Industrial Court and Jurisdiction over International Labour Treaties under the Third Alteration Act" (2011) 5:4, *Labour Law Review (NJLIR)*, cited in Onomrerhinor, "A Re-Examination of the Requirement of Domestication", *supra* at 23. The Third Alteration Act is available at http://nicn.gov.ng/publications (accessed 4 June 2019).
127 Section 254(c)(2).
128 Nwapi, "International Treaties in Nigerian and Canadian Courts" at 38.
129 The repugnancy tests are still applied to customary laws, which are observed in the Southern parts of Nigeria. Sharia, however, is largely codified.

Now that the Shari'a code has been reintroduced in these northern states as part of the criminal [and customary] law, it constitutes a deviation from the original understanding of the Shari'a as essentially regulating the personal lives of its adherents. There are many objections to the Shari'a code. There is no doubting the fact that Shari'a law is a religious law founded on the Qu'ran. It then follows that adopting and enforcing any religious penal law is tantamount to adopting a state religion, which is prohibited by the Nigerian Constitution and could constitute a violation of freedom of religion – a right that is universally recognized.[130]

When a more progressive approach is taken towards the application of international reproductive health law in Nigeria, what would follow is, hopefully, a more effective implementation of such laws. The first step to an effective implementation of reproductive health law, it is submitted, is an adoption of a rights-based approach to reproductive health in Nigeria. Our existing laws should be reviewed to reflect an understanding of the changing times as well as the dynamism of the 21stcentury. A great way to achieve this is to reconsider the dualist model of domestication of international law.

Section 36 of the Nigerian Constitution guarantees access to court for citizens. Yet, the issue of access to court goes beyond the theoretical constitutional guarantee. Along with the benefits of a rights-based framework under domestic law, there must be *practical* access to court backed-up with assurance of fair-hearing. Various factors militate against practical access to court and opportunity for fair hearing. These include financial incapacity in meeting legal expenses, a corrupt justice system, long delays in the hearing of claims and insensitivity of the government, among others.[131] For the courts to be empowered to perform their roles in the promotion of reproductive health rights, all the non-legal factors that militate against realistic access to courts by aggrieved persons must be addressed.[132]

---

130 Okeke, "The Use of International Law" at 427–428.
131 See B. Odunsi, "Unfair Fair Hearing and Unequal Religious Equality: The Facts and Fictions of Constitutional Guarantee of Equality in Nigeria" 35 *Indian Socio-legal Journal* at 61–66. See also D.A. Ijalaye, "Justice as Administered by the Nigerian Courts" in *Justice Idigbe Memorial Lecture Series Five* (Benin City: University of Benin, 1992) at 9–10.
132 *Ahamefule v Imperial Medical Centre and Molokwu*, Suit No. ID/1627/2000 (Ikeja Judicial Division of the Lagos High Court, Nigeria) illustrates how a court, through the conduct of a judge, can compound the problems of individuals who are already experiencing prejudice and whose rights have been transgressed. In that case, the defendants' counsel urged the court to require that the plaintiff, who was HIV-positive, produce a medical expert who would ascertain that the plaintiff would not infect other people present in the courtroom if he were allowed into the courtroom. The court held: "[H]aving listened to the arguments of both counsel on the issue of the risk of an HIV patient-plaintiff giving evidence in court . . ., I am of the opinion that the view of the learned counsel for the defendants should be respected in law in view of the fact that life has no duplicate and must be [guarded] jealously. It is hereby ordered that an expert opinion be heard on the subject-matter either from an expert in Nigeria or from any other part of the world where research had been fully carried out [*sic*]". See *Ahamefule v Imperial Medical Centre and Molokwu*, Appeal No. CA/L/514/2001, delivered on 21 April 2004.

# 10 On the margins of law

## Examining the limits of legislative initiatives on maternal mortality in South Africa and Nigeria

*Arooj Shah, Simisola O. Akintola
and Irehobhude O. Iyioha*

### Introduction

On 12 November 2015, the World Health Organization (WHO) issued a heartening statement: maternal deaths worldwide have dropped by nearly half since 1990.[1] However, in spite of this global drop, not all countries have experienced similar declines. Developing countries, including South Africa and Nigeria, continue to represent 99% of maternal deaths.[2] In South Africa and Nigeria alone, an estimated 59,500 women die each year due to complications during pregnancy and childbirth.[3] This number is decreasing at a staggeringly slow pace. Since 2010, South Africa experienced an average increase in maternal deaths at an annual rate of 1%,[4] while Nigeria experienced an average decline of 2% annually.[5] Both rates are far below the 7.5% annual decline necessary to achieve the Sustainable Development Goals (SDG) of improving women's health by reducing the maternal mortality ratio by 2023.[6]

According to the UN International Children's Emergency Fund (UNICEF) and WHO, research indicates that maternal mortality generally is preventable because the vast majority of maternal deaths could be averted with access to qualitative medical care.[7] What is less clear is why the enabling legal environment

---

1 World Health Organization (WHO), Press Release, "Maternal deaths fell 44% since 1990 – UN" (12 November 2015), available at WHO, www.who.int/news-room/detail/12-11-2015-maternal-deaths-fell-44-since-1990-un (accessed 22 May 2019).
2 *Trends in maternal mortality: 1990 to 2015: Estimates by WHO, UNICEF, UNFPA, World Bank Group and the United Nations Population Division* (Geneva: WHO, 2015) at 16, available at http://apps.who.int/iris/bitstream/handle/10665/194254/9789241565141_eng.pdf;jsessionid=B8ABEE8724C8F98410176BE00F4738CA?sequence=1 (accessed 22 May 2019) ('*Trends in Maternal Mortality*').
3 Ibid. at 19, 55.
4 Ibid. at 75.
5 Ibid. at 74.
6 *Transforming Our World: The 2023 Agenda for Sustainable Development*, GA Res A/RES/70/1, UNGOAR, 70th Sess, Supp No 49, UN Doc 15–16301 (E) 1 at 16 (2015) ('SDG Resolutions').
7 "Maternal and Newborn Health" (November 7, 2016), available at UNICEF www.unicef.org/health/index_maternalhealth.html (accessed 22 May 2019); *Strategies Toward Ending Preventable Maternal Mortality (EPMM)* (Geneva: WHO, 2015).

that supports healthcare delivery and undergirds women's right to reproductive healthcare and the cohort of domestic and international rights around bodily security, health and well-being have not affected the rate of maternal mortality effectively.

In 2000, world leaders met for the UN Millennium Summit in New York and passed the UN Millennium Declaration.[8] One of the targets of the Millennium Declaration was the reduction of maternal deaths by three quarters.[9] This commitment, first captured in Millennium Development Goal (MDG) 5, is now contained in SDG 3. MDG 5 was a commitment to improving maternal health by reducing the maternal mortality ratio (MMR) by three-quarters between 1990 and 2015. SDG 3 is a pledge to ensure the promise to improve maternal health issued in 2015 includes a commitment to reducing the MMR to 70 deaths per 100,000 live births by 2023.[10] The resolve of the international community and individual states to reduce maternal mortality is not new; however, not much progress has been recorded in some countries such as South Africa and Nigeria since the articulation of this commitment, and this is borne out by the statistics.

Globally, an estimated 303,000 maternal deaths occurred in 2015, a decline of over 43% from levels recorded in 1990.[11] However, sub-Saharan Africa bore 66% (201,000)[12] of this figure and southern Asia had 22% (66,000)[13] of the burden, which in total accounted for 88% of the global burden in 2015. At the country level, two countries account for a third of global maternal deaths: Nigeria at 19% (58,000) and India at 15% (45,000).[14] What this implies is that the decline of 43% has not translated to a significant reduction in maternal deaths in sub-Saharan Africa in spite of the laws, policies and international conventions that countries in sub-Saharan Africa have ratified and supported. When human immunodeficiency virus (HIV) related deaths are factored in, the data indicates that HIV directly or indirectly causes a significant number of maternal deaths in sub-Saharan Africa, including in South Africa and Nigeria. In Nigeria, it is estimated that 1 in 4 maternal deaths occur in women living with HIV.[15] Similarly, in South Africa, an estimated 1 in 3 maternal deaths are HIV related.[16]

A number of factors affect the successful reduction of maternal deaths, including HIV-related maternal deaths, and overall improvements in health.

8 *United Nations Millennium Declaration*, GA Res A/RES/55/2, UNGOAR, 55th Sess, Supp No 49, UN Doc 00 55951 (2000).

9 Ibid. at para 19.

10 SDG Resolutions, *supra*.

11 *Trends in Maternal Mortality* at 20.

12 Ibid. at 16.

13 Ibid.

14 *Trends in Maternal Mortality* at 19.

15 J. U. Onakewhor et al., "HIV-AIDS Related Maternal Mortality in Benin City, Nigeria" (2011) 64:2 *Ghana Medical Journal* 54 at 54 ('Onakewhor, "HIV-AIDS Related Maternal Mortality in Benin City, Nigeria"').

16 Coceka N. Mnyani et al., "Trends in Maternal Deaths in HIV-infected Women, on a Background of Changing HIV Management Guidelines in South Africa: 1997 to 2015" (2017) 20:e25022 *JIAS* 1 at 1 ('Mnyani, "Trends in Maternal Deaths in HIV-infected Women"').

Notable portions of these factors are legislative frameworks and policies and the impact of such laws and policies at curbing maternal deaths. It is, therefore, important to question the effect of existing laws and policies relevant to maternal health in the selected jurisdictions. Assessment of law's effect is a complex project. The effectiveness of a law depends on a broad of range of factors, including the law's objectives, its language and composition, its interpretation and considerations around the reception of and compliance with the law, among several others.

Drawing on different theoretical perspectives on the relationship between law and socio-cultural norms and on experiential evidence from relevant health legislation and policies and their operation in South Africa and Nigeria, this chapter addresses a number of factors that complicate the effectiveness of law and policymaking on maternal mortality in South Africa and Nigeria. First, we discuss the data on maternal mortality in South Africa and Nigeria, including data on HIV-related maternal deaths. Next, we discuss summarily some of the factors that affect the effectiveness of law, and then we address the socio-cultural causes of maternal deaths generally, as well as the political, legal and economic problems associated with poor maternal health. Following this analysis, we examine domestic and international laws and policies in South Africa and Nigeria regarding abortion and reproductive healthcare, including the constitutions of both countries, the Choice on Termination of Pregnancy Act[17] (CTOPA) and National Health Act[18] (South African NHA) in South Africa, and the National Health Act[19] (Nigeria NHA) and other healthcare policies in Nigeria. In the context of these laws, we examine: (1) whether and how these laws address the problems of inaccessible and inadequate healthcare services, including abortion services that contribute to unacceptably high maternal mortality rates; and (2) why South Africa's liberal laws on abortion fail to ameliorate the problem of illegal and clandestine abortions among South African women.

Finally, drawing on Iyioha's thesis on substantive legal effectiveness (SLE) in Chapter 2 to explain the problems with these legislated attempts at reducing or eradicating maternal mortality, we assess whether there can be adequate reduction of mortality among pregnant women through legislative and on-the-ground efforts without holistic attention to a range of issues that determine the effectiveness of laws and policies. Some of these issues include factors bearing on law's objectives, their compatibility with extant or accepted social or cultural norms, as well as latent and patent statutory objectives; others include harmonization of statutory provisions, legislative gaps, and infrastructural limitations. We conclude, drawing on tools for assessing law's effect offered under the concept of SLE, that given law's aspiration towards justice, legislated efforts

17  No. 92 of 1996, as amended ('CTOPA').
18  No. 12 of 2013 ('South Africa NHA').
19  No. 8 of 2014 ('Nigeria NHA').

that do not give due attention to these factors are bound to be limited in their effect.[20]

## Maternal mortality in South Africa and Nigeria: data and matters arising

Despite significant declines in maternal mortality globally,[21] South Africa and Nigeria have failed to keep pace with global trends. In Nigeria, maternal deaths decreased from 1,170 per 100,000 births in 2000 to 814 per 100,000 births in 2015.[22] South Africa did not experience a steady decrease. Instead, it experienced a slight increase from 2000 to 2010.[23] However, according to a 2015 WHO report, since then, the MMR in South Africa has decreased to 138 per 100,000 births.[24] This decrease is attributable in large part to the success of antiretroviral (ARV) programs.[25] Still, the MMR in South Africa remains high, and like Nigeria, South Africa is not on track to decrease its MMR to the goal rate of less than 70 per 100,000 births by 2023.[26]

The reduction of maternal deaths with the introduction of ARV treatments in South Africa shows a link between HIV and maternal mortality.[27] This connection makes it critical for any analysis of maternal mortality to consider the influence of HIV in maternal health. In Nigeria, the prevalence of people aged 15–49 living with HIV is estimated to have slightly decreased from 3.6% in 2000 to 2.8% in 2017.[28] The estimates on South Africa reveal a starkly different story. As of 2017, 18.8% of people aged 15–49 are estimated to be living with HIV in South Africa – a significant increase from the estimate of 13.4% in 2000. In both countries, HIV contributes to a large number of maternal deaths.[29] Part of the focus in this chapter is on addressing why such problems persist in the region, specifically

---

20 See Iyioha on 'Substantive Effectiveness' in Chapter 2 of this volume for further discussion of these principles.
21 *Trends in Maternal Mortality* at 15.
22 Ibid. at 74.
23 Ibid. at 75.
24 Ibid.
25 J. Moodley and R. Pattison, "Improvements in Maternal Mortality in South Africa" (2018) 3:1 *SAMJ* S4 at S5–S6.
26 World Health Organization, *Health in 2015: From MDGs to SDGs* (Geneva: WHO, 2015) at 72, available at WHO, http://apps.who.int/iris/bitstream/handle/10665/200009/9789241565110_eng.pdf?sequence=1 ('*Health in 2015*').
27 For a study on the link between HIV and maternal mortality, see Basia Zaba et al., "Effect of HIV Infection on Pregnancy-related Mortality in Sub-Saharan Africa: Secondary Analyses of Pooled Community- based Data from the Network for Analysing Longitudinal Population-based HIV/AIDS Data on Africa (ALPHA)" (2013) 381 *Lancet* e1763.
28 UNAIDS, "Nigeria: HIV Prevalence among Adults (15–49)" (2018) *AIDSinfo*, available at UNAIDS http://aidsinfo.unaids.org (accessed 22 May 2019).
29 Mnyani et al., "Trends in Maternal Deaths in HIV-infected Women", *supra*; Onakewhor et al., "HIV-AIDS Related Maternal Mortality in Benin City, Nigeria", *supra*.

in the selected jurisdictions, against the backdrop of seemingly progressive legal frameworks aimed at addressing HIV and maternal mortality.

## Maternal mortality

The definition of maternal death is unsettled. However, all definitions acknowledge that maternal death relates to or arises from pregnancy. According to the WHO:[30]

> A maternal death is the death of a woman while pregnant or within 42 days of the termination of pregnancy, irrespective of the duration and the site of the pregnancy, from any cause related to or aggravated by the pregnancy or its management but not from accidental causes.

Most definitions draw a distinction between direct maternal deaths that result from obstetric complications, including problems during pregnancy, delivery or management of the two, and indirect deaths that are the result of pre-existing diseases or a disease developed during pregnancy but not related to obstetrics. Some scholars dispute the necessity for such a distinction, arguing that it may result in the view that indirect maternal deaths are less important.[31] Still, the WHO continues to distinguish between direct and indirect maternal deaths.[32] There may be good reason for this, considering many maternal deaths are not caused by the obstetric process. About 80% of maternal deaths worldwide are caused by direct causes including bleeding (primarily), infections and unsafe abortions, while the other 20% are due to indirect causes such as malaria, HIV and poor health.[33] Understanding the underlying cause of maternal deaths may help policymakers fashion appropriate responses.

Statistics on maternal mortality are further divided by the specific cause of death. In Nigeria, the leading causes of maternal mortality are haemorrhage, infection, unsafe abortion, hypertensive disease and obstructed labour, which together account for more than 70% of maternal deaths.[34] The major causes of

30 World Health Organization, *WHO Guidance for Measuring Maternal Mortality from a Census* (Geneva: WHO, 2013) at 2, available at WHO, http://apps.who.int/iris/bitstream/handle/10665/87982/9789241506113_eng.pdf?sequence=1 (accessed 22 May 2019).
31 Thomas van den Akker, "Maternal Mortality: Direct or Indirect Has Become Irrelevant" (2017) 5:12 *Lancet* e1181.
32 See definitions of "direct obstetric deaths" and "indirect obstetric deaths" in World Health Organization, *The WHO Application of ICD-10 to Deaths During Pregnancy, Childbirth and the Puerperium: ICD-MM* (Geneva: WHO, 2012) at 9, available at WHO, http://apps.who.int/iris/bitstream/handle/10665/70929/9789241548458_eng.pdf?sequence=1 (accessed 22 May 2019).
33 Boniface Oye-Andeniran et al., "Causes of Maternal Mortality in Lagos State, Nigeria" (2014) 7:3 *Annals of Tropical Medicine and Public Health* 177 at 178.
34 Joseph Nnamdi Mojekwu and Uche Ibekwe, "Maternal Mortality in Nigeria: Examination of Interventions" (2012) 2:20 *International Journal of Humanities and Social Science* 135 at 137.

maternal mortality in South Africa are similar: unsafe abortion, haemorrhage, hypertension and infections, including sepsis.[35] Maternal mortality is often also the result of HIV, which necessities a closer examination of HIV prevalence in the selected countries. Rates of HIV infection have declined by 35% worldwide since 2000,[36] including in sub-Saharan Africa, a region in which the majority of HIV-positive people around the world live.[37] Despite these drops, HIV remains a critical public health concern in Nigeria and South Africa, chiefly because of the integral role it plays in maternal deaths in both countries.[38]

In Nigeria, an estimated 3.1 million people live with HIV.[39] This number has remained more or less stable since 2010.[40] The number of people living in South Africa with HIV is significantly more problematic. As of 2017, an estimated 7.2 million people live with HIV in South Africa – a 1.7 million increase since 2010.[41] The high rate of HIV infection in Nigeria is the result of a number of causes: a misconception that there is a low risk of infection, multiple sexual partners, limited access to healthcare and stigma surrounding HIV.[42] Similar risk factors contribute to the prevalence of HIV in South Africa.[43]

In both countries, HIV plays an undeniable role in maternal deaths. One study in Nigeria found that 1 in 3 maternal deaths occur in women living with HIV.[44] In South Africa, it is estimated that one-third of maternal deaths are HIV related.[45] Further, women with HIV are eight times more likely to die during or shortly after pregnancy than women without HIV in sub-Saharan Africa,[46] and maternal deaths caused by infections such as sepsis, malaria and tuberculosis are more likely to occur in women who are HIV-positive.[47] The reality that the risk of maternal mortality is greater in women with HIV reveals the subtle way in which HIV undermines maternal health. It is due to the prevalence of HIV-related

---

35 Mnyani et al., "Trends in Maternal Deaths in HIV-infected Women" at 1.
36 UNAIDS, "Global: New HIV Infections (all ages)" (2018) *AIDSinfo*, available at UNAIDS, http://aidsinfo.unaids.org (accessed 22 May 2019).
37 Clifford O. Odimegwu, Joshua O. Akinyemi and Olatunji O. Alabi, "HIV-Stigma in Nigeria: Review of Research Studies, Policies, and Programmes" (2017) *AIDS Research and Treatment* 1 at 1 ('Odimegwu et al., "HIV-Stigma in Nigeria"').
38 Onakewhor et al., "HIV-AIDS Related Maternal Mortality in Benin City, Nigeria" at 54.
39 UNAIDS, "Nigeria: People living with HIV" (2018) *AIDSinfo*, available at UNAIDS, http://aidsinfo.unaids.org (accessed 22 May 2019).
40 Ibid.
41 UNAIDS, "South Africa: People living with HIV" (2018) *AIDSinfo*, available at UNAIDS, http://aidsinfo.unaids.org (accessed 22 May 2019).
42 Odimegwu et al. "HIV-Stigma in Nigeria" at 2.
43 W.S. Linganiso and J.M.T. Gwegweni, "What Perpetuates the Spread of HIV/AIDS in Rural South African Communities? A Closer Look at Social Factors" (2016) 3:1 *Austin Journal of Public Health Epidemiol* 1.
44 Onakewhor et al., "HIV-AIDS Related Maternal Mortality in Benin City, Nigeria" at 54.
45 Mnyani et al., "Trends in Maternal Deaths in HIV-Infected Women" at 1.
46 Tamil Kendall et al., "Eliminating Preventable HIV-Related Maternal Mortality in Sub-Saharan Africa: What Do We Need to Know?" (2014) 67:4 *Journal of Acquired Immune Deficiency Syndromes* S250 at S250.
47 Ibid. at S254.

maternal mortality that an analysis of maternal mortality in sub-Saharan Africa must attend to HIV and consider the role of overall HIV reduction in reducing maternal mortality.

### Matters arising

The data suggests that domestic laws and government policies in South Africa and Nigeria aimed at reducing rates of maternal mortality, either directly or indirectly, have not achieved projected results. Global efforts to combat the issue have also failed to have the desired effect. To understand why laws have been unable to provide a solution, it is necessary to recognize the underlying causes of maternal mortality. Latent factors create the conditions for the ailments that are the immediate, directly measurable causes of maternal mortality.

There are several important socio-economic factors that result in high levels of maternal mortality in the selected countries. One of the major causes of maternal mortality is a lack of access to reproductive healthcare and services.[48] Even when women have access to healthcare, they may not receive qualitative, life-saving services.[49] Others may not wish to seek healthcare during their pregnancy out of fear they will be stigmatized for their HIV-positive status. Alternatively, women may be forced by the circumstances to undergo unsafe abortions in spite of the availability of legal abortion. The former is true in countries with restrictive abortion laws and policies such as Nigeria, as is the latter even in states with more liberal abortion laws such as South Africa, which has one of the most liberal abortion laws in the world. Other cultural factors contributing to maternal mortality in the region include early child marriage, female genital cutting and gender inequality, which are discussed in depth in the next section.

Summarily, other factors can be traced to the failure of law-makers to fashion holistic and effective laws – laws that consider the underlying causes of maternal mortality and that attempt to address these causes in their conception and actualization. For example, a law aimed at giving due recognition to women's human rights and that facilitates or exhorts their right of access to reproductive health services would likely fall short of its goal if it fails to recognize the critical role that access to safe and medically necessary abortions play in protecting maternal health.

High rates of maternal mortality in the selected jurisdictions may also be traced to a failure to implement laws, including anti-discrimination laws, that have the potential of making healthcare more inclusive for women living with HIV. Given the multi-faceted nature of the problem of maternal mortality, laws and policy

---

48 Mojekwu and Ibekwe, *supra* note 34 at 137; Comfort Chukuezi, "Socio-cultural Factors Associated with Maternal Mortality in Nigeria" (2010) 1:5 *Research Journal of Social Sciences* 22 at 22–23.

49 Kayode T. Ijadunola et al., "New Paradigm Old Thinking: The Case for Emergency Obstetric Care in the Prevention of Maternal Mortality in Nigeria" (2010) 10:6 *BMC Women's Health* 1 at 4.

responses need to address or at least be cognizant of the diverse factors that complicate and exacerbate the problem. Thus, rather than focusing on purely legal solutions, a holistic approach to reducing maternal mortality in South Africa and Nigeria is necessary if some progress is to be made. Before examining the limits of law's capacity to address maternal mortality in South Africa and Nigeria through Iyioha's theory of substantive effectiveness, this chapter turns to address more substantively the cultural and normative reasons for high rates of maternal mortality in the region, starting with a summary outline of some relevant considerations in the assessment of a law's effectiveness.

## Assessing law's effectiveness: some considerations

Whether a law is deemed effective depends on a broad range of factors relating to, among others, the objectives of the given law, its language and construction, the interpretive lenses through which a court assesses its provisions and the external considerations that determine reception and compliance with the law – such as ideas around the correctness of the norms sought to be advanced. These factors are present in the gap between the conception and passage of a law, as well as in its implementation.

Thus, the mere passage of a law or the existence of rights does not necessarily translate to public compliance or effective outcomes. Additionally, scholars in the field agree that the existence of penal sanctions does not always correlate to conformance with changes in statutes.[50] This is particularly the case where the law seeks to change enjoyable habits (such as smoking, drinking, drugs or sex) or habits embedded in cultural[51] or religious practices to which people are committed.

While the objective of a body of laws and policies governing healthcare delivery, especially reproductive healthcare, may be geared towards averting or diminishing a significant health risk such as maternal deaths, yet a closer examination of the laws and policies may reveal discrepancies between patent and latent objectives.[52] Laws that purport to 'protect' women's health can have other underlying goals, including limiting access to morally controversial procedures, such as abortion services.

In other cases, a law's objective may be patently expressed to curtail a right recognized by the international legal community. For example, in sub-Saharan African countries where abortion remains criminalized on broad grounds, clandestine and illegal abortions and a lack of prenatal care have been identified as underlying causes for the high prevalence of maternal mortality, thus highlighting links between restrictive reproductive health laws and policies and maternal mortality.

50 George P. Fletcher, *Basic Concepts of Legal Thought* (Oxford: Oxford University Press, 1996) at 29.
51 For instance, the resistance by religious leaders in the northern part of Nigeria to the Polio Eradication Initiative (PEI), on the grounds that it was a ploy by the West to reduce the Muslim population worldwide.
52 See Iyioha, Chapter 2 of this volume, for a summary analysis.

Another issue at the core of any assessment of law's limits and effectiveness is enforcement. Knowledge of prohibitions and regulations by law enforcement agencies, as well as the rate and consistency of policing and enforcement, can impact the success rate registered for given laws, policies and interventions.[53] Also, the enforcement of legislation entails personal burdens and opportunity costs. This can be the case where enforcement of a desired policy may be prohibitively expensive and divert resources away from still more important goals that a state may wish to pursue. Indeed, successive governments in sub-Saharan Africa have signed on to treaties in the area of maternal health without investing the necessary economic and human resources necessary to reduce or ameliorate the incidence of maternal deaths.

Finally, an effectiveness analysis may sometimes require a compatibility assessment between extant norms and a proposed law. In this regard, laws designed to ameliorate given health problems and which introduce norms counter to existing practices and values may prove counterproductive, thereby exacerbating the problems they were supposed to resolve, or at the very least face challenges with compliance. As Lewis et al. show in Chapter 3 on female genital cutting, this is often the case with cultural practices or morally divisive procedures where perspectives on the prohibited act are deeply entrenched, rightly or wrongly, in cultural or traditional values. The result of the discrepancy between socio-cultural norms and law is that the given law drives the practice underground. These summative challenges illustrate that the methods of law and the legal process do not always achieve the desired goals.

Central to some of the above examples of the factors implicated in the assessment of law's limits and its effect is the relationship between law and social norms and how this relationship might affect compliance with domestic and international reproductive health laws. This subject – partly explored by Odunsi and Adewole in Chapter 9 and Iyioha in Chapter 2 – has particular relevance in the context of sub-Saharan Africa and other African states whose ways of lives are rooted in strongly held cultural beliefs.

## Maternal mortality: the role of culture and other normative values

### *Maternal mortality, culture and norms*

Previous research focusing on biomedical causes and treatments for maternal mortality have largely neglected the reality that in countries in which maternal mortality remains high, culture and traditional health practices play a significant role in the process of pregnancy and childbirth.[54] Tradition and cultural practices

---

53  Ibid.
54  S. E. Geller et al., "Postpartum Hemorrhage in Resource-poor Settings" (2006) 92:3 *International Journal of Gynecology & Obstetrics* 202.

remain dominant influences in a woman's life from her birth to adulthood and these factors directly affect her decisions during pregnancy and childbirth.[55]

Culture influences maternal health in many dimensions. For instance, culture influences the way in which pregnancy, antenatal, and postnatal care, as well as childbirth are viewed in Nigeria and other sub-Saharan African states.[56] Nigeria, like most African nations, has rich cultural heritage and practices, which include close and extended family ties, adequate care for new mothers for 40 days after delivery and prolonged breastfeeding,[57] and embedded in these rich cultural values are some negative practices that affect the health of women, many of which are still ongoing in Nigeria in spite of the various conventions, laws and policies on maternal health. For example, a significant percentage of mothers are delivered by untrained Traditional Birth Attendants (TBAs) and traditional healers. In the Nigerian rural society, a pregnant woman has been said to prefer being delivered by a village birth attendant than going to a hospital.[58] Genital tract infection and sepsis can occur after such deliveries, especially where the delivery is not conducted in a sterile environment, as is usually the case in home delivery in most developing nations.[59]

Furthermore, in spite of international legal norms protecting the autonomous choice of women, women are culturally expected to seek the approval of their spouses in decisions relating to their health, especially in pregnancy or pregnancy-related matters. In some settings, the fear of reprisal from disapproving husbands or others may lead many to resort to clandestine treatment, especially in the use of family planning.[60] As Kowalewski et al. have noted, "women are controlled by local customs", and a woman is often unable to make any decision on her own without her husband's approval or without her husband first reaching a decision on the matter.[61] These restrictions mean that women are dependent on the decisions of others about receiving medical attention, whether to delay or prevent pregnancy, have antenatal examinations during pregnancy or arrange for skilled delivery attendants, among others. In Nigeria, in spite of Section 42 of the Constitution of the Federal Republic of Nigeria as amended, which constitutionalizes

55 L.L. Wall, "Dead Mothers and Injured Wives: The Social Context of Maternal Morbidity and Mortality among the Hausa of Northern Nigeria" (1998) 29:4 *Studies in Family Planning* 341.
56 O.A. Erinosho, *Sociology for Medical, Nursing, and Allied Professions in Nigeria* (Ijebu Ode, Nigeria: Lucky Odoni Enterprises, 2005).
57 E.M. Alabi, Newsletter, "Cultural practices in Nigeria" (1990) *Inter-African Committee on Traditional Practices Affecting the Health of Women and Children* No. 9.
58 D.A. Onyeabochukwu, "Cultural Practices and Health: The Nigerian Experience" *Journal of University of Nigeria Medical Students*.
59 C. Okolocha et al., "Socio-cultural Factors in Maternal Morbidity and Mortality: A Study of a Semi-urban Community in Southern Nigeria" (1998) 52:5 *Journal of Epidemiology Community Health* 293.
60 United Nations Population Fund, *Lives Together, Worlds Apart: Men and Women in a Time of Change* (United Nations Population Fund, 2000) at 27.
61 Marga Kowalewski, Albrecht Jahn and Suleiman S. Kimatta, "Why Do At-Risk Mothers Fail to Reach Referral Level? Barriers beyond Distance and Cost" (2000) 4:1 *African Journal of Reproductive Health* 100 at 105.

women's legal equality in Nigeria, women are dependent on others to make decisions relating to their health.

### The problem of early marriage

Early marriage accounts for about 23% of maternal mortality due to severe haemorrhage resulting from obstructed and prolonged labour. The narrow pelvis of adolescents may also result in stillbirths as well as vesico-vaginal fistula.[62] After delivery, a genital tract infection can occur, especially if the delivery is not conducted in a sterile environment, as in the case of home delivery. According to Ufford and Menkiti[63] and the 1999 Nigerian Demographic and Health Survey (DHS), many maternal deaths occur because of early childbearing. Adolescents suffer disproportionately from complications related to childbearing because their bodies are not fully developed.[64] Galadima, a state project manager at the Abuja-based Society for Family Health (SFH),[65] affirmed that early marriage increases the risk of maternal death due to the likelihood of complications. Under-aged women are more susceptible to maternal morbidity and, according to Graczyk,[66] are unlikely to be able to discuss their reproductive health with their husbands or seek healthcare.

Early or child marriage is a violation of fundamental human rights. By international conventions, 18 years has been established as the legal age of consent to marriage.[67] However, due to inconsistencies in legislation and the absence of any specific stipulation for a minimum age for marriage, early marriages continue to take place with impunity in many areas of Nigeria as a means of preserving chastity. For instance, Section 18 of the Matrimonial Causes and Marriage Act allows persons under the age of 21 to get married, provided parental consent is sought

---

62  A fistula is a hole that results when tissue in the woman's vaginal region loses blood supply due to the pressure placed on it during an obstructing labour.

63  Judith Ufford and Miriam Menkiti, "Delivery Care is Key for Maternal Survival: A Story of Two States in Nigeria" (2001) *Population Reference Bureau*, available at PRB, www.prb.org/deliverycareiskeyformaternalsurvivalastoryoftwostatesinnigeria/ (accessed 22 May 2019).

64  A. E. Idowu and A. E. Asakitikpi "Religion and the Quality of Maternal Health in Badagry, Lagos State" (2008) 4:1,2 *Nigeria Sociological Review* 129–140.

65  Ibrahim Abdul'Aziz, "HEALTH-NIGERIA: Little Progress on Maternal Mortality" (2008) *IPS Correspondents*, available at www.ipsnews.net/2008/07/health-nigeria-little-progress-on-maternal-mortality/ (accessed 22 May 2019).

66  Kathryn Graczyk "Adolescents Maternal Mortality: An Overlooked Crisis" (2007) *Advocates for Youth*, available at www.advocatesforyouth.org/storage/advfy/documents/fsmaternal.pdf (accessed 22 May 2019).

67  *Universal Declaration of Human Rights*, GA Res 217A (III), UNGAOR, 3rd Sess, Supp No 13, UN Doc A/810 (1948); Convention on the Elimination of All Forms of Discrimination against Women, 18 December 1979, 1249 UNTS 13 (entered into force 3 September 1981) (CEDAW); *Convention on the Rights of the Child*, 20 November 1989, 1577 UNTS 3 (entered into force 2 September 1990); *African Charter on the Rights and Welfare of the Child*, 1 July 1990, CAB/LEG/153/Rev.2 (entered into force 29 November 1999).

and obtained.[68] An official report on Nigeria's implementation of the Convention on the Rights of the Child prepared for the 38th Session of the Committee on the Rights of the Child acknowledges that "the age of marriage is a highly controversial issue and varies from place to place".[69] In northern Nigeria, where the majority of girls face the prospect of early marriage – and which has resulted over the years in a large number of cases of vesico-vaginal fistula, 14 years (or the given period before the second menstrual cycle of a girl) is an acceptable age of marriage. In the southern, more liberal part of Nigeria, the acceptable age for marriage varies between 16 and 18 years of age.[70] Although it is not precise, the existing legal framework sets the age of maturity at 18 years.[71] Similarly, the Committee on the Elimination of Discrimination Against Women (CEDAW Committee) has urged Nigeria to "ensure full compliance with the UN Convention on the Rights of the Child and the Child Rights Act of 2003, which set the statutory minimum age of marriage at 18 years in all parts of the country".[72] This medley of laws, which are not in harmony with each other, complicates the law on child marriage, opening up the unabated spectre of negative health outcomes, inclusive of maternal mortality.

A more stable, consistent and effective legal framework on the age of maturity in Nigeria must be adopted, combined with a harmonization of all laws to reflect a national stance on the age of maturity. Maternal deaths arising from early marriage can be reduced and ultimately, eradicated where the age of maturity under the law is objectively, rather than subjectively, specific, with 18 years adopted as the age of maturity and for marriage and related legal matters.

## Law and culture: some theoretical perspectives

One of the functions of law is to effect change on a given subject matter of interest. In the area of maternal health, however, law – as articulated in legislative provisions – or government policies have not been able to match societal aspirations for a significant reduction of maternal mortality. In the preceding section, we explored the role of culture in this state of affairs. In this section, we explore

68 Order 1, Rule 4 of the Nigerian *Matrimonial Causes Rules* defines a child as a person under 21 years.

69 E.E.O. Alemika, *Report on the implementation of the Convention on the Rights of the Child by Nigeria: A report prepared for the Committee on the Rights of the Child 38th Session* (Geneva: World Organization Against Torture and Clean Foundation, 2005) at 11.

70 National Population Commission, *Nigeria Demographic and Health Survey 1999* (Abuja, Nigeria: National Population Commission, 2000), available at www.dhsprogram.com/pubs/pdf/FR115/FR115.pdf (accessed 22 May 2019).

71 Section 31 of the Child's Rights Act, 2003, No 26 of 2003. Also see the Constitution of the Federal Republic of Nigeria, No 24 of 1999 ('Nigerian Constitution') which sets the age of maturity at 18 for many provisions.

72 Committee on the Elimination of Discrimination against Women, *Concluding Comments: Nigeria*, CEDAW/C/2004/I/CRP.3/Add.2, OCHCR, 13th Sess, UN Doc 04–22037 (E) (2004).

theories around the relationship between law and culture to examine how socio-cultural norms contribute to limiting law's effectiveness.

The prevailing culture in a society plays an important part in creating and maintaining situations of stratification and control. According to Turner, not only does the dominant culture determine the reality in which particular individuals live, but it also reflects the interests and worldviews of dominant world groups.[73] In this circuitous sense, cultural categories make an important contribution to the beliefs and attitudes of individuals. Turner opines that social life is a creation of culture, and that individuals create meaning through the cultural contents to which they are exposed in the course of their daily lives.[74] In other words, cultural practices that contribute to maternal mortality are ingrained in the social life of the people, and legal rules, regulations and conventions that do not reflect these social facts may not have any relevant impact on legal subjects. This observation is explored substantively in Chapter 2, where Iyioha discusses social facts, their constitutive role in lawmaking, and their impact on law's effectiveness.

Menachem Mautner discusses three approaches to understanding the relationship between culture and law.[75] The first approach views a nation's culture as constitutive of law. This approach is based on the historical school of law, which arose in German jurisprudence in the first half of the 19th century. This school of thought views law as a product of a nation's culture and as embedded in the daily practices of its people. According to the historical school, statutes are not meant to create law; rather, their function is to reflect existing social practices. And just as each group has its own language, expressing a unique national spirit, it also has its own distinctive law.[76] This approach to understanding the relationship between law and culture would suggest that the popularity of some practices – for example, the preference of traditional birthing systems over modern antenatal care – in some regions indicates a failure of health policy to reflect the cultural preferences of a number of women. However, this seemingly simplistic view of the relationship between law and culture using the example of preferred birthing practices does not capture the preferences of a significant segment of the population who prefer modern reproductive health systems. The relationship between law and culture and the impact of their disconnection on the effectiveness of law is much more complicated than this.

In fact, jurists and anthropologists are not in agreement on the connection between law and culture.[77] Some anthropologists argue that in many societies, customary laws are sufficient for the governance of the community, obviating the

---

73 Graeme Turner, *British Cultural Studies: An Introduction*, 3rd ed. (London: Routledge, 2003) at 33–40, 53, 56.
74 Ibid. at 39–40.
75 Menachem Mautner, "Three Approaches to Law and Culture" (2011) 4 *Cornell Law Review* 839.
76 Ibid.
77 Dennis Lloyd and Michael Freeman, *Lloyd's Introduction to Jurisprudence*, 7th ed. (London: Sweet & Maxwell, 2016) at 921–922.

need for a second body of norms to codify or confirm what is already agreed upon as governing norms. If this argument is taken at face value, it is then arguable that the sufficiency of customary values as the governing norms in some communities may be a reason why the various international conventions and domestic health policies are not impacting maternal mortality rates in Nigeria.

This argument is definitely not without criticism. As much as it seems to describe the connection between law and culture within societies with deep connections to their cultures and attempts to explain why existing laws do not have the desired effect on maternal mortality rates, it also creates a problem – that of determining which of the numerous cultural practices or norms within a given society can be defined as governing norms or law. Many societies are not defined by single cultures, thus making the claim to agreed-upon social values as constitutive of governing norms or law problematic. Indeed, as Cowan et al. have noted, a culture is a "field of creative interchange and contestation",[78] and can transform to embrace new ways of living and being.[79] Furthermore, individuals are at any given time subject to the influence of a host of values, norms, and social facts, making a cause-and-effect analysis of the disagreement between norms and law a complicated exercise.

However, recognizing the validity of this viewpoint does not invalidate the fact that where norms are defined, verifiable, and commonly held, they can serve as counternarratives to the universality of foreign value systems or internationally recognized norms. The ideological conflict between different worldviews or world cultures, between human rights in the West and Chinese traditions in the East or African belief systems in the South, is evidence of this. What begins to emerge, taking into consideration the arguments put forward by Iyioha, Lewis et al., Cao and Sta. Maria[80] in this volume, is that whether a given set of norms is determinative of law in any given milieu is often as much a function of the prevailing norms and nature of the society (with regard to their openness to progressive or at best new ideas), as it is of the politics of governance and of the trajectory chosen by those who wield the most political influence or power. The ultimate decision is, no doubt, often based on a weighing of interests, including the political and the economic, often (and unfortunately) unconnected to the interests of the women who are supposedly the 'beneficiaries' of the law.

A second approach to understanding the connections between law and culture, known as the constitutive approach, was developed in American jurisprudence in the 1980s. This approach views law as participating in the molding and constitution of culture and thereby in the constitution of people's minds, practices, and social relations. It thus views the relationship between law and culture as working in the opposite direction to the postulation of the historical school. In

---

78 See Jane K. Cowan, Marie-Bénédicte Dembour and Richard A. Wilson, "Introduction" in *Culture and Rights: Anthropological Perspectives* (Cambridge: Cambridge University Press, 2001) at 5.
79 See Iyioha, Chapter 2 of this volume.
80 See Chapters 2, 3, 4 and 6 of this volume.

both, however, law is an inseparable dimension of social relations. This view of the relationship between law and culture may be validated by the example of progressive laws, for example, those redefining the boundaries of marriage, the family and parenthood, when such laws take root and flourish. In this instance, societal perspectives may be interpreted as gradually bending towards recognition and acceptance of the new and progressive legal norm.

A third approach, found in 20th-century Realist Anglo-American jurisprudence, views the law that the courts create and apply as a distinct cultural system. Legal realism developed a descriptive argument contending that legal formalism fails to accurately portray legal decision-making processes. Karl Llewellyn, a leading realist, refuted legal formalism, arguing that law practitioners internalize a formalist culture in the course of their studies and professional activity, and this internalization comes to constitute, direct and delimit the way practitioners think, argue and resolve cases, and provide justifications for their arguments.[81] Llewellyn's argument was premised on the position that the contents of law are organized in certain categories and that there are certain recurrent modes of thinking and arguments in the law that lawyers internalize in the course of their professional lives. These contents of law and modes of thinking, as well as arguments prevalent in the law, not only pervasively structure the way lawyers function in the legal profession but also constrain the options available to them.

Llewellyn's arguments assume the law to be the outcomes of a judge's decision rather than the product of a rational and deductive reasoning process based on pre-established legal rules. In this position is a clear recognition and acceptance of the biases, preferences or predilections of individual judges, which can infiltrate the decision-making process. While such biases may be legitimately based on culture and other prevalent norms, they may equally arise from utterly inexcusable motives. In either case, legal realism would seem to lend credence to the notion that law is not immune from the influence of non-legal norms and other externalities, thereby allowing concepts of what is culturally right or wrong to permeate and, at some level, direct the course of the adjudicatory process.

This view of the application of legal rules discountenances legal formalism's claims to neutrality and impartiality, as well as its separation of "fact from value",[82] and this has significant relevance for our analysis of the legal order in operation in Nigeria. Insights from positivism suggest that there is no necessary relationship between law and morality. As a theory of law, positivism postulates that laws and their operation derive validity from the fact of having been enacted by a recognized authority and having originated logically from existing decisions in a precedential system. Summarily, the term positivism has a number of meanings as described by Hart. For example, laws are commands – a meaning associated with the postulations of Thomas Hobbes. Further, legal decisions can be deduced from predetermined rules without recourse to social aims, policy or

---

81 K.N. Llewellyn, "The Case Law System in America" (1988) *Columbia Law Review* 88 at 989.
82 Margot Stubbs, "Feminism and Legal Positivism" (1986) *Australian Journal of Law and Society* at 67 ('Stubbs, "Feminism and Legal Positivism"').

morality. Positivism also represents the thesis that law is as it is laid down and should be applied as such devoid of other extraneous considerations, such as religion or morality.

It is worthwhile to examine these claims about law and its operation in the case of African states, such as Nigeria, where culture, tradition and social norms play a significant role in defining – at least in the social realm – what is acceptable practice. What is obvious in a cursory examination of legislative and judicial practice in Nigeria is that laws are authoritatively passed by a recognized body of lawmakers at the national assembly or state houses of assembly; there is adherence to judicial precedents in the inherited British tradition; customary laws exist alongside other sources of Nigerian law, such as received English law, Nigerian legislation, delegated legislation and case law; and the legal system is deemed closed, internally coherent and without any express connections to morality.[83] Thus, on its face, the Nigerian legal order is clearly positivistic, with much outward evidence of judicial effort to deliver justice within a supposedly autonomous system.

Yet, given the pluralism of the country's legal system – which itself is a corollary of the diverse cultural values and norms that coexist with statutory law, as well as the morally conservative leanings of these cultures, it is not at all difficult to imagine that the interpretation of laws necessarily involves a consideration of both competing statutorily or customarily defined legal norms and a diverse range of socio-legal and moral norms, especially as embedded in the consciousness of the judges themselves. Thus, the 'justice' delivered by the system, as is "innately" the case with positivism,[84] is very often conservative. There is much "interpretive latitude" in judicial powers to "incorporate a value input" that represents the cultural worldviews of the populace.[85] In light of this, the formal legalism that operates in Nigeria's positivistic legal order would appear to be a "veneer",[86] one that leaves much room for judicial creativity in the application of rules, many of which are – by legislative design – already reflective of the moral and cultural values of the public.

In the context of our discussion on maternal mortality, these legal traditions – complicated by the unique context of an African state where there has been a transplantation of foreign legal traditions (and norms) – suggest that the legitimacy of Western concepts of women's health rights would be measured through existing laws on women's health rights (limited as they are) as well as through the lenses of local customs and norms that are deemed not to be repugnant to

---

83 See Irehobhude O. Iyioha, "Pathologies, Transplants, and Indigenous Norms: An Introduction to Nigerian Health Law and Policy", in I. O. Iyioha and R. N. Nwabueze, eds., *Comparative Health Law and Policies: Critical Perspectives on Nigerian and Global Health Laws* (London: Ashgate, 2015).

84 See generally, Stubbs, "Feminism and Legal Positivism", *supra*. For particular references, see pp. 64 and 79.

85 Ibid. at 84.

86 Ibid. at 68.

natural justice, equity and good conscience. The new, transplanted norms on women's rights are susceptible to being invalidated through normative comparisons against local value systems. While, as noted above, Nigerian courts may invalidate customary laws that are deemed repugnant to a sense of natural justice, equity and good conscience, it remains contentious what traditional norms and practices would be so regarded given the entrenchment, in the ethos of the people, of many local norms and values that are the target of the women's rights movement.

We draw a few conclusions from the above analysis against the foregoing discussion on the relationship between law and cultural norms: the relationship between cultural and moral norms and law in Nigeria as expressed in the legal process reflects a commitment to the different tenets of positivism.[87] However, the prevailing tradition in lawmaking and adjudication reveals a legal methodology that fails to limit judicial creativity just as much as it fails to guarantee neutrality.[88] While the system professes no necessary connection between law and the extensive body of moral rules that suffuses its legal rules, yet in the practice of law itself are often traces of an amalgam of both the written content of rules and the notions of the ideal in the public sphere – commonly held moral values that are substantially conservative and contrarian to universal understandings of women's rights. Morality in Nigeria is itself significantly entrenched in the religious, social, cultural and traditional values of the country's diverse peoples, thus fostering a sometimes conflicting maze of legal rules as between the largely Christian South and the predominantly Muslim North.[89]

For this and other reasons discussed in the foregoing, in interrogating law's capacity to reduce or ameliorate maternal mortality in the African region, we consider pluralism in the legal system to be a primal impediment to the realization of women's health rights in Nigeria, categorizing it as falling within the internal elements of law – and inherently as part of internal limits – because the plurality of social facts that circumscribe women's rights locally are themselves often embedded within or constitute bodies of customary laws, and sometimes entrenched within statutory law. An example of the latter is Nigeria's law on abortion. However, as Odunsi and Adewole show in Chapter 9 of this book, these same issues – to the extent that they expose a 'moral' bias for certain laws and, therefore, raise a problem of 'moral correctness' – can equally be read as falling within external limits.

## Legislation and policies targeted at maternal mortality

Against the background of the foregoing discussion, what progressive legislative efforts are in place in South Africa and Nigeria to address maternal mortality? In this section, we analyze the domestic and international laws and policies in

---

87  For further discussion of these tenets, see Iyioha, Chapter 2 of this volume.
88  See Stubbs, "Feminism and Legal Positivism" at 73.
89  Ibid.

South Africa and Nigeria aimed at reducing or eliminating maternal deaths. Laws that address maternal mortality, either directly or indirectly, take various forms. They may allow women to access safe abortions, thereby having the capacity to prevent deaths caused by unsafe abortions. They may prohibit discrimination against people living with HIV in order to prevent healthcare providers from denying access to reproductive healthcare services to women living with HIV. Others may be designed to increase access to affordable, quality healthcare to ensure that women have the resources and services they require during childbirth and pregnancy. Having discussed HIV-related mortality at some level, we focus on laws and policies that target unsafe abortions and inadequate or unaffordable healthcare – two primary reasons for maternal deaths worldwide.

South Africa and Nigeria have vastly divergent domestic laws on abortion rights. South Africa has liberal abortion laws that recognize women's right to reproductive autonomy, while Nigeria has restrictive abortion laws that stifle the ability of Nigerian women to choose their own reproductive health outcomes. In contrast, South Africa and Nigeria share similar laws and policies on access to healthcare. The right to health is constitutionalized in both South Africa and Nigeria and both countries have made legislative efforts towards universal health coverage. Despite providing such legal protections, maternal mortality continues to plague South Africa and Nigeria at devastatingly high rates, highlighting that liberal laws may not be enough on their own to curb maternal mortality.

Though their domestic laws have some inconsistencies, South Africa and Nigeria have both ratified a number of similar international Agreements that have provisions related to reproductive healthcare, including the International Covenant on Economic, Social and Cultural Rights (ICESCR)[90] and CEDAW.[91] The persistence of maternal deaths in South Africa and Nigeria in the face of laws and policies that aspire to reduce or eliminate maternal deaths necessities an examination of their effectiveness. Before turning to this analysis in the succeeding section, this section analyzes the state of abortion and healthcare laws in South Africa and Nigeria.

### Laws on unsafe abortions

Unsafe abortions are defined as abortions conducted by a person that lacks the skills necessary to provide the procedure or in an environment that is ill-suited for the procedure.[92] Each year, millions of women die as a consequence of unsafe abortions.[93] In Southern Africa, an estimated 120,000 women underwent unsafe

---

90 *International Convention on Civil and Political Rights*, 19 December 1966, 999 UNTS 171 (entered into force 23 March 1976) [ICESCR].
91 CEDAW, *supra*.
92 World Health Organization, "Preventing Unsafe Abortion", available at www.who.int/reproductivehealth/topics/unsafe_abortion/hrpwork/en/ (accessed 22 May 2019).
93 Lale Say et al., "Global Causes of Maternal Death: A WHO Systematic Analysis" (2014) 2:6 *Lancet Global Health* e323.

abortions and of those 500 died.[94] This figure is disheartening not only because of how high it is, but also because deaths caused by unsafe abortions are preventable. Deaths and other health complications due to unsafe abortions can be avoided by making reproductive health resources and services available to women.

One way to ensure that women have access to abortions is by legalizing abortions. Ensuring that women can attain abortions without legal reprisal facilitates the shift of the procedure from one that is conducted underground in unsafe conditions and by unqualified individuals, to above-ground facilities such as hospitals and clinics designed to provide medical services. This is the approach taken in South Africa. In South Africa, two seminal domestic laws govern abortions: the Constitution of South Africa[95] and the CTOPA.[96] The South African Constitution is one of the world's most progressive and robust constitutions in terms of the human rights protections it affords. Most notable, pursuant to Section 12(2), women have the right to make decisions concerning their reproduction and control over their bodies.

Shortly after passing the South African Constitution, South Africa enacted CTOPA, which came into force in 1997. The South African Constitution is celebrated as providing the legal framework that enabled CTOPA.[97] CTOPA is a comprehensive legislation that governs abortions in South Africa. CTOPA validates the truism that women have a fundamental right to govern their bodies and reproductive capacities.[98] Section 2 of CTOPA provides that a pregnancy may be terminated for any reason up to the twelfth week of pregnancy.[99] Between the 13th and 20th week of pregnancy and with the approval of a medical practitioner, an abortion may be approved in limited circumstances, including when continued pregnancy poses a risk to the health of the woman or fetus or when social or economic hardship to the woman will result.[100] After the 20th week, a woman may only receive an abortion if, in the opinion of a medical practitioner, continuing the pregnancy poses a danger to the woman or fetus.[101]

CTOPA also clarifies where an abortion may be performed. Legal abortions in South Africa must be completed at an approved facility or one that has, amongst other resources, the appropriate surgical equipment, infection control measures and access to emergency centres or facilities.[102] Abortion providers that are not

94 World Health Organization, *Unsafe Abortion: Global and Regional Estimates of the Incidence of Unsafe Abortion and Associated Mortality in 2008* (Geneva: WHO, 2011) at 19, 28.
95 No 109 of 1996 [South African Constitution].
96 CTOPA, *supra*.
97 Rachel Rebouche, "The Limits of Reproductive Rights in Improving Women's Health" (2011) 63 *Alabama Law Review* 1 at 9 ('Rebouche, "The Limits of Reproductive Rights in Improving Women's Health"').
98 CTOPA, *supra*, preamble.
99 Ibid., s 2(1)(a).
100 Ibid., s 2(1)(b).
101 Ibid., s 2(1)(c).
102 Ibid., s 3(1).

authorized to perform abortions may face a fine or imprisonment not exceeding 10 years.[103]

While CTOPA attempts to provide broad access to abortion services for South African women, it fails to make provisions for clinical referrals to address the case of healthcare professionals who object to the provision of abortion services on the grounds of conscience. In fact, the law "purposefully"[104] excludes the right to conscientious objection and what health professionals are to do in such circumstances, a deliberate legislative omission that is nonplusing considering the widespread moral objections to abortion in the country and across the region.

Furthermore, it would appear that in the drafters' attempt to avoid the horrors of United States abortion litigation and the claw-backs of women's rights to access the service, CTOPA advances the similar worrisome counselling services on options that United States abortion laws often require of women before and after obtaining an abortion.[105] With reference to latent objectives of a law discussed above, these types of mandatory options and counselling provisions are intended to deter women from obtaining an abortion. Regardless of the drafters' intention in the case of CTOPA, the provision, though non-mandatory, implicitly and yet possibly inadvertently sends out the same message of caution to women on a supposition that women only require further information from a 'counsel' at the point of service and they would change their minds about the procedure – a supposition that is not borne out on the facts regarding women's decision-making on abortion.

In contrast to South Africa's liberal abortion laws, Nigeria's abortion laws are highly restrictive. Two different laws govern abortions in Nigeria. In northern Nigeria, the Penal Code[106] applies, and in southern Nigeria, the Criminal Code[107] regulates abortions. Under both statutes, abortion is explicitly prohibited, except when necessary to save the life of the woman. Though similarly worded, the Criminal Code has been interpreted to permit abortions in a border range of circumstances. Specifically, abortions in southern Nigeria may be performed when continuation of the pregnancy would result in physical or mental suffering to the woman.[108]

The domestic abortion laws in South Africa and Nigeria are vastly different. In many circumstances, women in South Africa receive abortions without legal sanctions. Women in Nigeria, on the other hand, are not granted the same rights except in very limited circumstances. Yet, the experiences of millions of women seeking access to abortion under both jurisdictions are remarkably similar, a fact that raises questions about the effectiveness of South Africa's CTOPA – a problem that we address below.

---

103 Ibid., s 10(1)(d).
104 Rebouche, "The Limits of Reproductive Rights in Improving Women's Health" at 18–21.
105 Ibid.
106 No. 9 of 2008, ss 228–230.
107 No. 25 of 1960, ss 232–234.
108 Irehobhude O. Iyioha and Remigius N. Nwabueze, *Comparative Health Law and Policy: Critical Perspectives on Nigerian and Global Health Law* (Surrey: Ashgate, 2015) at 119.

Both South Africa and Nigeria are both bound by CEDAW, one of the most significant international conventions with respect to women's rights, which targets discriminatory and customary practices that are grounded in the unfounded and patriarchal idea of women's inferiority.[109] Article 12 of CEDAW requires states parties to take measures to ensure women have access to healthcare services, including reproductive healthcare treatments. Nothing in CEDAW explicitly requires states parties to legalize abortion. However, the CEDAW Committee has commented that liberalizing abortion laws are integral to achieving the goals of Article 12.[110] It is apparent from a review of the domestic legislation in Nigeria that it has not fulfilled this obligation under CEDAW.

### The legal environment for affordable, quality healthcare

A lack of availability of quality, affordable healthcare is also a critical indicator of maternal mortality and health. Women who are unable to access healthcare services or those forced to deal with ill-trained healthcare providers, such as medical service providers who lack the skills to assist pregnant women with HIV, are more susceptible to maternal death. South Africa and Nigeria have generous domestic legal frameworks that provide for access to health services. In the context of the international laws that bind both countries, South Africa and Nigeria are both states parties to ICESCR and CEDAW – two significant, binding conventions that call for access to healthcare.

In South Africa, the right to health is codified in Article 27 of the South African Constitution, the highest law in the country. Article 27 explicitly provides that everyone has a right to access healthcare services, including reproductive healthcare and emergency medical treatment. Further, it requires the government to take measures, within its means, to ensure the realization of these rights. The government has taken steps to give effect to this provision. Most significantly, South Africa enacted the South African NHA, which obligates public clinics to provide free health services to pregnant and lactating women (including free termination of pregnancies).[111] This coverage was specifically provided to, *inter alia*, address the issue of maternal deaths.

Similarly, in Nigeria, the right to health is codified in section 17(3)(d) of the Constitution of the Federal Republic of Nigeria,[112] which obliges the Nigerian state to direct its policy towards ensuring that all persons have access to adequate

---

109 Oluseyi Olayanju, "Analysis of the Legal and Policy Framework Applicable to Combat Vesico Vaginal Fistula in Nigeria and Systemic Challenges to their Implementation" (2017) 43:1 *Commonwealth Law Bulletin* 3 at 10.

110 Committee on the Elimination of Discrimination against Women, *General Recommendation No 24: Article 12 of the Convention (Women and Health)*, A/54/38/Rev.1, OCHCR, 20th Sess (1999).

111 Section 4; Jerome A. Singh, Michelle Govender and Nilam Reddy Singh, "South Africa a Decade after Apartheid: Realizing Health through Human Rights" (2005) 12:3 *Georgetown Journal on Poverty Law & Policy* 355 at 364.

112 *Nigerian Constitution, supra.*

healthcare. This constitutional obligation was not adequately realized until 2014 when the Nigerian NHA – a comprehensive healthcare legislation designed to transform the health system through robust regulation – was enacted.[113] Prior to the Nigerian NHA, only a few Nigerian states took steps to create conditions to enhance healthcare accessibility by providing free maternal health services, setting up maternal childcare centres, or connecting rural women with health services.[114] However, with the passage of the Nigerian NHA, it is apparent that the federal government of Nigeria is alive to the urgent need for suitable reproductive healthcare in the country.

Nigeria also has a number of policies that deal with maternal health. As Odunsi and Adewole explain in Chapter 9 of this book, Nigeria has implemented a number of national policies on reproductive and sexual healthcare that date back to the 1990s. The 2001 Reproductive Health Policy and Strategy[115] (Reproductive Health Policy) is one of the policies put in place by the Federal Ministry of Health to achieve quality reproductive and sexual health for all Nigerians. The Reproductive Health Policy expresses the commitment of the government of Nigeria to effectively address reproductive health challenges including those that impact the current trend of high maternal mortality rate. One of the goals and objectives of the Reproductive Health Policy is to reduce maternal morbidity and mortality due to pregnancy and childbirth by 50%.[116] Some other targets of the policy are to (1) increase access to qualitative and affordable maternal and child health services including post-abortion care by 40% and (2) increase access to reproductive health information and services by 50%.[117]

In 2011, the Federal Ministry of Health adopted the Integrated Maternal, Newborn and Child Health Strategy.[118] This policy has the commendable target of instituting a basic health insurance scheme that provides free services to pregnant women.[119] On paper, it appears that the country has achieved this goal with the enactment of the Nigerian NHA.

South Africa and Nigeria have ratified many international instruments relevant to the reduction of maternal mortality. By doing so, they have obligated themselves to enact measures that give effect to the various provisions of the instruments, including those dealing with maternal health. Dealing explicitly with maternal health, the ICESCR requires states parties to take steps to provide for "the reduction of the stillbirth rate and of infant mortality and for the healthy development of the child".[120] The UN Committee on Economic, Social and

---

113 Ibid., preamble.
114 Mojekwu and Ibekwe, "Maternal Mortality in Nigeria", at 138.
115 Federal Ministry of Health (Nigeria), National Reproductive Health Policy Strategy to Achieve Quality Reproductive and Sexual Health for All Nigerians (2001).
116 Ibid. at para 3.2.1.
117 Ibid.
118 Federal Ministry of Health (Nigeria), *Integrated Maternal, Newborn and Child Health Strategy* (2007).
119 Ibid.
120 ICESCR, *supra*, art 12(2)(a).

Cultural Rights, the body responsible for monitoring this treaty, has stated that this treaty obligation must be

> Understood as requiring measures to improve child and maternal health, sexual and reproductive health services, including access to family planning, pre- and post-natal care, emergency obstetric services and access to information, as well as to resources necessary to act on that information.[121]

The ICESCR also codifies the right to health, generally. Article 12.1 of the ICESCR codifies the principle of the right to health, and Article 12.2(d) requires states parties to work towards creating an environment that assures people have access to medical services.

Like the ICESCR, CEDAW also deals with maternal mortality. Pursuant to Article 12.1 of CEDAW, states parties must take appropriate measures to eliminate discrimination in the context of healthcare, including with respect to family planning. Article 12.2 further requires states parties to

> ensure to women appropriate services in connection with pregnancy, confinement and the post-natal period, granting free services where necessary, as well as adequate nutrition during pregnancy and lactation.[122]

The above provisions impute duties and obligations on states parties to provide women with adequate healthcare services during all stages of their pregnancy. As states that have ratified the above conventions, Nigeria and South Africa are under a legal obligation to take steps towards the realization of the intent of these provisions – in this case, reducing maternal mortality. Yet, high rates of maternal mortality persist in South Africa and Nigeria, with no sign of reducing at a rate necessary to meet the SDG target ratio by 2023. The question then turns on why, specifically, what accounts for the slow progress towards eradicating or significantly lowering maternal mortality. What insights do theory and practice afford? Next, we determine why these provisions have failed to address maternal mortality in any meaningful way.

## Assessing effectiveness

The literature on law's limits and effectiveness canvasses a number of parameters to apply in assessing law's effect. Chapter 2 offers a summary of some of the relevant considerations, some of which we summarily revised above. Here we zero in on key strands of the considerations offered in Chapter 2 that we deem particularly germane to the problem of maternal mortality.

---

121 UN Economic and Social Council, *General Comment No. 14: The Right to the Highest Attainable Standard of Health (Art. 12 of the Covenant)*, E/C.12/2000/4, CESCR, 22nd Sess, UN Doc GE.00–43934 (E) (2000) at para 14.
122 Art. 12.2, CEDAW, *supra*.

Thus, employing Iyioha's theory of substantive effectiveness to critique the utility of laws in South Africa and Nigeria that purport to reduce maternal deaths, this section determines that laws in both countries, including international laws that bind both, are inherently inadequate at addressing maternal mortality. Laws in South Africa and Nigeria are not only limited by internal factors in their objects, language and construction but also external factors regarding the socio-economic context in which they are implemented.

### Abortion rights

On its face, South Africa's abortion laws are liberal and have laudable objectives. They are designed to ensure that women have access to legal abortion services. Nigeria, on the other hand, does not have similar abortion laws. Nigeria's laws explicitly limit women's reproductive health choices. Remarkably, in spite of these vastly different legal positions on abortion, women in both countries are still forced to turn to backstreet service providers to receive pregnancy terminations, even when doing so puts their life in danger. South Africa's liberal abortion laws should, in theory, reduce the number of unsafe abortions and maternal deaths caused by unsafe abortions. However, this has not been the reality. Women in South Africa still access illegal, unsafe abortion services at an alarmingly high rate. South Africa's CTOPA fails the most basic test of legal effectiveness, which Iyioha terms in this book[123] as formal legal effectiveness.

An examination of abortion laws in South Africa and Nigeria reveals the internal limits that prevent the laws in either country from reducing maternal deaths. South Africa's abortion law, CTOPA, has laudable objectives: to codify women's equality and reproductive health rights. However, there are significant gaps in the law as currently composed. CTOPA does not include provisions that cover conscientious objections to abortions, a gap that has resulted in confusion regarding the legal obligations of reproductive healthcare providers in the performance of abortions or in their referral obligations to women who could have been directed to abortion service providers.[124] In Nigeria, the anti-choice laws are neither in their objectives nor construction sufficient to reduce maternal deaths arising from illegal abortions.

It is important to reiterate that, unlike the assumptions that can be made of the United Kingdom's female genital cutting law discussed in Chapter 3 by Lewis et al., this statutory loophole was intentional. The drafters of South Africa's CTOPA deliberately left out a conscientious objection provision[125] in the hopes of escaping some of the consequences following *Roe v. Wade*[126] and the contentious and disparate abortion regulations that the decision spawned across

---

123 See Iyioha, Chapter 2 of this volume.
124 Rebouche, "The Limits of Reproductive Rights in Improving Women's Health" at 27–30.
125 Ibid.; Charles Ngwena, "Conscientious Objection and Legal Abortion in South Africa: Delineating the Parameters" (2003) 28:1 J Judicial Science 1 at 9.
126 *Roe v. Wade*, 410 U.S. 113 (1973).

states in the United States.[127] This deliberate omission has thus opened up the law to much uncertainty and ambiguous interpretation by frontline healthcare professionals who must act on the basis of their own interpretations of the law.

Furthermore, evidence emerging from the experiences of women in the United States suggests that CTOPA's non-mandatory counselling requirement ultimately is not in the best interest of women. Counselling provisions intended to discourage women from accessing a given reproductive health service that are presented as purely 'informational' fit the typeset of latent statutory objectives; and where they appear not to, as might be the case with CTOPA's provisions, they remain problematic because millions of women with poor or no education may not know that the provision is non-mandatory.

The liberal abortion laws in South Africa are further limited by external considerations. There are a number of systemic failures that hinder women's right to choose in South Africa: (1) minimal infrastructure such as healthcare facilities to support pregnancy termination procedures;[128] (2) lack of training regarding abortion services for healthcare providers;[129] and (3) extreme underfunding for healthcare services.[130] Also, many South African women do not have enough information about their rights, further hindering their ability to access legal abortion services.[131] In addition to these barriers to implementation, the prevailing cultural and religious norms in South Africa severely jeopardize women's reproductive rights. Women who try to access abortion services often face stigma and discrimination from not only healthcare providers, but also others in their social circles that disagree with the ideals underlying reproductive health rights.[132] The social repercussions for accessing abortion services prevent many women from accessing their legal rights. Nigeria shares many of these problems. As is obvious from the restrictive abortion laws in the country, perceptions about contraception and abortion in Nigeria, on paper and in society, do not accord with contemporary understandings of women's health rights.

### Healthcare inaccessibility and unaffordability

The fact that South Africa and Nigeria both have instituted frameworks to provide healthcare coverage to their citizenry, including pregnant women, ought to

---

127  Rebouche, "The Limits of Reproductive Rights in Improving Women's Health", *supra.*
128  Camilla Pickles, "Lived Experiences of the Choice on Termination of Pregnancy Act 92 of 1996: Bridging the Gap for Women in Need" (2013) 29 *SAJHR* 515 at 516–518 ('Pickles, "Lived Experiences of the Choice on Termination of Pregnancy Act 92 of 1996"').
129  Ibid.
130  Ibid.
131  Ibid., 519–520; Cathi Albertyn, "Claiming and Defending Abortion Rights in South Africa" (2015) 11:2 *Direito GV Law Review* 429 at 444 ('Albertyn, "Claiming and Defending Abortion Rights in South Africa"').
132  Pickles, "Lived Experiences of the Choice on Termination of Pregnancy Act 92 of 1996" at 519–522; Albertyn, "Claiming and Defending Abortion Rights in South Africa" ibid. at 444.

result in reduced rates of maternal mortality. However, South Africa and Nigeria continue to struggle with a high level of maternal deaths due to inaccessible and inadequate reproductive health services. An examination of the internal characteristics of South Africa and Nigeria's healthcare laws and the external limitations of these laws confirms why this is the case.

Internally, the provisions with respect to healthcare in the South African Constitution and Nigerian Constitution are fundamentally flawed. The South African Constitution limits the state's obligation to enact measures to give effect to the right to health. The state is only required to do what is within its means to provide healthcare to citizens.[133] This entitles the state to evade its obligations to provide the infrastructure and resources necessary to give effect to the right to health by prioritizing other interests and citing a lack of resources for healthcare. The right to health codified in the Nigerian Constitution has similar problems. The right to health is contained in Chapter 2 of the Nigerian Constitution, titled "Fundamental Objectives and Directive Principles of State Policy".[134] The socio-economic rights contained in this chapter are non-justiciable, meaning the state cannot be held legally accountable for failing to give effect to these rights through the courts.[135] However, based on 2015 amendments that now support justiciability of educational and maternal health rights, Nigerian women may now be able to use this chapter of the Constitution to demand recognition of their healthcare rights. Yet, the feasibility and success of this remains debatable due to the structural, financial and informational barriers that limit women's ability to use rights and the legal system in their favour.

South Africa and Nigeria have both enacted measures to realize the right to health codified in their constitutions and international conventions to which they are signatories. The South African NHA and Nigerian NHA are two such measures, which provide for, *inter alia*, universal healthcare coverage. In principle, then, women in both countries should have access to affordable healthcare services. However, this goal has not been realized in either country, signifying issues with implementation and other external factors. This lack of universal coverage and access to quality healthcare services in South Africa and Nigeria in the face of laws that provide for same confirms that access to healthcare in principle is insufficient. To ensure true access to healthcare that effectively reduces maternal deaths, not only must healthcare be affordable, the healthcare provided must also be of a high standard, with service providers receiving training on how to treat and manage women with obstetric complications or pregnant women with HIV.

---

133 South African Constitution, *supra*, art 27.
134 Fundamental Objectives and Directive Principles of State Policy, Chapter II, Constitution of the Federal Republic of Nigeria, 1999.
135 Olaolu Opadere, "Non-Justiciability of Fundamental Objectives: Paradox and Bane of Governance in Nigeria" (2018) 74 *Journal of Law Policy & Globalization* 37 at 40–42; Andra Le Roux-Kemp, "The Recognition of Health Rights in Constitutions on the African Continent: A Systematic Review" (2016) 24:1 *African Journal of International Comparative Law* 142 at 148.

286 Arooj Shah et al.

Healthcare laws in South Africa and Nigeria are limited by similar external factors that contribute to their ineffectiveness. In both countries, the socio-economic contexts in which the countries' healthcare laws operate explain why the laws are inadequate. Both countries struggle with extremely underfunded healthcare systems, due in part to a lack of political will to ensure universal coverage for all.[136] The lack of healthcare funding in South Africa and Nigeria has resulted in a number of similar barriers to healthcare in both countries, including (1) overcrowded healthcare facilities with long wait times; (2) poor-quality general and maternal health services due in part to lack of qualified healthcare professionals, and lack of resources, such as medical equipment; and (3) underserved rural communities in which women have to travel considerable distances at their own expense to access healthcare services.[137]

The persistent inaccessibility of healthcare in South Africa and Nigeria means that reproductive healthcare continues to remain out of reach for many women. However, this inaccessibility is not experienced equally. Instead, marginalized women bear the most consequences of South Africa and Nigeria's fragmented healthcare systems.[138] Those with sufficient means are often able to travel abroad for quality healthcare services or turn to private healthcare service providers that provide quality services.

What the foregoing analysis shows is that the mere passage of laws does not necessarily lead to positive health outcomes. South Africa's and Nigeria's abortion laws and healthcare laws are limited in their ability to positively increase health outcomes for women due to a number of internal and external factors. Without societal reforms and adequate implementation, including sufficient funding, such laws fail to reduce maternal deaths meaningfully.

## Conclusion: moving forward

William Easterly, a commentator on health, argues that pressing for the right to health sometimes leads to a distortion of health priorities thus diverting resources to non-pressing areas of health with the most advocacy.[139] Easterly claims that concentrating on the right to health leads to resources being spent inefficiently, such as focusing on HIV/AIDS and malaria to the detriment of other areas of

136 Rebouche, "The Limits of Reproductive Rights in Improving Women's Health" at 34.

137 Ibid.; Bronwyn Harris et al., "Inequities in Access to Health Care in South Africa" (2011) 32:Supp 1 *Journal of Public Health Policy* S102 ('Harris et al., "Inequities in Access to Health Care in South Africa"'); Chimaraoke Izugbara, Frederick Wekesah and Sunday Adedini, *Maternal Health in Nigeria: A Situation Update* (Nairobi, Kenya: African Population and Health Research Centre, 2016); Mojekwu and Ibekwe, "Maternal Mortality in Nigeria", *supra*; Pickles, "Lived Experiences of the Choice on Termination of Pregnancy Act 92 of 1996", *supra*.

138 Harris et al., ibid. at S116.

139 William Easterly, "Human Rights Are the Wrong Basis for Healthcare" (12 October 2009) *Financial Times (North American Edition)*, available at FT, www.ft.com/content/89bbbda2-b763-11de-9812-00144feab49a (accessed 22 May 2019).

health. Easterly is right that focusing on single health issues can have negative effects on the overall health system. For example, it has been argued that as more money is spent on HIV/AIDS programs, the proportion of attended births falls.[140] In the context of reproductive rights, it can be argued that focusing on singular issues related to women's health generally may also be detrimental to the specific realization of women's reproductive health rights. Yet, the preceding discussion has shown that there are inefficiencies in enacting laws that are intended to reduce maternal deaths when various factors that cumulatively restrict women's reproductive healthcare are not considered or duly addressed.

Our research and analysis suggests that attention to the connections between HIV and maternal deaths, hospital infrastructural developments, and curbing the high rates of fatality from illegal abortions will go a long way towards addressing the high rate of maternal mortality in both South Africa and Nigeria. It is indisputable that reducing the maternal death ratio in South Africa and Nigeria requires instituting measures for the prevention of maternal deaths and their causes as well as the promotion of maternal health.[141] Such measures further include, but are not limited to, creating comprehensive training and awareness programs for healthcare providers, educating women about their rights and allocating resources more effectively to ensure that healthcare services are available.

In implementing the above reforms, it remains necessary for legislative and policy frameworks to be tailored to address the salient problems that weaken the effectiveness of legislation, with particular regard to those discussed in this chapter. The task of changing norms and having those changes reflected in legislation must be deliberate and strategic. In this exercise, clear and honest objectives, language choice, harmonization of legal provisions and unambiguous provisions go a long way towards ensuring women have improved access to reproductive healthcare and are protected from early pregnancy-related mortality.

140 Marcus Haacker, ed., "HIV/AIDS: Development Impact and Policy Challenges", in M. Hannam and J. Wolff, eds., *Southern African: 2020 Vision – Public Priorities for the Next Decade* (London: e9 Publishing, 2010).
141 US Department of Health and Human Services, *Healthy People 2010: Understanding and Improving Health*, 2nd ed. (Washington, DC: US Government Printing Office, 2000).

# Index

Note: Page numbers in *italic* indicate a figure and page numbers in **bold** indicate a table on the corresponding page.

*A, B, and C v Ireland* (2010) 72
*Abacha v Fawehimi* (2000) 242
*Abdulaziz, Cabales and Balkandali v The United Kingdom* (1985) 132–4
Aboriginal Healing Foundation 223
abortifacients 102n22, 164, 166–8, 172, 175–6
Abortion Act of 1967 (UK) 47n138, 55, 100n12
abortions and abortion law 1–2, 8–11, 15–16, 99–100; abuse and 18–19; 'backstreet' abortions 11, 35, 99, 102–3, 121, 283; in Canada 21, 28, 47, 49, 58–9, 63; in China 10–11, 21, 61, 75–6, 99–121, 130; consent and medical care 51n158; economics and 201–2; emergency 71–2, 72n44; forced 113, 115, 116n81, 117, 120, 130; gender-specific reformative laws 32, 37–8; international norms and law on 210; in Nigeria 15–16, 40, 49, 57n201, 248–50, 251n96, 253, 258, 277–84; permissive abortion laws 49; in the Philippines 29, 159, 162, 166–8, 172, 179–80; population politics and 59; portability requirements and 50–1; post-abortion care 234, 281; *R. v Morgentaler* (1988) 49–50, 56–7; *Roe v Wade* (1973) 56–9, 283–4; religious and moral opposition to 54–7; in Senegal 48–9, 48n140; in South Africa 15–16, 35, 40, 55, 254–5, 264–6, 277–84; statistics about 113; Substantive Legal Effectiveness (SLE) and 9; therapeutic 47–50, 48n141; in the United Kingdom 49, 55; in the United States 28, 41–2; unsafe 71–2, 100, 201, 253, 255, 264–6, 277–80, 283; violence against women and 18–19
abstinence 158, 200, 253; improving 207–11; independent 216; limited 197; social 207–8
Act for Collecting and Managing the Social Maintenance Fee (China) 113
Adelson, Naomi 215
Afghanistan *184*, 195
Africa: abortion access in 19; contraceptive prevalence in 205, *206*; education in 199, *200*; female genital cutting (FGC) in 78–9; maternal mortality in *183*, 184, 261; patriarchy in 252, 280; reproductive health services in 195–6; women's labour in 185–6; *see also* Nigeria; Senegal; South Africa
African Commission on Human Rights 7
agency 1–2, 4; child marriage and 190–2, 258; in China 121; economics and 188–92, **190**; expanding 198–202, *200*, 210–11; of Indigenous women in Canada 217, 221, 229, 231; in Nigeria 50, 258; in South Africa 55; in the Philippines 179
*Ahamefule v Imperial Medical Centre and Molokwu* 259n132
Alaattinoglu, Daniela 150
Alcover Jr., Jun 163
Alexy, Robert: on correctness 4, 22n13, 43n113; dual-nature thesis of 27,

43, 68–9; efficacy-oriented concepts of law 25, 25n34; on human rights and morality 4, 75–6; on positivism vs non-positivism 67–9, 72; on social efficacy 22–4, 22n13, 26–7, 43, 67; on the nature of law 22; on the validity of law 28n47, 29

Alliance for Nationalism and Democracy (ANAD) Party-List 163

Allott, Anthony 22n13, 26, 30, 39–40, 45

Amnesty International 1, 66n10

*Andrews v Law Society of British Columbia and the Attorney General of British Columbia* (1989) 31–2

*AP Garcon and Nicot v France* 127

Aquino III, President Benigno 178

Armenia *191*

Arroyo, Gloria Macapagal 153

*AS v Hungary* (2004) 72, 137–9, 141, 149

Asia: contraceptive prevalence in 205, *206*; education in 199, *200*; female genital cutting (FGC) in 78–9; maternal mortality in *183*, 261; *see also* China; Philippines

Atienza, Jose L. 173

authoritarianism 2, 147

Badji, Mamadou 48–9

Baines, Beverley 31n69, 32n72

Bangladesh: abortion in 202; agency and reproductive health outcomes in 192; healthcare access in 202–3; labour in 186–8, 200–1; maternal mortality and 186–8, 202–3

Bar Human Rights Committee of England and Wales (BHRC) 84

Barangay Ayala Alabang 171–4

Barlow, Kevin 219, 222n59

Belém do Pará Convention 135, 145, 148–9

Benin (country) 187

Bierling, Ernst Rudolf 25

Bindel, Julie 83

Bolivia 7; *IV v Bolivia* 146–8, 151

Borrows, John 224, 228

Boyer, Yvonne 213–14, 216, 216n22, 222, 229–30

Burkina Faso 187, 196

Burundi 184

Cambodia *191*, 196, 202

Cameroon 190, *191*

Campaign on Accelerated Reduction of Maternal and Child Mortality (CARMMA) 255

Canada: abortions and abortion law in 21, 28, 47, 49, 58–9, 63; *Andrews v Law Society of British Columbia and the Attorney General of British Columbia* (1989) 31–2; *Eldrige v British Columbia (Att. Gen.)* 33n73; equality in 34, 34n76, 89–90, 221–2; history of the law on abortion in 55–7; Prince Edward Island (PEI) 29, 49, 55–6, 58, 159; *R. v Morgentaler* (1988) 49–50, 56–7; rule of law in 215–16, 221; sex equality cases in 31n69; social norms in 14, 63, 120; Supreme Court of 31, 49–50, 81, 89–90; *Symes v Canada* (1993) 33n73; Truth and Reconciliation Commission of Canada 222–3; *see also* Indigenous women

Canada Health Act (1985) 50–1

Canadian Aboriginal AIDS Network (CAAN) 218, 219, 225, 225n72

Canadian Criminal Code (1985) 49

Canadian HIV/AIDS Legal Network 219–20, 222

Canadian Medical Association 47

capital punishment 25n32, 40, 245

Catholic Church 73n50, 154, 156, 158–9, 162–5, 173–4, 177–8

Cayetano, Alan Peter 160

Cayetano, Pia 162, 164

CEDAW *see* Convention on the Elimination of All Forms of Discrimination Against Women (CEDAW)

Center for Reproductive Rights 147

Central African Republic 184

Centre for Reproductive Rights 138

CERD *see* Convention on the Elimination of Racial Discrimination (CERD)

Chad *183*–4

Charter on Human and Peoples' Rights on the Rights of Women in Africa (Maputo Protocol) 48, 135, 135n83, 239, 242, 242n49, 245, 246n70

*Chavez v Peru* (2003) 146–8

child marriage 190–1, 250; polygyny and 238, 253; in Nigeria 238, 243, 258, 267, 270–1

Child Rights Act (Nigeria) 245, 248–9, 271

China 7, 10–11, 21, 59, 99–121; abortifacients in 102n22; abortion law and population policy in 110–14; abortions and abortion law in 10–11, 21, 61, 75–6, 99–121, 130; Act for Collecting and Managing the Social Maintenance Fee 113; constitution of 106–7, 109; contraceptives in 75, 109, 111, 113, 119; Convention on the Elimination of All Forms of Discrimination Against Women (CEDAW) 76; Cultural Revolution 106–7, 106n41, 107n42, 112; economics and employment in 105, 119–20, 119n93; equality in 10–11, 99, 103, 107, 120–1; ethnic minorities in 195; Eugenic Demographic Policy 114; eugenics in 111–12, 114–15; famine in 106n41, 110, 112; Feng Jianmei case 72, 72n41, 115; General Principles of the Civil Code (1986) 101; Glorious Mother 111; Great Leap Forward 106–7, 106n41, 107n42; liberalization of law and 114–19; National People's Congress (NPC) 107, 109, 114n71; out-of-quota births 113, 115, 116n81, 118, 130; patriarchy in 104, 117; power and rights in Chinese jurisdiction 108–10; premarital sex in 102, 118–19; pro-natalist policy in 109–12, 109n51; rule of law in 107; social norms in 59; social taboos in 118; Substantive Legal Effectiveness (SLE) in 102–4, 121; Theory of Five Organs 101; two-child policy 114n74; women in imperial China 105; women's agency in 121; *see also* Confucianism

Choice on Termination of Pregnancy Act (CTOPA) (South Africa) 16, 35, 55, 254, 262

Code of Medical Ethics (Senegal) 48, 48n141

Code on Maternal and Infant Health Care (China) 114

Code on Population and Family Planning (China) 114

Colombia 199

compliance: Compliance Theory of legal effectiveness 35–6, 35n78, 61, 77, 80–1, 246; popular 22, 29, 36, 81, 246; sanctions and 22n13, 25n32, 27n43, 29, 40, 62, 267; *see also* policing and enforcement

conception (of life) 28, 159–60, 164, 167–8, 172–4 *see also* contraceptives

conditional cash transfer (CCT) programs 198–9, 203

Confucianism 10, 101, 103–5, 117–21; communist legal system and 105–8; *li* (self-controlled order) 105, 118–19; power and rights under 108–10; 'Three Obedience' 105

contraceptives 24; abortifacients 102n22, 164, 166–8, 172, 175–6; in China 75, 109, 111, 113, 119; condoms 118n86, 172–3, 189, **190**; conscientious objection among healthcare providers 54–5; economics and 186, 191–2, 194–5, 198, 201, 204; international norms and law on 233, 251, 253; mifepristone and misprotal 102n22; in Nigeria 284; in Pakistan 205; in Peru 147; in the Philippines 51, 152, 157–8, 164–8, 171–7; promotion of 124–5, 124n14, 124n15; regional trends in 205–6, *206*; in South Africa 255; in the United States 127; *see also* abortions; sterilization

Convention on the Elimination of All Forms of Discrimination Against Women (CEDAW) 2, 11–12, 19, 40; in China 76; economics and 209–10; forced sterilization and 134, 135–9, 139n118, 142; General Recommendations 134, 134n80; intersectionality and 124, 128; *L.C. v Peru* (2011) 210; in Nigeria 239, 245, 271, 277, 280, 282; Optional Protocol to (2000) 136–7; in the Philippines 153, 165, 173, 173n76, 176, 179; *Pimentel v Brazil* (2011) 210; in South Africa 280, 282; in the United Kingdom 65, 84, 92

Convention on the Elimination of Racial Discrimination (CERD) 134–5, 134n80

correctness 4, 6, 9–12, 21–8; in abortion law in China 103–5, 121–3; compliance and 22n13, 39, 80; limits of law and 42–3, 46, 53–5, 57; in perceptions of law in Nigeria 233, 250; positivism vs. non-positivism 67–9, 71, 74; Substantive Legal Effectiveness (SLE) and 60–4, 67, 90, 94–6; validity of the law and 22–3, 22n13, 23n22, 39

Côte d'Ivoire 190, *191*

Council of Europe: Commissioner for Human Rights 142; Convention on Preventing and Combating Violence Against Women and Domestic Violence (2011) 134, 134n78; Gender Equality Strategy 2018–2023 140; Istanbul Convention 134, 140, 145; Strasbourg Declaration 140; *see also* Convention on Preventing and Combating Violence Against Women and Domestic Violence

Crenshaw, Kimberlé 36n84, 129–32, 135–6, 140

criminal intent 82, 82n99, 90, 94–6

criminal liability 82n99, 245

'critical race feminism' 70

CTOPA *see* Choice on Termination of Pregnancy Act (CTOPA) (South Africa)

Cultural Revolution 106–7, 106n41, 107n42, 112

Czech Republic 7, 141–4

Czyzewski, Karina 214–15, 222

death by stoning 237–8, 238n22

death penalty 177n94, 238n22

Defensor-Santiago 159–60

democracy 3, 7, 14, 254

Democratic Republic of Congo 184

Deng Xiaoping 112

*DH v Czech Republic* (2007) 139n115, 141, 143

Dharmasena, Dhanuson 87–8, 94

Dingake, OBK 216

disability 36n84, 124n15, 126–7

Easterly, William 286–7

*Ebralinag v Division Superintendent of Schools* 169

economics and employment; in China 105, 119–20, 119n93; economic factors and reproductive health 185–8; in Nigeria 239, 252, 258; maternity leave 239

ECt.HR *see* European Court of Human Rights (ECt.HR)

education: high school education 199; in Kenya 198, 200; legal empowerment and 210–11

Ejercito-Estrada Jr., Jose 'Jinggoy' 160–1

*Eldrige v British Columbia (Att. Gen.)* 33n73

Enrile, Juan Ponce 159

equality 2–3, 6; abortion rights and 55; *Andrews v Law Society of British Columbia and the Attorney General of British Columbia* (1989) 31–2; in Canada 34, 34n76, 89–90, 221–2; in China 10–11, 99, 103, 107, 120–1; economics and 182, 188–90, **190**, 194, 211; *Eldrige v British Columbia (Att. Gen.)* 33n73; 'equality potential' 138; feminism and 69–72; human rights and 123; international norms and law on 65, 99, 132–3, 139–40, 179; intersectionality and 36n84; jurisprudence 21; litigation 33–4, 33n73; modern equality doctrine 31, 31n68, 69–70, 71n31; in Nigeria 235, 245, 250, 266, 269–70, 283; in South Africa 254–4, 266, 283; substantive 2–3, 31–4, 34n76, 69–70, 70n31, 89, 131, 139; *Symes v Canada* (1993) 33n73; in the United Kingdom 89–90, 133; *see also* inequality

Equality Now 83, 88

Escudero, Francis 'Chiz' 160

*Estrada v Escritor* (2003) 169

Ethiopia 204–5

Eugenic Demographic Policy (China) 114

eugenics 12–13; in China 111–12, 114–15; forced sterilizations and 123–6, 124n15; in the Philippines 157–8

Europe; education in 199, *200*; maternal mortality in *183*; migration in 82–3; *see also* Ireland; United Kingdom

European Commission against Racial Intolerance (ECRI) 142

European Convention on Human Rights and Fundamental Freedoms 140

European Court of Human Rights (ECt.HR) 7, 11–12; *A, B, and C v Ireland* (2010) 72; *Abdulaziz, Cabales and Balkandali v The United Kingdom* (1985) 132–4; *AP*

*Garcon and Nicot v France* 127; *AS v Hungary* (2004) 72, 137–9, 141, 149; *DH v Czech Republic* (2007) 139n115, 141, 143; on forced sterilizations 139–44; jurisprudence of the 139–41; *Silguero v Portugal* (1999) 134n74; *VC v Slovakia* (2009) 141–3; on the *X-Case* 72n45

Factories Act (Nigeria) 252
Fadeyi, A. 232n1
*Familias en Accion* program 199
famine 106n41, 110, 112
female circumcision *see* female genital mutilation
female empowerment 10–11, 73–4; access to abortion and 10–11; formal legal effectiveness and 36; legal empowerment 210–11; in the Philippines 153; programs 200
Female Genital Cosmetic Surgery (FGCS) 88–9
female genital cutting *see* female genital mutilation
female genital mutilation 2, 8–10, 19, 32, 37; culture and 58, 250n92; international norms and law on 66n10, 245–6; in Nigeria 234, 239, 245–6, 253; *see also* UK Female Genital Mutilation (FGM) Act
feminism 2–6, 9–12, 24, 69–74, 88–9; in China 100–5, 121–2; critical race feminism 70; critique of rights instruments 128; cultural feminism 69, 71; feminist jurisprudence 67–8, 104–5; Indigenous Feminist Legal Theory (IFLT) 14–15, 131, 212n8, 213, 224–31; liberal or second wave feminism 69–70; post-modern 69–71, 76; third wave 70–1; Western notion of a global feminist theory 65–6, 76, 98
Feng Jianmei 72, 72n41, 115
Ferrari, Vincenzo 30
FGC (female genital cutting) *see* female genital mutilation
FGM *see* female genital mutilation; UK Female Genital Mutilation (FGM) Act
FIGO *see* International Federation of Gynaecology and Obstetrics (FIGO)
forced sterilization 8, 11–12, 32, 122–51; *Chavez v Peru* (2003) 146–8; in China 116n80, 117;

Convention on the Elimination of All Forms of Discrimination Against Women (CEDAW) 135–9; eugenics and 124–8; European Court of Human Rights on 139–45; Inter-American system 145–50; international case law on 134–50; intersectionality and 128–34; *IV v Bolivia* 146–8, 151; of Roma women 137–44
FORWARD 83
Friedman, Lawrence 30
Fujimori, Alberto 146–8
Fuller, Lon L. 24n29

Gambia 184
Gandhi, Mahatma 158
gender: adverse gender norms 1, 194; Indigenous norms 226, 236; transgender persons 127, 129n42, 223n65, 225; *see also* equality; feminism; patriarchy
General Principles of the Civil Code (China) 101
genocide 134, 148
Ghana 187, 192, 203, 257
global South 2, 7–9, 14, 20–1
Glorious Mother 111
*Gonzales v Carhart* (2007) 56
Great Leap Forward 106–7, 106n41, 107n42
gross domestic product (GDP) 189
Guidelines on Medical Management of Victims of Violence, Post-Abortion Care Training Manual (Nigeria) 234n7
Guinea 184
Guttmacher Institute 192

Haiti *184, 191*
Halappanavar, Savita 71–2
Hart, H.L.A. 23, 24n29, 274
Hart-Fuller debate 20
Hawkins, Kimberly 219–21
healthcare access 182–5; antenatal care 192, 194–6, 203, 205, 269, 272; economic factors and 185–97, *190, 191, 193*; education and sexual autonomy *191*; *Eldridge v British Columbia (Att. Gen.)* 33n73; external limits to law 188–97; healthcare workers' objections to contraception 54; improving

health outcomes 198–211; limited accountability in 197, 207–11; mandatory reporting 86–7; mutually reinforcing constraints and 192–7, *193*; portability requirement 50–1; Traditional Birth Attendants (TBAs) 235, 269; voucher-based programs 202–3; women's agency and 188–92, 198–202, **190**, *191*

HIV/AIDS: education and 200, 253; forced sterilization of women with 150; among Indigenous women of Canada 14, 212–13, 218–23, 225–9; international norms and law on 136, 150; maternal mortality and 1, 261–7, 285–7; in Nigeria 15, 234, 259n132, 261–7, 277, 285–7; in South Africa 15, 255, 261–7, 277, 285–7

Hobbes, Thomas 274

Home Affairs Select Committee (HASC) 84, 89

Honduras *191*, 210–11

Horton, Richard 215

Hu Jintao 109

human rights 1–3, 6–12, 15, 18–20; effectiveness of law and 74–8; equality and 123; intersectionality in adjudicating 123n10, 124, 128–34, 137–40, 145–51; morality and 4, 75–6; universality of 74–8; *see also* international law and norms

human trafficking 245

Hungary: *AS v Hungary* (2004) 72, 137–9, 141, 149

I-ACHR *see* Inter-American Court of Human Rights (I-ACHR)

*Ibidapo v Lufthansa Airlines* (1997) 256

immigration/migration 82–3, 132–3, 195

India: child marriage in *191*; constitution of 71, 210; education in 186–7; inheritance laws in 201; *Jaitun v Maternal Home MCD, Jangpura & Others* 209; *Janani Suraksha Yojania* program 204; *Laxmi Mandal v Deen Dayal Harinagar Hospital & Others* (2008) 209; maternal mortality and healthcare in *193*, 196–7, 204, 207–10, 261; Sangha women 207

Indigenous women 212–31; HIV/AIDS among 14, 212–13, 218–23, 225–9; Indigenous Feminist Legal Theory (IFLT) 14–15, 131, 212n8, 213, 224–31; Indigenous law as a determinant of health 222–4; patriarchy and 212, 214–15, 226; state law as a determinant of health 213–22; women's agency 217, 221, 229, 231

inequality 9, 18; in Africa 235, 250, 266; effectiveness of law and 36, 60, 70, 72; international norms and law on 140, 211; intersectionality and 36n84; poverty and 188–90, **190**, 194; social hierarchy and 31, 31n69

injustice 24, 24n23; extreme injustice 24, 68, 72, 74, 76, 79; Radbruch on 24, 24n23, 68, 72; social injustice as a collective phenomenon 151

Integrated Maternal, Newborn and Child Health Strategy, Federal Ministry of Health (Nigeria) 281

Inter-American Commission on Human Rights 7, 124; *Chavez v Peru* (2003) 146; jurisprudence of the 145, 145n165

Inter-American Convention on the Prevention, Punishment and Eradication of Violence Against Women (Belém do Pará Convention) 135, 145, 148–9

Inter-American Court of Human Rights (I-ACHR): *IV v Bolivia* (2016) 146–8, 151; *Xákmok v Paraguay* (2012) 210

International Conference on Population and Development (ICPD) 125, 179–80, 180n102, 240, 254

International Covenant on Civil and Political Rights (ICCPR) 134n80, 238, 240

International Covenant on Economic, Social and Cultural Rights (ICESCR) 134, 134n80, 209, 240, 277, 280–2

International Covenant on the Elimination of all forms of Racial Discrimination (ICERD) 240

International Federation of Gynaecology and Obstetrics (FIGO) 126

international laws and norms: on abortions 210; on contraceptives 233, 251, 253; on equality 65, 99, 132–3, 139–40, 179; on female genital mutilation 66n10, 245–6; on forced

sterilizations 134–51; on HIV/
AIDS 136, 150; intersectionality in
human rights adjudication 123n10,
124, 128–34, 137–40, 145–51; on
maternal mortality 260–1; morality
and 249–50; on sex work 245; *pacta
sunt servanda* 256; reception in
Nigeria 256–9; reception in South
Africa 254–6; Substantive Legal
Effectiveness (SLE) and 233; *see also
specific international organizations
and litigation*
International Planned Parenthood
Federation 158
Interrights 140
intersectionality 8, 11, 31n69,
36, 36n84, 70; Convention on
the Elimination of All Forms of
Discrimination Against Women
(CEDAW) and 124, 128; equality
and 36n84; forced sterilization and
128–34; in human rights adjudication
123n10, 124, 128–34, 137–40,
145–51; Indigenous women of
Canada 224n71, 231; political 130–2,
147; representational 132, 138–9,
144; structural 130
Intimate Partner Violence (IPV) 18–19,
65, 251–2
intrauterine devices (IUDs) 116,
116n80, 172–3
Ireland 54, 101; Eighth Amendment
101n17; Savita Halappanavar case in
71–2; *X Case: Attorney General v X*
(1992) 72, 72n44, 72n45
Islam: Maliki School of jurisprudence
237–8; Quran 237, 237n19; religious
dress 132, 139n122; Sharia law
236n11, 237, 237n20, 238n22,
248–9, 258–9, 258n129
Istanbul Convention 134, 140, 145
*IV v Bolivia* 146–8, 151
Iyioha, Irehobhude O. 1–16, 16–64;
economics and the limits of law 185,
188, 192–3; forced sterilizations 122,
144; Indigenous feminist legal theory
and 213, 228; international women's
health law 233, 237, 246; law and
women's agency in China 102–4,
120–1, 120n98; limits of the UK
Female Genital Mutilation Act 80–1,
82n99; maternal mortality in Nigeria
and South Africa 253–5, 262, 267–8,

272, 283; reproductive health law in
the Philippines 155, 159–60, 180

*Jaitun v Maternal Home MCD,
Jangpura & Others* 209
*James M. Imbong et al. v Hon. Paquito
N. Ochoa* 166n55
*Janani Suraksha Yojania* program 204
Japan 125n16
jurisprudence 1–8; Anglo-American
273–4; equality jurisprudence 21;
of the European Court of Human
Rights 139–41; feminist 67–8,
104–5; German 272; human rights
7; of the Inter-American Commission
145, 145n165; judicial evasion 73;
Maliki School of 237–8; positivist
vs. non-positivist 4, 6–9; substantive
effectiveness 17–64; Western legal
4–6, 72, 272–4; *see also* law; law,
effectiveness of; international law and
norms

Kelson, Hans 10, 66, 74
Kenya 40, 198, 200, 202–3
Kinh ethnic group 195
Kyrgyzstan *184*

*L.C. v Peru* (2011) 210
La Encanada Health Centre 146
Lady Health Worker program 205
*Lancet* 192
Latin America 19, 19n9, 71;
contraceptive prevalence in *206*;
education and *200*; fertility rates in
186; Indigenous women in 195;
maternal mortality in *183*; monism in
240; *see also individual countries*
Law on Reproductive Health
(Senegal) 47–8
law: binary character 27; as compelling
action 39; curative/facilitative 38;
customary 6, 15, 105, 236–7, 236n11,
258n129, 259, 272–3, 275–6;
economic limits of 192–211; efficacy-
oriented concepts of law 25; eight
principles of legality 24n29; feminist
legal theory 69–74; hermeneutic
effect of laws 54; legal formalism 4–5,
274–5; meaning of 22–5; nature of
20n12, 69–74; patent or declared
purpose of the law 41; philosophical
perspectives and definitions of 25–9;

positivism vs. non-positivism 67–9; quantitative aspect of 51n159; separation or separability thesis 67–8; Sharia 236n11, 237, 237n20, 238n22, 248–9, 258–9, 258n129; threshold of validity 28; *see also* international law and norms; law, internal and external limits of; positivism; *specific legislation and litigation*

law, effectiveness of 17–64; authoritative issuance 22, 22n13, 24–7, 27n43, 43, 52, 67, 102; Compliance Theory of 35–6, 35n78, 61, 77, 80–1, 246; correctness and the limits of law 53–7; defining 30–1; elastic concept of 31; equality and 31–4; formal legal effectiveness 36–40; human rights and 74–8; judicial decisions 56; language and normative ends 44; of laws barring female genital mutilation 78–80; law's normative content and 51–3; linguistic and interpretative limits 44–60; meaning of 29–30; morality and 74–8; Outcomes Theory of 34–5; patent and latent objectives and 40–2; reasons for ineffectiveness 40–42; resource-based factors 6; social efficacy 22–4, 22n13, 26–7, 43, 67; Socio-legal Theory of 35–6; theories of 34–6; universality of difference and 74–8; women's health and the limits of law 57–60; *see also* compliance; law, internal and external limits of; Substantive Legal Effectiveness (SLE)

law, internal and external limits of 6–7, 9, 13–4, 21–5, 24n29, 27, 42–64; in China 104; correctness and 53–7; economics and women's agency 185, 188–98, **190**, *191*, *193*, 211; international reproductive health law and 233–4, 249, 255; language and law's normative ends 44; law's normative content 51–3; linguistic and interpretative limits 44–51; in the Philippines160, 180; Substantive Legal Effectiveness (SLE) and 60–4, 94–6; in the United Kingdom 75–6, 93–6; women's health and 57–60; women's health in Nigeria and South Africa 267, 274–6, 284–6

*Laxmi Mandal v Deen Dayal Harinagar Hospital & Others* (2008) 209

LEAF *see* Women's Legal Education and Action Fund (LEAF)

Lemmens, Trudo 33n74

*li* (self-controlled order) 105, 118–19

Liberia 184

Llewellyn, Karl 274

MacKinnon, Catherine 34, 34n76

Magna Carta of Women (MCW) 152–4, 179–81

Mali 189, 203

Maliki School of jurisprudence 237–8

mandatory reporting 86–7

Mao Zedong 106, 106n41, 107n42, 109n51, 110–11

Maputo Protocol 48, 135, 135n83, 239, 242, 242n49, 245, 246n70

marital consent 168, 201

Marriage Act (Nigeria) 239, 270–1

Maternal and Child Health Strategic Plan for 2012–2016 (South Africa) 254–5

maternal mortality and morbidity 1–2, 8, 15–16; in Africa 235; declines in 205–6, 208; international norms and law on 260–1; legislative initiatives to combat in Nigeria and South Africa 260–87; in Nigeria 253, 260–87; in Peru 192, 208; by region 182–6, *183*, *184*; in South Africa 255, 260–87; vesico-vaginal fistula 270–1, 270n62

Maternal Mortality Ratio (MMR) 182–6, *183*, *184*, 192, 194–7, 260–1, 263

Matthews, Richard 216n21, 217, 222

Mautner, Menachem 272

McLachlin, Chief Justice Beverley 31–2, 31n68, 70n31

*Mental Health Trust, Acute Trust & The Council v DD and BC, The* (2015) 126n27

Mestanza Chav, Maria Mamerita 146

Mexico 198, 203

*MHWUN v Minister of Health & Productivity & Ors* (2005) 242n49

Middle East: contraceptive prevalence in *206*; education in *200*; female genital cutting (FGC) in 78–9; maternal mortality in *183*

mifepristone and misprotal 102n22

Mohamed, Hasan 87n109

morality 4, 6, 8–13, 15, 40–6; correctness 21–9, 22n16, 23n22,

24–7, 67–71, 95, 250, 276; healthcare access and provider bias 40; international norms and law and 249–50; in Nigeria 253, 274–6; in the Philippines 154, 156–8, 161, 179; separability thesis and law 67
Mozambique 190, *191*
Muslim women *see* Islam
My Health, My Voice program 208

Naffine, Ngaire 24n26, 34, 120
Namibia 192, 250n93
Napoleon, Val 224, 224n71, 226, 229
National Adolescent Health Policy (Nigeria) 239
National Family Planning/Reproductive Health Service Protocol (Nigeria). 234n7
National Health Act (Nigeria) 16, 239, 246–9, 253
National Health Act (South Africa) 16, 262
National Health Insurance Act of 1995 (Philippines) 166
National People's Congress (NPC) 107, 109, 114n71
National Policy on Maternal and Child Health, 1994 (Nigeria) 239
National Policy on the Elimination of Female Genital Mutilation (Nigeria) 239
National Reproductive Health Policies (Nigeria) 234, 239
National Training Manual on Integration of Reproductive Health and HIV Services (Nigeria) 234n7
Nepal *191*, 196, 210
New Culture Forum 83, 84n103
Ngwena, Charles 3
Nigeria; *Abacha v Fawehimi* (2000) 242; abortions and abortion law in 15–16, 40, 49, 57n201, 248–50, 251n96, 253, 258, 277–84; *Ahamefule v Imperial Medical Centre and Molokwu* 259n132; child marriage in 238, 243, 258, 267, 270–1; Child Rights Act (2003) 245, 248–9, 271; constitution of 238–9, 243, 244n60, 257–8, 269–70, 280–1; contraceptives in 284; Convention on the Elimination of All Forms of Discrimination Against Women (CEDAW) 239,

245, 271, 277, 280, 282; economics and employment in 239, 252, 258; effectiveness of law in 282–6; equality in 235, 245, 250, 266, 269–70, 283; Factories Act (1990) 252; Guidelines on Medical Management of Victims of Violence, Post-Abortion Care Training Manual 234n7; healthcare access in 280–3, 284–6; HIV/AIDS in 15, 234, 259n132, 261–7, 277, 285–7; *Ibidapo v Lufthansa Airlines* (1997) 256; influence of received English law 233; Integrated Maternal, Newborn and Child Health Strategy, Federal Ministry of Health 281; law and culture in 267–6; Marriage Act (1990) 239, 270–1; maternal mortality in 253, 260–87; Matrimonial Causes Act 1990) 239; *MHWUN v Minister of Health & Productivity & Ors* (2005) 242n49; morality in 253, 274–6; National Adolescent Health Policy (1995) 239; National Family Planning/Reproductive Health Service Protocol 234n7; National Health Act (2014) 16, 239, 246–9, 253; National Policy on Maternal and Child Health (1994) 239; National Policy on the Elimination of Female Genital Mutilation (1998 and 2002) 239; National Reproductive Health Policies (2010 and 2017) 234, 239; National Training Manual on Integration of Reproductive Health and HIV Services 234n7; Police Act 252; polio eradication in 267n51; positivism in the Nigerian context 237, 241, 274–6; premarital sex in 250n92; reception of international norms and law in 256–9; reproductive health law and international law 234–54; Reproductive Health Policy and Strategy (2001) 239, 281; Same Sex Marriage (Prohibition) Act (2014) 249; *Sidi v Sha'Aban* 237n19; social norms in 15–16; Substantive Legal Effectiveness (SLE) in 262, 267, 283; Supreme Council for Sharia in Nigeria 249; Supreme Court of 242, 256; Trafficking in Persons (Prohibition) Law Enforcement and Administration Act 245; Violence

Against Persons (Prohibition) Act (2015) 239, 245–6; women's agency in 50, 258
Nigerian Labour Act (2010) 239
Nigerian Penal Code (1963) 237
norms *see* international law and norms; social norms
North America 28, 205 *see also* Canada; Mexico; United States
Nowgesic, Earl 223
Nwabueze, R.N. 243

Orientalism 132
Outcomes Theory of legal effectiveness 34–5, 77, 80–1
out-of-quota births 113, 115, 116n81, 118, 130
Outcomes Theory of legal effectiveness 34–5

Pakistan 133, 5, 205
Papua New Guinea *184*
Paraguay 210
Partial-Birth Abortion Ban Act (2007) 56
paternalism 12, 120, 123
patriarchy: in Africa 252, 280; in China 104, 117; heteropatriarchy 212, 214–15; Indigenous 212, 214–15, 226
Peru 7; contraceptives in 147, 205; Fujimori's population programme 146–8; genocide of Quechua-speaking people in 148; healthcare access in 198–9, 208, 210; maternal mortality in 192, 208
Peruvian Truth Commission 148
Philippines 152–81; abortions and abortion law in 29, 159, 162, 166–8, 172, 179–80; *Alliance for the Family Foundation Philippines, Inc. (ALFI)* (2015) 176; Barangay Ayala Alabang 171–4; Catholic Church 73n50, 154, 156, 158–9, 162–5, 173–4, 177–8; Cheaper Medicines Act (2008) 166; constitution of 157n14, 168; contraceptives in 51, 152, 157–8, 164–8, 171–7; Convention on the Elimination of All Forms of Discrimination Against Women (CEDAW) 153, 165, 173, 173n76, 176, 179; culture, religion, and tradition (CRT) in 12,

154–7, 162, 166–81; *Ebralinag v Division Superintendent of Schools* 169; *Estrada v Escritor* (2003) 169; eugenics in 157–8; Executive Order (E.O.) No. 003 173; Family Code 158; Implementing Rules and Regulations (IRR) 167–8, 170; *James M. Imbong et al. v Hon. Paquito N. Ochoa* 166n55; Magna Carta of Women (MCW) 152–4, 179–81; morality in 154, 156–8, 161, 179; National Health Insurance Act of 1995 166; premarital sex in 158, 165, 172; Republic Act 152–3, 166, 170; Responsible Parenthood and Reproductive Health Act of 2012 (RPRHA) 12–13, 44, 51, 58, 154–62, 171–80; Sanggunian Barangay 172; social norms in 13; Supreme Court of 13, 155–6, 166, 170, 176, 176n90, 178–9; women's agency in 179
*Pimentel v Brazil* (2011) 210
Pinzon-Rondon, Angela Maria 215, 221
Planned Parenthood 19n9, 158
pluralism 3; cultural 74; legal 15, 221; pluralistic legal system 235, 275–6; plurality of experiences 225–6; religious 237n20
Police Act (Nigeria) 252
policing and enforcement; criminal intent 82, 82n99, 90, 94–6; death by stoning 237–8, 238n22; death penalty 177n94, 238n22; female genital mutilation 37, 87–9; harassment of sex workers 139–40; Peru's population programme 146; violence against women and 58, 220, 252–3, 256; of women's bodies 4, 73; *see also* compliance; violence against women
polio eradication 267n51
polygyny 238, 253
population politics 59
populism 2, 7
portability requirement 50–1
Portugal 7
positivism 4–5, 20, 20n12, 22n16, 23–7, 24n23, 24n29, 67–77; compliance theory of law and 35–6; legal effectiveness and 29–30, 60, 81, 97; legalism entrenched in 39; morality and 274–6; in the Nigerian

context 237, 241, 274–6; non-positivism 4–6, 20, 23–4, 54, 67–7, 147
Posner, Eric A. 51n160
practical well-being approach 76
premarital sex 191; in China 102, 118–19; in Nigeria 250n92; in the Philippines 158, 165, 172
Prentice, Tracey 226–7, 229
Prince Edward Island (PEI) 29, 49, 55–6, 58, 159
*Progress/Oportunidades* program 203
Prohibition of Female Circumcision Act (UK) 84
Project Prevent 127
pro-life groups 28, 154, 156, 159
pro-natalist policy 109–12, 109n51
prostitution *see* sex work
Protection of Life During Pregnancy Act, The (2013) 73, 73n49

Quran 237, 237n19

R. *v Morgentaler* (1988) 49–50, 56–7
Radbruch, Gustav 24n23, 68, 72–6
Rahman, Anika 82n99
Razack, Sherene 130, 133, 214n8
Reading, Charlotte 219–20
Recto, Ralph 158, 161
religion 2, 7; culture, religion, and tradition (CRT) in the Philippines 12, 154–7, 162, 166–81; opposition to abortion 54–7; pluralism 237n20; religious dress 132, 139n122; *see also* Catholic Church; Islam; morality
Reproductive Health Policy and Strategy (Nigeria) 239, 281
reproductive health *see* female genital mutilation; forced sterilizations; healthcare access; maternal mortality
reproductive rights *see* abortion and abortion law; healthcare access
Republic Act (Philippines) 152–3, 166, 170
Responsible Parenthood and Reproductive Health Act of 2012 (RPRHA) 12–13, 44, 51, 58, 154–62; challenges to implementation 171–6; in the medical-legal arena 176–80; opposition to 162–71
re-victimization 131
Revilla Jr., Ramon 'Bong' 161

RH Law *see* Responsible Parenthood and Reproductive Health Act of 2012 (RPRHA)
*Roe v Wade* (1973) 56–9, 283–4
Roma people 137–44
Romania 202
RSA *see* South Africa
rule of law 71, 76–7; in Canada 215–16, 221; in China 107; economics and the 194–5, 194n65
Rule of Law Index 221
Rwanda 204

SAHAYOG 208
Same Sex Marriage (Prohibition) Act (Nigeria) 249
Sampford, Charles 22n13
Sanger, Margaret 158
Sanggunian Barangay 172
Sangha women 207
Saunders, Alison 88
Saving Mothers, Giving Life Program 206
Schuck, Peter H. 46, 51n159, 56–7
SDGs *see* United Nations Sustainable Development Goals (SDGs)
Sen, Amartya 188
Senegal 47–8, 48n140, 77, 204; abortions and abortion law in 48–9, 48n140; Code of Medical Ethics (1967) 48, 48n141; Law on Reproductive Health (2005) 47–8; *State v Astou Diop* (2009) 48, 48n140; *State v Landing Massaly* (2008) 48; *State v Mouscoye Sane* (2008) 48
sex work 139–40; among Indigenous women in Canada 219–20, 222, 227; international norms and law on 245
Sharia 236n11, 237, 237n20, 238n22, 248–9, 258–9, 258n129
*Sidi v Sha'Aban* 237n19
Sierra Leone 89, 91, 183–4, *184*, 196, 203
*Silguero v Portugal* (1999) 134n74
Sloane, Robert D. 76
Slovakia 7, 141–4
social norms 6, 51–3, 51n160; in Canada 14, 63, 120; in China 59; economic limits of law and 189, *193*, 211; language and 61–2; in Nigeria 15–16; relationship with law 25n34, 26–30, 35, 51–3; in South Africa 15–16; in the Philippines 13

Socio-Legal Theory of Legal
Effectiveness 35–6
Somalia 79, 82, 98, 184
Sorsogon 13, 155, 156, 174–6, 177
Sotto III, Vicente 'Tito' 157–61
South Africa 7, 15–16, 40; abortions
and abortion law in 15–16, 35,
40, 55, 254–5, 264–6, 277–84;
Choice on Termination of Pregnancy
Act (CTOPA) (1996) 16, 35, 55,
254, 262; Constitution of the
Republic of South Africa (1996)
254; contraceptives in 192, 255;
Convention on the Elimination of
All Forms of Discrimination Against
Women (CEDAW) 280, 282; equality
in 254–5, 266, 283; healthcare access
in 280–3, 284–6; HIV/AIDS in 15,
255, 261–7, 277, 285–7; Maternal
and Child Health Strategic Plan for
2012–2016 (South Africa) 254–5;
maternal mortality in 255, 260–87;
maternal mortality law and culture in
267–76; National Health Act (2013)
16, 262; reception of international
norms in 254–6; reproductive health
law and international law 254–6;
social norms in 15–16; Substantive
Legal Effectiveness (SLE) in 255,
262, 267, 283; women's agency in 55
Spain 7
Sri Lanka 194, 197, 205–6
*State v Astou Diop* (2009) 48, 48n140
*State v Landing Massaly* (2008) 48
*State v Mouscoye Sane* (2008) 48
stereotypes: embedded into
international law 132; gender 149,
252n98; HIV/AIDS stigma and 220,
228–9; of Indigenous women 228–9
sterilization *see* forced sterilization
Stopes, Marie 124
Strasbourg Declaration on the Roma 140
Stubbs, Margot 5, 23–4
*Subsidio Educativo* program 199
Substantive Effectiveness *see* Substantive
Legal Effectiveness (SLE)
Substantive Legal Effectiveness (SLE)
6, 9–10, 16, 27; in China 102–4,
121; concept of 60–4; defining
effectiveness 30–1; economics and
185, 193, 198; feminism and 70–1,
76–8; forced sterilizations and 124;
formal legal effectiveness vs. 21, 102;

international law and 233; in Nigeria
262, 267, 283; in South Africa 255,
262, 267, 283; and the UK Female
Genital Mutilation (FGM) Act 66,
89–98
Sudan (South) 184
Supreme Council for Sharia in Nigeria
249

Tanzania 202
Thailand 193
Theory of Five Organs 101
Therapeutic Abortion Committees
(TAC) 47
Timor-Leste *184*
Toubia, Nahid 82n99
*Towne v Eisner* (1918) 45n123
Traditional Birth Attendants (TBAs)
235, 269
Trafficking in Persons (Prohibition) Law
Enforcement and Administration Act
(Nigeria) 245
transgender persons 127, 225; self-
identification 127, 129n42; two-spirit
Elders 223n65, 225
TRAP laws (Targeted Restrictions on
Abortion Providers) 32, 41
Trimmer, Alexandra 144
Truth and Reconciliation Commission
of Canada 222–3
Turkey 198

Uganda *191*, 192, 200, 202,
206–7, 209
UK Female Genital Mutilation Act
10, 65–98; amendments to 85–8;
criminal propensity/intent 94–5;
effectiveness of 78–82; Female
Genital Cosmetic Surgery (FGSC)
and 88–9; health professionals
uncertainties about 93–4; scale and
history of 82–5; socio-economic
factors impeding 90–3; Substantive
Legal Effectiveness (SLE) of 89–97
United Kingdom; *Abdulaziz, Cabales
and Balkandali v The United
Kingdom* (1985) 132–4; Abortion
Act of 1967 47n138, 55, 100n12;
abortions and abortion law in 49, 55;
Court of Protection 126; equality
in 89–90, 133; National Health
Service 88; Prohibition of Female
Circumcision Act (1985) 84; *The*

*Mental Health Trust, Acute Trust &*
*The Council v DD and BC* (2015)
126n27
United Nations Children's Fund
(UNICEF) 195–6, 209, 260–1
United Nations Committee on
Economic and Socio-Cultural Rights
165, 244
United Nations Conference on Women
in Beijing in 147, 232n1, 240, 254
United Nations Convention Against
Torture (1984) 238, 239–40
United Nations Convention against
Torture and other Cruel, Inhuman
or degrading Treatment or
Punishment 238
United Nations Convention on the
Rights of the Child (CRC) 85, 239,
245, 248, 271
United Nations Declaration on Social
Progress and Development (1968)
233n4
United Nations Declaration on the
Elimination of Violence Against
Women (DEVAW) 18, 135
United Nations International
Conference on Population and
Development (ICPD) 179–80,
180n102, 204
United Nations Millennium
Declaration 261
United Nations Population Fund
(UNFPA) 189–90, 194, 255
United Nations Resolution XVIII:
Human Rights Aspects of Family
Planning 233n4
United Nations Special Rapporteur on
Violence Against Women 148–9
United Nations Sustainable
Development Goals (SDGs) 65, 182,
211, 254, 260–1, 282
United States: abortions and abortion
law in 28, 41–2; contraceptives in
127; *Gonzales v Carhart* (2007)
56; Partial-Birth Abortion Ban Act
(2007) 56; Supreme Court 41, 59;
*Roe v Wade* (1973) 56–9, 283–4;
*Towne v Eisner* (1918) 45n123;
TRAP laws (Targeted Restrictions on
Abortion Providers) 32, 41; *Whole*

*Woman's Health v Hellerstedt*
(2016) 41
Universal Declaration of Human Rights
135, 174, 240
U-Report system 209

Vakulenko, Anastasia 139n122
*VC v Slovakia* (2009) 141–3
Vermette, D'Arcy 212, 216–17
vesico-vaginal fistula 270–1, 270n62
Vienna Declaration and Programme of
Action (1993) 240
Vietnam 195
Violence Against Persons (Prohibition)
Act, 2015 (Nigeria) 239, 245–6
violence against women 1, 9, 32,
36–7, 58; HIV/AIDS and 220,
227; Intimate Partner Violence
(IPV) 18–19, 65, 251–2; statistics
18–19; UN initiatives against 65,
92–3, 134–5; *see also* female genital
mutilation; forced sterilization
voucher-based programs 202–3

*Whole Woman's Health v Hellerstedt*
(2016) 41
widowhood practices 105, 246, 250, 253
wife hospitality 250
Women's Legal Education and Action
Fund (LEAF) 31, 130–1
World Bank: 2012 World Development
Report (WDR2012) 182, 185, 189,
192–3, 197, 211; on income and
women's agency 189, *191*, *193*, 201
World Health Organization (WHO) 65,
66n10; on female genital mutilation
78, 83–4, 95; on forced sterilization
150; on maternal mortality 260–1,
263–5

*X Case: Attorney General v X, The*
(1992) 72, 72n44, 72n45
*Xákmok v Paraguay* (2012) 210

Yemen *184*

Zambia 192, 205, 206
Zika virus 19, 19n9
Zimbabwe *191*, 199, 204
Zoppei, Verena 30–1, 35n78, 38–9, 46